THE NATURE OF WAR
IN THE
INFORMATION AGE

Cass Series: Strategy and History
Series Editors: Colin Gray and Williamson Murray
ISSN: 1473-6403

This new series will focus on the theory and practice of strategy. Following Clausewitz, strategy has been understood to mean the use made of force, and the threat of the use of force, for the ends of policy. This series is as interested in ideas as in historical cases of grand strategy and military strategy in action. All historical periods, near and past, and even future, are of interest. In addition to original monographs, the series will from time to time publish edited reprints of neglected classics as well as collections of essays.

THE NATURE OF WAR IN THE INFORMATION AGE

Clausewitzian Future

DAVID J. LONSDALE

King's College London,
Based at the Joint Services Command and Staff College, UK

FRANK CASS
LONDON • NEW YORK

First published in 2004 in Great Britain by
FRANK CASS

and in the United States of America by
FRANK CASS
270 Madison Ave,
New York NY 10016

Website: www.frankcass.com
Frank Cass is an imprint of the Taylor & Francis Group

Transferred to Digital Printing 2005

British Library Cataloguing in Publication Data

Lonsdale, David J.
The nature of war in the information age: Clausewitzian
future. – (Cass series. Strategy and history; 9)
1. War 2. Strategy 3. War – Technical innovations 4. Military
art and science – Data processing 5. Information warfare
I. Title
355'.02

ISBN 0-7146-5546-5 (hbk)
ISBN 0-7146-8429-5 (pbk)
ISSN 1473-6403

Library of Congress Cataloging-in-Publication Data

Lonsdale, David J.
The nature of war in the Information Age: Clausewitzian future /
David J. Lonsdale.
    p.   cm. – (Cass series – strategy and history; 9)
Includes bibliographical references and index.
    1. War. 2. Information warfare. 3. World politics – 21st century.
I. Title. II. Series.
U21.2.L66 2004
355.02 – dc22

                                              2003065325

Typeset in 10.5/12pt Aldine 721 by Frank Cass

Dedicated to the memory of
Minnie Lonsdale (1908–1998)

Contents

Series Editor's Preface

I admit to feeling a particular satisfaction, even some pride, in adding David Lonsdale's study of *The Nature of War in the Information Age: Clausewitzian Future* (henceforth referred to as *Clausewitzian Future*) to the series. I attended the birth, and witnessed the maturing, of Dr Lonsdale's project. This is an important book. In point of fact, whether or not readers find its very clear argument persuasive, the opportunity to publish books such as Dr Lonsdale's is precisely why Williamson Murray and myself created this new series on 'Strategy and History'. It was, and remains, our intention especially to encourage authors who strive to marry strategic theory with historical evidence. Rephrased, we believe strongly in the continuing importance of developing strategic ideas in the context of a proper respect for historical experience. When all is said and done, even though the strategic historical record often will be ambiguous, contested, and annoyingly partial, it happens to be the only *evidence* available to us, albeit always only imperfectly so.

Clausewitzian Future is a book with several layers. Pre-eminently, it offers an interpretation of the strategic implications of the information age. The author boldly ventures the new concept of what he terms the 'infosphere', as a fifth geostrategic dimension to join the land, sea, air and space. However, in the course of making such sense as can be made of the recent innovations in information technology, Dr Lonsdale also writes penetratingly about the nature of war and strategy. With ample and detailed historical illustration from many periods, the book considers the information revolution in long historical context. The author is not shy of ranging from the ancient Near East to the present day and then on into the future. In short, *Clausewitzian Future* is a broad-gauged study of the fundamentals of war and strategy, which happens to be keyed to an issue-set of our time, the implications of information technologies. The study provides understanding of where we are and where we might be going, strategically; it develops that story with reference to historical experience; and it has significant things to say about the theory of war and strategy. In that last regard, as the sub-title advertises explicitly, the great Prussian is accorded his due.

Clausewitzian Future hammers yet another nail in the coffin of the argument that technological change can alter the nature of war. To refer to the book's principal title, *The Nature of War in the Information Age*, that nature is the same as it was in all past and in all future ages! Clausewitz could hardly have been clearer on this central issue. He wrote: 'All wars are things of the *same* nature.' A little earlier he advised as follows: 'But war, though conditioned by the particular characteristics of states and their armed forces, must contain some more general – indeed a universal element with which every theorist ought above all to be concerned.' He conceived of war as having two natures, objective and subjective. The former was the universal element that persists regardless of time, belligerents, issues, technology or other shifting contextual matters. Indeed, war is necessarily defined by its objective nature. If war were to change its nature it would become something else. The latter, war's subjective nature, is what we mean when we refer to the 'character' of war. That character inherently is highly variable and dynamic.

Far from being an abstruse scholastic point, it is essential to distinguish with the utmost clarity between war's eternal nature and its ever-changing character. On page one of *On War* Clausewitz tells us that 'war is nothing but a duel on a larger scale', and that it is an '*act of force to compel our enemy to do our will*'. Lest he had been insufficiently plain, he proceeded to emphasise that the object of war is 'to impose our will on the enemy'.

What does all this have to do with the IT (information technology) revolution, if such it be? Not for the first time in the 170 years since its first published appearance, Clausewitz's general theory of war is dismissed by many as yesterday's theory for yesterday's political and strategic context. On the one hand, there are people who are simply confused between the nature and character of war. Radical changes in the latter, most typically those associated with cumulatively dramatic technological advances (machine-guns, air power, nuclear weapons and, now, the exploitation of the computer), lead some commentators into the error of believing that everything about war will change. On the other hand, there are theorists who, while not confused between war's nature and character, nonetheless are convinced that Clausewitz wrote only for a particular era, one that now has passed. The most common reason for this mistake is traceable to an inaccurate understanding of Clausewitz's famous 'trinity'. The information age, Dr Lonsdale's focus, allegedly is promoting a 'globalization' that is eroding the sovereignty, even the relevance, of states. If Clausewitz theorised for a world of sovereign states with governments that controlled armies somewhat subject to the passions of the people, how can he still be relevant as warfare becomes less and less the business of states?

The answer is that Clausewitz did not postulate, *primarily*, a 'remarkable trinity' of the people, the commander and his army, and the government. That was his secondary trinity. His primary trinity is 'composed of primordial violence, hatred, and enmity'; 'the play of chance and probability'; and of 'its [war's] element of subordination, as an instrument of policy'. In other words, for Clausewitz's theory, it really does not matter whether war, understood as organised violence for political purposes, is conducted by states, tribes, transnational groups, or whatever. There was no 'Clausewitzian era', now purportedly defunct, because he theorised for all historical contexts.

David Lonsdale has undertaken to test the salience of classical strategic thought to the still emerging new realities of the information age. *Clausewitzian Future* is a most welcome addition to the thin population of studies that successfully relate strategic ideas from a general theory of war to the all too obvious changes in war's material culture. We are very pleased to add this title to the series.

Colin S. Gray
Series Co-Editor

Acknowledgements

I would like to thank Colin S. Gray, who has not only given me immeasurable support in the writing of this book, but also introduced me to the love of Strategic Studies. I am also indebted to colleagues from my time at the Centre for Security Studies, University of Hull, whom it was a pleasure to work with. In particular, I would like to thank Eric Grove, Adam Baddeley, Malcolm Davis and James Kiras for their long discussions that proved a constant source of joy and inspiration. The final stages of this book were made much easier thanks to the support of my new colleagues at the Joint Services Command and Staff College. In particular, I would like to thank Matt Uttley for his support and advice. Finally, and most importantly, I would like to express my sincere gratitude to my family, who have shown unfailing support throughout my academic career.

List of Abbreviations

ACTS	Air Corps Tactical School
AI	artificial intelligence
APC	armoured personnel carrier
ATO	Air Tasking Order
AWACS	Airborne Warning and Control System
AWE	Advanced Warfighting Experiment
BAT	Brilliant Anti-Tank (submunition)
BDA	Bomb Damage Assessment
C^2	command and control
C^4I	command, control, communications, computer applications and intelligence processing
CBO	Combined Bomber Offensive
CEC	Co-operative Engagement Capability
COA	course of action
COIN	counterinsurgency
DARPA	Defense Advanced Research Projects Agency
DBK	Dominant Battlespace Knowledge
DIA	Defense Intelligence Agency
DISA	Defense Information Systems Agency
EMP	electromagnetic pulse
EMS	electromagnetic spectrum
EW	electronic warfare
EXFOR	Experimental Force
FSR	Field Service Regulations
GAO	General Accounting Office
GIE	Global Information Environment
GPS	Global Positioning System
GWAPS	*Gulf War Air Power Survey*
HE	high explosives
HUMINT	human intelligence resources
IADS	Integrated Air Defence System
ICBM	intercontinental ballistic missile

ISR	intelligence, surveillance and reconnaissance
IW	information warfare
JCS	Joint Chiefs of Staff
JIT	just-in-time
KLA	Kosovo Liberation Army
KTO	Kuwaiti Theatre of Operations
LGBs	laser-guided bombs
MBT	main battle tank
MEW	Ministry of Economic Warfare
MIE	Military Information Environment
MOOTW	military operations other than war
MTR	Military Technical Revolution
NCW	Network Centric Warfare
NII	National Information Infrastructure
NSA	National Security Agency
NSI	National Strategic Infrastructure
NVA	North Vietnamese Army
OODA	observation–orientation–decision–action
PCCIP	President's Commission on Critical Infrastructure Protection
PGMs	precision-guided munitions
PSN	public switched network
PSO	peace support operations
RMA	Revolution in Military Affairs
ROE	rules of engagement
SAS	Special Air Service
SEAD	Suppression of Enemy Air Defences
SIW	Strategic Information Warfare
SLBM	submarine-launched ballistic missile
SOS	system of systems
SSBN	Soviet ballistic missile nuclear submarine
TLAM	Tomahawk land attack missile
UAV	Unmanned Aerial Vehicle
UCAV	Unmanned Combat Aerial Vehicle
USAF	United States Air Force
USMC	United States Marine Corps
USN	United States Navy
USSBS	United States Strategic Bombing Survey
VTC	video teleconferencing
WMD	Weapons of Mass Destruction

Introduction

The proliferation of information technology, what Winn Schwartau describes as 'computers everywhere',[1] has spawned a profusion of speculations concerning the changing nature of societies and economies. Indeed, the period covering the late twentieth century and the early years of the twenty-first is now commonly accepted as being the 'information age'. Running alongside the debate concerning the socio-economic implications of this new epoch, and at times converging with it, is a field of literature ruminating over the impact the information age will have on war and strategy. A 'Revolution in Military Affairs' (RMA) is said to be underway. The debate surrounding this RMA formed into its current manifestation after the 1991 Gulf War. However, over a decade later, and even in the aftermath of the terrorist attacks of 9/11, the debate continues. In January 2002, Admiral Cebrowski, a leading exponent of the RMA concept 'Network Centric Warfare', argued, 'the most important transformation that we're facing is the transformation from the Industrial to the Information Age'.[2] Reflecting the more cautionary side of the discourse, in a study of the 2001–2 campaign in Afghanistan, Stephen Biddle advises against the desire to transform the United States' (US) military too radically.[3] For some, including the US Secretary of Defense Donald Rumsfeld, the 2003 invasion of Iraq represented an early test for a partially transformed US military.[4] Similarly, the new strategy of 'shock and awe', so prominent in the Pentagon's plans for the invasion of Iraq, was said to have been enabled by new technology; was designed to go beyond the Powell Doctrine's emphasis on overwhelming force; and would help to minimise casualities.[5] Clearly, the RMA is still a live issue, and its proponents continue to peddle their wares. Therefore, it is as important as ever to test the validity of those works that promote radical change. In the context of this book, the term 'RMA literature' is used to refer collectively to those works that generally subscribe to the notion that revolutionary change, fuelled by the information age, is occurring.[6]

This study begins from the premise that information represents an ever-present dimension of warfare and strategy. Indeed, information warfare (IW), a dominant buzzword in the RMA literature, has been a constant feature of conflict. Field Marshal Slim's account of the Burma campaign indicates just how important information has been historically. Slim noted that a fundamental difference between the Japanese and Allied forces during the early Japanese successes was that the Japanese possessed good information, whereas 'It is no exaggeration to say that we had practically no useful or reliable information of the enemy strength, movements, or intentions.'[7] Similarly, Napoleon's use of a cavalry screen and Hannibal's deception at Lake Trasimene are classic examples of information warfare.[8] Nonetheless, many writers on this subject claim that, although not new, information warfare has been transformed by new technologies.[9]

Though it is reasonable to suggest that the information age will affect the conduct of warfare and strategy, the advocates of the RMA are on less safe ground when they proclaim, as William E. Odom does, that 'the very nature of war is changing'.[10] For the purposes of this study war is defined in Hedley Bull's language as 'organised violence carried on by political units against each other'.[11] In reference to strategy, Colin S. Gray defines it as 'the use that is made of force and the threat of force for the ends of policy'.[12] Similarly, strategy is defined by Carl von Clausewitz as 'the use of engagements for the object of the war'.[13] Andre Beaufre, in his definition of strategy, focuses attention on the interaction between belligerents: 'the art of the dialectic of two opposing wills using force to resolve their dispute'.[14] An alternative definition that draws its inspiration from those of Clausewitz, Gray and Beaufre, may describe strategy as *the art of using military force against an intelligent foe(s) towards the attainment of policy objectives.*[15] To summarise: war is a purposeful act of actual or threatened physical violence which takes place within a dialectic relationship.

In general, the RMA literature implicitly suggests that the ever-increasing use of advanced information systems in the battlespace, and the more general implications of the proliferation of information technology, indicate that information may be achieving a more direct and decisive role in warfare. Indeed, Eliot Cohen argues, 'Information and the ability to process it is at the heart of modern conventional warfare.'[16] This thought is echoed in *Joint Vision 2020*, the US Joint Chiefs of Staff's (JCS's) perspective on future war.[17] In the theoretical literature primary exponents of such ideas are Alvin and Heidi Toffler. In their influential work *War and Anti-war: Survival at the Dawn of the 21st Century*, the Tofflers declare that the coming change is a momentous one in human history. They postulate that humanity is entering its third wave of civilisation. In the wake of the agricultural and industrial waves, man is now entering the information wave of his existence. Both in the battlespace and within society at large, knowledge is becoming the central resource. At the heart of their work is the notion that the manner in which a society operates, and in particular how it produces wealth, will generally determine how it wages war.[18] Sections of the RMA literature even raise questions concerning the continuance of man's role in conflict. This latter point is superlatively underlined by J. F. C. Fuller's identification of what he defines as the hidden impulse in the technological epoch of war, which is: 'The elimination of the human element both physically and morally, intellect alone remaining.'[19] This is particularly evident in writings on the future of war in the air, where Unmanned Aerial Vehicles (UAVs) are trumpeted as the next step in airpower platform development.[20] Taken together, all of the above changes have led the more extreme elements of the RMA literature to indicate that alterations to the character of war may be of such proportions that the nature of war itself is transformed.

Although a clear and unanimous definition of the nature of war does not exist, it is fair to say that the activity of warfare is generally understood to be constituted of certain characteristics. This subject will be addressed fully in Chapter 1. At this stage, it is sufficient to note that war is perceived as a human contest in the pursuit of policy objectives, and is infused by chance, uncertainty, violence and physical exertion. This description reflects the Clausewitzian paradigm, and is enshrined within a number of concepts to be found in *On War*. Of particular relevance are the 'trinity', 'climate of war' and 'friction'. Taken together, these three concepts encompass the true nature of war.

Increasingly, concepts and capabilities associated with the information age – such as Dominant Battlespace Knowledge (DBK), Network Centric Warfare (NCW), Strategic Information Warfare (SIW), stand-off precision munitions and UAVs – are challenging some of the main characteristics that constitute the Clausewitzian worldview. If the predictions of the RMA enthusiasts come to pass, and Clausewitz's theories look increasingly jaded, then a gap will be left in the theoretical literature. This gap may be filled by another of the classical works, such as Sun Tzu's *The Art of War*. Alternatively, we may have to turn towards the writings of the information age to seek an understanding of the nature of war in the future. At minimum, strategists may have to supplement the established theories with more recent works that take greater account of the coming changes.

These thoughts are not merely idle academic theorising. Strategic Studies is a practical subject. An enhanced dimension of strategy (in this case the infosphere) offers new methods through which to pursue strategic objectives, and also creates new vulnerabilities. Any fundamental change to the character of warfare will require appropriate alterations in how to prepare for, and fight, future conflicts. Likewise, a proper understanding of strategy in the information age may present actors with new and more effective ways to achieve their strategic goals. Gray summarises why this debate matters when he notes: 'The stakes are very high indeed ... the subject of the RMA is the prevention, conduct, and outcome of wars.'[21] Bearing in mind the costs, including opportunity costs, and lead-time required for major defence procurement projects, a well-informed understanding of warfare in the information age is required now. How one adapts to an emerging RMA can have important consequences. German adaptation to armoured forces, wireless radio and airpower endowed them with a relative advantage that became evident in the years 1939–41. However, this same example reveals how transitory such an ascendancy can prove to be, and how the operational superiority of an RMA does not automatically translate into a theory of strategic victory. Therefore, there are dangers both in not exploiting an RMA sufficiently and also in placing all your strategic eggs in the RMA basket.

In light of the above remarks, it is the objective of this book to draw the implicit assumptions of the RMA literature into the open and, from there, to test the hypothesis that the information age will witness a fundamental change to the nature of warfare.

THE RMA DEBATE

The RMA debate encompasses a wide array of topics of strategic interest; therefore, the relevant literature covers a number of areas, and can be divided into a number of categories. Within the literature that deals explicitly with the conduct of warfare, three broad areas of debate can be identified. The first of these is concerned with information age warfare as it is applied to the battlespace. This covers the character of conflict, as well as the forces and operations that will characterise it. An associated area deals with issues of command in the information age. The subject of command is of particular interest to this book because it is an area in which the balance between the human dimension and the role of technology is particularly important. Also, the subject of command presents us with Clausewitz's concept of the 'military genius'.[22] The military genius provides many of the answers to the problems raised by the nature of war. Therefore, changes to the nature of war will have to be reflected within the function of command.

A third section of the literature deals with what has been termed Strategic Information Warfare. In ways reminiscent of the early air power theorists of the interwar years, this section of the literature focuses upon 'strategic' war waged against information age infrastructures.[23] Whilst the

4

methods employed in SIW can be utilised to support operations in the battlespace, the literature often expresses the notion that SIW could be the dominant, perhaps decisive, strategy of choice for the twenty-first century. Akin to the early airpower theorists, some writers imply that a new centre of gravity has developed, which if targeted could produce decisive leverage. Alternatively, perhaps an old centre of gravity has been rediscovered. The centre of gravity in question is the interdependence of modern societies and economies. This time the reference is to information age societies rather than their industrial forerunners. The interdependencies and dependencies may be greater, the infrastructure could be more vulnerable and the weapons more accurate and reliable. If this is the case, then the future of warfare may become increasingly characterised by SIW. However, whether this method of conflict has the potential for independent and decisive strategic effect will be explored in Chapter 4.

There is a distinct technological bent to much of the RMA literature. Consequently, the debate over information age warfare has helped to refocus attention on the role technology plays in strategy. Opinion is sharply divided on this issue. At the one extreme, Fuller is unequivocal about the role of technology in deciding the outcome of a conflict: 'Tools or weapons, if only the right ones can be discovered, form ninety-nine per cent of victory.'[24] Whereas, although Martin van Creveld recognises that technology permeates all aspects of warfare, he suggests that its limitations are more important than its advantages.[25] For Michael Howard, the technological dimension of strategy is but one amongst four. The other dimensions in Howard's taxonomy are *operational, social and logistical.* Howard argues that the relative dominance of each dimension is dependent upon circumstance.[26] Similarly, Gray asserts that as a dimension of strategy: 'technology is important. But historical evidence suggests that the outcomes to none of the wars in modern history among the great powers have plausibly been determined by superiority in weapons technology.'[27] Throughout this study, Gray's multidimensional approach is utilised as an antidote to the bouts of reductionism prevalent in some of the RMA literature.

As noted, discourse on the information age RMA formed into its present manifestation after the 1991 Gulf War.[28] However, the broader theoretical foundations of the debate, and the historical evolution of the technology and operations which form the core of information age warfare, can be traced back much further. In the mid-1980s the Soviet Marshal Nicolai Ogarkov began hypothesising about what he termed a 'Military Technical Revolution' (MTR). Ogarkov identified developments in computers, space surveillance and long-range missiles as the defining characteristics of this MTR.[29] One can go even further back than this though. In a material sense, World War II bore witness to significant exploitation of the electromagnetic spectrum (EMS), long-range missiles and the early development of precision munitions.[30] Alternatively, Jonathan Bailey posits that the genesis of the modern style of warfare – including information age warfare – is directly a result of the development of indirect artillery fire in 1917–18.[31] And, as already mentioned, information warfare is readily identifiable in past conflicts reaching back into antiquity.

Clearly, depending upon one's perspective the current debate has a variety of possible theoretical and material origins. This is further exemplified by the concepts of integration and jointness. Although both of these concepts are fashionable within the information age warfare literature, they also resonate throughout history. Williamson Murray notes that it was the Germans' combined-arms framework that allowed them such an edge in the exploitation of the tank in armoured warfare in World War II.[32] The fourth century BC exhibits even more ancient exponents of integration. Both Alexander the Great and his father Philip II of Macedonia led armies that derived much of their effectiveness from their proficiency in combined arms.[33] The conundrum of whether the concepts of integration and jointness have greater salience in the information age than in the past is perhaps best summed up by former Chairman of the Joint Chiefs of Staff John M. Shalikshili: 'The nature of modern warfare demands that we fight as a joint team. This was important yesterday, it is essential today, and it will be even more imperative tomorrow.'[34] Hence, the increasing focus on systems in the information age.

Within the information age literature, the concept of integration is best exemplified by the work of Admiral William Owens and Martin Libicki. In Owens' vision, a 'system of systems' (SOS) can be created through the integration of three areas of technology. These are: intelligence, surveillance and reconnaissance (ISR); command, control, communications, computer applications and intelligence processing (C^{4}I); and precision force. Owens insists that the RMA, as exemplified by the system of systems, represents a new appreciation of joint military operations, and depends on the contributions of all the services, and a common military doctrine.[35] Libicki's speculations on the future battlespace share a number of common features with those espoused by Owens. Libicki's concept of the 'Mesh' foresees an ever more ubiquitous coverage of the battlespace by sensors, and an ever closer relationship between sensors and shooters. The ultimate expression of this relationship comes in the form of fire-ant warfare, in which a myriad of sensors either cue a host of miniprojectiles, or indeed merge to a point where the sensors are also simultaneously the shooters.[36] In fact, the merger of sensors and

6

shooters is already upon us. This development is apparent in a number of weapon systems, most notably infrared-guided missiles and acoustic-based autonomous systems such as the Brilliant Anti-Tank (BAT) submunition.[37] What distinguishes Libicki's vision from the weapon systems of today is the ubiquity of multispectral sensors to form a mesh which no manned platform can evade. Libicki comes to the conclusion that 'By 2015, visibility is even more likely to equal death on the battle-field.'[38] On a practical level, the US Army has been developing higher levels of integration. In 2003, the 4th Infantry Division, the so-called 'digital division', was deployed to Iraq during the war to overthrow Saddam's regime.[39] Likewise, significantly improved levels of integration have achieved operational reality in the United States Navy's (USN) Co-operative Engagement Capability (CEC). Increasing levels of digital connection amongst units and weapon systems have led sections of the RMA literature to place networks at the centre of future conflict. Notable in this respect are the writings of Arquilla and Ronfeldt and the afore-mentioned concept of Network Centric Warfare.[40]

A key operational goal that could be made possible by the levels of integration mentioned above is Dominant Battlespace Knowledge. DBK builds upon the information coming from ISR assets, and produces knowledge of the enemy system, identifying key nodes and weaknesses, as well as marrying weapons to targets. A related concept is 'situational awareness'. This operational concept seeks the acquisition of a real-time image of the battlespace that includes knowing the disposition and location of both friendly and hostile forces. The objective is the creation of a transparent battlespace. Efforts to realise these operational concepts work to remove the fog of war from the battlespace for one's own forces, whilst increasing it for the enemy. Clearly, the attainment of these goals would go some way towards undermining an important element of the Clausewitzian paradigm. Of a similar ilk is 'information dominance'. Arquilla defines information dominance as 'Knowing everything about an adversary while keeping the adversary from knowing much about oneself.'[41] To Arquilla's definition, one might add that information dominance also includes: *knowing everything about oneself while keeping the adversary from knowing much about himself.* Achieving these objectives is increasingly being regarded as the primary operational goal, as a prerequisite to undertaking more traditional operations such as winning command of the air.[42] Achieving information dominance is also said to facilitate the exploitation of 'control warfare', as opposed to strate-gies characterised by manoeuvre or attrition.[43]

Other important buzzwords reverberating throughout the RMA liter-ature are 'simultaneity' and 'non-linearity'. Rather than a campaign being characterised by front lines, and a series of related but independent opera-

7

tions, campaigns in the information age will allegedly take the form of simultaneous attacks throughout the breadth, depth and cyberspace of the battlespace. The objective is to impose complete systemic shock upon the enemy.[44] In this sense it is often claimed that the tactical, operational and strategic levels are merging to a point where a single action proves to be decisive.[45] Thoughts such as these appear to resonate with the quest for decisive battle. At one level this emphasis on the decisive clash of arms has a certain Clausewitzian ring to it. However, often it misses the essence of Clausewitzian thought by all but ignoring the relationship between military means and policy ends. It also ignores the paradoxical logic of strategy and exhibits the danger of falling into the fallacy of the final move.[46] Finally, it has the tendency to reduce the complex, interactive activity of strategy to the mere bombardment of hostile forces.

Although the RMA literature displays certain common features, such as its emphasis on regular warfare[47] and its astrategic outlook, it does not present a homogeneous view of the future. In contrast to the above undue emphasis on battle, a section of the literature recoils somewhat from the use of destructive and violent force, and instead seeks decision through disruption and/or information dominance.[48] Lawrence Freedman postulates that the primacy of these concepts may have its roots in the cultural bias of the United States.[49] Whatever its origins, disruption is being hailed as the replacement for war based around destruction.[50] A further concept which reflects both the socio-political attitudes of the United States – which in some sections of the US policy-making establishment have created a culture of casualty aversion – and the technological advances of the information age is Edward Luttwak's notion of 'post-heroic warfare'. This mode of operation stresses forms of conflict that minimise contact between forces, and thereby hopefully reduce casualties.[51]

Finally, a higher tempo of operations is an important feature in visions of the RMA battlespace. Real-time information allied to DBK is said to facilitate a significantly higher tempo of operations relative to the enemy. This condition allows one's forces to operate inside the decision-making cycle of the adversary. The philosophical father of this concept is Boyd's OODA cycle.[52] Whilst the quest for a higher tempo is an admirable search for an advantage, an overemphasis of this can entail an astrategic, one-dimensional perspective of war, and ignorance of the human element in warfare. This latter error is particularly pertinent in regard to command issues. The search for an ever-higher tempo could lead to the temptation to remove the human actor from the decision-making loop and perhaps replace him with artificial intelligence (AI). This, in conjunction with the increasing promotion of the network C^2 structure, raises serious questions about the human dimension of command that is enshrined in the ideal of Clausewitz's military genius.

If the above visions of the future battlespace are taken too seriously there could be significant implications for the structure of forces in the information age. Libicki's work in particular explicitly signals the demise of the manned platform. He propounds that in the contest between stealth and the Mesh, the ubiquitous sensors will be victorious.[53] Libicki follows through the logic of the omnipotent Mesh to conclude that warfare will cease to be a force-on-force experience, and will increasingly be characterised by hide-and-seek, with the seekers having the edge. The notion is mass of effect rather than the massing of force.[54] Alternatively, the information age may facilitate the conduct of 'postmodern warfare', in which precise, distant bombardment dispenses with the need to deploy ground forces in a combat role and thereby relegates them to a constabulary function.[55] Many of these notions are not only astrategic and ignore the paradoxical logic of strategy; they also implicitly rely upon unrealistically effective operations, and thereby seemingly ignore the presence of friction.

As mentioned earlier, the art of command is an important testing ground for the interplay between humans and technology. In this respect, there has been a great deal of attention paid to potential changes in command style and structures. Aside from the use of AI to improve information handling and increase tempo, an area that has received a great deal of this attention is the structure of command systems. It is often noted in the literature that the hierarchical structure of current military command systems is inappropriate when faced with 'command networks' that are facilitated by the information age. These networks are based around a more equitable dispersal of power amongst more equal units. This creates a more flexible system, with a quicker information flow, and without a recognisable head that can be decapitated. Most notable in this field is the work of Arquilla and Ronfeldt.[56] As the debate has matured, hybrid concepts have appeared which attempt to marry military traditions with the challenges and opportunities of the information age.[57] It is predicted, often within military circles, that tying concepts such as DBK to network forms of C^2 will give lower echelons greater leverage.[58] The emphasis is on information flow and C^2 structures.

Acting somewhat as a counterbalance to these views, much of the broader command literature is infused with a greater emphasis on the role of human characteristics in the art of command. This is evident in the writings of many of those responsible for command, from the first-century Greek Onasander, to the writings of modern commanders.[59] The central role of the individual human commander is a shared theme in all three of the classical works. With Napoleon as their model, both Clausewitz and Jomini place the individual in centre stage. However, reflecting their differing perceptions on the predictability of war, Jomini sees the role of the commander as that of applying his identified principles of war, whereas for Clausewitz it is the traits of the military genius that are required to deal with the uncertainty and stresses of war. In Sun Tzu's work the human side of command is revealed as a contest of wits that includes understanding and playing upon the characteristics of the opposing general. For the future, a synthesis is required which can accommodate the advantages offered by AI and networks, but which does not forgo the requisite human features of command. War and command are both simultaneously human activities, but are also composed of a series of processes in which infrastructures and information are significant enablers.

The RMA literature that advocates many of the above revolutionary changes is not without its detractors. As the debate has matured, a number of writers have appeared to challenge many of the features of the RMA literature and offer more balanced appraisals on the future of warfare. Prominent amongst these are Riper and Scales, and Gray. Occasionally, individual essays make an important and striking contribution to the debate. In this latter category, Brian Holden Reid's 'Enduring Patterns in Modern Warfare' is worthy of particular note,[60] as is Biddle's 'Land Warfare: Theory and Practice'.[61] The cautionary remarks of these authors stem from an appreciation of many of the key elements of strategy, such as friction, policy requirements and asymmetrical forms of warfare. When considering the latter of these, the range of options available to a foe facing an RMA force are many and varied. They range from the employment of Weapons of Mass Destruction (WMD) to the adoption of various styles of irregular warfare.[62] One of the most troublesome asymmetrical responses in the long run will be the use or threat of WMD, especially nuclear weapons. Nuclear weapons can be used as weapons of mass disruption (through the production of an electromagnetic pulse that destroys electronic circuits);[63] as the means to deliver large amounts of destructive force to negate the qualitative advantage of an RMA foe; or as a deterrent force. Some strategies designed to offset RMA competence may actually serve to reinforce the potential changes in the nature of war. This is potentially the case in the use of SIW.

The SIW debate exhibits important similarities to the early musings on conventional strategic bombing. Although there has yet to emerge an information age variant of Douhet, making ambitious claims concerning the independent war-winning potential for SIW, some have come close. Schwartau is notable for postulating that this form of information warfare will become the dominant form of state conflict in the information age.[64] If this indeed becomes the case, then our understanding of the nature of war will need some reworking.

This facet of the information warfare debate has received a great deal of attention in both academic and policy circles. A significant moment in the recognition of this issue was President Clinton's issue of an Executive Order establishing the President's Commission on Critical Infrastructure Protection.[65] As concern over this threat has intensified, a host of organisations have been established to manage the problem. Indeed, in the aftermath of 9/11 the leading governmental organisations within the United States were brought together within the new Department of Homeland Security.[66] The bulk of the current literature displays a level of concern that is consistent with the spirit of the Presidential Executive Order, although there are a few notable dissenting voices that play down the threat from SIW.[67] Amongst the concerned fraternity, the most extreme proponents warn of the shutdown of information age societies in the wake of an attack. At minimum it is predicted that the economic competitiveness of a society would be seriously compromised.[68] There are a plethora of facts and figures that reveal both the growing dependence on information assets, and the related level of vulnerability. One of the most telling of these is the fact that 97 per cent of the US GDP exists as cybercash, meaning that it exists only on computers. A much-vaunted figure is that 95 per cent of government and military communications travel along private lines.[69] It is also important to note that the power grid; transportation network; telecommunication network; water supply system; financial and banking services; emergency services; and many other central sectors of post-industrial societies rely upon computer networks, and are therefore potentially vulnerable to SIW attack. Just-in-time (JIT) inventory control and management systems have become embedded in the National Strategic Infrastructure (NSI) of the United States.[70] This latter development allows a greater exploitation of efficiencies, but at the same time creates a certain amount of fragility within the system, as the fuel crisis demonstrated in the United Kingdom in September 2000.

The foundation for the ideas of the SIW literature is the notion that a late-industrial or information age society is increasingly dependent upon information and the required infrastructure.[71] Information is increasingly being discussed as a strategic asset. Consequently, these assets represent valuable targets through which to exert leverage and pursue policy objectives against such societies. A notable feature of SIW is that the capabilities required to wage such a campaign are widely available.[72] This means that potentially a small group or even an individual can cause substantial damage when utilising this form of warfare. However, some authors argue that a large-scale campaign requires substantial resources.[73]

Molander et al. have identified two categories of SIW. Alongside the Homeland variety as discussed above, they correctly note that an SIW capability can be used to disrupt military operations.[74] A seminal RAND study on SIW identifies four distinct theatres of operations in which the US deploying overseas forces could be attacked. These are: US Zone of Interior; Intercontinental Zone of Communications and Deployment; Allied Zone of Interior; and the Battlefield.[75] In this vein, troop deployments, communications and logistics present valuable targets. Logistics could prove a particularly inviting target as information age militaries increasingly adopt JIT logistics to increase efficiency and reduce their vulnerable logistics tail.[76]

The final area of the RMA debate that will be dealt with in this book concerns the geopolitical ramifications of the information age. The accessibility and flexibility of information power has led a number of writers to proclaim the demise of the nation-state and the growing insignificance of physical geography and proximity in international politics.[77] The radical nature of such claims testifies to the scope and reach of the changes the information age will allegedly usher in. As is the case with the other ambitious claims of the RMA literature, a more balanced strategic analysis of the geopolitical implications of the new epoch suggests that the changes will be less drastic than is often claimed.

Reflecting the broad scope of the information age RMA literature, this work will cover a range of diverse, if related, subjects. However, the homogeneity of the work is provided by the fact that in one way or another the various subsets of the RMA debate challenge the Clausewitzian paradigm. Therefore, this book will take the form of an analysis of the challenges posed to the Clausewitzian nature of war. Before embarking upon this task, Chapter 1 is devoted to an exploration of the various facets that make up this nature of war. Simultaneously, the opportunity is taken to examine the perspectives of Sun Tzu and Jomini. This exercise serves as the basis for a later comparison of the three great works in light of the changes wrought by the information age. In the case of Sun Tzu, this is especially important because his work has been touted as more relevant to the information age than Clausewitz. In this respect Libicki and Shapiro describe Sun Tzu as 'an icon in this pantheon'.[78] Whereas, Jomini deserves attention since his work has perhaps been underestimated, and therefore The Art of War may benefit from the exposure of the information age.

The subsequent four chapters will explore the areas of strategy that have attracted the most attention in the RMA literature and which offer the most significant changes, and therefore present the most direct challenges to the nature of war as outlined in On War. To this end, Chapter 2 assesses the fortunes of Clausewitz's 'climate of war' in the future battlespace. This analysis is undertaken within a framework composed of the five essential features of strategy: the demands of policy;

the paradoxical logic (dialectic nature of strategy); the various geographic settings in which strategy is conducted; the polymorphous character of war; and finally the fifth, generic factor that underpins all the others: the fact that war is a human activity.

Chapter 3 retains the focus on the battlespace but concentrates on the art of command. An entire chapter is devoted to this area to reflect the significance of the human element in war, and in particular Clausewitz's emphasis on the military genius as the instrument through which to deal with the complexities and uncertainties of warfare. Particular attention is focused upon the development of AI and the rise of the network structure. In different ways, these two developments both challenge the prominence of the individual human commander.

Moving beyond the battlespace, the fourth chapter deals with SIW. This new form of waging war holds the potential to amend the nature of warfare if it can prove to be independently decisive. In the absence of any historical case studies of a substantial SIW campaign, the theory and practice of strategic bombing is utilised as an informative analogy. It is suggested that many of the same factors that have retarded the strategic potential of strategic bombing will place similar restraints on SIW, in which case the revolutionary potential of SIW will be curtailed.

The penultimate chapter broadens the scope of the book and considers the strategic and geopolitical ramifications of the rise of information power. This includes an analysis of the infosphere as the fifth dimension of strategy, the flexible and accessible nature of information power and how this newly empowered dimension will interact with the more established environments.

Finally, the work concludes with an assessment of the Clausewitzian nature of war in light of the changes likely to occur in the information age. From this, the continued relevance of the three great works of strategic theory is assessed. It is concluded that in the most important respects Clausewitz's work remains the most useful work of theory. Nevertheless, in the same manner by which Brodie and Gray suggest that *On War* requires supplementation to reflect certain changes over time and shortcomings in the text, to cope with the nuclear revolution for example, the works of theory that reflect the information age are examined to assess whether they have anything to add to the established treatises. The main objective of this book is to present a balanced assessment of the nature of war in the information age, and consequently to appraise whether Clausewitz's work remains 'not simply the greatest but the only truly great book on war'.[79]

NOTES

1. Winn Schwartau, *Information Warfare: Cyberterrorism: Protecting Your Personal Security in the Electronic Age*, 2nd edition (New York, Thunder's Mouth Press, 1996), Ch. 2, pp. 71–86.

2. Quoted in United States Department of Defense, *Secretary Rumsfeld Speaks on '21st Century Transformation' of US Armed Forces* (transcript of remarks and question and answer period), www.defenselink.mil/speeches/2002/s20020131-secdef.html.

3. Stephen Biddle, *Afghanistan and the Future of Warfare: Implications for Army and Defense Policy* (Carlise, PA, Strategic Studies Institute, US Army War College, 2002).

4. Julian Borger and Richard Norton-Taylor, 'US Generals Embrace New Kind of Warfare', *Guardian*, 22 March 2003, p. 4.

5. Oliver Burkeman, 'Shock Tactics', *G2, Guardian*, 25 March 2003, pp. 2–3.

6. MacGregor Knox and Williamson Murray offer an alternative term to describe the RMA enthusiasts by referring to them as 'technological utopians'. Williamson Murray and MacGregor Knox, 'Conclusion: The Future Behind Us', in Williamson Murray and MacGregor Knox (eds), *The Dynamics of Military Revolution, 1300–2050* (Cambridge, Cambridge University Press, 2001), p. 179.

7. Robert B. Asprey, *War in the Shadows* (London, Little, Brown, 1994), p. 419.

8. David Chandler, *The Campaigns of Napoleon*, (London, Weidenfeld & Nicolson, 1966), p. 165, and Nigel Bagnall, *The Punic Wars: Rome, Carthage and the Struggle for the Mediterranean* (London, Pimlico, 1999), pp. 180–3.

9. See Dorothy E. Denning, *Information Warfare and Security* (Boston, MA, Addison-Wesley, 1999), p. 14, and Martin Libicki and Jeremy Shapiro, 'Conclusion: The Changing Role of Information in Warfare', in Zalmay Khalizad, John P. White and Andrew W. Marshall (eds), *Strategic Appraisal: The Changing Role of Information in Warfare* (Santa Monica, CA, RAND, 1999), p. 437.

10. William E. Odom quoted in A. J. Bacevich, 'Preserving the Well-Bred Horse', *National Interest*, 37 (1994), p. 46. This proclivity to postulate that the nature of war is changing is widespread. See also Jeffrey McKitrick, James Blackwell, Fred Littlepage, George Kraws, Richard Blanchfield and Dale Hill, 'The Revolution in Military Affairs', www.airpwr.maxwell.af.mil/airchronicles/battle/chap3.html. Similarly, David C. Gompert makes the same claim. See David C. Gompert, 'The Information Revolution and US National Security', *Naval War College Review*, 51, 4 (1998), p. 29. Other examples can be found in Ch. 1, p. 19 of this book.

11. Hedley Bull, *The Anarchical Society: A Study of Order in World Politics* (London, Macmillan, 1977), p. 184.

12. See Colin S. Gray, *Modern Strategy* (Oxford, Oxford University Press, 1999), p. 17.

13. Carl von Clausewitz, *On War*, trans. Michael Howard and Peter Paret (London, David Campbell, 1993), p. 146.

14. Andre Beaufre, *An Introduction to Strategy: With Particular Reference to the Problems of Defence, Politics, Economics, and Diplomacy in the Nuclear Age* (London, Faber & Faber, 1965), p. 22.

15. For a range of definitions of strategy see John Baylis and James J. Wirtz, 'Introduction', in John Baylis, James Wirtz, Eliot Cohen and Colin S. Gray (eds), *Strategy in the Contemporary World: An Introduction to Strategic Studies* (Oxford, Oxford University Press, 2002), p. 4.

16. Eliot Cohen, 'Technology and Warfare', in John Baylis, James Wirtz, Eliot Cohen and Colin S. Gray (eds), *Strategy in the Contemporary World: An Introduction to Strategic Studies* (Oxford, Oxford University Press, 2002), p. 247.

17. *Joint Vision 2020* (Washington, DC, US Government Printing Office, 2000).

18. Alvin and Heidi Toffler, *War and Anti-war: Survival at the Dawn of the 21st Century* (London, Little, Brown, 1994). An even more radical vision of the changes to come in both society and warfare is to be found in Michael Vlahos, 'The War after Byte City', *Washington Quarterly*, 20, 2 (1997), pp. 39–72.
19. J. F. C. Fuller, *Armament and History: A Study of the Influence of Armament on History from the Dawn of Classical Warfare to the Second World War* (London, Eyre & Spottiswoode, 1946), p. v.
20. For example, see Major Chip Thompson, 'F-16 UCAVs: A Bridge to the Future of Air Combat', *Aerospace Power Journal*, Spring 2000, www.airpower.maxwell.af.mil/airchronicles/apj/apj00/spr00/thompson.htm.
21. Colin S. Gray, 'A Contested Vision: The RMA Debate Today', paper presented at The Royal Institute of International Affairs conference 'Revolution in Military Affairs? Challenges to Government and Industry in the Information Age', Chatham House, London, 21–22 May 1997, p. 10.
22. For a description of military genius see Clausewitz, *On War*, Book 1, Ch. 3, pp. 115–131.
23. See Ch. 4, pp. 137–8, for a discussion on the misuse of the term 'strategic'.
24. Fuller, *Armament and History*, p. v.
25. Martin van Creveld, *Technology and War*, revised and expanded edition (New York, Free Press, 1991).
26. Michael Howard, 'The Dimensions of Strategy', in Lawrence Freedman (ed.), *War* (Oxford, Oxford University Press, 1994).
27. Gray, *Modern Strategy*, p. 37.
28. See Stephen Biddle, 'Land Warfare: Theory and Practice', in John Baylis, James Wirtz, Eliot Cohen and Colin S. Gray (eds), *Strategy in the Contemporary World: An Introduction to Strategic Studies* (Oxford, Oxford University Press, 2002), p. 104.
29. For a discussion of the development of the RMA see James R. Blaker, *Understanding the Revolution in Military Affairs: A Guide to America's 21st Century Defense*, Progressive Policy Institute, Defense Working Paper 3 (Washington, DC, January 1997).
30. See Guy Hartcup, *The Silent Revolution: Development of Conventional Weapons 1945–85* (London, Brassey's, 1993).
31. Jonathan Bailey, *The First World War and the Birth of the Modern Style of Warfare*, The Occasional, 22 (Camberley, Strategic and Combat Studies Institute, Joint Services Staff College, 1997).
32. Williamson Murray, 'Armoured Warfare: The British, French, and German Experiences', in Williamson Murray and Allan R. Millett (eds), *Military Innovation in the Interwar Period* (Cambridge, Cambridge University Press, 1996), p. 40.
33. See Arther Ferrill, *The Origins of War: From the Stone Age to Alexander the Great* (London, Thames & Hudson, 1985). J. F. C. Fuller mirrors Ferrill's assessment that Phillip II created the all-arms tactical organisation that was an enabling factor in Alexander's successes. See Fuller, *Armament and History*, p. 39. Lieutenant-Colonel Stephen J. Kirin also notes that Field Marshal Slim was a great exponent of the art of synchronisation. See Lieutenant-Colonel Stephen J. Kirin, 'Synchronisation', *Naval War College Review*, 49, 4 (1996), pp. 7–21.
34. Joint Chiefs of Staff, 'Joint Vision 2010: America's Military – Preparing for Tomorrow', *Joint Force Quarterly*, 12 (1996), pp. 34–49.
35. Admiral William A. Owens, 'The Emerging System of Systems', *Military Review*, 75, 3 (1995), pp. 15–19. See also Admiral William A. Owens, 'Introduction', in Stuart E. Johnson and Martin C. Libicki (eds), *Dominant Battlespace Knowledge*, Revised Edition (Washington, DC, National Defense University, 1996), pp. 1–14.
36. These thoughts, and many others on the subject of the information age battlefield, are

developed by Libicki in his work, *The Mesh and the Net: Speculation on Armed Conflict in an Age of Free Silicon*, McNair Paper 28 (Washington, DC, National Defense University, Institute for National Strategic Studies, 1996).

37. Marvin G. Metcalf, 'Acoustics on the 21st Century Battlefield', *Joint Force Quarterly*, 10 (Winter 1995–96), pp. 44–7. For further details on autonomous weapons see Michael Sovereign, 'DBK with Autonomous Weapons', in Johnson and Libicki (eds), *Dominant Battlespace Knowledge*, pp. 103–13.

38. Martin C. Libicki, 'Technology and Warfare', in Patrick M. Cronin (ed.), *2015: Power and Progress*, www.ndu.edu/ndu/inss/books/2015/chap4.html.

39. It was thought that the War for Iraq would represent the first battlefield test for the 4th Infantry Division. However, the digital division never engaged in any large-scale conflict. See Ewen MacAskill and Stuart Millar, 'America's Digital Division – the Biggest Advance in Warfare since the Tank', *Guardian*, 7 April 2003, p. 7.

40. Most of Arquilla and Ronfeldt's work on this subject can be found in John Arquilla and David Ronfeldt (eds), *In Athena's Camp: Preparing for Conflict in the Information Age* (Santa Monica, CA, RAND, 1996). For NCW see Vice-Admiral Arthur K. Cebrowski, 'Network-Centric Warfare: An Emerging Military Response to the Information Age', Command and Control Research and Technology Symposium, 29 June 1999, and Stanley B. Weeks, 'US Maritime Doctrine and Manoeuvre Warfare', New Dimensions: Maritime Manoeuvre and the Strategic Defence Review, Conference at the University of Hull, 2 July 1999.

41. John Arquilla, 'The Strategic Implications of Information Dominance', *Strategic Review*, 22, 3 (1994), p. 25.

42. See Lt-Col. Michael R. Nifong, 'The Key to Information Dominance', *Military Review*, 76, 3 (1996), and Phillip L. Ritcheson, 'The Future of "Military Affairs": Revolution or Evolution?', *Strategic Review*, 24, 2 (1996), pp. 31–40, and General Gordon R. Sullivan, 'A Vision for the Future', *Military Review*, 75, 3 (1995), pp. 5–14.

43. See Arquilla, 'The Strategic Implications of Information Dominance'. On this issue Gray correctly alerts us to the fact that such claims as these present a false distinction amongst these three styles of warfare. See Gray, *Modern Strategy*, pp. 159–62, 176–9.

44. For a discussion of many of the operational concepts in the RMA literature see Colin S. Gray, *The American Revolution in Military Affairs: An Interim Assessment*, The Occasional, 28 (Camberley, Strategic and Combat Studies Institute, 1997), p. 10.

45. For example, see Jeffrey R. Cooper, 'Another View of the Revolution in Military Affairs', in Arquilla and Ronfeldt (eds), *In Athena's Camp*, p. 129.

46. The concept of the paradoxical logic of strategy is enunciated in the work of Edward Luttwak. Its essence is 'nothing fails like success'. Whether by overreaching itself or by instigating countermeasures from the enemy, a successful strategy, tactic or technology will provide diminishing returns over time, or may be negated completely. See Edward N. Luttwak, *Strategy: The Logic of War and Peace* (Cambridge, MA, Belknap Press, 1987).

47. This point is made in Christopher Jon Lamb, 'The Impact of Information Age Technologies on Operations Other Than War', in Robert L. Pfaltzgraff, Jr and Richard H. Shultz, Jr (eds), *War in the Information Age: New Challenges for US Security Policy* (Washington, DC, Brassey's, 1997), p. 247.

48. These sentiments can be found variously in the works of Arquilla and Ronfeldt, and Libicki. See the discussion of this subject in Ch. 2.

49. L. Freedman, *Information Warfare: Will Battle Ever Be Joined?*, International Centre for Security Analysis (Launch), 14 October 1996.

50. John Arquilla and David Ronfeldt, *The Advent of Netwar* (Santa Monica, CA, RAND, 1996).

51. Edward N. Luttwak, 'A Post-Heroic Military Policy', *Foreign Affairs*, 75, 4 (1996),

pp. 33–44.

52. For a description and analysis of the OODA loop, see Grant T. Hammond, *The Mind of War: John Boyd and American Security* (Washington, DC, Smithsonian Institution Press, 2001), and David S. Fadok, *John Boyd and John Warden: Air Power's Quest for Strategic Paralysis* (Maxwell Air Force Base, AL, Air University Press, 1995).
53. Libicki, *The Mesh and the Net*.
54. Libicki, 'Technology and Warfare'.
55. This notion is discussed in Captain Chris Parry, 'Some Recent and Emerging Themes in Maritime Warfare', New Dimensions: Maritime Manoeuvre and the Strategic Defence Review, Conference at the University of Hull, 2 July 1999.
56. Arquilla and Ronfeldt, *The Advent of Netwar*, and Ashley Craddock, 'Netwar and Peace in the Global Village', an interview with John Arquilla, *Wired*, 5.05, May 1997.
57. See Captain John Bodnar and Second Lieutenant Rebecca Dengler, 'The Emergence of the Command Network', *Naval War College Review*, 49, 4 (1996), pp. 93–107.
58. Joint Chiefs of Staff, 'Joint Vision 2010: America's Military – Preparing for Tomorrow', p. 41.
59. See the chapter 'Onasander', in G. Chaliand, *The Art of War in World History: From Antiquity to the Nuclear Age* (Berkeley, CA, University of California Press, 1994), pp. 154–6 and Archibald Wavell, *Generals and Generalship* (London, Times Publishing, 1941). For an example of command in the Gulf War of 1991, see General Sir Peter de la Billiere, *Storm Command* (London, HarperCollins, 1992).
60. See Paul Van Riper and Robert H. Scales, Jr, 'Preparing for War in the 21st Century', *Parameters*, 27, 3 (1997), pp. 4–14, Gray, *The American Revolution*, and Brian Holden Reid, 'Enduring Patterns in Modern Warfare', in Brian Bond and Mungo Melvin (eds), *The Nature of Future Conflict: Implications for Force Development*, The Occasional, 36 (Camberley, Strategic and Combat Studies Institute, Joint Services Staff College, 1998), pp. 15–30.
61. Stephen Biddle, 'Land Warfare: Theory and Practice', in Baylis, Wirtz, Cohen and Gray (eds), *Strategy in the Contemporary World*, pp. 91–112.
62. For the classic explanation of the challenges posed by irregular warfare, or 'small wars', see C. E. Callwell, *Small Wars: A Tactical Textbook for Imperial Soldiers* (London, Greenhill Books, 1990).
63. Charles S. Grace, *Nuclear Weapons: Principles, Effects and Survivability*, Land Warfare: Brassey's New Battlefield Weapons Systems and Technology Series, Vol. 10 (London, Brassey's, 1994). See Ch. 7 for details of the EMP effects of nuclear weapons, and
    possible defensive measures in the face of such effects.
64. Schwartau, *Information Warfare*, pp. 27–8.
65. A copy of this Executive Order can be found at the following website: www.infowar.com/CIVIL_DE/Cyberwar.html-ssi. This project has been described by former Deputy Attorney-General Gorelick as the equivalent of the Manhattan project. See John Carlin, 'The Netizen: A Farewell to Arms', *Wired*, 5.05, May 1997.
66. For details on governmental responses to this issue see Robert F. Dacey, *Critical Infrastructure Protection: Significant Homeland Security Challenges Need to Be Addressed* (Washington, DC, United States General Accounting Office, July 2002), www.gao.gov/cgi-bin/getrpt?GAO-02-918T.
67. In the United Kingdom Lawrence Freedman is one of the few writers to have written on this issue. See his paper, *Information Warfare: Will Battle Ever Be Joined?*
68. P. G. Neumann, 'Security Risks in the Computer-Communication Infrastructure', Written testimony for the US Senate Permanent Subcommittee on Investigations of the Senate Committee on Governmental Affairs, 25 June 1996, p. 41.
69. The cybercash figure was taken from Schwartau, *Information Warfare*, p. 43. See

Schwartau, *Information Warfare*, p. 48 for details concerning usage of private lines by the military and government.

70. Peter A. Wilson, 'The Transformation of Military Power, 1997–2027', paper presented at the 1997 Pacific Symposium, Honolulu, Hawaii, 28–29 April 1997, p. 5.
71. An early identification of this threat within US policy circles can be found in S. Nunn, 'Opening Statement', US Senate Permanent Subcommittee on Investigations Hearing on Security in Cyberspace, 25 June 1996.
72. The ease with which hacking techniques can be obtained is noted in Schwartau, *Information Warfare*, p. 39, and John M. Deutch, 'Foreign Information Warfare Programs and Capabilities', Statement for the Record to the US Senate Committee on Governmental Affairs; Permanent Subcommittee on Investigations, 25 June 1996, p. 3
73. See Schwartau, *Information Warfare*.
74. See Roger C. Molander, Andrew S. Riddile and Peter A. Wilson, 'Strategic Information Warfare: A New Face of War', *Parameters*, 26, 3 (1996), www.carlisle-army.mil/usawc/Parameters/96autumn/molander.htm, and Douglas Waller, 'Onward Cyber Soldiers', *Time International*, 21 August 1995, pp. 31–2.
75. Molander *et al.*, 'Strategic Information Warfare', p. 85
76. Peter A. Wilson, *Preparing for Early 21st Century War: Beyond the Bottom-Up Review*, CGSC Monograph, 'Toward 2000' Series, 5 (Centre for Global Security Cooperation).
77. See Michael Vlahos, 'The War after Byte City', pp. 39–72, Jessica T. Mathews, 'Power Shift', *Foreign Affairs*, 76, 1 (1997), pp. 50–66.
78. Libicki and Shapiro, 'Conclusion', p. 439.
79. Bernard Brodie, 'The Continuing Relevance of *On War*', in Carl von Clausewitz, *On War*, trans. Michael Howard and Peter Paret (London, David Campbell, 1993), p. 57.

1

Classical Strategic Thought and the Nature of War

'The central ingredients of military victory or defeat will continue to reflect the enduring nature of war at least as much as the transient means used to prosecute it.' [1]

INTRODUCTION

Before undertaking an analysis of any subject, it is often necessary to define some of the main terms used. In the context of this book a satisfactory understanding of the word 'nature' is required. The ultimate objective of this work is to test the continued validity of the fundamentals of warfare, the constants if you will, those elements which are the very essence of war across both time and place, rather than its more transient features. Words such as 'nature' are often used rather loosely, both in general language and more importantly within the academic and professional literature. It is not unusual to come across works in which analysts clearly state that the nature of warfare will change. In *The Future of Warfare* Francois Heisbourg confidently claims that a series of technological, political, social and economic changes 'are transforming the nature of warfare'.[2] Similarly, Arquilla and Ronfeldt argue that the information revolution will bring the next shift in the nature of warfare.[3] Even more ambitiously Robert R. Leonhard asserts that the information age represents the greatest change to the nature of war.[4] These are substantial claims that should not go unchallenged. Therefore, the first step in verifying these assertions is to understand what the nature of warfare actually is.

According to one dictionary definition, 'nature' refers to 'a thing's essential qualities'.[5] In this sense the nature of warfare is different from its character. The character of war, or rather its style, is a constantly changing phenomenon; it is less absolute. For example, the Napoleonic Wars were clearly of a different character to the campaigns in the Pacific during World War II. Features of the latter such as carrier-borne aircraft, strategic bombing (including the use of atomic weapons) and island hopping distinguish it from the former. The forces, tactics and operational art employed vary depending upon a number of factors. These include the period of history one is considering, which security communities are engaged, the technology in use and the policy objectives to be attained. These self-evident truths should not be taken as evidence that the character of war is of little importance. Understanding the character of a particular war is an important prerequisite to its successful conduct. However, in relation to this work, of even greater significance is the possibility that the character of war could change to such an extent that the nature of war itself may be altered. Consequently, this work will test the hypothesis that a dynamic relationship exists between the character and nature of war, and that the changes wrought by the information age will be so momentous that the nature of war itself will be transformed. In theory, if all wars were concluded by calculations of 'information dominance', or through information attacks against information infrastructures, warfare would all but cease to be a violent activity. Should that come to pass, the nature of warfare would have been altered by a change in the character of war. Such possibilities may explain the proclivity of certain authors to proclaim the rise of Sun Tzu at the expense of Clausewitz, since the former is noted for his admonition to achieve victory without fighting.[6] However, thus far, although the character of war has proved mutable, the nature of warfare has been resistant to significant or permanent change.

In light of the above thoughts, the main objective of this chapter is to define the nature of warfare, as it is traditionally understood. This will be achieved using various accounts and memoirs of war, as well as the three great works of classical strategic thought: Carl von Clausewitz's *On War*, Sun Tzu's *The Art of War* and Baron Antoine Henri de Jomini's *The Art of War*. In this sense, the fate of these three works, and especially *On War*, are entwined with that of the nature of warfare itself. The historical record is also utilised in the endeavour to understand the true nature of war. The value of using history in an attempt to understand warfare is well expressed by Moltke, who described military history as 'the most effective means of teaching war during peace'.[7]

Any attempt to capture the essence of an activity as complex as war is self-evidently a large undertaking, and will ultimately fail to accurately reflect the true reality. James Kiras is convincing when he declares, 'Definitions rarely convey the complexity of a subject in either theory or practice.'[8] It is because of this that we turn to the theories of Clausewitz, Sun Tzu and Jomini to act as aids in the task. Clausewitz identifies the value of theory in this respect when he notes: 'Theory exists so that one need not start afresh each time sorting out the material and ploughing through it, but will find it ready to hand and in good order.'⁹ So, strategic theory provides an important conceptual tool for our analysis. Still, an important question remains: why choose these particular works of theory from amongst the mountain of literature that has been written on the subject of war? The answer to this question lies in the fact that these three works are regarded as the founders of modern military thought, and as performing the role of enabling students of war to understand the central elements of the activity.¹⁰ The language and ideas expressed in these works permeate a great deal of modern military doctrine and academic work on war. With regard to understanding the nature of war this is particularly the case for Clausewitz's work. There is perhaps no better example of this than the United States Marine Corps' (USMC) doctrine manual *Fleet Marine Force Manual 1 'Warfighting' (FMFM-1)*. Clausewitzian ideas and language dominate this document. Indeed, *Warfighting* stipulates that Clausewitz's *On War* is 'the definitive treatment of the nature and theory of war'.¹¹ *Warfighting* regards both Clausewitz and Sun Tzu as essential reading for any marine officer.¹² Clausewitz and Sun Tzu's influence can be seen in many other doctrinal works, including *British Defence Doctrine: Joint Warfare Publication (JWP) 0-01*.¹³ Although not as obvious as the other two theorists, Jomini's influence can also be detected in modern military thought. Daniel Moran notes that the principles of war upon which modern military doctrine is based are all reminiscent of Jomini's ideas.¹⁴

As previously noted, this book does not rest its understanding of the nature of war solely upon these three works. Memoirs and accounts of warfare play an equally valid role in understanding war's true nature. However, a further validation of using the three chosen works of theory emanates from the fact that all of the three great theorists were practitioners of war, and therefore their works are the theoretical representations of their real experiences. It follows from this discussion that, since it is the works of Clausewitz, Sun Tzu and Jomini which have been most influential in shaping our understanding of the nature of war, it is these three works which will be examined to discern how relevant they remain, and consequently whether the pre-information age concept of the nature of warfare retains its relevance.

Why is it important to understand the nature of war? There are two main answers to this question. The first concerns a purely academic interest which stems from man's desire to understand the world around him and in particular the activities in which he engages. Since war can be such an important event for the individual, the state or indeed the whole international system, a desire to better comprehend it is understandable. However, there are more practical reasons to engage in an attempt to grasp the essence of war. This relates to how actors prepare for hostilities. What one perceives as the nature of warfare greatly influences the development of doctrine, force composition and training. Clausewitz himself noted that the nature of war affects which forces will be used.[15] Turning once again to the USMC, *Warfighting* declares: 'our understanding of the nature and the theory of war ... must be the guiding force behind our preparation for war'.[16] If we take for example the training and education of officers, this is based on the established belief that war is a political, chaotic, violent, uncertain and human activity. It follows that, if the nature of war should be altered by the information age, then the whole panoply of war preparation (including military culture) will require amendment in order to prepare for a very different kind of conflict than has occurred historically.

THE GENESIS OF STRATEGIC THOUGHT

Before embarking upon an analysis of the nature of war, it is important to describe briefly the influences upon the three classic theorists. Any thinker, including the author of this book, will be influenced by their experiences and the intellectual environment of their time and place. Indeed, Roger Parkinson has identified a vital relationship between Clausewitz's experiences and his writings.[17] In the context of understanding the true nature of war these influences must be considered. It may transpire that each theorist's notion of warfare is more a reflection of his experiences and his intellectual environment than a representation of the immutable reality of war. When we come to analyse the nature of warfare in the information age it may be profitable to consider that our own perspective will be coloured by our own times and culture. Western attitudes at the turn of the twenty-first century are wont to emphasise less destructive forms of warfare or, at least, a conduct of warfare which is more sensitive to casualties (in terms of both combatants and civilians).[18] It is worth considering that this particular mindset of the information age, rather than the reality of war, may lead us to reject the classical strategists too readily. In this sense, the RMA literature may represent no more than a political, social or intellectual fad.

Both Jomini and Clausewitz witnessed and indeed participated in the Napoleonic Wars. In this sense they both witnessed a time when, through political, technological, organisational and operational changes, warfare became much more total, embracing as it did on the French side the fervour of the revolution and the utilisation of a large part of the nation's resources and effort.[19] As an aside, it is interesting to note that the French revolution in warfare was eventually defeated by armed forces and societies, especially the British, which operated in more traditional ways.[20] This is perhaps an early warning to those who equate the exploitation of an RMA with final victory. It is not only the general trends of the time that influence the theorist. More individual experiences can partly account for the fact that different theories can emerge from the same environment. For example, Jomini served primarily as a staff officer. John Shy notes that this experience with the general staff influenced Jomini to adopt a planning-based approach to the subject of war. This may explain his greater emphasis on concepts such as lines of operation.[21] In broad philosophical terms both Jomini and Clausewitz display a tendency for the Enlightenment's propensity towards rational analysis.[22] Christopher Bellamy focuses attention upon their use of Newtonian concepts such as 'mass', 'momentum' and 'force'. Moreover, Bellamy notes that both of them also base their theories in a strictly linear formula.[23] Jomini in particular displays a very Newtonian approach in his quest to discover the fundamental principles underpinning the activity of war. Whereas Jomini is criticised for failing to escape the rationalism of the eighteenth century,[24] Clausewitz managed to create a synthesis of the Enlightenment's rationality and the non-rational approach of German Romanticism with its greater emphasis on the psychological, emotional, metaphysical and intuitive.[25]

Sun Tzu on the other hand represents the Taoist tradition with its emphasis on non-material force-multipliers. In this sense, Thomas Cleary suggests that Sun Tzu's theory bears the hallmark of Taoism, 'the ancient tradition of knowledge'.[26] Michael Handel concludes from this that for Sun Tzu war in its ideal form becomes an intellectual and metaphysical exercise rather than a physical one.[27] Similarly, van Creveld notes that for Sun Tzu war is a necessary evil that nonetheless represents a departure from cosmic harmony. It follows that, should conflict be unavoidable, violence should be kept to a minimum.[28] Like Clausewitz and Jomini, Sun Tzu was also writing at a time regarded as one of revolutionary change in the art of warfare.[29] Griffith notes that war in the age of Sun Tzu was more total, in the sense that it was less ritualistic, and less restricted to campaigning seasons. Conscript standing armies under the control of professional officers were increasingly common, and general staffs had begun to appear.[30] The careers of the three great theorists may suggest that significant works of theory are more likely to appear in times of revolutionary change in warfare. Should this be the case, perhaps we can expect an important work to emerge from the information age to supplement or even replace the current dominant treatises.

THE NATURE OF WAR – THE ROLE OF POLICY

Any attempt to extract an understanding of the nature of war from the three great works of theory quickly runs into a series of apparent contradictions amongst the works. There are a number of possible outcomes from these contradictions. It may be that the true nature of war lies within a synthesis of all three works. This still leaves the question of whether this synthesis has been left outdated by the information age. Alternatively, it may be that each of the works represents a vision of warfare that is not universal. Rather, each one is more or less appropriate to a certain time and place, in which case one is perhaps more appropriate to the information age than the others. The following sections of this chapter will extract the main elements relating to the nature of warfare from the three works, and conclude by attempting to produce a coherent appreciation of war's nature.

War is an extremely diverse activity, with many facets that could conceivably be regarded as part of its 'nature'. One such element that lays a controversial claim to being embedded in the nature of warfare is the 'policy rationale'. This is most famously declared in Clausewitz's oft quoted assertion: 'We see, therefore, that war is not merely an act of policy but a true political instrument, a continuation of political intercourse, carried on with other means.'[31] This constituent of war unifies the three theorists. However, the notion that this represents an abiding component of war's nature has not gone unchallenged. This principle element of *On War* has been questioned by some of the biggest names in the field of modern military studies. John Keegan opens his work *A History of Warfare* with the following bold statement: 'WAR IS NOT THE continuation of policy by other means' (emphasis in the original).[32] Keegan's main criticism of Clausewitz boils down to this: because in many cases, and throughout most of history, war has been harmful, even fatal, to those security communities who have conducted it, it cannot be regarded purely as a rational instrument of policy. Keegan goes on to argue that war is often a cultural and/or ritualistic activity. In response to this criticism, Christopher Bassford correctly notes that Keegan's analysis is based upon a very narrow interpretation of Clausewitz's work. As Bassford argues, Clausewitz was certainly not postulating that warfare was always undertaken in a rational manner. Indeed, the Romantic influence in Clausewitz suggests that he fully accepted a non-rational tendency in war.[33] It has also been noted that the Clausewitzian trinity reveals that its author understood that war was not a finely controlled, purely rational activity. The trinity consists of 'primordial violence', 'chance and probability' and 'the role of policy'.[34] Mark T. Clark suggests that the first two features of the trinity can be regarded as non-rational forces.[35] Similarly, Gray describes the trinity as a flexible concept encompassing both rational and non-rational elements.[36] Rather than portraying war as a sterile activity, Clausewitz noted that policy objectives give birth to war, and therefore they should guide how it is waged. Policy is also one of the factors which helps prevent warfare from escalating to its extreme. If Clausewitz can ever be said to have proffered advice, it is that war should never be conducted in accordance with its own independent rationale. Rather, actions should always be undertaken with the policy objective as the guiding factor.[37]

Martin van Creveld is also guilty of basing his criticisms of Clausewitz on very strict and narrow interpretations of concepts central to the Prussian's work. Akin to Keegan, van Creveld allocates a narrow definition to the concept of 'a continuation of policy'. His interpretation restricts Clausewitz's work as being appropriate only to the post-1648 Westphalian world, and therefore relevant only to state-to-state conflict.[38] These precepts lead van Creveld to conclude that *On War* is of limited value in understanding the entire spectrum of warfare. In his book *The Transformation of War* van Creveld also breaks down the motivations for warfare into many categories, within which politics is a distinct motivation. In this context van Creveld once again relies upon narrow and restrictive definitions. For him politics is merely concerned with secular state interests: 'Thus, strictly speaking, the dictum that war is the continuation of politics means nothing more or less than that it represents an instrument in the hands of the state.'[39]

An illuminating example of how van Creveld restricts his analysis to narrow and rigid distinctions is in his section regarding religion as an influence and motivation in war. He claims that the influence of religion on warfare declined in post-1648 Europe.[40] There are two predominant reasons why this surely draws the line too strictly between religion and what van Creveld regards as politics. First, religious doctrine often underpins political sentiment, even to this day. Second, both politics and religion are concerned with how societies conduct and organise themselves. In this sense, to classify wars of religion and those with political motives as mutually exclusive is to draw artificial distinctions. Of course this is not to suggest that religion and politics are one and the same. Rather, it is merely to suggest that a war waged to decide which religious group or doctrine should hold sway is not so different from wars waged to decide which political grouping or ideology should dominate a territory or population. Both religious and political rationales have resulted in wars waged to expand the authority of one group at the expense of others. Also, as the case of Philip II of Spain reveals, war can be waged by a state for reasons of religion and 'secular politics' simultaneously. Philip II's conflicts in the sixteenth century were concerned with promoting the security interests of Habsburg Spain, as well as being part of the Counter-Reformation.[41] Indeed, in Philip II's foreign policy religion and state interests cannot be separated.[42]

Clausewitz's work can be taken on the basis that 'policy' refers to any objective for which war is waged, in which case his central point remains that war, being nothing more than a continuation of this motivation, should not have a rationale independent from this guiding objective. Policy may concern religious issues, territorial disputes, resources or indeed important cultural events. In Book Eight, Chapter Six of *On War*, Clausewitz himself declares, 'Policy, of course, is nothing in itself; it is simply the trustee for all these interests against other states ... we can only treat policy as representative of all interests of the community.'[43] Along similar lines, William R. Hawkins declares: 'War is about politics, and politics is about the governing of land and people.'[44]

One can argue endlessly over what Clausewitz's exact thoughts were on these issues. However, in one sense this does not really matter. If the point in question is how relevant *On War* is to understanding the future of warfare, then adopting a more general interpretation of Clausewitz's work, in which 'policy' or indeed the term 'interests' is more inclusive, not only makes *On War* more universal, it also presents us with a theory for understanding almost any war regardless of it motivations.

Clausewitz's work can also be interpreted as more universal in relation to what van Creveld describes as 'wars of existence' (war in its most total form). In these instances, van Creveld argues that the means and ends have merged to a point where distinctions between them have become meaningless, and any cost/benefit analysis becomes equally redundant. Rationality, which van Creveld associates with 'state interests', has become equally irrelevant.[45] The first response to this argument is that the decision to wage a war of existence is often just that, a decision. Bernard Brodie is persuasive when he argues, 'war is an act of choice'.[46] A choice has been made to resist. An actor can always decide not to fight and therefore surrender, in which case a choice has been made based upon some form of cost/benefit calculation of fighting or surrender. It may have been decided that subjugation to enemy rule entails fewer or more acceptable costs than those associated with armed resistance. Even when the decision to fight has been taken, and all a state's resources are committed, rational calculations may still be in play. Any war of existence, even a seemingly suicidal large-scale nuclear war, can involve rational calculations concerning interest. After all, 'better dead than red' is a statement that implies choice. Again, there is no better way of defending *On War* than to turn to the writings of Clausewitz himself. When discussing how the French Revolution brought about changes to warfare which pushed it towards its absolute, Clausewitz asserts that 'these changes did not come about because the French government freed itself, so to speak, from the harness of policy; they were caused by the new political conditions which the French Revolution created'. He continues, 'It follows that the transformation of the art of war resulted from the transformation of politics. So far from suggesting that the two could be disassociated from each other, these changes are a strong proof of their indissoluble connection.'[47] More extreme circumstances or policy objectives may simply result in more extreme efforts. However total a war becomes, means still have to be matched correctly to the ends. World War II can surely be regarded as a war of existence in Europe, and especially on the Eastern Front, and yet both sides still had to decide which particular means to utilise in which proportion and how much effort would be expended against which targets. In other words, the means–ends relationship still functions in such circumstances. Also, as Gray and Kahn assert, even though large-scale nuclear war would in all likelihood result in a pyrrhic victory, preparations should be undertaken to use nuclear forces in a manner that offers the best chance of victory and/or damage limitation.[48] Matching means to ends in this ultimate war of existence also serves the policy objective of a more credible deterrence posture. As Gray asserts, strategy does not cease to operate in the nuclear realm; rather it becomes a more challenging task.[49]

Clausewitz undoubtedly constructed his theory within a worldview that he was most familiar with. This happened to be based around state, land-based conflict. It is also worth noting that many of van Creveld's thoughts in *The Transformation of War* are worthy of consideration. The future of warfare may rest predominately with irregular conflict. He is also certainly correct to highlight the dangers of preparing for the wrong type of war. Of course, Clausewitz was also perfectly aware that one should identify and understand what sort of war one was about to undertake: 'The first, the supreme, the most far-reaching act of judgment that the statesman and commander have to make is to establish by that test the kind of war on which they are embarking.'[50] In the end, a less rigid interpretation of Clausewitz's theory leaves us with a work which is far more universal than either van Creveld or Keegan give it credit for. Basic Clausewitzian concepts, such as the fact that a war should be conducted in line with its motivating influence, or that warfare is prevented from escalating to its extreme by amongst other things its policy considerations, ensure that *On War* is a useful and productive work. This view is diametrically opposed to van Creveld's view, based as it is on narrow and rigid definitions, that Clausewitz's work is counterproductive to understanding the future of warfare. Too much emphasis is placed on a literal and misguided interpretation of the trinity.[51] Self-evidently warfare has not only been waged by nation-states. To re-emphasise: a less rigid reading of Clausewitz presents us with a body of work that can be applied to wars fought for various policy ends (even as an important cultural activity) and by various types of actors. In fact, it is possible to see the trinity more as an analogy to the nature of warfare, rather than as a strict comment on the kind of actors who conduct war. Katherine L. Herbig interprets the trinity in this manner, stressing that it regards warfare as being composed of violence, chance and subordination as an instrument of policy.[52]

In conclusion, based on a more inclusive reading of Clausewitz and the history of war, the policy rationale stands as the first element in the nature of warfare. War cannot begin without a rationale; otherwise it is just mindless violence. To reiterate Bull's definition, war is distinguished from other human activities by resort to organised violence for policy objectives. Policy gives birth to the child of war. Therefore, this work will not be testing whether the information age will change this element of warfare. The information age may create new motivations for the resort to war,[53] but it will not produce wars that are not the continuation of policy. Political factors can of course influence the conduct of war. This was Clausewitz's central notion, namely that political factors are one element that prevents war reaching its absolute state. In this sense, the information age may witness a change in the nature of war, brought about by a policy rationale aimed at limiting destruction.[54] This latter objective itself may partly be a product of an omnipotent media and information technology. The power of the policy rationale is once again revealed in this example, and consequently reaffirms that policy is inexorably entwined with war.

THE NATURE OF WAR – 'THE CLIMATE OF WAR'

As previously noted, war is a varied activity. Each war is unique. The policy rationale and the character of each war can differ enormously. However, after examining the three works of theory, as well as various historical and personal accounts of war, a number of key elements seem to appear in most wars, and consequently can be said to lie at the heart of the debate concerning the nature of warfare. These represent the main areas of dispute amongst the three classic works. Several words or phrases may be used to describe these elements, but fundamentally they can be described as 'uncertainty', 'violence and destruction', 'chance and narrow friction' and 'human factors'.[55] Taken together these produce a vision of war that is uncertain, violent and ultimately a human activity at both the physical and psychological levels. Clausewitz amalgamated this combination of elements into the concept 'the climate of war'.[56] *Warfighting* divides the nature of warfare into a slightly higher number of elements, although the end result is much the same as the 'climate of war'. For the USMC the nature of warfare consists of friction, uncertainty, fluidity, disorder, the human dimension, violence and danger, moral and physical forces.[57]

Uncertainty

Uncertainty is at the heart of Clausewitz's theory of war. On this point he was unequivocal: 'In war everything is uncertain.'[58] Jack Belden makes this same point more poetically, although no less starkly: 'Uncertainty is in the very air which a battle breathes ... So I say the unknown is the first-born son of combat and uncertainty its other self.'[59] John Ferris and Michael Handel declare that this lack of certainty is the condition in which military genius reveals itself.[60] It is within this first element of war's nature that the first contradictions appear between the works of theory. This is particularly the case between Clausewitz and Sun Tzu. In contrast to Clausewitz, Sun Tzu implies that many things can be known in war. Indeed, Lawrence Freedman goes as far as to suggest, 'Sun Tzu believed that perfect knowledge could be obtained.'[61] In Sun Tzu's theory a general should have good knowledge of his enemy, his own forces, the terrain and the weather.[62] Throughout his treatise Sun Tzu implies that victory is best assured through knowledge and flexibility: in other words, knowledge of the situation and then adaptation to it. Jomini seems to fall somewhere between the other two writers. Jomini follows Clausewitz's logic quite explicitly at times. For example, he notes the inevitability of uncertainty and inaccuracies in information.[63] More importantly he writes that perfect information on the enemy is impossible, and indeed that it is this fact that distinguishes the theory of war from its practice. Like Clausewitz he ultimately feels that the answer to this problem is the natural talent and experience of the general.[64] However, Jomini does advise, much like Sun Tzu, that one should know the enemy.[65] Also, although not explicit in his writings, Jomini does appear to imply that certain bits of knowledge can be ascertained. For example, he assumes that the decisive point, a notion central to his theory of waging war successfully, can be identified, whether it is the enemy forces' weak point or a geographical feature.[66] To use an information age concept, Jomini's identification of the decisive point appears to imply that one can have 'Dominant Battlespace Knowledge'.

The issue of uncertainty reveals differing opinions on both the potential role and value of information in war. Clausewitz, in contrast to Sun Tzu, does not regard the answer to the dilemma of uncertainty to be the acquisition of more information. Rather, he notes that the good general must accept uncertainty and rely upon his intuitive abilities. Clausewitz indeed postulates that guesswork plays a significant part in war.[67] David Kahn correctly notes that Clausewitz is not totally dismissive of the value of collecting information, but ultimately he concludes that its value is strictly limited. This limitation is due to a number of factors, in particular the play of chance, the incomplete nature of information gathered and the human tendency to adopt a worst-case scenario mindset, and thereby overestimate the enemy's strength and capabilities. As Michael Handel notes, in this sense Clausewitz regards intelligence as another source of friction in war.[68] Therefore, information has limited value in warfare. Jomini places a somewhat higher emphasis on the value of information, in that he notes that information on the enemy's proceedings is vital.[69] He continues this line of thinking by noting, 'A general should neglect no means of gaining information on the enemy's movements.'[70] In contrast to Clausewitz, Jomini's writings on information are far more extensive, and even include reference to information security and encryption.[71]

Unlike Clausewitz, rather than relying upon such metaphysical factors as the intuition and natural talent of the general, Sun Tzu sees the route to victory through knowledge.[72] In fact, Sun Tzu's analysis, indeed his advice, rests heavily upon the ability of a commander to control and manipulate information. This goes to the heart of his statement that 'All warfare is based upon deception.'[73] In order to deceive the enemy effectively, one must exert control over information. Sun Tzu's emphasis on information is no more obvious than in his last chapter, 'Employment of Secret Agents'.

So whose perspective on uncertainty and information most accurately represents the true nature of warfare? Certainly, Sun Tzu's theory is full of sound advice. Having thorough knowledge of oneself, the enemy and the environment in which a war will take place is good to have. If you can have better knowledge than the enemy, either through deception or superior collection and analysis, then all the better. This truism is as applicable in the strategic realm as it is in the tactical and operational settings. However, this perspective may represent an ideal rather than a true representation of war. In this sense Clausewitz seems much closer to the mark. In his time the battlefield was a place of great confusion and uncertainty. According to contemporary accounts, the battlefields of the Napoleonic Wars were more often than not veiled in a true fog of war due to the smoke from musket and artillery fire.[74] Accounts of war since the time of Clausewitz only reaffirm the omnipotence of uncertainty on the battlefield. These thoughts do not mean that Sun Tzu has little of importance to say in this respect. In relation to the value of information Sun Tzu's analysis appears far more appropriate. Clausewitz's comments on the value of intelligence are far too negative, and his one-and-a-half-page treatment of intelligence is indicative of this.[75] In the final analysis of uncertainty on the battlefield, Clausewitz identifies two factors that lead one to assume that it will be a constant feature of war. The first of these concerns the impossibility of calculating moral forces in battle, in which case war can never be accurately estimated.[76] The second factor also concerns human factors, more precisely in the form of human interaction.[77] To these thoughts one can add the fact that the intentions of an opponent are very difficult to discern with any degree of accuracy. T. E. Lawrence describes well the complex nature of war which is constructed of both tangible and intangible elements: 'Nine-tenths of tactics were certain enough to be teachable in schools; but the irrational tenth was like the kingfisher flashing across the pool, and in it lay the test of generals.'[78] Ultimately, Jomini's assessment presents perhaps the most balanced analysis of uncertainty and information. Whilst recognising that certainty can never be attained, Jomini still values the role of information in the art of waging war.

Violence and Destruction

An element as central to war as uncertainty is 'violence and destruction'. *Warfighting* declares starkly that 'the means of war is force, applied in the form of organised violence'.[79] Here again we note a clash between the views of Clausewitz and Sun Tzu. Clausewitz, and to a slightly lesser extent Jomini, perceive war as a violent activity with battle and the destruction of the enemy's forces as the main features. In contrast, Sun Tzu is noted for advocating victory without fighting and bloodshed.

This division between Clausewitz and Sun Tzu may not be as absolute as is often portrayed. There are a few occasions in *On War* when Clausewitz accepts that battle and the destruction of the enemy are not always required for victory. These instances in the Prussian's work may help extend the relevance of Clausewitz should warfare in the information age become less violent. For example, Clausewitz acknowledges that there are 'shortcuts to peace'. In this respect he notes that the seizure of lightly or undefended provinces may tip the balance against an enemy who is already fearful of the final outcome.[80] On another occasion Clausewitz recognises that at times the odds prior to battle can be so decisive that one side will capitulate without combat. He postulates that, to bend the enemy to your will, you must 'either make him literally defenceless or at least put him a position that makes this danger probable'.[81] Michael Handel suggests that in Clausewitz's theory this victory without fighting can be achieved by two methods. The first is 'war by algebra', in which a rational calculation of strength prior to battle produces a decisive prediction of the outcome, upon which one side capitulates. Alternatively, manoeuvre on the battlefield can create a similar decisive imbalance of capabilities. Handel goes on to suggest that for Clausewitz the former cannot be considered war proper, whereas the latter can.[82] Handel's identification of this distinction in *On War* between war by algebra and victory through manoeuvre is questionable. This is an important point when one is considering Clausewitz's relevance in an age where information dominance prior to battle could decide the outcome. A different interpretation of *On War* from that of Handel's suggests that Clausewitz perceived victory through both 'algebra' and 'manoeuvre' as relating back to the physical act of war. Clausewitz's thoughts on this subject are best expressed by the following two extracts. 'When one force is a great deal stronger than the other, an estimate may be enough. There will be no fighting: the weaker side will yield at once.'[83] However, two pages before this Clausewitz notes: 'it is inherent in the very concept of war that everything that occurs *must originally derive from combat*' (emphasis in the original).[84] From this latter statement we can conclude that capitulation without fighting, whether this emanates from calculations of combat strength or positions brought about by manoeuvre, always relates back to what would occur if combat took place. And therefore, war by algebra still relates back to fighting and therefore war proper. Clausewitz's concern about war by algebra was that it appeared to regard war as being bereft of emotion.[85]

On War is one of those works in which the reader can find a maxim to support a wide range of contradictory arguments.[86] Therefore, it is important to recognise the general ideas that underpin the whole treatise. In this sense, those moments in which Clausewitz identifies non-violent means to victory, although significant, ultimately do not detract from his central belief in the significance of battle.[87] On the very first page of Book One, Chapter One, Clausewitz states: 'War is thus an act of force to compel our enemy to do our will.' He develops this thought: 'Force – that is, physical force ... is thus the means of war.'[88] Later on he proclaims: 'Essentially war is fighting, for fighting is the only effective principle in the manifold activities generally designated as war.'[89] More starkly he notes that violent resolution is the first-born son of war, and that the supreme law is force of arms.[90] At times Clausewitz is even more explicit than this: 'it is always true that the character of battle, like its name, is slaughter, and its price is blood'.[91] And finally to distinguish war from other activities he notes: 'War is a clash between major interests, which is resolved by bloodshed – that is the only way in which it differs from other conflicts.'[92] What does this imply for both Clausewitz and indeed war, if war ceases to be characterised by violence?

Clausewitz clearly did not want to leave the reader in any doubt about the destructive nature of battle. He had himself witnessed the physical ravages of war, including the destructive French retreat from Moscow. Ultimately, he emphasises the 'dominance of the destructive principle', and the direct annihilation of enemy forces.[93] For Clausewitz, war is a physical act of force, and, even if fighting does not actually occur in a conflict, the result still relates back to this. In this sense, fighting and the destructive principle are central to warfare. Others, such as Michael Howard, echo these thoughts. Howard notes that the engine of change in battle is the infliction of human suffering through violence. From this he deduces that, because armies are designed for fighting, military history must primarily be about battle.[94]

On the issue of violence and destruction Sun Tzu lies at the other end of the spectrum. In complete contrast to the principle of destruction, he advocates the value of taking things intact. Again, this attitude may be a reflection of the period in which Sun Tzu wrote. Cleary suggests that during the era of the Warring States conflict was regarded as destructive and counterproductive, even for the victor.[95] Samuel Griffith contends that for Sun Tzu war is not about bloodshed or indeed destruction; rather it is essentially a battle of the wills. Cleary comments: 'in Sun Tzu's philosophy the peak efficiency of knowledge and strategy is to make conflict altogether unnecessary'.[96] Griffith goes on to suggest that for Sun Tzu, even in those circumstances in which war has to be waged, it should be concluded with three objectives very much to the fore. These are: it should be completed in the shortest possible time; with the least expenditure of lives and effort; and with as few casualties inflicted on the enemy as possible.[97] The reader may note that these sentiments have a very contemporary ring to them. The principle of leaving enemy forces and property intact is in stark contrast to the principle of destruction. Sun Tzu's *The Art of War* also makes reference to the fact that battle is a dangerous affair, and perhaps this also underscores the preference to avoid it if possible.[98] This is a view shared by Vegetius, who regards battle as a risky affair because of the play of chance.[99] Being a pragmatic man, Sun Tzu realised that battle would not only reduce one's own forces, but would also reduce the resources of the enemy, resources which one could put to good use in the aftermath of victory. *The Art of War*'s advice is best summed up in the phrase 'conquer by strategy'.[100] This statement seems to advocate an approach in which victory should first be sought through attacking the enemy's plans; then his alliances; and finally, should these fail, battle must be undertaken. Sun Tzu's approach on this issue can be best represented by three extracts from his work: 'Thus, those skilled in war subdue the enemy's army without battle.' 'Your aim must be to take All-under-Heaven intact. Thus your troops are not worn out and your gains will be complete.' And perhaps most famously of all Sun Tzu wrote: 'For to win one hundred victories in one hundred battles is not the acme of skill. To subdue the enemy without fighting is the acme of skill.'[101] It is interesting that in the second of these extracts Sun Tzu states that complete gains are best assured through non-destructive means. Again this is in contrast to Clausewitz and Jomini, both of whom suggest that victory must be exploited through pursuit of the enemy. It is during the pursuit that most destruction can be inflicted on one's adversary.

It is interesting to note that once again Jomini appears to have a foot in each of the two camps. Jomini recognises the value to be gained from destruction of enemy forces, but he is never as explicit as Clausewitz. Indeed, with his emphasis upon the value of lines of operation, in particular with reference to threatening the enemy lines of communication, he seems to acknowledge that victory is attainable through decisive manoeuvre without bloodshed and destruction.[102] In fact, Crane Brinton, Gordon A. Craig and Felix Gilbert argue that Jomini was more concerned with the acquisition of territory than with the destruction of the enemy's forces.[103]

The Christian crusades to regain the Holy Lands present an interesting case that demonstrates both the potential and the limits of non-violent means to achieve one's objectives. The particular crusade in question is the thirteenth-century campaign by Frederick II. By means of a treaty with the Sultan of Egypt, Frederick reclaimed a great deal of the Holy Lands, including for the first time in 42 years the city of Jerusalem and a safe route for Christian pilgrims to the Holy Sepulchre. Frederick achieved all of this with a force far inferior to that at the disposal of the Sultan. His achievement is no more starkly outlined than in his own letter to Henry III of England:

> For in these few days, by a miracle rather than by strength, that business has been brought to a conclusion which for a length of time past many chiefs and rulers of the world amongst the multitude of nations have never been able until now to accomplish by force, however great.[104]

There are two main reasons why Frederick was able to retake the Holy Lands without resorting to war. The first relates to his close political relationship with the Sultan. Frederick had for some time been in secret correspondence with the Egyptian leader. Alongside exchanging gifts and embassies, they had reached an agreement by which Frederick would be given Jerusalem in exchange for aiding the Sultan in his attempts to take Damascus from his brother Corraden. Within the final treaty, Muslims retained the Temple Area and in particular the Dome of the Rock in Jerusalem. Second, as G. A. Campbell notes, the Sultan was at that time facing a rebellion of fellow Muslims against his rule. He feared an alliance between Frederick and these rebellious Muslims, and therefore opted for the treaty with Frederick. The fact remains that, whether primarily through fortune or astute political insight, Frederick was able to take advantage of the political situation and achieve his objective without resorting to war. It is worth noting that he achieved this despite the fact that Pope Gregory IX was openly attempting to sabotage the crusade. However, the limits of Frederick's success are reflected in the fact that he left the Christian-held Holy Lands in an unstable and vulnerable condition. The truce failed to hold, and eventually Jerusalem fell to al-Nasir Daud, King of Transjordania.

Richard of Cornwall, the brother of Henry III, repeated Frederick's feat in 1241. Taking advantage of a civil war amongst the Muslims, Richard once again retook control of Jerusalem without resorting to war. However, the inability to cement Christian domination of the Holy Lands ended in bloody tragedy for Christians in the area. The new Sultan of Egypt, in alliance with Barbacan's Khorasmians, retook most of Palestine. The Christians in Jerusalem were slaughtered, and their religious and cultural artefacts and properties were destroyed.[105]

As with the issue of uncertainty, the majority of historical evidence heavily supports Clausewitz's explicit approach to the issue of fighting, violence and destruction in war. There are of course exceptions to this. Alongside the above example from the crusades, Clausewitz himself makes reference to the battle of Ulm, in which Napoleon secured victory without the need to resort to battle.[106] But as already mentioned, the threat of fighting and violence often underpins these exceptions. It is hard to disagree with Peter Paret's analysis that the bottom line is that in all wars violence is always the essence.[107] We can assume that Sun Tzu, as a practitioner of war, surely was aware of the occurrence of violence and bloodshed in warfare. Once again his thoughts expressed in *The Art of War* are perhaps best regarded as advice espousing an ideal rather than reflecting reality. A synthesis of Clausewitz and Sun Tzu's thoughts, in which the introduction and level of violence is a decision to be taken, portrays a position on this subject that takes account of the needs of strategy. Whether, and how much, violence and destructive force is required will depend upon the objective sought and the relative circumstances of the belligerents. In this sense, T. E. Lawrence is right to disavow an undue emphasis on battle within the context of the Arab uprising against the Turks during World War I. In this context, set-piece battles would normally prove disadvantageous to the Arab forces. Therefore, Lawrence places greater emphasis on the moral rather than the physical struggle.[108] Gray refines this train of thought somewhat by stating that the enemy can be defeated either physically or by breaking his will.[109] The subtleties and judgments that lie at the heart of this issue can also be found in the writings of Mao. On the one hand he advocates avoiding battle if circumstances are unfavourable, yet on the other hand he seeks the annihilation of enemy forces.[110]

Although in certain circumstances violence and destructive force may not be required to achieve one's policy objectives, in terms of war preparation, violence must be taken as a given element in the nature of war. For war to become and remain non-violent would require the agreement of all potential belligerents. As long as the political objective is of a certain import, the desire to gain an advantage by raising the level of conflict to violence may be too great. The enemy can usually reintroduce violence, and therefore one must be prepared for such an eventuality.

Human Factors
Any analysis of the nature of warfare cannot ignore what is perhaps one of its most basic elements. Regardless of what character a war assumes, it is always a human activity, in that humans do the fighting and also that war is a contest between opposing human wills. The involvement of humans is central to the existence of the climate of war, the trinity and friction more generally.[111] That being the case, war is imbued with human traits, emotions, concerns and factors. Based upon his after-action surveys of combat troops, the work of S. L. A. Marshall displays an acute awareness of how understanding and dealing with human nature is central to the successful conduct of war.[112] The importance of taking account and dealing with the human side of war is dealt with more fully in the chapter relating to command. At this stage it is merely necessary to show that human factors have a dominant and vital role in warfare. The human dimension accounts for a great deal of what Clausewitz described as the climate of war. As already mentioned, Clausewitz suggests that uncertainty is compounded by human perceptions. Likewise, chance and friction (which will be dealt with shortly) are partly the product of human actions. However, since war will always be orchestrated by humans regardless of who, or what, does the actual fighting in the battlespace, this section will concentrate upon issues relating to the other two elements of the climate of war, namely 'danger and exertion'. These two prominent features of war directly impact upon a crucial range of issues that come under the heading of 'moral forces'. Equally, they are credited with affecting the ability to think and act effectively, and thereby place further limits on the conduct of war. Indeed, it has been noted that humans can only operate continuously for four days before they shut down.[113]

When considering the issue of danger, warfare becomes a very personal endeavour.[114] Keegan, in *The Face of Battle*, correctly argues that for the individual soldier war is not about big issues and policy aims; rather it is about personal survival.[115] Ardent du Picq states simply that the battlefield is dominated by fear.[116] Specialist 4 Bill Beck describes how fear struck in the battle for the Ia Drang Valley in Vietnam: 'While Doc Nall was there with me, working with Russell, fear, real fear, hit me. Fear like I had never known before.'[117] *Warfighting* reiterates this thought by stating that leaders must understand and cope with fear in the battle-space.[118] The following account of one private's experience at the Battle of El Alamein is as good as any expression of these truisms:

> Everyone was shouting, screaming, swearing, shouting for their father, shouting for their mother, I didn't know whether to look at the ground or at the sky, someone said look at the ground for spider-mines, someone said look at the sky for the flashes, shells were coming all ways, the man next to me got hit through the shoulder, he fell down, I looked at him and said 'Christ', and then ran on, I didn't know whether to be sick or dirty my trousers.[119]

For Clausewitz, danger and physical effort are contributory factors to friction in war. Indeed he notes that, because the limits of physical effort cannot be measured accurately, it makes the estimation or understanding of friction uncertain.[120] This in itself goes further towards making war an activity that is far from controllable or an activity that can be reduced to simple calculations. Returning briefly to the subject of destruction, Clausewitz rightly identifies factors such as fatigue, exertion and privation as separate destructive forces in war.[121] The existence of human limitations, in both the physical and psychological realms, places limits on what armed forces can do, in which case war is prevented further from reaching its absolute form.[122]

The human element imbues war with powerful moral forces. War is essentially a battle of wills. Indeed, van Creveld notes that war is always a duel between two moral forces and that any analysis of war that ignores passionate emotions is without value.[123] This places psychological considerations at the heart of warfare. Reflecting these thoughts, Sun Tzu notes that the primary target in war is the opposing commander's mind.[124] In this sense, the Chinese theorist reflects well the intellectual competition at the heart of war, and the significance of the emotions of the commander. A similar thought is echoed by Jomini when he states that war is an impassioned drama, although his tendency to perceive victory in geometric lines of operations seems somewhat at odds with any particular emphasis on moral forces.[125]

One way in which the emotional and psychological side of man reveals itself is the often-overlooked prevalence of psychological casualty rates. Keegan reveals that, according to a British Army senior psychiatrists' report from World War II, of all battle casualties between 10 and 15 per cent were of a psychiatric nature during the active phase of the Battle of France in 1940. During the early days of the Normandy battle the figures were between 10 and 20 per cent. Just as interesting in reference to the limits of man's endurance in war, he notes that virtually all soldiers involved in continuous or semi-continuous combat broke down.[126] John Ellis alerts us to a real testimony that highlights the human and psychological impacts of combat. An officer of the 1st Scots Guards in World War II reports: 'how I hate shells. I have seen strong, courageous men reduced to whimpering wrecks, crying like children.'[127] However, human emotions do not have only negative effects in the conduct of war. Gray asserts that human factors can be one means to overcome an imbalance in technology and numerical inferiority.[128]

Displaying his synthesis of Enlightenment and Romantic thought, Clausewitz perceives physical and psychological factors forming an organic whole.[129] Whilst admitting that physical factors dominate combat, he also reflects at length on the centrality of morale effect in battle.[130] All the theorists under consideration agree on the decisiveness of the intellectual and moral strength of man, particularly the commander.[131] Ellis highlights the vital role played by officers in helping their men deal with the fear and chaos of battle.[132] Indeed, the more successful commanders have usually been aware of man's dominant role in warfare. Mao is one such example. He was an insurgent leader, who not only revealed an understanding of the political considerations inherent in an insurgency, but also was acutely aware that man was decisive in war.[133]

The human dimension of warfare is one area in which the character of war can affect its nature. If war remains an activity that is ultimately characterised by combat in which man is in conflict with man, then human factors and considerations will remain paramount. In relation to this both Clausewitz and Jomini espouse the centrality of infantry in warfare. In a passage that has interesting implications for the current trend towards stand-off weaponry, Clausewitz states: 'the actual core of an engagement lies in the personal combat of man against man. An army composed simply of artillery, therefore, would be absurd in war.'[134] Some may argue that these sentiments are merely a reflection of the unmechanised character of warfare that was witnessed by these two theorists. However, the role of close infantry combat is just as noticeable in many wars of the modern period. Battles in World War II, a war that is frequently portrayed as one dominated by armour and manoeuvre, were often decided by infantry forces.[135] Moving from history to possible futures, van Creveld argues that a future dominated by irregular conflict will continue to place infantry forces, or their equivalent, at the centre of warfare.[136] This focus on the role of infantry will be further enhanced if forecasts concerning the increasing urbanisation of warfare come to pass. Indeed, in the War for Iraq, Coalition urban operations were characterised by combined arms forces.

What are the implications of these truisms? As is argued in some detail in Chapter 3, dealing with the human side of warfare must be one of the commander's main preoccupations, whether that involves motivating men to engage the enemy regardless of their fear, or whether it simply means ensuring that the mail gets through from home. Another outcome of these considerations is that armed forces cannot simply be regarded as symbols on a map, or a collection of technologies that can be counted and reduced to quantifiable analysis. Rather, they are social organisms in which personal dynamics and relationships are critical to their functioning.[137] Consideration of the human dimension is a significant concern in the preparation for, and conduct of, war.

Chance and Friction

Thus far this chapter has noted that war can be considered as a human activity imbued with non-rational forces. War is also an uncertain and somewhat chaotic undertaking. Taken together, these features suggest that war is far from being a wholly predictable activity. These difficulties are further compounded by the play of chance and the occurrence of friction. When added together with the dialectic element of strategy, and the challenges of matching means to ends, this list produces Clausewitz's unified concept of general friction.[138] In the Clausewitzian paradigm the concept of friction is a central feature of war's true nature: 'Friction is the only concept that more or less corresponds to the factors that distinguish real war from war on paper.'[139] The occurrence of friction could have important implications for those who predict that revolutionary changes will emanate from the operational performance of RMA capabilities. As Clausewitz himself notes when defining friction: 'Countless minor incidents – the kind you can never really foresee – combine to lower the general level of performance, so that one always falls short of the intended goal.'[140] Whilst stressing the role friction will play in future conflicts, it is important to note that even Clausewitz did not overplay its invincibility. He suggests that human characteristics such as determination can go some way towards overcoming friction.[141] Gray also notes that other steps can be taken to help limit its influence on performance. These include: good and ample equipment; high morale; rigorous training; imaginative planning; historical education; combat experience; and sensitivity to potential problems.[142] The means by which friction can be dealt with again reveal the value to be gained by identifying, understanding and preparing for those features that make up the nature of war.

An element which itself is prominent within the broader concept of friction is the role of chance. In Clausewitz's view the element of chance is never absent from war. Consequently, guesswork and luck also play a significant role in warfare.[143] Jomini is likewise explicit on the omnipotence of chance. He notes that chance events 'are risks which cannot be foreseen nor avoided'.[144] Taken together, both narrow friction and chance propel warfare further from being an activity that can be controlled with any degree of certainty and completeness. To some extent Sun Tzu appears to offer a different perspective. Far from seeing war as a chaotic undertaking, Sun Tzu implies that with the right knowledge and mindset warfare can be highly malleable. In the chapter 'Energy', Sun Tzu provides a picture of combat that appears chaotic, but in fact 'there is no disorder'. Organisation and good communications are the means by which order is produced from seeming disorder.[145] This latter point is interesting in reference to the current emphasis on digitisation and the attendant improvements in C^2 of forces. In this sense, it is easy to see why Sun Tzu is popular in the information age. In fact, Arquilla and Ronfeldt go further than just promising a reduction in friction. Instead, they suggest that the Clausewitzian emphasis on friction should be replaced by a vision of war in which the manipulation of entropy is the key.[146]

In concluding this section it is perhaps best to regard Sun Tzu's work as looking towards an ideal, in which the chaotic world of warfare is to a large extent under the control of a good general with the required knowledge at his disposal. When considering this overoptimistic perspective there is some justice to criticise Sun Tzu for failing to include enough consideration of an intelligent foe. An intelligent foe would also be capable of utilising Sun Tzu's advice, on issues such as deception for example, and therefore warfare may become more chaotic and chance-ridden for the commander on the receiving end of these actions. The fact that warfare is a human interaction creates uncertainty, chance, friction and a certain level of chaos. However, Sun Tzu, not unlike Clausewitz, is a useful reminder that certain actions can be taken, including the accumulation of knowledge and more efficient organisation, which can reduce the play of chance and friction. This is a subject to which we will return in later chapters. Overall, it is important to bear in mind these thoughts regarding the ways in which friction and chance can be alleviated, whilst still retaining the fundamental notion that the nature of warfare includes a heavy element of chance and friction.

CONCLUSION

Any attempt to capture the nature of warfare in writing is bound to be inadequate to some degree. Reducing an activity as complex, varied and impassioned as war to a few concepts is somewhat artificial. Yet, as noted at the beginning of this chapter, understanding the nature of warfare is important in order to prepare and equip oneself adequately. To reiterate Clausewitz's opinion on this issue, theory helps make understanding this subject a manageable exercise. In this vein, the three classical works of theory have been utilised, alongside recorded experience, to act as a basis for that understanding. So, how do the great theorists fare in our quest for a literary manifestation of war's true nature? Clausewitz comes closest to putting the nature of war into a theoretical framework. With regard to the other great works: Sun Tzu also has some useful observations and advice to offer. Whereas Jomini, although useful in that he often claims the middle ground between the other two, is perhaps too prescriptive, too readily engages in reductionism and perhaps devotes too much of his work to operational concepts for him to be considered as a first-rate, universal theorist. However, it is worth considering that by occupying the middle ground Jomini's work could be revived in the information age.

What does the nature of warfare consist of? Uncertainty seems to be a prevalent factor throughout warfare in the pre-information age. This results from a number of factors, many of which centre on information. These include the fact that information is rarely in real time; is often incomplete; contains contradictions; and is subject to human perceptions and interpretations. To this list we can also add the ever-present play of friction and chance. And finally, uncertainty emanates from the fact that war is an activity characterised by human interaction. War is fought against an intelligent foe whose intentions can never really be known with absolute certainty. From this we can deduce that Clausewitz is more useful than Sun Tzu in understanding the uncertain element of war. Sun Tzu may be criticised for promoting advice which indirectly implies that warfare and information are more controllable than they really are.

However, the Clausewitzian model may not be as useful with regard to the value of information and knowledge. In this sense, Sun Tzu's emphasis on the value of knowledge is more practical. This latter point does not invalidate Clausewitz's focus on uncertainty. Rather, it is to say that alongside the character of the commander, which Clausewitz viewed as the means to deal with uncertainty, we should also value information as a means to help diminish the fog of war, and value knowledge to help shed light upon our foe's intentions. In the final analysis, it has to be concluded that uncertainty has always been present in warfare.

The historical evidence also indicates that violence and destruction are usually evident in warfare. There are times when resort to the destructive principle can prove counterproductive. The efficacy of certain counterinsurgency and counterterrorism campaigns may be reduced by the application of destructive force. More positive and productive measures may be required to achieve one's objectives in such cases. Likewise, as already noted in reference to the crusades of Frederick II and Richard of Cornwall, the objectives of a war can sometimes be achieved without resort to fighting. Although, as these attempts at recapturing the Holy Lands reveal, an enemy left intact can at some point in the future reintroduce the destructive principle very much to your disadvantage. This is not to criticise the activities of these crusaders, who simply did not have the resources available to destroy their rivals and thereby reclaim the Holy Lands for Christianity in perpetuity. It is merely sufficient to note that the Roman Republic had few problems with Carthage after the city and the Carthaginian civilisation were destroyed in 146 BC.

The campaigns of Alexander the Great present an instructive case in which one can detect a synthesis of Clausewitz and Sun Tzu on the issue of violence and destruction in war. J. F. C. Fuller notes that Alexander learned from his father, Philip II, that military force was not the sole weapon, nor the most puissant, in strategy. Fuller postulates that, with the limited resources at his disposal, Alexander could never have conquered the Persian Empire if he had relied upon fighting alone. To rule the hostile Persian population would have necessitated enormous garrisons to administer and secure Alexander's conquered territory. To deal with this, and perhaps for religious reasons, Alexander adopted a policy of unification with the Persians. He did not destroy Persian administration in the areas he conquered; in fact he often employed the local Satraps and shared authority with them. He also took measures such as adopting Persian court etiquette and took to wearing Persian clothes. Rather than always destroying his enemies, Alexander often employed them, and in fact helped them develop, as is revealed through the many cities he built east of the Tigris. In this sense, the case of Alexander reveals the advantages of leaving things intact, and therefore also highlights the limits of the principle of destruction. Alexander's example suggests that in certain circumstances following Sun Tzu's advice can produce positive strategic outcomes. Yet, it should be noted that Alexander could not have undertaken his unification of the two cultures without the success he gained on the battlefield. In the final analysis it has to be noted that Alexander created the opportunity for his policies of unification through violent warfare, and it was only after his battlefield victories that he could reap the benefits of his benevolence.[147]

Overall, history conclusively reveals that war is usually a violent activity. Therefore, one should prepare for war with this very much at the forefront of one's mind. This has implications for procurement policies, as well as the training of future warriors. Strategy however is a complex beast. As Clausewitz expressed in *On War*, the policy objective should dictate the level of violence and destruction to be used. One has to factor the resistance of the enemy into this calculation also. It is the judgment of the strategist that must find the correct balance between the violent nature of war and the demands of policy.

The bottom line in this discussion is that warfare, above all else, is a human activity. This is true both in terms of the units that actually do the fighting, and in reference to the fact that it is an activity best thought of in terms of human interaction. This fact endows warfare with many of the elements that have been discussed in this chapter. However they choose to organise themselves politically or socially, and whatever terms they employ to describe the motivations behind their decision to wage war, humans fight each other for human reasons. As a result of this, the 'climate of war' and the 'trinity', and therefore the work of Clausewitz, come very close to defining the true nature of warfare. The rest of this book will be devoted to an exploration of warfare in the information age, to assess whether *On War* will continue to best reflect the nature of war. Alternatively, the work of either Jomini or Sun Tzu may prove more fruitful. Or finally, maybe the character of war will change so significantly that new theorists will have to be utilised to understand the nature of warfare in the information age. Because Strategic Studies is a practical subject, any work that has become anachronistic should not serve as the basis for military education and preparation for war.

NOTES

1. Van Riper and Scales, 'Preparing for War in the 21st Century', p. 6.
2. Francois Heisbourg, *The Future of Warfare* (London, Phoenix, 1997), p. 1. A similar argument is made by Christopher Coker when he asserts that 'post-modern war' represents a transformation of Clausewitz's 'true nature of war'. See Christopher Coker, 'Post-modern War', *RUSI Journal*, 143, 3 (1998), p. 7.
3. John Arquilla and David Ronfeldt, 'Cyberwar is Coming', in John Arquilla and David Ronfeldt (eds), *In Athena's Camp: Preparing for Conflict in the Information Age* (Santa Monica, CA, RAND, 1996), p. 25.
4. Robert R. Leonhard, *The Principles of War for the Information Age* (Novato, CA, Presidio Press, 1998), p. 6.
5. Joyce M. Hawkins (ed), *The Oxford Reference Dictionary* (London, Guild Publishing, 1987), p. 559.
6. See John Arquilla and David Ronfeldt, 'A New Epoch – and Spectrum – of Conflict', in John Arquilla and David Ronfeldt (eds), *In Athena's Camp: Preparing for Conflict in the Information Age* (Santa Monica, CA, RAND, 1996), p. 18, and also James Adams, *The Next World War: The Warriors and Weapons of the New Battlefields in Cyberspace* (London, Hutchinson, 1998), p. 93.
7. Quoted in David J. Lemelin, 'Force XXI: Getting it Right', *Military Review*, 76, 6 (1996), p. 81.
8. James D. Kiras, 'Terrorism and Irregular Warfare', in John Baylis, James Wirtz, Eliot Cohen and Colin S. Gray (eds), *Strategy in the Contemporary World: An Introduction to Strategic Studies* (Oxford, Oxford University Press, 2002), p. 212.
9. Clausewitz, *On War*, p. 163.
10. See Crane Brinton, Gordon A. Craig and Felix Gilbert, 'Jomini', in Edward Mead Earle (ed), *Makers of Modern Strategy: Military Thought from Machiavelli to Hitler* (Princeton, NJ, Princeton University Press, 1943), pp. 80–3, and Michael I.

43

Handel, *Masters of War: Classical Strategic Thought*, second, revised edition (London, Frank Cass, 1996), p. 16.

11. H. T. Hayden (ed.), *Warfighting: Manoeuvre Warfare in the US Marine Corps* (London, Greenhill, 1995), p. 43.

12. Ibid, pp. 43, 54.

13. See *British Defence Doctrine: Joint Warfare Publication (JWP) 0-01* (London, HMSO, 1997).

14. Daniel Moran, 'Strategic Theory and the History of War', in John Baylis, James Wirtz, Eliot Cohen and Colin S. Gray (eds), *Strategy in the Contemporary World: An Introduction to Strategic Studies* (Oxford, Oxford University Press, 2002), p. 24.

15. Clausewitz, *On War*, p. 342.

16. Hayden, *Warfighting*, p. 66.

17. Roger Parkinson, *Clausewitz* (London, Wayland Publishers, 1970), p. 9.

18. See for example Edward N. Luttwak, 'Towards Post-Heroic Warfare', *Foreign Affairs*, 74, 3 (1995), and Luttwak, 'Post-Heroic Military Policy'.

19. This is not the place to enter into the Revolution in Military Affairs (RMA) debate, either in a general sense, or in particular reference to whether one can regard the Revolutionary and Napoleonic period as representing a revolutionary change in warfare. The following works are good places to begin exploring the merits of the RMA hypothesis. Bacevich, 'Preserving the Well-Bred Horse', A. F. Krepinevich, 'Cavalry to Computer: The Pattern of Military Revolutions', *National Interest*, 37 (1994), and Gray, 'A Contested Vision'.

20. See Peter Paret, *Understanding War: Essays on Clausewitz and the History of Military Power* (Princeton, NJ, Princeton University Press, 1992), p. 16. Christopher Bellamy also notes that the armies which defeated Napoleon, again notably the British, used old-fashioned tactics. See Christopher Bellamy, *Knights in White Armour: The New Art of War and Peace* (London, Hutchinson, 1996), p. 36. Similarly, Azar Gat notes that the British Army of the Napoleonic era was an eighteenth-century institution. Azar Gat, *The Development of Military Thought: The Nineteenth Century* (Oxford, Clarendon Press, 1992), p. 4.

21. John Shy, 'Jomini', in Peter Paret (ed.), *Makers of Modern Strategy: From Machiavelli to the Nuclear Age* (Oxford, Clarendon Press, 1986), p. 157.

22. See Martin van Creveld, *The Art of War: War and Military Thought* (London, Cassell, 2002), p. 105, and Moran, 'Strategic Theory and the History of War', p. 20.

23. Bellamy, *Knights in White Armour*, p. 42.

24. Brinton *et al.*, 'Jomini', p. 90

25. Michael I. Handel, 'Introduction', in Michael I. Handel (ed.), 'Clausewitz and Modern Strategy', special issue of *Journal of Strategic Studies*, 9, 2/3 (1986), p. 6.

26. Thomas Cleary, 'Translator's Introduction', in Sun Tzu, *The Art of War*, trans. Thomas Cleary (Boston, MA, Shambhala, 1988), p. 2.

27. Handel, *Masters of War*, pp. 74, 19.

28. Van Creveld, *The Art of War*, pp. 29, 37.

29. Michael D. Krause, 'Getting to Know Jomini' (Book Review), *Joint Forces Quarterly*, 7 (1995), p. 128.

30. Samuel B. Griffith, 'Introduction', in Sun Tzu, *The Art of War*, trans. Samuel B. Griffith, (London, Oxford University Press, 1971), pp. 33–5, and van Creveld, *The Art of War*, pp. 33–4.

31. Clausewitz, *On War*, p. 99.

32. John Keegan, *A History of Warfare* (London, Pimlico, 1994), p. 3.

33. Christopher Bassford, 'John Keegan and the General Tradition of Trashing Clausewitz: A Polemic', *War in History*, 1 (1994), pp. 325–6.

34. For an explanation of the trinity see Clausewitz, *On War*, p. 101.
35. Mark T. Clark, 'The Continuing Relevance of Clausewitz', *Strategic Review*, 26, 1 (1998), p. 58.
36. Gray, *Modern Strategy*, p. 111, and Edward J. Villacres and Christopher Bassford, 'Reclaiming the Clausewitzian Trinity', www.clausewitz.com/CWZHOME/Trinity/TRINITY.htm.
37. For a fascinating discussion on the relationship between political leadership and the military see Eliot A. Cohen, *Supreme Command: Soldiers, Statesmen, and Leadership in Wartime* (New York, Free Press, 2002).
38. Martin van Creveld, *The Transformation of War* (New York, Free Press, 1991), pp. 41, 36.
39. Ibid., p. 125.
40. Ibid., p. 141.
41. See Geoffrey Parker, 'The Making of Strategy in Habsburg Spain: Philip II's "bid for mastery," 1556–1598', in Williamson Murray, MacGregor Knox and Alvin Bernstein (eds), *The Making of Strategy: Rulers, States, and War* (Cambridge, Cambridge University Press, 1994), pp. 115–50, and Geoffrey Parker, *The Grand Strategy of Philip II* (New Haven, CT, Yale University Press, 1998), p. 286.
42. A similar argument to this can be found in James Kiras' aforementioned work 'Terrorism and Irregular Warfare', in which he uses the attacks of 9/11 to emphasise the relationship between politics and religion.
43. Clausewitz, *On War*, p. 733.
44. William R. Hawkins, 'Imposing Peace: Total vs. Limited Wars, and the Need to Put Boots on the Ground', *Parameters*, 30, 2 (2000), p. 79.
45. Van Creveld, *The Transformation of War*, pp. 142, 155.
46. Bernard Brodie, *War and Politics* (London, Cassell, 1973), p. 2.
47. Clausewitz, *On War*, p. 737.
48. See Gray, *Modern Strategy*, especially Chs 11 and 12, and Herman Kahn, *On Thermonuclear War* (Princeton, NJ, Princeton University Press, 1960).
49. Gray, *Modern Strategy*, p. 278. See also Malcolm R. Davis and Colin S. Gray, 'Weapons of Mass Destruction', in John Baylis, James Wirtz, Eliot Cohen and Colin S. Gray (eds), *Strategy in the Contemporary World: An Introduction to Strategic Studies* (Oxford, Oxford University Press, 2002), p. 255.
50. Clausewitz, *On War*, p. 100.
51. Villacres and Bassford, 'Reclaiming the Clausewitzian Trinity'.
52. Katherine L. Herbig, 'Chance and Uncertainty in *On War*', in Michael I. Handel, (ed.), 'Clausewitz and Modern Strategy', special issue of *Journal of Strategic Studies*, 9, 2/3 (1986), p. 97.
53. Although most will surely still be covered by Thucydides' taxonomy: 'honour, fear, and interest'. Thucydides, *History of the Peloponnesian War*, trans. Rex Warner (London, Penguin, 1972).
54. Although, as is argued in Ch. 2, this is unlikely to be the case.
55. For a discussion of the difference between narrow and general friction see Barry D. Watts, *Clausewitzian Friction and Future War*, McNair Paper 52 (Washington, DC, Institute for National Strategic Studies, National Defense University, October 1996), especially Ch. 4.
56. Clausewitz, *On War*, p. 120.
57. Hayden, *Warfighting*, pp. 38–42.
58. Clausewitz, *On War*, p. 156.
59. Quoted in John Ellis, *The Fighting Man in World War II: The Sharp End of War* (London, Book Club Associates, 1980), p. 99.
60. John Ferris and Michael I. Handel, 'Clausewitz, Intelligence, Uncertainty and the

Art of Command in Military Operations', *Intelligence and National Security*, 10, 1 (1995), pp. 1–4.

61. Lawrence Freedman, *The Revolution in Strategic Affairs*, Adelphi Paper 318 (Oxford, Oxford University Press, 1998), p. 60.

62. In the chapter entitled 'Terrain', Sun Tzu states: "Know the enemy, know yourself; your victory will never be endangered. Know the ground, know the weather; your victory will then be total." Sun Tzu, *The Art of War*, trans. Griffith, p. 129.

63. Baron Antoine Henri de Jomini, *The Art of War* (London, Greenhill Books, 1996), pp. 196–7.

64. Ibid., pp. 268–9.

65. Ibid., p. 207.

66. Ibid., p. 187.

67. Clausewitz, *On War*, p. 96.

68. David Kahn, 'Clausewitz and Intelligence', in Michael I. Handel (ed.), 'Clausewitz and Modern Strategy', special issue of *Journal of Strategic Studies*, 9, 2/3 (1986), p. 118, and Michael I. Handel, 'Clausewitz in the Age of Technology', in Michael I. Handel (ed.), 'Clausewitz and Modern Strategy', special issue of *Journal of Strategic Studies*, 9, 2/3 (1986), pp. 66–7.

69. Jomini, *The Art of War*, pp. 268–9.

70. Ibid., p. 273.

71. Ibid., p. 259.

72. Sun Tzu, *The Art of War*, trans. Griffith, pp. 144–9.

73. Ibid., p. 66.

74. For an account of the conditions on Napoleonic battlefields, see John Keegan, *The Face of Battle* (London, Barrie & Jenkins, 1988).

75. See Clausewitz, *On War*, Book 1, Ch. 6.

76. Ibid., p. 216.

77. Ibid., p. 161.

78. T. E. Lawrence, *Seven Pillars of Wisdom* (Ware, Wordsworth Editions, 1997), p. 183.

79. Hayden, *Warfighting*, p. 41.

80. Clausewitz, *On War*, p. 105.

81. Ibid., p. 85.

82. Handel, *Masters of War*, p. 219.

83. Clausewitz, *On War*, p. 110.

84. Ibid., p. 108.

85. Ibid., p. 84

86. For an excellent discussion on the potential to misunderstand elements of *On War* see Raymond Aron, *Peace and War: A Theory of International Relations*, trans. Richard Howard and Annette Baker Fox (London, Weidenfeld & Nicolson, 1966), especially Ch. 1.

87. Gray, *Modern Strategy*, p. 104.

88. Clausewitz, *On War*, p. 83.

89. Ibid., p. 145.

90. Ibid., p. 113.

91. Ibid., p. 307.

92. Ibid., p. 173.

93. Ibid., pp. 269–70.

94. Quoted in Keegan, *The Face of Battle*, pp. 28–9.

95. Cleary, 'Translator's Introduction', p. 5.

96. Ibid., p. 1.

97. Sun Tzu, *The Art of War*, trans. Griffith, p. 39.

98. This point is raised by one of Sun Tzu's commentators, Wang Hsi. Sun Tzu, *The Art of War*, trans. Griffith, p. 78.
 99. Vegetius, *Vegetius: Epitome of Military Science*, trans. N. P. Milner (Liverpool, Liverpool University Press, 1993), p. 108.
100. Van Creveld, *The Art of War*, p. 41.
101. See Sun Tzu, *The Art of War*, trans. Griffith, pp. 77–9.
102. Hew Strachan, *European Armies and the Conduct of War* (London, George Allen & Unwin, 1983), p. 61.
103. Brinton *et al.*, 'Jomini', p. 88.
104. See Robert Payne, *The Crusades* (Ware, Wordsworth Editions, 1998), p. 317.
105. For accounts of these events, see Payne, *The Crusades*, and G. A. Cambell, *The Crusades* (London, Duckworth, 1935).
106. Clausewitz, *On War*, p. 309.
107. Paret, *Understanding War*, p. 109.
108. T. E. Lawrence, 'Guerrilla Warfare', in Gerard Chaliand (ed.), *The Art of War in World History: From Antiquity to the Nuclear Age* (Berkeley, CA, University of California Press, 1994), pp. 882–6.
109. Gray, *Modern Strategy*, p. 210.
110. See Mao Tse-Tung, *Selected Military Writings of Mao Tse-Tung* (Beijing, Foreign Languages Press, 1963).
111. Gray persuasively argues: 'in war and strategy people matter most'. See *Modern Strategy*, p. 97. See also p. 26 in which Gray asserts that 'people and politics' represent one of the dimensions of strategy.
112. See S. L. A. Marshall, *Men Against Fire: The Problem of Battle Command in Future War* (New York, William Murrow, 1947).
113. Watts, *Clausewitzian Friction and Future War*, pp. 30, 82.
114. Ellis, *The Sharp End of War*, p. 97.
115. Keegan, *The Face of Battle*, p. 42.
116. Ibid., p. 61.
117. Quoted in Lt-Gen. Harold G. Moore (Ret.) and Joseph L. Galloway, *We Were Soldiers Once ... and Young* (London, Corgi, 2002), p. 118.
118. Hayden, *Warfighting*, pp. 40–1.
119. Ellis, *The Sharp End of War*, p. 111.
120. Clausewitz, *On War*, p. 135.
121. Ibid., p. 243.
122. Watts, *Clausewitzian Friction and Future War*, p. 30.
123. Martin van Creveld, 'The Eternal Clausewitz', in Michael I. Handel (ed.), 'Clausewitz and Modern Strategy', special issue of *Journal of Strategic Studies*, 9, 2/3 (1986), pp. 38, 46.
124. Sun Tzu, *The Art of War*, trans. Griffith, p. 41.
125. Jomini, *The Art of War*, p. 344.
126. Keegan, *The Face of Battle*, p. 288.
127. Ellis, *The Sharp End of War*, p. 69.
128. Gray, *Modern Strategy*, p. 97.
129. Clausewitz, *On War*, p. 216.
130. Ibid., pp. 162, 300.
131. See for example Sun Tzu, *The Art of War*, trans. Griffith, p. 39, and Jomini, *The Art of War*, p. 290.
132. Ellis, *The Sharp End of War*, p. 228.
133. See Griffith, 'Introduction', p. 54, and Mao, *Selected Military Writings of Mao Tse-Tung*.
134. Clausewitz, *On War*, p. 338. See also Jomini, *The Art of War*, p. 290.

135. Keegan, *The Face of Battle*, p. 254, and Ellis, *The Sharp End of War*, p. 72.
136. Van Creveld, *The Transformation of War*, p. 212.
137. See Keegan, *The Face of Battle*, pp. 42, 46–7, 62. See also Marshall, *Men Against Fire*, pp. 149–51.
138. Watts, *Clausewitzian Friction and Future War*, p. 30. In his excellent study on future war Watts identifies the following taxonomy for the unified concept of general friction: danger; physical exertion; uncertainties and imperfections in information; friction in the narrow sense of the resistance within one's own forces; chance events; physical and political limits on the use of military force; unpredictability stemming from interaction with the enemy; disconnects between ends and means in war. See Watts, *Clausewitzian Friction and Future War*, p. 32.
139. Clausewitz, *On War*, p. 138.
140. Ibid., p. 138.
141. Ibid.
142. Colin S. Gray, *War, Peace, and Victory: Strategy and Statecraft for the Next Century* (New York, Simon & Schuster, 1990), pp. 107–8.
143. Clausewitz, *On War*, p. 96.
144. Jomini, *The Art of War*, p. 42.
145. Sun Tzu, *The Art of War*, trans. Griffiths, pp. 92–3.
146. John Arquilla and David Ronfeldt, 'Information, Power and Grand Strategy: In Athena's Camp – Section 1', in John Arquilla and David Ronfeldt (eds), *In Athena's Camp: Preparing for Conflict in the Information Age* (Santa Monica, CA, RAND, 1996), p. 156.
147. For details of these campaigns, see J. F. C. Fuller, *The Generalship of Alexander the Great* (Ware, Wordsworth Editions, 1998), Nicholas Hammond, *The Genius of Alexander the Great* (London, Duckworth, 1998), and Robin Lane Fox, *Alexander the Great* (Harmondsworth, Penguin, 1986).

2

The Future Battlespace

'We are in the midst of a dramatic change in the relationship between technology and the nature of warfare.'[1]

INTRODUCTION

The future battlespace is the realm of infinite possibilities. That is not what some of the RMA literature would have us believe. In their different ways, many of the RMA enthusiasts each portray a vision of the future that is narrow and often ignorant of strategic considerations. This chapter will analyse and challenge the central tenets of the RMA literature. Of course, the literature in question is plentiful; consequently it contains a host of different visions of the future. However, certain themes can be identified. Indeed, it is these central themes which present the most direct challenge to the nature of warfare as outlined in the previous chapter.

What are these central themes? The contemporary RMA hypothesis is fuelled by the increased application of IT to the battlespace and the consequent digitisation of forces. From this, the prime commodity and engine of change is 'information'. As Robert R. Leonhard has noted: 'If twenty-first century warfare has any theme, it is information.'[2] On occasion, some of the RMA devotees refine their visions to promote the concept of 'knowledge' above that of information. In this way, knowledge is merely information with meaning and understanding attached to, or extracted from, it. Another important component of some of the literature is an emphasis on the relationship between the increased availability of real-time information and precision-guided munitions (PGMs). Taken together, these developments allegedly establish assured destruction in the battlespace.

The claims that emanate from the above themes offer a radical vision of the future, one that goes a significant way towards rendering the

Clausewitzian paradigm anachronistic. The promise of an increasing abundance of information has led some writers to proclaim the significant decline of uncertainty in war. They postulate that operational concepts such as high levels of 'situational awareness' and 'Dominant Battlespace Knowledge' will facilitate a lifting of the fog of war for friendly forces. Also evident is a proclivity to view war merely as an act of bombardment, in which victory is assured through the destruction of enemy targets with stand-off PGMs. At a 1999 conference, Captain Chris Parry of the Royal Navy predicted that heavy ground forces would never again engage the enemy close in. Rather, ground forces would merely fulfil a constabulary function and consolidate a victory already won by distant firepower.[3] Similarly, the authors of Network Centric Warfare subscribe to the belief that destruction of 50 per cent of the enemy's assets automatically translates into victory.[4] Predictions such as these reflect both emerging capabilities and an alleged sensitivity to casualties in Western societies and polities.[5] Extreme manifestations of these trends are 'Post-Heroic Warfare' and 'Virtual War'.[6] Indeed, Libicki argues that, due to sensitivity to casualties, the United States must adopt and perfect stand-off warfare.[7] As this chapter will contend later, these theories may fufil the requirements of perceived domestic political requirements, and in that sense make the military instrument more politically usable, but this certainly does not necessarily represent good strategy.[8] A related consequence of the reconnaissance–strike complex (the linking of reconnaissance assets and PGMs) is the demise of the manned platform, either to be replaced by unmanned vehicles or miniprojectiles, or indeed rendered partially obsolete by the concepts of 'virtual presence' and 'air occupation'.[9] The latter exhibits striking similarities to control from the air, and in this sense it suffers from similar limitations as expressed by General Schwarzkopf: 'There is not a military commander in the entire world who would claim he had taken an objective by flying over it.'[10] In our efforts to understand this removal of man from the battlefield we can again look towards a combination of technological determinism and socio-political considerations. To reiterate, Fuller may have identified this trend as far back as 1946, when he describes a hidden impulse in technological development, which has as its objective 'The elimination of the human element both physically and morally, intellect alone remaining'.[11] Chapter 3 of this book will explore whether artificial intelligence will pose a challenge to Fuller's last refuge of man's role in warfare.

The conclusion to be drawn from the above predictions is that an increased ability to gather and disseminate information, allied to the assumed reliability of PGMs, creates a battlespace in which the conflict over information is perceived to be the key to success. In this vein, Libicki foresees a battlespace that is characterised by 'hide-and-seek' warfare rather than a 'force-on-force' experience.[12] Likewise, Admiral Owens has claimed, 'If you see the battlefield, you win the war.'[13] Alvin Toffler has joined this fray by stating explicitly: 'The wars of the future will increasingly be prevented, won or lost based on information superiority and dominance.'[14] Aside from this emphasis on information, Lawrence Freedman has identified in the RMA literature a desire for victimless war, typified by the achievement of victory through disruption rather than destruction.[15] Christopher Coker proclaims that the ultimate manifestation of post-modern war is 'humane warfare', in which the mission is to neutralise rather than kill.[16] Evidently, these visions of future war do not fit well with the emphasis placed on violence and destruction in the Clausewitzian nature of warfare. The notion of victory through information dominance reads like the theory of war by algebra, which Clausewitz largely dismissed.[17] Finally, although rarely explicit in the RMA literature, there does appear to be a reduced emphasis on friction in much of the enthusiasts' work.[18] By significantly removing humans from the battlespace, by reducing or eliminating violence and destruction and by lifting the fog of war, the RMA visionaries are going some way towards removing significant causes of friction. This implicit reduction of friction perhaps explains why they can make such confident claims regarding the efficacy of RMA forces and operations in the future battlespace. An example of this can be found in the concept of 'effects-based planning': 'Modelling this concept is a planning and analytical tool that *accurately depicts* the intercourse among enemy economic, political, military, and social structures and predicts the impact of operations on many target sets in these categories' (emphasis added).[19]

Should the future battlespace resemble the visions outlined above, in which war is a significantly less uncertain activity; is concluded with little or no violence; is to a large extent devoid of human involvement at the sharp end; and is much less vulnerable to friction; then modern warfare would be almost unrecognisable to Clausewitz. In many respects, certainly in relation to the climate of war, the nature of warfare would have been transformed. Such a change would have a number of important implications, and therefore these claims are worthy of study. Bearing in mind the role of theory in the education of officers, changes as radical as those proffered in the RMA literature would make Clausewitz's work much less meaningful. In this respect, Mackubin Thomas Owens reports that a US Army general has declared that technological advances will soon result in the end of Clausewitz.[20]

Aside from the educational ramifications of change, there are more direct and practical implications. As previously noted, one's understanding of the nature of warfare significantly influences how one prepares to wage war, and with what kind of equipment. Predicting, and preparing for, the character of future wars is a difficult and uncertain undertaking. Too much enthusiasm for the latest fad can leave you ill prepared for the next war. In the 1950s an overemphasis on nuclear weapons detracted from the conventional warfighting capabilities of the United States.[21] Relating that period to the current RMA, Paul Van Riper and Robert H. Scales, Jr, in an extremely well-balanced appraisal of twenty-first-century warfare, offer the following warning: 'What overconfidence in nuclear weapons produced then, overconfidence in the microchip threatens to reproduce today.'[22] Similarly, an emphasis on limited war theory in the pre-Vietnam War era is also criticised for distorting US performance in that conflict. In particular, Harry G. Summers bemoans the proclivity in limited war theory to rid war of its passion and emotions, and attempt to reduce it to an academic model.[23] Much of the current RMA literature also fails to give due credit to the intangible forces at play in war. There are obvious procurement implications to this debate. Peter A. Wilson, whilst a senior consultant at RAND, noted that in order to fund the current RMA the 'radicals' are prepared to cut infrastructure and force structure. In particular, he notes that the US Army would feel the brunt of any cuts.[24] Evidence of this can be found in Campen's assessment that the RMA enables the development of a much smaller force structure.[25] An early manifestation of this was witnessed in the War for Iraq. In particular, it is reported that Secretary of Defense Rumsfeld planned on the basis that a smaller 'transformed' force would be able to achieve the same results as an older, much larger force.[26] Note that the invasion was carried out with approximately 250,000 troops, as opposed to the 500,000 used for Desert Storm in 1991. Despite the success of the invasion, Coalition forces found themselves stretched at times. This became a particular problem as troops got bogged down in urban operations around Umm Qasr, Basra and An Nasiriyah. One result of this overstretch was that the long lines of communications became vulnerable to Iraqi hit-and-run tactics. If one considers the length of time taken for British forces to clear Umm Qasr and Basra, it is fair to speculate that the transformed US military would have struggled to achieve its objectives as rapidly and with such low costs, without British participation. One should also remember that Iraqi forces performed poorly and only managed sporadic resistance. How would the United States have coped with a more astute guerrilla campaign?

Bearing in mind the opinions of those such as Captain Parry, one can envisage a procurement policy which emphasises sensors and stand-off munitions, such as increased numbers of TLAMs, at the expense of armoured and infantry forces. Indeed, prior to the Kosovo campaign Benjamin Lambeth notes that the prevailing US approach to the use of force could be characterised as 'cruise missile diplomacy'.[27] Donald

Rumsfeld is said to prefer the use of long-range precision weapons to ground forces.[28] In this sense, political attitudes can have a significant influence upon the development of military technology.[29] This chapter will return later to the debate concerning the value of ground forces. At this juncture it will suffice to note that, although TLAMs are a very effective means to deliver explosives, they cannot patrol the streets of Belfast or Basra, nor could they have rooted out insurgents in Malaya.

The danger exists that an overly enthusiastic implementation of the RMA could establish military and strategic cultures that are ill suited to cope with the gamut of future conflicts and enemies. Williamson Murray is correct to draw our attention towards the fact that military culture, through which military organisations develop an understanding of the nature of warfare, is a central component of military effectiveness.[30] In this respect, we should be wary of further moves towards the 'humanisation' of warfare.[31] Alongside the principle of 'Economy of Force', this desire to 'humanise' war appears implicitly to underpin the current promotion of disruption at the expense of destruction. The inherent danger in this honourable solecism is no better described than by Clausewitz, who warned:

> The fact that slaughter is a horrifying spectacle must make us take war more seriously, but not provide an excuse for gradually blunting our swords in the name of humanity. Sooner or later someone will come along with a sharp sword and hack off our arms.[32]

Another flaw in an RMA-based military culture is an increased emphasis on technology.[33] Important as it is, technology only represents one dimension of strategy.[34] Although Cohen is right to conclude that a technological edge is often important, if not always decisive,[35] the other factors, which include the human dimension of war, may be more influential in deciding success or failure.

The above discussion reveals that perceptions of the future nature of war will have significant implications for future strategic performance. Preparing for a very different kind of war to that which actually occurs could leave you materially and culturally at a significant disadvantage. Therefore, this chapter will examine the main challenges suggested in the RMA literature to the Clausewitzian nature of warfare. This will consist of an analysis of how resilient uncertainty, humans, violence/destruction and friction will prove to be in the information age. This chapter will not contain a detailed account of the future technologies and operations that may characterise the future battlespace. This is impossible to do with any degree of accuracy, since no one security community can control the future development of warfare. Instead, the analysis will explore the most prominent predictions in the RMA literature, within a framework constructed of the factors that most heavily influence the conduct of war. These factors are: strategy; geography; the existence of an intelligent enemy (the paradoxical logic of strategy); the fact that war can take many forms (the character of war is polymorphous and therefore the belligerents have a number of options available to them with regard to the style of conflict they adopt); and finally that war is a human activity. Taken together, these factors prevent war from attaining any degree of uniformity. However, this work does not reject the notion that the information age will impose some changes on the conduct of war. In this vein, the chapter will conclude with a speculative assessment of what significant changes could occur. This raises an important point. Gray, who notes that dangers exist if you buy into an RMA too enthusiastically, also correctly observes that there are also pitfalls for those who do not adapt sufficiently to the changing character of war.[36]

AN UNCERTAIN FUTURE

As noted in the previous chapter, uncertainty lies at the heart of the Clausewitzian concept of war. The expectation of uncertainty influences the conduct of war, including approaches to command and control, and doctrine, and demands the holding of reserve forces to safeguard against the unexpected. Indeed, the USMC has described its doctrine of 'Manoeuvre Warfare' as a culture designed to cope with the fog, chaos and friction inherent in war.[37] Uncertainty may be a rudimentary characteristic of the Clausewitzian paradigm, but it has been subject to some of the most severe challenges to be found in the RMA literature.

Although at times even the most strident RMA enthusiasts qualify their optimism concerning the levels of certainty attainable, their general message proclaims that the fog of war is a malleable phenomenon that can be lifted or increased as required. For example, Admiral Owens, one of the most ardent RMA theorists, has admitted that the system of systems will not see everything. Rather, it will *reduce* the fog and friction of war. This is a welcome statement, although one which is at odds with most of his less restrained assertions: 'technology could enable US military forces in the future to lift the "fog of war" … battlefield dominant awareness – the ability to see and understand everything on the battlefield – might be possible'.[38] Similarly, in the aptly titled *Lifting the Fog of War* he proclaims: 'This new revolution challenges the hoary dictums about the fog and friction of war.'[39] Behind these claims lies the notion that layers of multispectral sensors, digitally linked to form a common picture of the battlespace, will be able to identify every physical instrument in a conflict. At the purely technological level this claim is not too outlandish. However, the omnipotence of friction and the mere existence of an intelligent enemy should cause one to be cautious of these claims. These two factors will undoubtedly reduce the efficacy of IT-based capabilities. Where the RMA literature becomes even more daring is when it claims an ability to translate this information into knowledge.[40] Note the excessive optimism in the definition of 'Information Dominance': 'Knowing *everything* about an adversary while keeping the adversary from knowing much about oneself' (emphasis added).[41] Over-confidence in IT encourages Jeffrey Cooper to declare that DBK allows the commander to transcend the problems of uncertainty.[42]

Taking the above claims too seriously could have ruinous conse-quences. It has been variously asserted that in a DBK future there are no requirements for mass, flank protection forces, or reserves, because part of the rationale for these forces is to deal with the unexpected.[43] The obvious danger with this emanates from the not unreasonable possibility that, whether due to friction within one's own forces or because of the actions of the enemy, the certainty that underpins the above claims could prove transient. Another cause for concern relates to the impact on doctrine and training. This relates to both the commander and the forces in his charge. At the risk of being glaringly obvious, it is worth noting that a military equipped and trained to operate in an environment characterised by certainty would surely struggle if deprived of its infor-mation crutch or faced with an unexpected development. It is profitable to remember that at present the USMC's entire doctrinal culture is premised on the expectation of uncertainty.

It should be clear from the discussion thus far that the author expects uncertainty to remain an ever-present factor in the battlespace. There are a number of different, if at times overlapping, reasons which lead to this conclusion. The first of these reasons relates to the aforementioned existence of an intelligent enemy. Any foe that is faced with an array of information-gathering devices will in all likelihood place significant weight on the art of *deception*.[44] Writers such as Libicki proclaim that deception will become increasingly difficult as the array of multispectral sensors increases.[45] However, one can only look to the historical evidence and conclude that it would take a seismic shift to end the continuous dynamic conflict between the hunters and hunted. Libicki underesti-mates the possibility that those wishing to remain unseen will be able to develop their techniques. In this respect, he appears to assume that those producing the mesh have a monopoly on technical and tactical develop-ments. To cite just one example, O'Hanlon suggests that an enemy facing the Brilliant Anti-Tank submunition can employ flares to confuse its infrared sensors, and/or create noise to jam its acoustic sensors.[46] Both the Gulf War of 1991 and the Kosovo conflict of 1999 reveal that the technologically disadvantaged can still deceive opponents fielding the most advanced information systems. During the Gulf War, the Coalition destroyed a substantial number of high-fidelity ballistic missile decoys. According to United Nations inspectors these decoys were only identifiable as fakes 25 yards away on the ground.[47] Similarly, Serbian camouflage and deception techniques significantly limited the numbers of military hardware destroyed by NATO in Kosovo.[48] NATO's difficulties in this respect were further compounded by the geography of Kosovo that hampered the effective operation of some air-based sensors.[49] Taken together, these factors produced a kill rate lower than in the 1991 Gulf War.[50] Assessing NATO's performance in Kosovo, Lambeth starkly concludes, 'NATO's effort to attack enemy ground units in the KEZ [Kosovo Engagement Zone] was essentially a failure.'[51] US forces in Afghanistan encountered similar problems. Even the significantly less sophisticated al Qaeda and Taliban forces proved adept at concealment, and displayed robustness in the face of heavy air assault. Again, the nature of the terrain was an added complicating factor for US operations.[52] It is interesting to note that advocates of the RMA often cite the writings of Sun Tzu because of his focus on the value of knowledge, and yet they appear to overlook his declaration that 'All warfare is based on deception.'[53] If they do not overlook this sentiment, then they are naively assuming that the art of deception rests only with the side fielding the RMA force.

Aside from acts of deception, there are other reasons why information on the battlespace can never be complete. This is the case because war does not consist purely of tangible physical objects to be counted and classified. At least as important, if not more so, to the outcome of any particular conflict are the intangibles, such as morale and level of training. This is one area in which gaps in 'knowledge' can occur most readily. *The Economist*, quoting an infantry colonel, expresses this dilemma well: 'No screen can convey perfect information: there is always more to know, like, are the enemy soldiers tired and hungry?'[54] In his work S. L. A. Marshall places a degree of emphasis on the role of incalculable factors such as the effects of terrain, weather and morale. The latter is particularly troublesome, because, as Marshall notes, morale is not a stable phenomenon; rather it tends to fluctuate.[55] Callwell adds yet another complication into this issue by correctly postulating that one cannot truly know the fighting quality of enemy forces until the conflict has actually got underway.[56] In reference to terrain, it could be argued that terrain analysis could predict the effects of a particular environment on a military operation. However, in contrast, Field Marshal Slim suggests from experience that one can never fully appreciate the impact of terrain until one is in it.[57] Similarly, Harold Winters *et al.* note that in general environmental factors are unpredictable.[58] Note how sandstorms delayed the advance of Coalition forces during the invasion of Iraq. Ground forces were all but rendered stationary and most of the Coalition's aircraft were grounded.[59] For a balanced appraisal on the significance of the intangible elements in war, we can turn once again to the USMC's *Warfighting* doctrine publication. *Warfighting* describes war as an interaction of moral and physical forces, the former having the greater effect in the outcome of a conflict.[60]

It is noteworthy, and of concern, that much of the RMA literature simply fails to mention intangibles such as morale. However, the literature is not totally devoid of such issues. For example, the Tofflers stress the importance of the 'knowledge terrain', which includes qualities of the enemy such as level of training, education and culture.[61] In this respect, the Tofflers are offering sound advice. However, much of this already comes under the rubric of 'strategic culture', in which case it is more profitable to explore the strategic culture literature, as it contains a number of cautionary points absent from the Tofflers' work. While it is certainly sensible to attempt to understand how a particular enemy usually thinks and acts, absolute knowledge is unattainable. The process of turning information into knowledge involves subjective interpretations. What passes for an appreciation of strategic culture can sometimes be no more than the creation or validation of stereotypes.[62] Consequently, the knowledge you have acquired or constructed does not necessarily represent reality. These comments are not designed to denigrate the value of acquiring knowledge on the enemy; rather they are designed to suggest that certainty is rarely, if ever, achieved.

In this exploration of the difficulties encountered in the quest for knowledge there is one very important factor still to mention, namely, intent. Being able to see all the enemy's physical assets is not the equivalent of knowing what he will do with them.[63] Although, Leonhard is right to suggest that by watching enemy logistical preparations one can gain some insight into his intentions.[64] Also, intelligence gathering, including the interception of enemy communications, can also help in this process. However, even when blessed with intelligence such as that garnered from Ultra during World War II, understanding the enemy's intentions is far from guaranteed. Despite the advantages offered to Allied commanders in the North African campaign, Rommel was still able to achieve surprise on a number of occasions.[65] The previous discussion of deception should also temper any undue optimism regarding the identification of enemy intentions. Finally, it is necessary to once again refer to the polymorphous character of war. Conflict is not restricted to conventional warfare composed of easily identifiable units and formations. Both Callwell and Lawrence remind us that irregular operations and formations mitigate the chances of quantifying enemy force structures and intentions.[66] On the issue of intentions, the USMC once again seems to have the most sensible viewpoint. *Warfighting* declares that the best one can hope for is to establish probabilities, to estimate the enemy's designs. However, some enemy actions will always come as a surprise, and these kinds of actions can often have the greatest impact on the battle.[67]

Aside from these two major obstacles to the pursuit of certainty, there are a host of other difficulties. One often noted in the literature is the potential for information overload. Indeed, Ferris and Handel identify this as one of the more prominent elements of uncertainty in the modern battlespace.[68] Rather than lifting the fog of war, too much information could thicken it, presenting a commander and his staff with too much data to understand in a reasonable time.[69] A possible future answer to this dilemma is the utilisation of artificial intelligence in the process of command. The following chapter will explore this possibility and suggest reasons why this may not present a credible solution to the problem of command in the information age. Another technological problem faced in Kosovo was that information flow was delayed substantially because of the lack of a high-volume data link.[70]

The environmental context in which a conflict occurs can also have a significant bearing on the chances of dispersing the fog of war. In this respect, the difficulties posed by wooded and jungle areas immediately come to mind. O'Hanlon notes that the sensors which collect information have a number of limitations. In general, he concludes that, although sensors will improve, the laws of physics, enemy countermeasures and natural cover will limit their potential.[71] For example, in the 1991 Gulf War the performance of infrared, electro-optical and laser systems suffered due to the weather, dust and smoke. There may well be technological solutions lurking in the future to mitigate some of the current problems and to help the seekers peer through what were once impenetrable screens. However, other environments, such as the growing urban environment, will present greater difficulties. This is not so much a result of the physical characteristics of these areas, although that is still clearly a problem, but is more to do with the density of population into which the enemy can blend. David Jablonsky reminds us of the obvious difficulties faced by US forces in Somalia in trying to identify enemy forces amongst the general population.[72]

Reference has already been made to the problems involved in the interpretation of information. The classic study of this subject is Roberta Wohlstetter's analysis of the Japanese attack on Pearl Harbor in 1941. Significantly for those who equate information and/or knowledge with victory, Wohlstetter concludes: 'Never before … have we had so complete an intelligence picture of the enemy.'[73] Despite this, the Japanese were still able to achieve surprise. Arab forces in 1973 and Iraq in its invasion of Kuwait in 1990 achieved similar strategic surprise. Although deception often played a role in these cases, with reference to Japan, Wohlstetter instead places greater emphasis on the problems of deciphering the useful information from the surrounding noise, and the subjective interpretation of information as a result of preconceived expectations of the enemy's intentions: 'In short, we failed to anticipate Pearl Harbor not for want of the relevant materials, but because of a plethora of irrelevant ones.'[74] Looking further back into history, Elizabeth I had acquired plans for Philip II's Armada of 1588. However, like Pearl Harbor, Spain's actual intentions were subsumed within a cacophony of other intelligence.[75] The above cases refer to what might be described as surprise at the strategic level, yet the fears and pressures confronted in the battlespace will surely produce similar mistakes in the use of information at the lower levels of strategy. T. E. Lawrence notes:

> There was a line of variability (man) running through all its estimates. Its components were sensitive and illogical, and generals guarded themselves by the device of a reserve, the significant medium of their art. Goltz had said that when you know the enemy's strength, and he is fully deployed, then you know enough to dispense with a reserve. But this is never. There is always the possibility of accident, of some flaw in materials, present in the general's mind: and the reserve is unconsciously held to meet it.[76]

Again, the ever-useful *Warfighting* assumes that information and instructions will be unclear and/or misunderstood during battle.[77] It is also worth remembering that Clausewitz discusses a 'psychological fog' that emanates from an emotional response to the suffering and hardship of battle, and therefore makes it 'hard to form clear and complete insights'.[78] The underlying point to be made is that even the possession of complete information does not guarantee certainty of understanding, nor the ability to act upon that information. Bennett cites the example of Crete in 1942 when General Freyberg, the Allied commander on Crete, lacked the resources to defeat the German assault he knew was coming.[79] Finally, information is ultimately handled by participating humans who may distort the data. Brodie notes that during Vietnam President Johnson placed too much faith in information that was biased and the product of excessive optimism.[80]

There are myriad factors that prevent information from fulfilling its operational and strategic potential. This does not mean that uncertainty cannot be reduced. Indeed, the increasing deployment of ever more enhanced sensors should help to increase the level of transparency in the battlespace. In this sense, 'Joint Vision 2010' is probably correct when it asserts that the likes of DBK will not eliminate the fog of war; rather they will merely increase transparency.[81] However, what will ensure the dominance of uncertainty more than anything is the inescapable fact that war is an interaction between intelligent foes.[82] In this respect, an intelligent foe can deceive his enemy; alternatively he can directly offset his opponent's information technology. Just as importantly, one can never know for sure how the enemy will react within the interactive activity that is war.

These conclusions suggest strongly that it would be wise to continue to prepare for war in the expectation of uncertainty. Kenneth F. McKenzie, Jr is right to warn us against the dangers of training for, and expecting, certainty.[83] Two doctrinal manuals, *Warfighting* and the 1986 version of the US Army's *FM 100-5*, both caution that creating a culture that expects certainty could result in the surrender of the initiative to the enemy as the elusive search for certainty dominates a commander's actions.[84]

A HUMAN FUTURE

Reference has already been made to what Fuller described as the hidden impulse to remove humans from the direct conduct of war. A number of concepts that underlie the current RMA appear to continue this process. This is not wholly surprising since the modern RMA is, to a significant degree, shaped by the United States. The strategic culture of the United States tends to place undue emphasis on technological answers to strategic questions.[85] Major Norman C. Davis of the USMC notes that for decades the United States has pursued the objective of replacing manpower with firepower.[86] In terms of protecting friendly lives, this is undoubtedly a laudable goal. However, the development of a force structure and strategic culture that reduces the ability to put men into 'harm's way' may not serve the cause of strategic efficacy.

Two main sources of change can be identified in this area. Those who seek and believe victory can be obtained by distant bombardment provide the first of these. This approach is typified by the opinions of men like Captain Parry, and was also reflected in NATO's strategy during the Kosovo conflict. In his memoirs, General Wesley Clark, the NATO commander in Kosovo, proffered the thought that the reluctance to enter a ground campaign could be an emerging pattern in US strategic culture.[87] In the conclusion to his book *The Next World War*, James Adams declares that stand-off will be the fundamental strategy of the future. More alarmingly, he goes on to postulate: 'fighting wars without casualties might seem a contradiction in terms, but there are systems in service or being developed that allow exactly that'.[88] On the basis of these ideas, Adams concludes that embracing stand-off equates to accepting a decreasing requirement for people to do fighting up close and personal.[89] In his work on post-heroic warfare, Luttwak complains at the cost of infantry and armoured forces and the corresponding shortage of cruise missiles. Although he recognises that ground forces are the most versatile expression of military power, he concludes that in the current political environment they are unusable in many instances.[90] Indeed, Biddle notes that this prevailing perspective requires a cultural need for the United States to adopt a post-heroic stance.[91] In light of the Kosovo conflict, one has to conclude that in many respects Luttwak's ideas were proven correct. There was certainly unwillingness on the part of NATO political leaders to risk deploying more casualty-prone ground forces. The conflict also uncovered a shortage of precision munitions in NATO arsenals.[92] However, 9/11 appears to have changed US approaches to war to some degree. Operations in Afghanistan represent somewhat of a compromise. The so-called 'Afghan Model' brings together the deployment of US special forces, airpower and indigenous allied forces (in this case, the Northern Alliance). Whilst US forces were indeed engaged in ground combat in Afghanistan, this approach has been criticised for relying too much upon local allies. This policy is blamed for the alleged escape of Osama Bin Laden at Tora Bora, where Afghan forces did a deal with the al Qaeda leadership.[93] The invasion of Iraq seems to represent a further shift away from post-heroic warfare. Substantial Coalition forces mounted a ground invasion and even engaged in urban operations. However, initially there was some criticism of the fact that too much reliance was placed upon technology, and in particular airpower, that resulted in too few ground forces.[94] As already noted, this led to vulnerable supply lines because the forces were not available to protect them in sufficient numbers. However, as in the 1991 Gulf War, Iraqi forces proved to be so inept that these Coalition deficiencies did not prove catastrophic.

An aversion to casualties also has implications for urban operations for security communities such as the United States. The proceedings of a 1998 conference on urban warfare reveal how influential the risk of casualties could prove to be in future US military operations. The summary of the conference concluded that sustained urban conflict was almost totally out of the question because of the potential casualties that could be sustained.[95] At one level the War for Iraq suggests that inhibitions to urban operations may be on the wane. Nonetheless, there was evidence that culturally the West had a serious aversion to urban warfare. Newspaper headlines such as 'Pentagon Plans for Worst Nightmare' are indicative of this prevailing attitude.[96] In the event, the Coalition managed to avoid sustained urban operations against a competent foe. In many important respects the War for Iraq was not a substantial test of Western attitudes and approaches to sustained urban warfare. However, interesting observations can be drawn from the battles for cities such as Basra and An Nasiriyah. In particular, whist airpower and PGMs can contribute to the urban battle, the fighting in Iraqi cities again shows that ground forces play the leading role.[97]

Strategy demands that the response to the current political environment is not to change force structure or avoid certain types of operations, but rather to attempt to change the current political psyche. Future enemies, plus the requirements of future strategy, may not play by the rules of post-heroic warfare. In this context, referring to the Confederacy's loss at the Battle of Gettysburg, Vincent J. Goulding, Jr comments: 'our 21st century Cemetery Ridge awaits us if we allow political expediency and transient technological advantage to become the determinant of successful military operations'.[98] Goulding wisely argues that decision makers must accept that mission success might entail casualties, and chastises the following statement by Don Snider, John Nagl and Tony Pfaff: 'if mission and force protection are in conflict, then we don't do the mission'.[99] Lambeth is clear about the responsibilities of civilian leaders when planning and conducting military operations:

> It follows that civilian leaders at the highest levels have an equal obligation to try and stack the deck in such a manner that the military has the best possible hand to play and the fullest possible freedom to play it to the best of its ability. This means expending the energy and political capital needed to develop and enforce a strategy that maximizes the probability of military success.[100]

Finally, in what is a praiseworthy article, Goulding bemoans the fact that aversion to casualties is reaching into peace support operations (PSO), and creates a situation in which US troops, cocooned within their fortified camps, cannot interact properly with the local inhabitants or understand the situation on the ground.[101]

The second, related, potential agent of change is an increased emphasis on unmanned platforms. Wilson observes that it is not just a sensitivity to casualties that drives these efforts. The desire for higher operational tempo, allied to the physical and mental limitations of humans, presents understandable motivations for the development of unmanned vehicles.[102] One of the most extreme versions of these ideas, and one which brings together the notions of war by bombardment and unmanned delivery systems, is Libicki's concept of fire-ant warfare. In this vision of the future, which is devoid of reference to strategic context, tiny sensors, emitters and microprojectiles dominate the battlespace. The existence of a fine 'Mesh' of sensors that covers the battlespace ensures that nothing the size of a manned platform can escape detection.[103] Even Libicki's concept of fire-ant warfare is surpassed by the aforementioned notion of 'virtual presence'. Interestingly however, at one stage Libicki does acknowledge that the best ground-based sensor is a digitally linked human.[104] Some authors even regard the primary future role of soldiers as that of sensors, and proclaim that army doctrine must change to reflect this.[105] In many respects, a key role of US special forces in Afghanistan was to act as sensors for cuing in PGM strikes.[106] There is, of course, a distinction between utilising humans merely as sensors, and perceiving them as broader instruments of strategy that may include the use of them for the delivery of firepower and 'control'.[107] It is also worth bearing in mind, as Lemelin argues, that an acknowledgement of the value of humans in warfare in some of the RMA literature may be no more than rhetoric.[108] Often, work by RMA enthusiasts begins with a declaration on the value and continued role of humans, only for the rest of the paper to focus entirely on the latest technology. Careful analysis of these issues is required because the procurement and military cultural implications of accepting these RMA visions on the future role of humans are very significant.

As in the case of uncertainty, there are a number of reasons to indicate that humans, and the platforms in which they travel, will continue to be put into harm's way, and will have to engage in direct and close combat with the enemy. These reasons emanate once again from the requirements of strategy. The central role of strategy is often overlooked in the RMA literature. For example, Admiral Owens concentrates his attention on the 'combat superiority' that can be garnered from long-range PGMs and enhanced delivery systems.[109] Whilst it is right and proper to stress the requirement for efficacy in combat, the real focus of attention should be on the attainment of 'strategic superiority'. To reiterate, strategy is concerned with the relationship between means and ends, in which means are represented by military instruments and the ends refer to policy objectives. In broader terms, the objective of war, to use Admiral J. C. Wylie's terminology, is to exert some measure of *control* over the enemy and/or the situation.[110] Wylie describes the method by which control is enforced: 'The ultimate determinant in war is the man on the scene with the gun. This man is the final power in war. He is control.'[111] The term 'control' accurately describes the broad objective of strategy, in that it engenders a notion of physical control over the land, its people, resources and thereby the issues at stake. As Gray and Corbett have both noted, land is where the final decisions will be made, because it is on land where humans dwell.[112] Control can be applied to a number of things, including the control or protection of populations, resources or territory for its own sake. In Kosovo, clearly airpower could not stop the ethnic cleansing of Albanians by Serb forces.[113] The possession of territory can serve many purposes, from the establishment of a security buffer zone, to fulfilling the requirements of political symbolism.[114] The deployment of ground forces can also display resolve and commitment to allies. In contrast to airpower, ground forces can provide prolonged presence. The history of warfare continually reaffirms Wylie's principle of the man on the scene with a gun. The conflict in Kosovo presents one of the most recent examples. The debate continues over whether the air campaign alone proved decisive. However, from a strategic perspective it is clear that one of NATO's primary objectives, the return of the Kosovar Albanians, could not be achieved without the physical presence of NATO ground forces in the Yugoslav province. More obviously, during the invasion of Iraq, despite the air campaign's 'shock and awe', Saddam's regime only fell when Coalition ground forces actually entered Baghdad. Not only did the appearance of US ground forces in Baghdad represent a physical representation of the end of Saddam's regime, they were also crucial in securing and protecting the valuable oil fields in the country.[115]

The value of ground forces, especially infantry, is further enhanced when the various possible contexts for future conflicts are considered. Much of the RMA literature focuses its attention on regular forms of warfare, and yet this is in direct contrast to a substantial body of work that foresees a future of low-intensity, irregular forms of conflict.[116] Indicative of the RMA literature's narrow focus is an article by Andrew Krepinevich written just two years before 9/11. When identifying the challenges of the twenty-first century, he focuses on technological developments such as space power, SIW and PGMs, with no reference to terrorism.[117] In the context of this chapter, the important implication of these ideas is, as Ralph Peters suggests, that irregular forms of conflict more often than not require the utilisation of infantry and special operations forces.[118] This truism was evident in British operations on the North West Frontier during the interwar period: 'The infantryman and pack mule reigned supreme in frontier warfare.'[119] In more recent history, as the United States discovered in Vietnam, indirect firepower can only achieve so much in a counterinsurgency (COIN) campaign. In this form of conflict the most useful military instrument is the light infantryman.[120] In Afghanistan, special forces represented the 'main effort' of US operations, and Biddle concludes that for the future an ample supply of skilled dismounted infantry is required.[121] An important component of a COIN campaign is the protection of the local population from coercion by the insurgents. In this respect, it is unlikely that the local inhabitants will attain a real sense of security from 'virtual presence'. As is the case in Kosovo, the perception of security begins with the immediate presence of an armed NATO soldier. Although it is questionable whether the future will be entirely or even predominately composed of irregular warfare, it is wise to anticipate that irregular operations will be required. The future, much like the past, will likely consist of a mixture of both regular and irregular forms of conflict, in which case future force structure and military culture must strike a balance between these differing needs. Occasionally, elements of the RMA literature do address irregular forms of warfare. However, often the focus is yet again on technological fixes to complex strategic issues.[122]

The future battlespace will take many different forms. A strong candidate in this respect is urban warfare. Daryl Press makes the point that wars have always drawn troops into cities, but this trend may increase in line with the increasing pace of urbanisation. It has been estimated that in 25 years 70 per cent of the world's population will reside in urban areas.[123] As Murray notes, there are a host of factors that endow urban areas with both political and military significance. Not only are they often key transportation hubs, and therefore have significant logistical importance; they also represent the political centres of power. Subsequently, cities have both physical and psychological resonance.[124] Indeed, the urban environment is an area that the USMC is currently taking very seriously.[125] Because of population density, the physical nature of the environment and possible strategic objectives, ground forces are likely to prove the most applicable and versatile expressions of military power in urban conflict.[126] The reconnaissance–strike complex would seem to have important, but limited strategic value in these operations. The nature of certain physical environments should influence future force structure.

At this stage it is important to outline the inherent advantages of infantry forces. These benefits have long been recognised. In the late fourth century Vegetius wrote, 'infantry are more vital to the state, as they can be useful everywhere'.[127] Furthermore, a point worth emphasising is Goulding's observation that a foot soldier is the most precise instrument of war.[128] S. L. A. Marshall also identifies the value of infantry, and yet he correctly balances this opinion with a recognition of the importance of firepower in combat: 'when decision is made possible through the attainment of a superiority in the striking (fire) power of the heavy weapons of war, they [the infantry] must go forward to claim the victory and beat down the surviving elements of resistance'.[129] This last quote by Marshall is important, in that it correctly presents the value of both distant firepower and close combat forces. Indeed, Biddle regards combined arms operations as one of the key elements of successful land warfare.[130] To this end, the comments in this section are not designed to denigrate the importance of firepower, which of course will continue to play a vital role in the defeat of enemy forces. Firepower made a notable contribution in Ia Drang Valley: 'a major difference between Lieutenant Colonel Nguyen Huu An of the People's Army of Vietnam and Lieutenant Colonel Hal Moore of the 1st Cavalry Division was that I had major fire support and he didn't'.[131] Nonetheless, in certain physical environments and in certain strategic contexts (COIN), heavy and distant firepower may prove counterproductive and strategically unusable, in which case ground forces with organic firepower will prove most effective. The significance of this point is evident when one considers Blaker's statement that the RMA force will contain little organic firepower.[132] Ground forces also enable control. Riper and Scales are once again correct when they conclude that ground forces give you resolution, durability and versatility.[133]

Once we accept the need physically to hold ground and to deploy infantry forces, then the requirement for manned platforms becomes clear. Again, Blaker's comments are of particular interest here, as he concedes that the RMA force is less able to hold and occupy territory.[134] A number of reasons promote the retention of manned platforms. Because men will have to be placed in harm's way, they will continue to require protected firepower and mobility. Armoured platforms such as tanks and armoured personnel carriers (APCs) provide these very capabilities.[135] The tank represents a good compromise between firepower, mobility and protection.[136] Indeed, the downing of US Apache attack helicopters during the invasion of Iraq has lead Charles Hayman, editor of *Jane's World Armies*, to argue that 'Against heavily fortified Iraqi positions there is no substitute for heavy armour and artillery.'[137] Peters, commenting on the experience of the United States in Mogadishu, argues that the protection provided by armour was sorely needed in Somalia.[138] The history of urban warfare is one in which armour often plays an important supporting role to infantry.[139] In the battle for Hue, organic firepower proved critical for the USMC, since ROE and the weather limited the applicability of support from the air.[140] Similarly, in the battle for Ban Me Thuot the North Vietnamese Army (NVA) relied upon combined arms organisations based around infantry and armour. This approach created self-sufficient units that possessed speed, mobility and striking power.[141] Aside from the protection offered, platforms such as the tank also provide much needed organic firepower. The main battle tank (MBT) and APC played crucial roles during the capture of Iraqi cities in 2003. During the capture of Basra, British forces mounted so-called 'thunder runs' with tanks thrusting into the urban environment as a signal to residents that the old regime had lost its grip on the city. An aide to Donald Rumsfeld noted, 'The British occupation of Basra was the pilot project for the US assault on Baghdad, using tank and armour thrusts to get control of a city without taking it house by house.'[142]

The RMA enthusiasts may ask why would organic firepower be required if one possessed a true reconnaissance–strike complex? The potential vulnerability of the networks that underlie such capabilities is a major concern. Such weaknesses that may be present in an RMA force may be enhanced by the paradoxical logic of strategy. If the strength of an RMA-based military resides in its digital networks, then these networks will likely be the most pressing target for an enemy. Also, as Colonel Volney J. Warner argues, 'Remoteness impairs effectiveness and invites countermeasures.'[143] Although a somewhat sweeping statement, in the light of the Kosovo conflict it is difficult to disagree with Colonel Warner substantially. For these reasons, it would seem somewhat of a gamble to remove organic firepower and rely solely upon distant, networked means of delivery. Looking to potential future operations and conflicts, Colonel Dick Applegate notes that the British Army may want to keep its organic firepower assets because in future multinational operations it may not have the Royal Air Force or Royal Navy on hand to provide such capabilities.[144] Equally, O'Hanlon notes that many of the tactics used by the North Vietnamese and Viet Cong forces to offset distant firepower are still applicable today. These techniques include: bunkers and tunnels, and 'hugging', to name but two.[145] In this respect, it is encouraging to see that, although the British Royal Artillery is sensibly planning to replace some of its heavy guns with precision missile systems, it is retaining some of its 105mm guns, and perhaps purchasing lighter short-range guns for the battlefield.[146] Tanks and their equivalents offer other advantages besides those already mentioned. As both Gadsby and Bellamy reveal, in Bosnia the British Challenger MBT proved an effective psychological instrument, in that it clearly represented an indication of British firepower to the warring parties.[147] In this respect, Bosnia showed armour to be far more versatile than is often assumed.

Identifying a need for manned platforms does not in itself negate the doubts concerning the alleged vulnerability of these instruments. So why is Libicki wrong to signal the end of the manned platform? Because manned platforms are required, those deploying them will devise ways to provide for their protection. Various methods could be deployed in this endeavour. These include plastic tanks with stealthy characteristics and electromagnetic armour, the employment of laser dazzlers and more simple decoy measures as used in Kosovo.[148] Peters raises a salient point when he asks the question: why should tanks not be able to enjoy the benefits of situational awareness?[149] At the technical level of strategy the devil is very much in the detail. Yet, for the purposes of this study the detail is not that important. What matters is the recognition of the paradoxical logic of strategy. Put simply, those deploying manned platforms will almost certainly develop means by which to offset the efficacy of Libicki's Mesh or its equivalent. Evidence of the ability of platforms to survive in the face of countermeasures is provided by airpower. Lambeth makes the salient point that only two US aircraft were lost to Serbian SAM (surface-to-air missile) fire during the Kosovo war.[150] And, whilst the Serbian Integrated Air Defence System (IADS) was never completely neutralised, NATO aircraft continued to increase their sortie rate during the war. Despite the continued development of anti-aircraft capabilities, aircraft have not only survived as viable instruments of strategy, but arguably have attained greater prominence in certain circumstances and contexts.[151]

Of course, some pieces of equipment do become obsolete, but something as important and fundamental as the manned platform, in all its guises, will in all likelihood find ways to remain viable. These thoughts do not mean that the world will stand still. Indeed, in the face of these threats armoured vehicles probably will have to change in response. Also, there is undoubtedly a future role for unmanned vehicles. For instance, Damian Kemp offers one of the most sensible evaluations concerning the future role of Unmanned Combat Aerial Vehicles (UCAVs). Kemp foresees UCAVs operating somewhere between cruise missiles and manned fighters.[152] There are certainly missions to which unmanned platforms are well suited. Both Kosovo and Afghanistan further revealed the utility of these vehicles in reconnaissance and command and control procedures, as well as some strike missions.[153] Afghanistan saw the first instance in which a Predator UAV launched a Hellfire missile to neutralise al Qaeda operatives.[154] This procedure was repeated in Yemen.[155] Suppresion of Enemy Air Defences (SEAD) is another area for which UCAVs are well suited.[156] However, Kosovo witnessed the importance of manned platforms in attacks on mobile ground targets. Despite errors such as the mistaken NATO bombing of a refugee column, Kosovo showed the political value of having pilots on the spot to verify target identification. The political nature of war will continue to place a premium on the skill and judgment of trained pilots to minimise strategically harmful mistakes.

Stand-off firepower certainly has a role to play. If strategy and the enemy allow, then utilising this method of delivery makes a great deal of sense. Biddle persuasively argues: 'The results thus suggest that where the troops on the ground are comparable ... American precision fires can make the difference.'[157] Likewise, the future should see a greater role for unmanned vehicles. Indeed, the United States is increasing the number of unmanned vehicles programmes and substantially increasing the budget for this area of development.[158] However, the requirements of strategy, allied to the fact that the future battlespace, and future adversaries, will take many guises, dictate that control will ultimately continue to be exercised by the man on the scene with a gun. In this context, Goodwin is correct to state that strategic success depends on control of land, people and resources.[159] This requirement, allied to the existence of the paradoxical logic, should ensure that the manned platform will continue to prove a viable instrument of war. These thoughts contrast sharply with Libicki's comment that stand-off warfare focuses not on controlling territory but on destroying adversaries.[160] Applegate could not be more correct when he states that 'we will still need the ability to generate mass and provide forces for endurance, and *maintain the capability and mental outlook necessary to conduct and sustain aggressive close combat*' (emphasis added).[161] The rationale for this statement is well described by Scales, who proclaims that an actor facing an opponent waging stand-off warfare would only have to avoid defeat by preserving his forces. He surmises that this is an achievable objective as long as countries such as the United States are not prepared to dominate on the ground.[162] Finally, we can turn once again to the insight of Stephen Biddle, who cautions, 'where coercion fails, brute force on land has been the final arbiter of disputes'.[163]

A VIOLENT FUTURE

Some of the most outlandish claims in the RMA literature concern the prominence of information-based warfare in deciding future conflicts. In its most extreme form, this section of the debate throws into question the most basic assumptions about warfare. Clausewitz defines war as 'an act of force to compel our enemy to do our will'. He goes on to define these concepts further: 'Force – that is, *physical force* ... is thus the means of war' (emphasis added).[164] Contrast these thoughts with Libicki's definition of information-based warfare: 'Information-based warfare is that which utilises information, especially computer-processed information, to impose one's will on the enemy.'[165] Often at the heart of these notions concerning the role of information is the idea that wars can be won with significantly less, or no, fighting and violence. As noted earlier, this emanates from two desires. The first is concerned with the principle of economy of force; the second is from the aspiration to humanise the act of war.[166] An extreme example of this latter desire can be found in the Kosovo conflict. The Dutch government delayed an attack on President Milosevic's villa for over a month because of fear of bombing a painting by Rembrandt. More telling was the refusal of NATO ambassadors to approve the bombing of Serbian army barracks for fear of causing too many casualties amongst Serbian conscripts.[167] In terms of the classical works of strategic thought, these ideas are often regarded as signalling the substitution of Sun Tzu for Clausewitz. To this end, the literature often recalls Sun Tzu's statement: 'For to win one hundred victories in one hundred battles is not the acme of skill. To subdue the enemy without fighting is the acme of skill.'[168] Although the desire to make war a less violent and destructive activity may at first appear to be an admirable objective, when one considers the nature of future war, the requirements of strategy and the actions of the enemy, the viability and wisdom of this vision is open to question.

Prominent in much of the RMA literature are references to the attainment of victory through the disruption rather than destruction of the enemy. Although more cautious in some of their claims than many of their colleagues, Arquilla and Ronfeldt still feel justified to declare that war is evolving into a less destructive pursuit: 'In the new epoch, decisive duels for the control of information flows will take the place of drawn-out battles of attrition or annihilation; the requirement to destroy will recede as the ability to disrupt is enhanced.'[169] In an optimistic appraisal of information-based warfare, Arquilla postulates that 'control warfare', which derives from information dominance, can achieve victory at a low cost in blood and treasure even against the strongest opponents.[170] What Arquilla seems to misapprehend is that it is not the strong opponents one should necessarily worry about; the real danger comes from those foes that are strategically adept. Similar ideas to those above are also at the heart of the US Navy's concept of Network Centric Warfare. One of the authors of the NCW literature unambiguously avowed that disruption is a preferable way to defeat the enemy.[171] In theory, victory through disruption is achieved by breaking the coherence of enemy forces, usually by attacking or disrupting his C^2 system. The objective is to paralyse his forces so that they cease to function as a viable whole. The assumption behind these claims is the optimistic hope that a disrupted force will sue for peace because this disruption has broken his will.

Related to the notion of victory through disruption is the belief that information has become the determining factor in any given conflict.[172] For example, Donald E. Ryan equates twenty-first-century warfare with the eighteenth century, in that information-based warfare attains victory without firing a shot.[173] Similarly, Alan D. Campen postulates that the Gulf War of 1991 'was the first war with a notion that an enemy could be brought to his knees by denial of information'.[174] Although Campen is correct to note that an asymmetry in information endowed the Coalition with an undoubted advantage, it is tempting to respond to his enthusiasm by pointing out that the Coalition's victory also required the destruction of Iraqi forces in the Kuwaiti Theatre of Operations (KTO). In 2003, although many Iraqi formations surrendered or melted away once their cohesion had been broken, a great deal of violence and destructive force was still required to remove the more stubborn elements of Saddam's forces. It is also important to reiterate the point that poor Iraqi performance flattered US technology in both 1991 and 2003.[175]

The tendency to overplay the significance of information in war has also crept into historical analysis. It is not uncommon for modern scholars to re-examine past conflicts and, with an information age perspective, discover that information was the key to many past campaigns. In his vigorous efforts to highlight the central importance of information, Leonhard makes the extraordinary claim that the Maryland campaign of 1862 was decided not by guns or cavalry, but rather by information. In contrast to these thoughts, it is more credible to recognise the value of information and yet also conclude that information was just one factor in the outcome of the conflict in question. In 1862, information did not kill a single soldier, destroy a single piece of artillery nor occupy a square inch of land.[176] Information may have enabled these actions, but it did not achieve them directly. Leonhard's claims are akin to the Tofflers' proclamation that software was the real star of the Gulf War.[177] This is rather like saying that fuel was the real star of Germany's victory over France in 1940. In both cases, software and fuel were significant enablers; after all, German panzers could not have advanced into France without fuel. But success in war relies upon a myriad of factors, including information, leadership, adequate technology, trained soldiers, morale and logistics, to name just six. To reduce success in war to one element is simply an act of reductionism. This tendency to oversimplify the conduct of war is often underpinned by a one-dimensional perspective of conflict in which the enemy plays a placid, even co-operative role. This is evident in claims that in future wars course and outcome will be one and the same, that due to the efficacy of the reconnaissance–strike complex surprise may become decisive and consequently there will be only one period of fighting.[178] Although historically some wars have been concluded by one action, one should not plan on the basis that this will invariably happen.[179] Placing too much faith in such actions presents the real danger of giving insufficient attention to the dialectic nature of strategy, and therefore the paradoxical logic is not given its due.

Libicki has written extensively on the issue of information as a deciding factor in future conflicts. As noted earlier, Libicki postulates that war will cease to be a force-on-force experience. Rather, it will be conducted along the lines of hide-and-seek. At times Libicki accepts that targets identified by the Mesh will still require destruction. However, he predicts also that recognised information superiority may compel the enemy to sue for peace.[180] This latter claim is not wholly unreasonable. It is not inconceivable, in permissive conditions, for a conflict to end once information dominance has been achieved. As previously noted, even

Clausewitz, who places significant emphasis on battle, recognises that on occasion the odds prior to battle could be so decisive that one side would capitulate without combat.[181] On balance, however, Libicki suggests that the transparency created by the information age will render the offensive use of physical force less viable. He has professed that physical expression of force acts merely to serve information.[182] If Libicki is not claiming that information will be decisive in the future, he is coming very close to it. Finally, a concept of future war with the primacy of information very much at its core is 'cyberwar'. When defining this concept, Arquilla and Ronfeldt unequivocally state that victory goes to those who have the better grasp of information.[183] Although varying in their levels of intensity, the above authors all have information at the heart of their visions of future war. Information is perceived to be the decisive factor in conflict. As noted, some even go as far as to suggest that disruption of a foe's C^2, or recognised information dominance, will prove independently capable of ensuring victory, thereby removing violence and destruction from the act of war. In procurement terms, one author's advice is 'Don't scrimp on C^3 to buy more bullets.'[184] Aside from de-emphasising the implements of firepower, there are obvious dangers in the formation of a military culture that expects the nature of war to be a significantly less violent undertaking.

Strategy is once again the leading element in the chorus of counter-claims against these information-dominated visions of the future. For instance, the demands of strategy may dictate that the enemy's forces should be physically destroyed. This is in direct contrast to claims that destructive force is wasteful.[185] Prior to D-Day, the Combined Chiefs of Staff issued the following directive to Eisenhower: 'You will enter the continent of Europe and, in conjunction with the other Allied Nations, undertake operations aimed at the heart of Germany and the destruction of her armed forces.' Eisenhower goes on to note, 'This purpose of destroying enemy forces was always our guiding principle.'[186] Likewise, the Union's strategy in the US Civil War was designed around a perceived need to destroy Lee's army.[187] Commenting on counter-guerrilla warfare, Leroy Thompson stipulates that the main military aim 'is to find, fix, and destroy them'.[188] Such operations reveal that the relationship between information and firepower is complementary. As Thompson asserts, the task of finding and destroying enemy guerrilla forces requires good information, usually from the local population.[189] Ironically, the quest for information dominance may also help retain the destructive nature of war. 'Joint Vision 2010' foresees information superiority campaigns that rely upon the physical destruction of enemy C^4I, as well as non-physical acts, including electronic warfare (EW) and intrusion into enemy networks.[190] Commenting upon the war on terrorism, Ralph Peters is somewhat stark, but still persuasive when he argues 'we will have to kill terrorists and their supporters until the hardcore terrorists are exterminated'.[191] These thoughts are not intended to suggest that the destruction of enemy forces is always a wise strategy; it is merely to note that certain circumstances conspire to create a situation in which one's objectives are most readily achieved through the annihilation of enemy forces. And whilst the war on terrorism requires an astute balancing of all of the instruments of grand strategy, military force must play a decisive role when dealing with hardcore al Qaeda operatives.

Of course, excessive firepower, or even battle itself, can prove counter-productive in strategic terms. In contrast to the Union's strategy during the US Civil War, it is argued that the Confederates' wisest course of action would have been to avoid battle, and thereby prolong the war in an attempt to break the will of the North.[192] An important part of strategic judgment is knowing when and when not to fight the enemy. Also, Leonhard is at least half-right when he notes that war is concerned with imposing one's will rather than killing.[193] However, against enemies such as the Third Reich and al Qaeda, destruction may be the most, if not the only, assured method of imposing one's will. In this sense, some enemies are not amenable to negotiation or coercion, have such extreme objectives and employ such destructive methods that their elimination is the only viable solution to the threat they pose. The decisive use of destructive force does not represent an oversimplification of grand strategy. Clausewitz is persuasive when he argues, 'the maximum use of force is in no way incompatible with the simultaneous use of the intellect'.[194] Also, disruption and destruction are not necessarily mutually exclusive approaches to war. Indeed, when destruction is required, it may often prove profitable to disrupt and then destroy. An opposing force that has lost its cohesion will in all likelihood present less effective resistance.

What is missing from the 'disruption' literature is recognition that the enemy's cohesion often can be broken through the application of firepower and physical destruction. Clausewitz recognised the effects physical destruction could have on the intangibles in war: 'Physical casualties are not the only losses incurred by both sides in the course of the engagement: their moral strength is also shaken, broken and ruined.'[195] The USMC declares that inherent in manoeuvre warfare 'is the need for violence, not so much as a source of physical attrition but as a source of moral dislocation'.[196] It seems that this form of moral dislocation is a far more potent weapon than simply disrupting the enemy through attacks against his C^{4}I networks. The former is arguably more difficult to recover from, and therefore has longer-lasting effects, with the added bonus of physically depleting the enemy's capabilities. When considering the most effective method of warfare, bearing in mind the strategic objectives of any campaign, it is difficult to disagree with Clausewitz's call for an uncomplicated approach.[197] NCW and its derivatives would seem to rely upon a very good understanding of the enemy's network structure and operational procedures. Likewise, Owen Jensen advocates operations that produce the minimum changes to behaviour required to fulfil the objectives.[198] Approaches such as these could potentially lead to overly complex and fine-tuned operations that are not as tolerant of error or change.[199] They also presume levels of precision which military instruments do not posses. Finally, as Clausewitz notes, rapid and simple enemy actions can wreck these fine-tuned operations.[200]

Staying with the demands of strategy, Wylie's concept of control may require the occupation of territory. Information dominance can help achieve this end, but cannot occupy territory nor protect nor control a population itself. A disrupted foe on the wrong end of an information asymmetry may still be in physical possession of 'key ground'. This scenario is reminiscent of the position the Iraqis found themselves in during the Gulf War of 1991. Despite the Coalition's information dominance, the liberation of Kuwait required the application of destructive physical force. More importantly, the policy objectives of the war called for the destruction of the Iraqi Republican Guard. It was believed that regional stability partly rested on the removal of the offensive threat posed by such forces. Rick Atkinson correctly notes that this objective did not require the obliteration of every last Republican Guard platoon; what was needed was the disabling of the Guard as an effective force.[201] However, some destruction was required. It is unlikely that mere disruption would have neutralised the threat to Iraq's neighbours posed by the Guard. To paraphrase the maritime strategist Julian Corbett, an enemy force that is merely disrupted poses a threat as a 'force in being'.[202] In the same manner by which an enemy fleet in being could dispute command of the sea, an enemy force in being in theory could dispute 'control'. Of course, the question of disruption and/or destruction is dependent upon circumstance and strategic objectives. However, a disrupted enemy surely has more potential to return as an effective force than one that is largely destroyed. It is interesting that the US Navy, from which NCW originated, appears to have ignored Corbett's writings on the threat posed by a fleet in being. As noted earlier, one of the authors of the NCW work expressed a preference for disruption as opposed to destruction. In response, it is sufficient to note that a disrupted enemy fleet can regain cohesion, while a sunken enemy fleet remains sunk.

When considering whether the future nature of warfare can be non-violent, it is important to reiterate the point that no one society controls the future of war. To cite just one example, Timothy L. Thomas notes that the Chinese will develop their own particular version of information warfare.[203] As other security communities develop their own versions of information age warfare, they may or may not reflect the non-violent proclivities in much of the RMA literature. War is an interactive activity in which an enemy can always reintroduce violence and destruction. To this end, Ignatieff observes, 'For the future depends not on us alone but on our enemies. They, like us, are drawing their own conclusions from the way we seek to avoid the mortal hazard of war.'[204] In fact, when faced by an RMA-competent enemy, it may prove strategically advantageous for a foe to wage a violent form of conflict. Coker remarks that, in contrast to Western attempts to humanise war, in other parts of the world war is becoming increasingly inhumane.[205] Charles Dunlap describes this technique, as a deliberate act of policy, as 'neo-absolutist war'. Referring to the incident in Somalia in which the body of a US serviceman was dragged through the streets of Mogadishu, Dunlap declares that a strategy of neo-absolutist war relies upon the leverage to be gained from the horror felt by a casualty-averse opponent to such a display.[206] Herein lies a potential vulnerability of a military/strategic culture that emphasises less destructive forms of warfare. Another method by which a foe can reintroduce extreme levels of violence is through the use of Weapons of Mass Destruction. Gray correctly points out that the twenty-first century is not only the information age; it is also the second nuclear age.[207] Interestingly, WMD may be the weapon of choice for an opponent facing a foe who is RMA competent. Indeed, Mike Moore suggests that pursuing the RMA will render the United States less secure precisely because it will encourage the proliferation of WMD.[208] Finally, the policy objectives of an actor may be best served by committing particularly savage acts of terrorism such as those of 9/11.

Strategic requirements, in addition to the actions of the enemy, will ensure that war remains a violent and destructive undertaking. Information has always been an important resource in the conduct of war. As Bennett reminds us, it facilitates a more economical use of force.[209] Information will retain a significant role in the future; indeed it is likely that it may become more directly relevant. However, Ajay Singh's comment that information is not an end in itself is right most of the time.[210] Although it is not impossible that a perceived information dominance or dislocation of the enemy could be enough to ensure victory, to raise the value of one factor in war, such as information, above the others commits the error of oversimplifying the conduct of war. R. L. DiNardo and Daniel J. Hughes reflect this well when they note that 'All the information in the world will not help poorly motivated, badly trained, and undisciplined soldiers led by indecisive leaders fighting without sound doctrine.'[211] To this list of disadvantages one could also add 'in the service of poor strategy'.[212]

A FUTURE OF FRICTION

Although the RMA literature does not directly discuss the banishment of friction from future war, much of the optimistic pronouncements concerning the efficacy of RMA forces at best undervalue the influence of friction, and at worst seem to ignore it completely. As an example, Colonel Owen E. Jensen, in a work that develops principles of third-wave warfare, advises readers to 'achieve total situation awareness'. He suggests further that they 'ensure rapid, insightful, accurate battle damage assessment'.[213] Similarly, Daniel T. Kuehl declares that one must have 'comprehensive situational awareness'.[214] While this is undoubtedly wise counsel, Colonel Jensen's work would benefit from a reaffirmation of Clausewitz's cautionary note that 'Everything in war is very simple, but the simplest thing is difficult ... so in war it is difficult for normal efforts to achieve even moderate results.'[215] In our understanding of the nature of war friction plays a critical role because 'friction is the only concept that more or less corresponds to the factors that distinguish real war from war on paper'.[216] That being the case, ignorance of friction in the planning and conduct of future operations, as with expecting certainty on the battlefield, could leave a force unprepared and ill equipped to cope with the reality of war. The phenomenon of friction in war is not an independently occurring factor. Rather, friction is the product of various other conditions. That being the case, in theory the removal or reduction of these factors should consequently remove or reduce friction. However, as will be shown, the causes of friction are so numerous and so inveterate to warfare that any study of the future must accept this element of the nature of war.

Clausewitzian friction has many sources. In his excellent work *Clausewitzian Friction and Future War,* Barry D. Watts identifies eight broad factors that produce the 'unified concept of general friction'. These factors are: danger; physical exertion; uncertainties and imperfections in information; resistance within one's own forces; chance events; physical and political limits on the use of force; unpredictability emanating from interaction with the enemy; and disconnects between ends and means.[217] Invariably, many of these different factors overlap and interact to enhance friction. It has already been argued that uncertainty and violence cannot generally or totally be removed from war. It was also shown that often strategy would demand the physical presence of humans. The continued presence of humans in the activity of war, both physically and mentally, helps ensure the existence of friction. These humans, exposed to the dangers and physical pressures of warfare, will, as Clausewitz noted, retain the potential for friction.[218] The next two causes of friction in Watts' taxonomy, chance events and limitations on the use of force, found expression in the 1999 Kosovo conflict. As described in greater detail in Chapter 4, the chance event of cloud cover significantly affected British bombing missions. Similarly, political concerns that compelled NATO bombers to operate above 15,000 feet helped limit the efficacy of operations, especially those against Serbian forces in Kosovo. This conflict also presents an example of how unpredictability can arise from interaction with the enemy. In this case, the Serbian intensification of ethnic cleansing impacted on NATO operations and strategy. As will also be argued in Chapter 4, NATO's bombing campaign revealed how friction can emanate from the choice of inappropriate means in the pursuit of the desired ends. What these examples, and the preceding sections of this chapter, reveal is that the entrenched, general sources of friction will continue to manifest themselves. Geography, an ever-present factor in the practice of strategy, contributes its own sources of friction: 'the landscape can sometimes present a tenacious friction that constrains, or even curtails, operations. Examples include Flanders during World War I and Burnside's American Civil War Mud March of 1863.'[219] Harold Winters, the author of these words, rightly accepts that technology can help reduce the friction produced by geo-graphy.[220] However, the negative influence of this feature of strategy will never be eradicated.

These constant, generic causes of friction may be joined by other sources of friction more prevalent in the information age. Riper and Scales suggest that the envisaged enlarged battlefields of the future, in which formations are further dispersed and operations are accelerated, will produce higher levels of friction. They suggest that the corresponding increase in danger and fatigue will be intensified by the negative psychological effects of a lack of proximity to other units, and the reduction in periods of inactivity. In short, the future battlefield could become a more stressful and exhausting place to be.[221] Information age operations and technology are not immune from the touch of friction.[222] This is a fact that *Joint Vision 2020* thankfully recognises: 'Information systems, processes, and operations add their own sources of friction and fog to the operational environment.'[223] Adams reports that during operations in Bosnia JSTAR images failed to reach their intended destination when a primary server crashed and a backup computer incorrectly sent the images to a fax machine, thereby making the pictures unintelligible.[224] Similarly, information overload caused enough friction in an Experimental Force (EXFOR) exercise to compel the headquarters' commanders to revert to following the battle on maps and acetate overlays.[225] It should be remembered that this occurred in a peacetime exercise, not within the stressful environment of battle. Watts' study highlights the possibility that novel weapon systems and operations associated with future warfare will in all likelihood create non-linear and unpredictable outcomes. He concludes that these non-linear dynamics, allied to human foibles, inaccessible information and increased opportunity for deception in an information-rich environment, all produce the potential for future friction.[226]

This emphasis on the pervasive nature of friction should not be taken as evidence that friction cannot be reduced or manipulated. It has already been noted in Chapter 1 that Clausewitz and Gray both indicate that friction can be reduced by various measures. The application of information technology, resulting in increased situational awareness, should help reduce friction that emanates from uncertainty. However, the potential for information overload and an increase in stress and lethality in the battlespace could somewhat counteract the reduction in friction produced by better battlespace awareness. On balance, it is not those sources of friction more specific to the information age that will ensure the survival of this constant feature of warfare. Rather, it is the more universal factors that form general friction that will ensure the continued relevance of the USMC's advice in *Warfighting* that 'the greater requirement is to fight effectively within the medium of friction'.[227]

INFLUENCES ON THE FUTURE BATTLESPACE

The character of the future battlespace will not be shaped exclusively by the technology and operations foreseen by advocates of the RMA. At least as significant in this respect will be the demands of strategy; interactions with the enemy; the polymorphous character of war; the physical environment in which war must be conducted; and the involvement of humans. These latter influences are the underlying factors that will ensure that the Clausewitzian nature of war retains validity. However, as noted throughout this chapter, much of the RMA literature either undervalues or ignores these influences on future operations. To avoid the mistake of preparing for the wrong kind of war, and to increase the chances of strategic success, military innovation should stress strategic requirements and be prepared for interaction with the enemy. James Fitzsimonds has noted what might be regarded as a theme of this study: 'the "goodness" of a military capability is ultimately determined by its contribution to the nation's strategic goals and the success of the strategic outcome'.[228]

The requirements of strategy, and the influence of policy more generally, will influence the conduct of warfare in a number of ways.[229] Policy objectives often require the physical presence of troops, and/or the destruction of enemy forces and resources. An example of this truism is counterinsurgency warfare. In such contingencies control of the population is often the key to success or failure.[230] Stand-off weapons simply cannot do this mission. To reiterate, Wylie's helpful concept of 'control' is defined as being concerned with 'influence' and/or 'unchallenged presence'.[231] The British experience in the American War of Independence reveals the complementary relationship that can exist between population control and destruction of the enemy. At minimum, strategic success required the presence of British forces to protect loyalist sympathisers and allow their numbers to grow. The destruction of Washington's army and the rebel militias would have contributed towards this protection, while at the same time reducing the will of the Patriots.[232]

The RMA literature should also take account of the fact that political concerns frequently place limitations on the use of force, in which case RMA-based forces will often be unable to reach, or indeed approach, maximum operational efficiency. The use of airpower in both the 1991 Gulf War and the 1999 conflict over Kosovo presents examples of the kind of limitations that can be placed on the military instrument. Airpower in these two conflicts presents a useful illustration for this discussion. In both cases, airpower to some degree represented the RMA vision of war by stand-off bombardment cued in by situational awareness assets such as JSTARS. With reference to the Gulf War, Riper and Scales remind us that the Al Firdos bunker incident reveals how political sensitivities 'routinely preclude the unconstrained employment of military means ... the mere possession of advanced technology is no guarantee of its practical utility'.[233] Kosovo is just as revealing. Concerns over Allied casualties obliged ground attack bombers to fly above 15,000 feet. Although the significance of this should not be overplayed, it did diminish the operational efficacy of some attacks, particularly as it made them more vulnerable to acts of Serbian deception. Other political restrictions emanated from the fact that the war was a Coalition effort and was therefore hostage to the unanimity principle within NATO.[234] Such limitations on the use of force will in all likelihood preclude the sufficient operational performance necessary to fulfil the hopes of RMA advocates like Parry. Ironically, the impulses which drive the desire for stand-off, post-heroic forms of war also place restrictions on operations, and in turn these may diminish the chances of success, in which case ground forces will often be required for the attainment of policy objectives.

The nature of warfare could in theory be affected by significant technological and operational innovation, but only if said innovations could be translated into assured success at the strategic level. Victory in war must be assessed at this higher level; tactical success is not sufficient. Success at the lower level, though beneficial, has little meaning if it cannot be translated into the attainment of policy objectives. That being the case, an RMA-based force (whether it be a force based around stand-off munitions or around information operations) that performs flawlessly at the tactical level does not guarantee victory. The continued need for traditional operations ensures that there will be no fundamental change in the nature of warfare. Poor friendly strategy, or indeed astute strategy by the enemy, can render tactical and operational success impotent. The most prominent example in the twentieth century of this truism is Nazi Germany. Although generally displaying high levels of competence in the tactical and operational realms, the Wehrmacht suffered from, and was ultimately destroyed by, disastrous strategic judgment.[235] Likewise, the great Carthaginian commander Hannibal could not translate a series of spectacular tactical and operational successes, most notably the battles of Cannae and Trasimene, into strategic victory over the Roman Republic. Hannibal's failure may have been the result of his poor strategic judgment. A contentious historical debate still rages over the question of whether he should have marched on Rome after Cannae. Alternatively, his failure may have emanated from Rome's adoption of Fabius Maximus' strategy of avoiding battle under anything but the most favourable circumstances. This Fabian strategy gave Rome the time it needed to mobilise its resources and regenerate its forces. The response of Fabius Maximus to Hannibal's tactical superiority once again highlights the dialectical nature of strategy.

Under certain circumstances destruction of the enemy's forces in the battlespace does translate into strategic victory. After all, Waterloo ended the career of Napoleon, and Alexander's victory over Porus at the battle of Hydaspes proved decisive. Every war is unique, and each opponent has unique vulnerabilities. Yet, success in war can only be measured in strategic terms. At times, the centre of gravity is the enemy's armed forces. In different circumstances the centre of gravity may be the enemy's will, capital or popular support. All told, the RMA literature is correct to stress the desire for tactical and operational superiority. Where it falls down is by not placing this tactical prowess into a larger strategic context.

The technological, political or social innovations that form the basis of an RMA can be utilised in the service of various objectives. In this sense, strategy can influence the development of an RMA in a more direct manner, and therefore each so-called RMA can have various manifestations. Strategic demands can shape how innovation is utilised. This is nowhere better demonstrated than in the different uses to which mechanised armour was put by various European countries. Nazi Germany's development of blitzkrieg strongly reflected strategic goals that called for rapid offensive operations. In contrast, France, which had a defensive strategic outlook, distributed its armour throughout its infantry formations to enhance the firepower of the defensive.[236] The current RMA at present reflects certain attitudes within the United States, with an emphasis on post-heroic warfare. This translates into the increased application of stand-off munitions at the expense of more vulnerable ground forces, or the application of information power as an alternative to deploying physical expressions of military power.[237] It also reflects a US proclivity to emphasise the technological dimension of warfare.[238] However, the United States cannot dictate the nature or character of future war. A more offensively minded, less casualty-sensitive foe could develop their own, very different, version of the information age RMA. Even within the realms of SIW, which on the surface appears to be a form of non-lethal warfare, an adversary could in theory inflict death and destruction by disrupting air traffic control systems, or attacking nuclear power stations.[239] The nature of warfare as reflected by the current US RMA advocates is just that, a US perspective on the subject.

The relationship between strategy and RMAs is not restricted to the former influencing the latter. RMAs can also affect the practice of strategy, and not always for the better. As mentioned earlier, a combination of technological developments and political sensitivities has produced concepts such as 'post-heroic warfare'. Admiral Owens has confidently claimed that the 'system of systems' has enabled a remarriage between US military capability and its foreign policy.[240] Although strategy is the art of the possible,[241] and domestic political support for military action is an important consideration, limiting oneself to military action that is firstly judged for its domestic acceptability is too restrictive.[242] Admittedly, this mismatch between external strategic demands and internal political necessity does create somewhat of a dilemma for the practitioner. The answer to this dilemma is not to limit one's strategic options too severely, and therefore adopt post-heroic warfare wholesale, because an intelligent enemy will soon ensure that these limited strategic options are insufficient. Instead, a more prudent approach is to change current sensitivities to the realities of war. However, this does not mean that the RMA should not be exploited in its potential to offer less direct and less lethal forms of warfare. Indeed, in this respect the current RMA can contribute positively to the practice of strategy. Adam J. Baddeley and Libicki correctly note that adding RMA capabilities to existing military resources enhances an actor's strategic flexibility, and may offer greater strategic efficacy under certain circumstances.[243]

Of just as much concern as post-heroic warfare is Leonhard's concept of 'option acceleration'. In this particular example of overplaying the potential of the RMA, Leonhard advocates the abandonment of the principle of 'objective' in war. Rather than conducting a campaign with a set strategic goal, Leonhard favours a situation in which IT facilitates the rapid creation of new strategic objectives as the situation changes in theatre. Leonhard's idea is summed up by the following statement:

'Mission creep is *good*! It is an expression of option acceleration.'[244] Although Leonhard is correct to note the value of flexibility in adapting strategic objectives to the changing reality, his notion should have every Clausewitzian reaching for the sanctity of *On War*. 'Option acceleration' surely falls within the realms of the military tail wagging the policy dog. It would also seem to have within it the clear potential for confused strategy and a lack of focus.

Strategy and policy will, and should, help shape the RMA. That being the case, the vision of the RMA as espoused by its most strident advocates is unlikely to be fulfilled in its entirety; nor will it represent the only possible version of an information age RMA. Strategic and political demands will at times call for the application of more traditional military forces and operations. These same demands could limit the operational efficiency of RMA-based capabilities.

Aside from the demands of strategy, the RMA will be shaped by the paradoxical logic. With its focus on the technological dimension, the RMA literature often overlooks the existence and influence of an intelligent enemy. General George Pickett splendidly expresses the omnipotence of this fundamental aspect of strategy in a famous quotation. When asked why the Confederates lost at Gettysburg, he replied, 'I think the Union Army had something to do with it.'[245] It is all too easy to focus on the performance of one's own side without taking sufficient account of the dialectical nature of strategy. Libicki, overestimating the omnipotence and invulnerability of the Mesh, acknowledges that deception and stealth will be utilised by those hunted by the Mesh, but then declares that multispectral sensors will ensure that the hunter triumphs in the final analysis.[246] In a similar vein, Admiral Owens gives only passing reference to countermeasures to the system of systems. He bases his confidence in the SOS on the robustness of modern communications technology, and the level of effort expended on the vulnerability question.[247] These statements of overconfidence focus primarily on the tactical and technical levels, and therefore fail to consider the application of paradoxical logic at the strategic level. This failure to address the issue of countermeasures at the strategic level shows yet again how many of the most strident advocates of the RMA restrict their analysis to the lower levels of strategy. As will be outlined below, an enemy wishing to counter an RMA-competent enemy can do so at all levels: technical, tactical, operational, strategic and political. One-dimensional thinking on this subject is nowhere better illustrated than in Leonhard, *The Principles of War for the Information Age*. As noted earlier, in an attempt to prove the value of information in war he uses the unusual counterfactual historical method of applying information age technology to historical campaigns. Leonhard declares that had Robert E. Lee possessed modern information assets he would not have committed the errors that he did in 1862.[248] Although this latter claim by Leonhard is undoubtedly true, he, like Libicki and Owens, underplays the dialectical nature of strategy. Technological monopolies are usually fleeting. Where a significant technological edge does exist, an intelligent enemy will be aware of this and react accordingly. This suggests that, in reference to Leonhard's own example, Lee would not have enjoyed the full potential benefits of his advanced information technology, at least not for long.

Unbridled confidence in the robustness of RMA capabilities to countermeasures should not go unchallenged. To declare that a techno-logical system is immune to the actions of the enemy is tantamount to declaring that a historic and unique change has occurred in strategy. It is a claim for the final move. Every weapon system is countered eventually to some degree. This fact does not render the system in question strate-gically impotent; after all, manned platforms such as tanks and planes have continued to play major roles in modern warfare, despite the level of effort expended to thwart them. What countermeasures have ensured is that the efficacy of these systems is offset to some degree. Therefore, this has meant that warfare is not dominated by any one capability; rather is it characterised by combined and joint operations. This point is illustrated by the history of airpower. Since its introduction, airpower has developed into an extremely important asset for most practitioners of war. Despite the advantages offered by operating in the third dimension, and despite its continued evolution, airpower still represents only one element amongst the gamut of military capabilities.[249] Even the opera-tional and strategic potential of nuclear-armed ballistic missiles can be offset by a series of countermeasures. These include civil defence, ballis-tic missile defence and deterrent forces.

An intelligent foe can find a manner of ways, across all the levels of strategy, to offset and diminish an RMA-competent enemy. Evidence of this is provided in a myriad of historical examples. At the technical and tactical levels there can be few more original countermeasures than the Roman Republic's introduction of the 'Corvus' to negate Carthaginian naval superiority. This particular innovation enabled the Romans to grapple, hold and board their enemy's vessels, and thereby bring to bear the strength of their infantry forces at sea.[250] More recently, aerial combat in World War II presents an example of how an advantage was trans-lated into an Achilles' heel by an adversary. Rearward-looking radar was fitted to British bombers to locate approaching German fighters. German jamming soon negated the initial success of these devices, and finally the radar became an Achilles' heel when German fighters used them to track the bombers.[251] The technologies that underpin the current RMA likewise have readily identifiable candidate vulnerabilities. GPS jammers could in theory inflict serious disruption on a digitised force, on the basis that modern navigation and guidance rely heavily upon this satellite-based system.[252] Indeed, it is reported that US forces destroyed a number of these jammers during the 2003 War for Iraq.[253] With a twist of irony, a future enemy could utilise information age capabilities to disrupt RMA-based forces. IW attacks could in theory disrupt logistics,[254] or attack the software which serves as the foundation upon which the whole RMA is built. Indeed, software is often identified as the key vulnerability in the information age.[255] Just as potentially vulnerable is the silicon circuitry that acts as the 'physical' basis for the RMA. Unless well hardened, IT is potentially vulnerable to either nuclear- or non-nuclear-induced electro-magnetic pulse (EMP).[256] The US Army's *FM 100-6 Information Operations* identifies a more subtle method. By degrading the integrity of the information within a system, an enemy can erode confidence in that information.[257] To summarise, Brown declares that 'there should be no doubt that components of the emerging SOS will be targets of offen-sive information warfare'.[258] The various merits of these different countermeasures are open to debate. However, once again, in a general sense the details do not matter. The purpose of discussing these few examples is to show that the dialectical nature of strategy at the techni-cal/tactical level will continue to operate in the information age.

Those faced with an RMA-equipped foe can opt for other, less techni-cal, countermeasures. The Serbian use of UN hostages as human shields in Bosnia illustrates how a simple act can negate the advantages conferred by millions of dollars' worth of RMA equipment.[259] Ground forces threatened by an enemy composed primarily of stand-off capabili-ties have various simple options available. These include dispersal, utilisation of the terrain and weather, and blending into local popula-tions, to mention just three.[260] On this latter point, Libicki admits that the omnipotent sensors of the Mesh cannot distinguish between a civil-ian and a guerrilla.[261] At another level, as exemplified by Fabius Maximus when facing the tactical superiority of Hannibal, the conventionally superior force can be denied victory if the enemy refuses to take the field. Of course, this particular countermeasure is not universally appropriate. Being unable to face the enemy in battle can have negative consequences. Indeed, although Fabius Maximus saved the Roman army from destruc-tion, his actions were not universally welcomed in Italy, primarily because his strategy enabled Hannibal to ravage the Italian country-side.[262] During the War for Iraq, the Coalition was surprised that Saddam's regime had been able to infiltrate paramilitary forces deep into the south of the country.[263] Whilst this did not affect the final outcome of the conflict, having to deal with these pockets of resistance delayed the capture of towns such as Umm Qasr and An Nasiriyah. Often these paramilitary forces were not uniformed and mingled with the local populace, thereby negating much of the advantage held by the technologically advanced Coalition forces.

A potential strength of the current RMA is that it enhances systems as well as individual weapons. However, even systems that seem dominant can be countered. The defensive systems in the early years of World War I, which had seemed so impregnable, were eventually overcome with a mixture of technology, tactics and operational art.[264] Likewise, in World War II, German U-boats, which had spectacular early levels of success against Allied shipping, were offset by intelligence (the breaking of Ultra), tactical/operational measures (the convoy system) and at the strategic level (US resources).[265]

An enemy is not restricted to offsetting a dominant capability through asymmetric countermeasures; he might also acquire similar capabilities. In this context, Michael L. Brown correctly identifies that a significant problem arises for the visions espoused in the RMA literature if the enemy acquires similar capabilities.[266] However, when discussing operational art the RMA literature indirectly assumes a monopoly of these capabilities. This is particularly evident in Arquilla's discussion of 'control warfare', which he presents as an alternative to the more traditional paradigms of attrition and manoeuvre.[267] History suggests that operational and organisational innovations that confer advantage are usually offset and/or copied, and therefore attritional forms of warfare often re-emerge. Holden Reid suggests that in both world wars of the twentieth century, once Germany had failed to achieve quick and decisive victories, attritional forms of warfare ensued.[268] Although Krepinevich is correct to note that exploiting an RMA first usually confers advantages, modern history reveals that these advantages are fleeting and sometimes do not translate into strategic success.[269] In this respect, the examples of Napoleon and Nazi Germany once again suggest that operational efficiency is no guarantee of strategic victory. With history in mind, it is reasonable to assume that any monopoly in RMA capabilities could be negated, and therefore any revolutionary operational breakthroughs would cease to offer the same returns, and attrition could re-emerge. Also, rather than signalling an escape from attrition, it is not unreasonable to assume that when both belligerents possess RMA forces they could find themselves locked into an attritional struggle centred around IT assets. Due to the dialectic nature of strategy the contemporary RMA does not signal an irrevocable shift away from attrition. History reveals that warfare tends to be composed of many different features and paradigms. For example, the Punic Wars were characterised by surprise, deception, manoeuvre and attrition. Any attempt to characterise this conflict, or any other, as being dominated by any one form or paradigm of warfare would be an act of reductionism.[270]

Much of the RMA literature fails to take sufficient account of the fact that warfare can assume various forms. Instead, the focus tends to be on high-intensity, regular conflict.[271] Faced with a conventionally superior enemy, a foe may well adopt an asymmetric form of warfare.[272] In this respect, the options include irregular warfare, SIW or escalating the conflict into the realms of WMD. *Joint Vision 2020* is clear that the biggest danger for the future is asymmetric opponents.[273] Lawrence Freedman points out just how insignificant the RMA was on 9/11: 'The attack was instigated using the most ancient of military technologies – the knife – in order to turn the most modern civilian aviation technology against the West.'[274] These thoughts are echoed by Senator Warner, a member of the US Senate's Armed Services Committee: 'Battlefields now are isolated individuals bringing about enormous devastation, utilizing weapons of mass destruction.'[275] Whilst advanced conventional forces have a role to play in the war against terrorism, whether that be in a reconnaissance sense or in operations against terrorist bases or sponsors, intelligence operatives and special forces undertake the main effort.

Commentating on WMD, Gray persuasively argues: 'the absolute quality to nuclear weapons about which Bernard Brodie and his collaborators wrote so eloquently in 1946 means that an information-led RMA might be trumped by the "old reliable" equalizer of a nuclear arsenal'.[276] At times, academic literature has a tendency to pigeonhole subjects. In this respect, it is all too easy to perceive the various futures in isolation from one another. To counter this, Gray performs a useful service by exploring how these various futures may interact.[277]

The above examples highlight a third underlying reason why the RMA vision will not come to pass in its entirety. Namely, an enemy, or indeed policy requirements, can impose a form of warfare that is less conducive to the current dominant vision of the RMA. Mao stipulates that many factors will determine the character of any particular war.[278] Following this logic, we can conclude that each conflict has its own complex character. There are various examples of wars which cannot easily be attributed a place on the spectrum of conflict. The American War of Independence, Napoleon's Peninsula campaign and Vietnam all display elements of both regular and irregular forms of conflict.[279] The fact that war can take many forms clearly implies that the future will not solely be comprised of conflict between regular, conventional forces. Consequently, the nature of warfare as espoused, directly or indirectly, by the RMA literature will not come to pass in its entirety. Those responsible for preparing for future war should take heed of Gray's assertion that war is a very adaptable phenomenon.[280] Applegate concludes that what is required is a broad range of capabilities to avoid disappearing up a strategic cul-de-sac.[281]

Too much emphasis on the RMA could leave a military both physically and culturally incapable of operating at lower or higher levels of intensity. To take irregular warfare as an example, the theoretical and historical literature suggests that forces optimised for regular operations often fail to cope effectively with the different challenges posed by this form of conflict. Murray and Knox note how, in Vietnam, 'technological sophistication [was] irrelevant to the war actually being fought'.[282] Callwell reminds us that the conduct of irregular warfare is a distinct art and that these forms of conflict present very diverse enemies and environments.[283] In contrast to the RMA literature's emphasis on quick and decisive operations with stand-off munitions, irregular conflicts are usually protracted, attritional and people intensive.[284] Lawrence describes wars against rebels as 'messy and slow'.[285] The British Field Service Regulations (FSR) of 1920 declares that the varied enemies and terrain encountered in irregular operations require significant modification to the principles for regular warfare.[286] These types of operations also pose problems for regular forces in terms of their organisation. In this context, Callwell declares: 'it is the elaborate organisation of the regular troops which cramps their freedom in the theatre of war'.[287] Moreman notes that British battalions trained for conventional war were often unprepared for tribal conflict.[288] Finally, irregular opponents can utilise terrain to enhance their operations.[289] In this way, both geography and irregular warfare combine to further complicate the campaign of a regular force.

However, the mismatch between conventional and unconventional capabilities and tasks is a circle that can be, and has been, squared. The Roman imperial army consisted of legions designed to cope with regular conflicts, and the *auxilia* that functioned at the lower levels of intensity.[290] Similarly, Alexander the Great displayed an ability to transform his force from the regular formations that faced Darius III's Persian field army to a much lighter capability during the conflicts with tribal enemies in more dense, mountainous terrain post-Guagamela. And, as already mentioned, the Afghan Model represents a case in which special forces operated alongside airpower assets such as B-52s against semi-regular opponents.

It is important to pay heed to Gray's salient point that too much can be made of the asymmetric threat. Placing too much emphasis on this threat could lead to the erroneous assumption that being conventionally superior is a distinct disadvantage.[291] As noted earlier, some of the current literature also overemphasises the 'coming anarchy'. It is also worth reiterating Baddeley and Libicki's assertion that the RMA has applicability within irregular warfare.[292] In particular, the RMA offers various methods to employ force that is supposedly less destructive. In theory, more discriminating capabilities could prove useful in irregular conflicts where minimum force is often required.[293] Being competent in the realm of conventional warfare is an advantage, so long as this competence does not leave your forces impotent in irregular conflicts.

The future strategic environment will undoubtedly require balanced forces that exploit elements of the RMA, without opting for the radical version with its attendant drastic force structure reductions. Numbers serve as a safeguard against unexpected counters to innovative operations. The theme of this book is not to denigrate the current RMA, which does offer some significant operational advantages, but rather to note that the version to be found in the RMA literature is not omnipotent, nor does it come with a strategic guarantee. In strategic terms the RMA itself is neutral; it is neither good nor bad. The danger lies with how it is utilised, and if it is allowed to affect radically the conduct of strategy, the content of military culture, and force structure.

A final underlying factor that will affect prospects for full realisation of the RMA is the inescapable reality of geography and the ubiquitous nature of the elements.[294] In this context, geography is taken to mean the physical environment in which strategy is conducted. Historically, geography has been a major influence on the conduct of operations. Clausewitz himself notes: 'geography and the character of the ground bear a close and ever-present relation to warfare'.[295] Of course, geography is not an unconquerable dimension of warfare. Indeed, some of the most outstanding operational successes have been such precisely because geographical obstacles were overcome. Alexander the Great was a prime exponent of this. His capture of the mountain fort of Aornus and his flanking manoeuvre to capture the Persian Gates from Ariobazanes are just two examples of Alexander's ability to turn geography to his advantage.[296]

An analysis of geography's role in strategy also reveals the presence of the paradoxical logic. An intelligent enemy can manipulate the physical environment to his advantage. For example, during the siege of the island city of Tyre in 333–332 BC, Alexander constructed a 200-foot-wide mole between the coast and the city. This enabled Alexander's land forces to attack the city directly.[297] In 1672, the Dutch responded to the French invasion by opening the dikes to flood the land and thereby hold back the invaders.[298] As Winters *et al.* indicate in their seminal work *Battling the Elements*, good generalship enhances and exploits geography to one's advantage.[299]

Military operations cannot be conducted without reference to geographical factors.[300] Terrain often shapes operations significantly. In this context, G. J. Ashworth suggests that the five most fundamental characteristics of urban warfare emanate from the physical urban environment. The geography of a large conurbation tends to fragment forces into small operational units such as squads or platoons; the environment favours close-range weaponry, in which case small units become dependent upon organic firepower; the presence of civilian lives and property can impose restraints on movement, fields of fire, targeting and weapon choice, and therefore Ashworth concludes that infantry are the most usable capability; the environment has a bias in favour of those on the defence; and it absorbs large amounts of manpower, often through the requirement for a rapid rotation of units due to the stress of urban operations.[301] From his study of the Russian campaign to capture Grozny in the First Chechen War, Anatol Lieven also notes that urban warfare is mainly conducted at the section level, and highlights the significance of infantry in such an environment: 'It cannot be emphasised too strongly, therefore, that the key to success in urban warfare is good infantry.'[302] Wilson concludes that an increased emphasis on urban operations 'will likely call for a more infantry intensive force structure. Preparing for urban combat runs counter to the current planning imperative, which calls for military operations that minimise US casualties.'[303] Many of these thoughts do not fit well with the proposed RMA, which therefore highlights the fact that the RMA is not omnipotent and cannot be applied regardless of geography.

The American Civil War reveals just how the pervasive reach of geography can extend into all the levels of strategy. Heavy undergrowth significantly shaped the outcome of the First Battle of the 'Wilderness' in 1863. Winters concludes that Hooker's failure to execute his masterful plan was the result of poor leadership plus the nature of the terrain: '[Hooker] let the vegetation fix his army.'[304] At the operational level, the geology of the Eastern Theatre of the American Civil War heavily influenced the campaigns there. Again, Winters is persuasive when he argues:

> It is clear that lines of movement for the largest maneuvers early in the war were based, more than any other factor, on [the] major geographic characteristics. Early in the conflict the Union would take full advantage of the Coastal plain and Chesapeake Bay to the East while the Confederates exploited the form and trend of the Appalachian topography.[305]

Terrain and geography were equally important in the Normandy campaign. Murray notes that from an Allied perspective Normandy possessed both advantages and obstacles. On the one hand, because it was flanked by swamp, the Seine and the Atlantic, and therefore offered the Germans only one avenue of approach, 'Normandy represented the ideal solution to the ... problem of achieving a lodgment on the European Continent.' On the other hand, the bocage presented the Germans with an ideal environment in which to conduct a defence in depth.[306] At the strategic level, Murray also correctly draws attention to the fact that geography exerts an influence on a defence community's strategic culture: 'the size and location of a nation are crucial determinants in the way its statesmen and military leaders think about strategy'.[307] Like the above conflicts, the physical environment heavily shaped the US war in Vietnam. To take just one example, in the Battle of Lam Son 719, the terrain neutralised many of the advantages of US air mobility and funnelled the advance into the Ye Pon river valley.[308] Likewise, urban warfare tends to mould itself around the physical environment. In this case, streets tend to channel operations. Geography can also neutralise the operational efficacy of certain war forms. In 1941, German blitzkrieg failed to replicate the success of 1940, partly due to the sheer geographic depth and width of the Soviet Union. Similarly, weather has proven to be an important influence on the conduct of operations. It played a debilitating role in both 1812 and 1941, and a weather front exerted enough friction on Burnside's famous 'mud march' in 1862 to block his plans completely.[309] The elements have proven to be an ongoing influence on war, as NATO air operations over Kosovo and dust storms during the invasion of Iraq indicate.[310]

However, as noted above, geography is not impenetrable. Certain technological, tactical and operational innovations can offset the influence of terrain and the elements. The current RMA, in particular the exploitation of GPS, has already reduced the significance of cloud cover and the featureless nature of desert terrain.[311] Yet, physical geography is so pervasive and so varied a dimension in warfare that its influence can never be reduced significantly. This is only intensified by the fact that the enemy can make use of geography and, therefore, the geographic and paradoxical logic factors interact. Indeed, this thought can be extended further to illustrate how four of the major influences on war can interact. Strategy may require operations to be conducted in an environment that is less conducive to an RMA force. The same policy rationale that dictated the location for operations may also call for the utilisation of infantry forces in close proximity with the enemy. This foe, taking note of both the environment and the conventional superiority of the enemy, may enact the paradoxical nature of strategy and opt to wage asymmetrical forms of warfare, perhaps concentrating on irregular operations (and thereby utilising the terrain to maximise small unit actions) and/or the employment of WMD.

CHANGES TO THE FUTURE BATTLESPACE

Although the future battlespace will not witness any fundamental alteration to the nature of war, certain changes are likely to occur. One possible change that has credibility is the notion that information may become more *directly* relevant in war. Information has always been important in warfare, as Peter Emmett correctly observes by citing Wellington's statement: 'All the business of war ... is to endeavour to find out what you don't know by what you do; that's what I called guessing what was at the other side of the hill.'[312] In war, knowledge of the whereabouts and disposition of enemy forces has always been important. However, information may be acquiring a more immediate role. For example, once foot soldiers of the Roman Republic commenced battle, the outcome would be decided more by their fighting skills, morale, discipline and tactical leadership than directly by their access to information – aside from the rudimentary information collected by their organic senses. The same still applies to the infantryman of today. Yet, many of the weapon systems of the information age rely more directly on information to function effectively. The most obvious examples are those munitions that rely upon GPS for their guidance. Better information gives many of these weapons an edge in conflict. Also, although it has been argued that political concerns, friction, the paradoxical logic and geography will in all likelihood diminish the operational potency of information-based warfare, it still seems likely that the reconnaissance–strike complex will result in more deadly forms of firepower. That being the case, Libicki's concept of hide-and-seek warfare has certain validity. As noted earlier, where Libicki perhaps falls down is by overplaying information operations at the expense of physical expressions of power. Overall, as will be argued in Chapter 5, control of the infosphere has attained an unprecedented significance in recent years. In this sense, Leonhard is right to argue that information management must be an integral part of warfighting, and that IT assets constitute part of combined arms warfare.[313]

Whilst recognising and accepting the growing significance of information, it is important not to become information-centric. Organising one's operations and doctrine around information would be a mistake. Libicki is incorrect in his assertion that physical force now 'serves' information.[314] If anything, the exact reverse is true. As noted in the USMC's *Warfighting*, waiting for that crucial piece of information could sacrifice the initiative. To this end, their citation of the following advice by General Patton still has resonance: 'A good plan violently executed now is better than a perfect plan next week.'[315] One example of placing far too much reliance on the promise of information is Campen's aforementioned assertion that the current RMA enables a downsizing of forces. Downsizing too vigorously entails unacceptable risks. In this sense, quantity serves as a safeguard against an intelligent enemy, poor strategy and friction, all of which can negate the operational efficiency of an RMA-based force. Thomas P. M. Barnett notes that the US Navy's sacrifice of ship numbers to technology is occurring at a time when the Navy is complaining about the stress these lower numbers place on operational tempo and global presence.[316]

Aside from the growing importance of information generally, another useful component of the RMA literature is its emphasis on the digitisation of the battlespace. All things being equal, a digitised force should be better able to co-ordinate its operations and thereby operate at a higher tempo. In addition, a common picture of the battlespace should facilitate more efficient command and control. In this respect, it would be a mistake to underestimate the value of digitisation as a force-multiplier. However, the historical record should instil caution into our thoughts on the long-term impact of digitisation. The experience of blitzkrieg in World War II reveals how successful operational innovation can be offset by a number of factors, including strategy, friction, logistics, resources, geography and will. Howard proclaims:

> The inter-war dream of swift, skilful units operating against each other's supply lines, securing maximum decisions with minimum cost, turned into the reality of huge armies with massive 'tails', highly vulnerable to enemy air attack and demanding logistical ingenuity to keep them moving at all.[317]

Similarly, it has been noted that, despite the addition of mechanised armoured forces, World War II eventually took on much of the character of World War I, with fortified positions being taken by large artillery barrages and infantry advances across open land.[318] In a broader sense, John Ellis notes that, rather than being won by brilliant operational manoeuvres, World War II became an attritional struggle that was decided by the balance of resources and production rates.[319] More recently, after-action reports on the conflict in Kosovo suggest that the success of the NATO campaign came close to being put in jeopardy by weapons shortages.[320] Operational innovation does not necessarily lead to strategic success; many things can stand in between these two conditions. As a final thought on this subject, it should be noted that for a digitised force to be operationally effective will still require factors such as training, good leadership, high morale and discipline.

This chapter has placed the role of humans at the heart of warfare, and has stated the need to retain the man on the scene with a gun as the ultimate guarantor of strategic success. However, this does not prevent unmanned vehicles of various designs performing useful functions in the future battlespace. Under certain circumstances there is no need to operate inhabited vehicles. For example, in the case of bombardment against static targets, stand-off munitions launched from UAVs or naval vessels could perform the job sufficiently, without the need to risk a pilot. This preservation of human life is not motivated purely by moral or political considerations, but also by the pragmatic need to preserve valuable and expensively trained pilots. In air-to-air combat UCAVs also have the advantage of being able to operate at higher G-forces. UAVs are already playing an increasingly important role in surveillance and reconnaissance activities. On the ground, Peters sensibly suggests that in extreme threat environments remotely operated unmanned tanks could prove more usable than their manned counterparts.[321] Nonetheless, strategic considerations dictate that humans cannot be removed from the sharp end of warfare altogether. Pilots will still prove valuable when attacking mobile targets, especially if the potential exists to inflict collateral damage. Kosovo revealed that visual identification of some kinds of targets was usually desirable, sometimes was critical and required a number of passes by the bombers. In this sense, pilots do not exist merely to push buttons that deliver munitions; they are also, and perhaps more importantly, expected to use their judgment when attacking a target. It has also been noted that humans in the cockpit have better situational awareness than a remotely piloted UCAV.[322] Manned vehicles with organic firepower also serve as a safeguard against potential future vulnerabilities of digital communication networks. The presence of humans in the front line is especially unavoidable on the ground. Control will often require the physical presence of troops. These troops will in turn require organic firepower, and vehicles that provide protection for manoeuvre and firepower. Some future version of the tank or APC would seem to fulfil these requirements as they have done in the past.

CONCLUSION

Within the current RMA literature there is an abundance of varying ideas concerning the future character of warfare. The most prominent amongst these include Libicki's visions of fire-ant and hide-and-seek warfare; Admiral Owens' system of systems; Arquilla's control paradigm; Parry's post-modern warfare; Luttwak's post-heroic warfare; Arquilla and Ronfeldt's cyberwar; and the US Navy's Network Centric Warfare. Taken together, these visions of information age warfare generally focus on regular, high-intensity conflict; information-dominated operations, with the battle over information proving decisive; the increasing fulfilment of Fuller's prophecy on the removal of humans from the activity of conflict; and an emphasis on less-destructive, less-attritional forms of warfare.[323] The RMA literature portrays war as a highly controllable activity and one dominated by technological prowess. This perspective contrasts sharply with the Clausewitzian nature of warfare as outlined in Chapter 1, with its emphasis on destruction, uncertainty, chance, friction and, above all, infused by policy and the role of humans.

In contrast to much of the RMA literature, this chapter has suggested that five central factors will prevent the above visions of the RMA developing sufficiently to change the nature of warfare. These are the demands of strategy and the influence of policy; the polymorphous character of war; the paradoxical logic of strategy; the physical reality of geography in which all warfare is conducted; and finally the human element. These five underlying factors mean 'control' requires the presence of humans, and at times may require the destruction of enemy forces; that the operational efficiency of the envisaged RMA will be reduced; and that uncertainty will remain an integral part of warfare. As Clausewitz himself indicated, 'the very nature of interaction is bound to make [war] unpredictable'.[324] The above thoughts can be refined further, so that war can be characterised by the Constant–Variable–Constant Model. Within this hypothesis the first set of constants that are always in play in whatever form are: policy demands, geography, the enemy and human involvement. As noted above, the existence of these factors produces a situation in which the whole phenomenon of war can never be characterised by one omnipotent form. Consequently, these four constants produce the variable factor that is the polymorphous character of war. In turn, this inability of war to assume just one overriding form ensures that the features that constitute the Clausewitzian nature of war (violence, uncertainty, chance and the human element) will remain constantly in play.

The future battlespace is not something that can be dictated and moulded by any one defence community. Acknowledging this fact, Dunlap notes: 'We must plan our weapons to fight war where, when, and how the enemy chooses.'[325] An example which draws together many of the elements discussed in this chapter is the loss of Varius' Roman legions in the Teutburg Forest. The legions of that period were considered to be at their peak, and the German tribal forces were equipped with inferior technology. The destruction of the legions can be attributed to a host of factors. Of particular note were geography, weather, clever diplomacy and strategy by Armitius (the German commander) and a lack of flexibility on the part of Varius in the face of guerrilla operations.[326] Information age warfare cannot develop as an abstract process isolated from strategic, paradoxical and geographic factors. Rather, future warfare will reflect these influences at least as much as, if not more than, it reflects the attitudes of the US defence community and the development of technology. It would be an error to undervalue the advantages offered by the information age. Yet, an equally damaging error would be to equate the RMA literature's vision of warfare with reality. Committing this particular mistake could allow these visions to dominate the development of military and strategic cultures, and procurement policies and/or dictate foreign policy. Future force structure, doctrine, strategy and general preparation for war should reflect the nature of warfare, not some idealised vision of the potential offered by the current RMA.

NOTES

1. General William Odom, quoted in David Jablonsky, 'US Military Doctrine and the Revolution in Military Affairs', *Parameters*, 24, 3 (1994), p. 18.
2. Leonhard, *The Principles of War for the Information Age*, p. 219.
3. Parry, 'Some Recent and Emerging Themes in Maritime Warfare'.
4. Vice-Admiral Arthur K. Cebrowski, 'Network-Centric Warfare: Its Origin and Future', *Proceedings*, 124, 1 (1998), p. 32.
5. Michael O'Hanlon describes how 'The RMA Movement' includes an emphasis on technology and sensitivity to casualities. See Michael O'Hanlon, *Technological Change and the Future of Warfare* (Washington, DC, Brookings Institution Press, 2000), p. 7.
6. Luttwak, 'A Post-Heroic Military Policy', and Michael Ignatieff, *Virtual War: Kosovo and Beyond* (New York, Picador USA, 2001).
7. Martin C. Libicki, 'Information and Nuclear RMAs Compared', *Strategic Forum*, 82, July 1996, www.ndu.edu/inss/strforum/forum82.html.
8. In fact, as David Tucker argues in relation to the US experience in Somalia, the public's perceived sensitivity to casualties may not be a true representation of their opinions. See David Tucker, 'Fighting Barbarians', *Parameters*, 28, 2 (1998), carlisle-www.army.mil/usawc/Parameters/98summer/tucker.htm.
9. This concept originated in the USAF, and, although it accepts that at times physical presence will be required, it does postulate: 'There is an informational form of presence – a virtual presence'. See Glenn W. Goodman, Jr, 'The Power of Information: Air Force Clarifies its Misunderstood Virtual Presence Concept', *Armed Forces Journal International*, July 1995, p. 24. For a critical assessment of 'virtual presence', see Squadron Leader Peter Emmett, 'Information Mania – A New Manifestation of Gulf War Syndrome?', *RUSI Journal*, 141, 1 (1996), pp. 19–26. For a discussion of 'air occupation' see Maj. Marc K. Dippold, 'Air Occupation: Asking the Right Questions', *Aerospace Power Journal*, Winter 1997, www.airpower.maxwell.af.mil/airchronicles/apj/apj97/win97/dippold.html.
10. Michael R. Gordon and General Bernard E. Trainor, *The Generals' War: The Inside Story of the Conflict in the Gulf* (Boston, MA, Little, Brown, 1995), p. 442.
11. Fuller, *Armament and History*, p. v.
12. See Martin C. Libicki, 'Technology and Warfare', and Lawrence E. Casper, Irving L. Halter, Earl W. Powers, Paul J. Selva, Thomas W. Steffens and T. LaMar Willis, 'Knowledge-Based Warfare: A Security Strategy for the Next Century', *Joint Force Quarterly*, 13 (1996), p. 83.
13. Admiral Owens quoted in Mackubin Thomas Owens, 'Technology, the RMA, and Future War', *Strategic Review*, 26, 2 (1998), p. 69. See also James Adams, 'Anoraks' Apocalypse', *Sunday Times, News Review*, 16 March 1997, p. 9. Arquilla and Ronfeldt provide a useful description of the current RMA at the operational level. See

'Cyberwar is Coming', p. 26.

14. Alvin Toffler, 'Looking at the Future with Alvin Toffler', www.usatoday.com/news/comment/columnists/toffler/toff05.htm.
15. Freedman, *Information Warfare*, p. 6.
16. Coker, 'Post-modern War', p. 14.
17. Clausewitz, *On War*, p. 84.
18. Murray and Knox note that from the perspective of the technological utopians war could become a frictionless engineering exercise. Murray and Knox, 'Conclusion: The Future Behind Us', p. 178.
19. Casper *et al.*, 'Knowledge-Based Warfare', p. 87.
20. Mackubin Thomas Owens, 'Technology, the RMA, and Future War', p. 64.
21. See Mackubin Thomas Owens, 'Vietnam as Military History', Review Essay, *Joint Force Quarterly*, 3 (1993–94), pp. 112–18.
22. Van Riper and Scales, 'Preparing for War in the 21st Century', p. 4. See also Ch. 4 of this book for an analysis of the difficulties faced by the USAF in Vietnam as a result of their pre-war emphasis on nuclear weapons, and Gray, *Modern Strategy*, p. 250.
23. Harry G. Summers, Jr, *On Strategy: A Critical Analysis of the Vietnam War* (Novato, CA, Presidio, 1982), p. 35.
24. Wilson, 'The Transformation of Military Power, 1997–2027', p. 4.
25. Alan D. Campen, 'Introduction', in Alan D. Campen (ed.), *The First Information War* (Fairfax, VA, AFCEA International Press, 1992), p. ix.
26. Bernard Weinraub and Thom Shanker, 'War on the Cheap?', *International Herald Tribune*, 2 April 2003, pp. 1–2.
27. Benjamin S. Lambeth, *NATO's Air War for Kosovo: A Strategic and Operational Assessment* (Santa Monica, CA, RAND, 2001), p. 179.
28. Weinraub and Shanker, 'War on the Cheap', pp. 1–2.
29. Cohen, 'Technology and Warfare', p. 237.
30. Williamson Murray, 'Does Military Culture Matter?', *Orbis*, 43, 1 (1999), pp. 27–42.
31. Holden Reid, 'Enduring Patterns in Modern Warfare', p. 20.
32. Clausewitz, *On War*, p. 309.
33. Major David J. Lemelin has criticised the US Army's Force XXI programme for putting technology centre stage, and only rhetorically acknowledging the human side of warfare. See Lemelin, 'Force XXI', p. 81. Similarly, O'Hanlon argues that high technology has become the defining characteristic of the US way of war. See O'Hanlon, *Technological Change and the Future of Warfare*, p. 1.
34. Gray, *Modern Strategy*, p. 37.
35. Cohen, 'Technology and Warfare', p. 239.
36. Gray, 'A Contested Vision'. This point is also strongly made in Krepinevich, 'Cavalry to Computer'. See also O'Hanlon, *Technological Change and the Future of Warfare*, pp. 24–6.
37. Hayden, *Warfighting*, p. 10.
38. For the more cautious appraisal see William A. Owens, 'Introduction', p. 12. The less restrained statement was quoted in Mackubin Thomas Owens, 'Technology, the RMA, and Future War', p. 63.
39. Admiral William Owens with Ed Offley, *Lifting the Fog of War* (New York, Farrar, Straus & Giroux, 2000), p. 15.
40. For more details on these issues, see Martin C. Libicki, *What is Information Warfare?*, ACIS Paper, 3 (Washington, DC, National Defense University, August 1995), www.ndu.edu/ndu/inss/actpubs/actoo3/aoo3cont.html, Libicki, *The Mesh and the Net*, and Owens, 'The Emerging System of Systems'.
41. John Arquilla and David Ronfeldt quoted in Arquilla, 'The Strategic Implications of Information Dominance', p. 25.

42. Jeffrey Cooper, 'Dominant Battlespace Knowledge and Future Warfare', in Stuart E. Johnson and Martin C. Libicki (eds), *Dominant Battlespace Knowledge*, revised edition (Washington, DC, National Defense University, 1996), p. 92.
43. See Leonhard, *The Principles of War for the Information Age*, and Richard J. Harknett, 'Information Warfare and Deterrence', *Parameters*, 26, 3 (1996), p. 102.
44. See *FM 100-6 Information Operations* (Washington, DC, Headquarters Department of the Army, 1996), p. 4-1, and Cebrowski, 'Network-Centric Warfare: An Emerging Military Response to the Information Age'. Bennett provides an excellent account of Allied deception in the D-Day operation, and quite clearly shows that the information one receives is not always beneficial; indeed it was detrimental to the Germans. Ralph Bennett, *Behind the Battle: Intelligence in the War with Germany 1939–1945* (London, Pimlico, 1999), pp. 259–69. See also Timothy L. Thomas, 'Kosovo and the Current Myth of Information Superiority', *Parameters*, 30, 2 (2000), carlisle-www.army.mil/ usawc/Parameters/00spring/thomas.htm.
45. See Libicki, *What is Information Warfare?*
46. Michael E. O'Hanlon, 'Beware the "RMA'nia"!', paper presented at the National Defense University, 9 September 1998. See also O'Hanlon, *Technological Change and the Future of Warfare*, p. 3.
47. Thomas A. Keaney and Eliot A. Cohen, *Gulf War Air Power Survey: Summary Report* (Washington, DC, 1993), p. 86.
48. See Nick Cook, 'War of Extremes', *Jane's Defence Weekly*, 7 July 1999, p. 21.
49. Lambeth, *NATO's Air War for Kosovo*, p. xvi.
50. Biddle, 'Land Warfare: Theory and Practice', p. 109.
51. Lambeth, *NATO's Air War for Kosovo*, p. 128.
52. For an analysis of US operations in Afghanistan, see Biddle, *Afghanistan and the Future of Warfare*.
53. Sun Tzu, trans. Griffith, p. 66.
54. 'The Future of Warfare', *Economist*, 8 March 1997, p. 24.
55. See Marshall, *Men Against Fire*, pp. 108–9, 179.
56. Callwell, *Small Wars*, p. 47
57. Field Marshal Sir William Slim, *Defeat into Victory* (London, Reprint Society, 1957), p. 22. This sentiment is shared by Marshall, *Men Against Fire*, p. 107.
58. Harold A. Winters, with Gerald E. Galloway, Jr, William J. Reynolds and David W. Rhyne, *Battling the Elements: Weather and Terrain in the Conduct of War* (Baltimore, MD, Johns Hopkins University Press, 1998), pp. 3–4.
59. James Meek, 'US Advance Grinds to Halt in Teeth of Storm', *Guardian*, 26 March 2003, p. 1.
60. Hayden, *Warfighting*, pp. 41–2.
61. Toffler and Toffler, *War and Anti-war*, p. 158.
62. For an assessment of strategic culture the following works offer a range of perspectives: Gray, *Modern Strategy*, especially Ch. 5, 'Strategic Culture as Context', G. Chaliand, 'Warfare and Strategic Culture', in Chaliand (ed.), *The Art of War in World History*, Carl G. Jacobsen (ed.), *Strategic Power: USA/USSR* (New York, St Martin's Press, 1990), Alastair I. Johnston, 'Thinking About Strategic Culture', *International Security*, 19, 4 (1995), Yitzhak Klein, 'A Theory of Strategic Culture', *Comparative Strategy*, 10, 1 (1991), pp. 3–23, Gerald Segal, 'Strategy and Ethnic Chic', *International Affairs*, 60, 1 (1983–84).
63. Campen, 'Introduction', p. 172
64. Leonhard, *The Principles of War for the Information Age*, p. 166.
65. Bennett, *Behind the Battle*, p. 86.
66. Lawrence, 'Guerrilla Warfare', p. 888, and Callwell, *Small Wars*, p. 47.
67. Hayden, *Warfighting*, p. 39.

68. Ferris and Handel, 'Clausewitz, Intelligence, Uncertainty and the Art of Command', pp. 42, 49.
69. This point is made in Ritcheson, 'The Future of "Military Affairs"', p. 35.
70. Lambeth, *NATO's Air War for Kosovo*, pp. 158–9.
71. O'Hanlon, 'Beware the "RMA'nia"!'. See also O'Hanlon, *Technological Change and the Future of Warfare*, p. 3.
72. Jablonsky, 'US Military Doctrine and the Revolution in Military Affairs', p. 30.
73. Roberta Wohlstetter, *Pearl Harbor: Warning and Decision* (Stanford, CA, Stanford University Press, 1962), p. 382.
74. Ibid., p. 387.
75. Parker, *The Grand Strategy of Philip II*, p. 215.
76. Lawrence, 'Guerrilla Warfare', p. 884.
77. Hayden, *Warfighting*, p. 40.
78. Quoted in Van Riper and Scales, 'Preparing for War in the 21st Century', p. 9. Similarly, Bennett comments: 'hindsight finds it easy to propose facile answers and actions which would never have entered the minds of men forced to make quick decisions in the heat of battle or in the moment of unguarded elation which may follow hard-won victory'. Bennett, *Behind the Battle*, p. 109.
79. Bennett, *Behind the Battle*, p. 80.
80. Brodie, *War and Politics*, p. 211.
81. See Joint Chiefs of Staff, 'Joint Vision 2010', p. 39.
82. Van Riper and Scales, 'Preparing for War in the 21st Century', p. 10.
83. Kenneth F. McKenzie, Jr, 'Beyond Luddites and Magicians: Examining the MTR', *Parameters*, 25, 2 (1995), p. 19.
84. See Hayden, *Warfighting*, p. 70, and *FM 100-5* cited in Murray, 'Does Military Culture Matter?', pp. 36–7.
85. See Colin S. Gray, *Nuclear Strategy and National Style* (Lanham, MD, Hamilton Press, 1986), p. 45.
86. Major Norman C. Davis, 'An Information-Based Revolution in Military Affairs', *Strategic Review*, 24, 1 (1996), p. 45.
87. Wesley K. Clark, *Waging Modern War: Bosnia, Kosovo, and the Future of Combat* (New York, PublicAffairs, 2001), p. 438.
88. Adams, *The Next World War*, p. 310. The quote was taken from p. 125.
89. Ibid., p. 125.
90. Luttwak, 'A Post-Heroic Military Policy', p. 38.
91. Biddle, *Afghanistan and the Future of Warfare*, p. 57.
92. Bryan Bender, 'US Weapons Shortages Risked Success in Kosovo', *Jane's Defence Weekly*, 32, 14, 6 October 1999.
93. Biddle, *Afghanistan and the Future of Warfare*.
94. Weinraub and Shanker, 'War on the Cheap', pp. 1–2.
95. Daryl G. Press, 'Urban Warfare: Options, Problems and the Future', summary of a conference sponsored by the MIT Security Studies Program, 20 May 1998, Hanscom Air Force Base, Massachusetts, p. 18.
96. Oliver Burkeman, Stuart Millar and Nick Paton Walsh, 'Pentagon Plans for Worst Nightmare', *Guardian*, 3 April 2003, p. 7.
97. For some less than convincing ideas about the role of airpower in urban warfare, see Capt. Troy S. Thomas, 'Slumlords: Aerospace Power in Urban Fights', *Aerospace Power Journal*, 16, 1 (2002), www.airpower.maxwell.af.mil/airchronicles/apj/apj02/spr02/thomas.doc.
98. Vincent J. Goulding, Jr, 'From Chancellorsville to Kosovo, Forgetting the Art of War', *Parameters*, 30, 2 (2000), p. 7.
99. Ibid., pp. 8–9.

100. Lambeth, *NATO's Air War for Kosovo*, p. 238.
101. Goulding, 'From Chancellorsville to Kosovo', p. 11.
102. Wilson, 'The Transformation of Military Power, 1997–2027', pp. 7–8. This point is reiterated by Adams, who correctly notes that Unmanned Combat Aerial Vehicles (UCAVs) can operate at significantly higher speeds and G-forces. See Adams, *The Next World War*, pp. 128–9.
103. See Libicki, *The Mesh and the Net*. In one of his latest works, Libicki argues that we are witnessing the sunset of platform-centric warfare. See Martin C. Libicki, *Illuminating Tomorrow's War*, McNair Paper 61, November 1999, www.ndu.edu/inss/ mcnair/mcnair61/m61cont.html.
104. Libicki, *What is Information Warfare?*
105. Brian Nichiporuk and Carl H. Builder, *Information Technologies and the Future of Land Warfare* (Santa Monica, CA, RAND, 1995), pp. 65–7.
106. Biddle, *Afghanistan and the Future of Warfare*, p. 1.
107. For a description of control see below.
108. Lemelin, 'Force XXI', p. 81.
109. Owens, *Lifting the Fog of War*, p. 208.
110. J. C. Wylie, *Military Strategy: A General Theory of Power Control* (Annapolis, MD, Naval Institute Press, 1967), p. 66. Clausewitz expressed a similar concept when he described the objective of war as 'an act of force to compel our enemy to do our will'. See Clausewitz, *On War*, p. 83.
111. Wylie, *Military Strategy*, p. 72.
112. Colin S. Gray, *The Leverage of Sea Power: The Strategic Advantage of Navies in War* (New York, Free Press, 1992), p. 4, and Julian S. Corbett, *Some Principles of Maritime Strategy* (London, Longmans, Green, 1919).
113. Lambeth, *NATO's Air War for Kosovo*, p. 121.
114. Van Riper and Scales argue that for less developed countries the conquest of land still holds great significance for the purposes of resource and/or population control, and to satisfy the need for political symbolism. That being the case, Western countries could easily be drawn into these conflicts. See Van Riper and Scales, 'Preparing for War in the 21st Century', p. 7. It is also worth noting that, despite the relatively long, if uneasy, peace in Europe, these motivations behind the conquest and occupation of land could once again become important in the Western world. Any suggestion that political boundaries in the West are stable in perpetuity is hard to accept because of the lack of historical precedent. See Freedman, *Information Warfare*, p. 12.
115. See Julian Borger, 'After the Onslaught, a Leap in the Dark', *Guardian*, 20 March 2003, p. 5.
116. When considering the future of irregular conflict, the writings of van Creveld and Ralph Peters are amongst the most prominent. In this genre the classic text is van Creveld's *The Transformation of War*. See also Ralph Peters, *Fighting for the Future: Will America Triumph?* (Mechanicsburg, PA, Stackpole Books, 2001). Although in this book the author uses the traditional terms of 'high' and 'low' intensity warfare, it should be noted that the validity of these terms has been questioned by various authors. Of particular value is Christopher Bellamy, *Spiral through Time: Beyond 'Conflict Intensity'*, The Occasional, 35 (Camberley, Strategic and Combat Studies Institute, Joint Services Staff College, 1998).
117. Andrew F. Krepinevich, 'Why No Transformation?', *Joint Force Quarterly*, 23 (1999–2000), p. 97.
118. Ralph Peters, 'After the Revolution', *Parameters*, 25, 2 (1995), p. 9, Loren B. Thompson, 'Low-Intensity Conflict: An Overview', in Loren B. Thompson (ed.), *Low-Intensity Conflict: The Pattern of Warfare in the Modern World* (Lexington, MA, Lexington Books, 1989), p. 22, and O'Hanlon, *Technological Change and the*

Future of Warfare, p. 128.

119. T. R. Moreman, 'Small Wars and Imperial Policing: The British Army and the Theory and Practice of Colonial Warfare in the British Empire, 1919–1939', in Brian Holden Reid (ed.), *Military Power: Land Warfare in Theory and Practice* (London, Frank Cass, 1997), p. 115.

120. Leroy Thompson, *Ragged War: The Story of Unconventional and Counter-Revolutionary Warfare* (London, Arms & Armour Press, 1996), p. 148.

121. Biddle, *Afghanistan and the Future of Warfare*, pp. iii, 56.

122. A particularly striking example of this is Col Jeffery R. Barnett, 'Defeating Insurgents with Technology', *Airpower Journal*, Summer 1996, www.airpower. maxwell.af.mil/airchronicles/ apj/barnett.pdf.

123. Press, 'Urban Warfare', pp. 3–4. The United Nations estimates that in developing countries the urban population grows by 150,000 each day. See Mark Hewish and Rupert Pengelley, 'Warfare in the Global City: The Demands of Modern Military Operations in Urban Terrain', *Jane's International Defense Review*, 31 (1998), p. 32.

124. Williamson Murray, 'Thinking about Cities and War', www.mca-marines.org/ Gazette/stanton.html.

125. For example, see USMC, *A Concept for Future Military Operations on Urbanized Terrain*, Marine Corps Concept Paper (Quantico, VA, USMC, 1997).

126. Timothy L. Thomas, 'The Battle of Grozny: Deadly Classroom for Urban Combat', *Parameters*, 29, 2 (1999), carlisle-www.army.mil/usawc/Parameters/99summer/ thomas.htm.

127. Vegetius, *Vegetius*, p. 30.

128. Goulding, 'From Chancellorsville to Kosovo', p. 10.

129. Marshall, *Men Against Fire*, p. 19. See also p. 51 in which Marshall claims that the core of tactics is putting down firepower on the decisive point.

130. This argument is central in much of Biddle's recent work. See his 'Land Warfare: Theory and Practice', and *Afghanistan and the Future of Warfare*. Similarly, Sir Timothy Garden notes that airpower is most effective when combined with surface forces. Timothy Garden, 'Air Power: Theory and Practice', in John Baylis, James Wirtz, Eliot Cohen and Colin S. Gray (eds), *Strategy in the Contemporary World: An Introduction to Strategic Studies* (Oxford, Oxford University Press, 2002), p. 147.

131. Moore and Galloway, 'We Were Soldiers Once', p. 121.

132. Blaker, *Understanding the Revolution in Military Affairs*, p. 22.

133. Van Riper and Scales, 'Preparing for War in the 21st Century', p. 12.

134. Blaker, *Understanding the Revolution in Military Affairs*, p. 16.

135. These characteristics of tanks are outlined in Brigadier A. C. I. Gadsby, 'Do We Still Need Tanks?', *RUSI Journal*, 142, 4 (1997), pp. 17–22.

136. Christopher Bellamy, *The Evolution of Modern Land Warfare: Theory and Practice* (London, Routledge, 1990), p. 25.

137. Quoted in Stuart Millar, 'Hi-Tech Arsenal Decisive – if Targets Can be Found', *Guardian*, 25 March 2003, p. 4.

138. Ralph Peters, 'The Future of Armoured Warfare', *Parameters*, 27, 3 (1997), p. 51. Some of the dangers of the improper use of armour in an urban environment are evident in the Russian experience in Grozny. See Thomas, 'The Battle of Grozny'.

139. See Ashworth's account of the battle for Groningen 13–16 April 1945. G. J. Ashworth, *War and the City* (London, Routledge, 1991), pp. 125–8, and Robert W. Lamont's discussion of the role of armour in Hue and Khorramshahr, Robert W. Lamont, 'A Tale of Two Cities – Hue and Khorramshahr', *Marine Corps Gazette*, 83, 4 (1999), pp. 22–4.

140. Andrew J. Lawler, 'The Battle for Hue City', http://www.geocities.com/Pentagon/ 6453/hue3.html.

141. Robert W. Lamont, 'Urban Warrior – A View from North Vietnam', www. geocities.com/Pentagon/6453/uwvietnam.html.
142. See Joseph Fitchett, 'British Influence US with Tactics in Iraq', *International Herald Tribune*, 24 March 2003, p. 4.
143. Col Volney J. Warner, 'Technology Favours Future Land Forces', *Strategic Review*, 26, 3 (1998), p. 41.
144. Col Dick Applegate, 'Towards the Future Army', in Brian Bond and Mungo Melvin (eds), *The Nature of Future Conflict: Implications for Force Development*, The Occasional, 36 (Camberley, Strategic and Combat Studies Institute, Joint Services Staff College, 1998), p. 81.
145. O'Hanlon, *Technological Change*, p. 117.
146. Hugh McManners, 'Smart Missiles to Spike the Army's Big Guns', *Sunday Times*, 11 October 1998, p. 7.
147. Gadsby, 'Do We Still Need Tanks?', pp. 19–20, and Bellamy, *Spiral through Time*, p. 22.
148. See Hugh McManners, 'Plastic Tank is Silent Killer of Battlefield', *Sunday Times*, 7 February 1999, p. 9, J. Reed, 'Protecting Armoured Vehicles against Helicopter Attack: Stealth, Smoke and Mirrors', *Asian Defence Journal*, July 1996, pp. 70–3 and Peters, 'The Future of Armoured Warfare'.
149. Peters, 'The Future of Armoured Warfare', p. 52.
150. Lambeth, *NATO's Air War for Kosovo*, pp. 110–11.
151. For example, Gray argues that Coalition airpower in the Gulf War of 1991 represented the 'leading edge'. Gray, *Modern Strategy*, p. 240.
152. Damian Kemp, 'Combat Drones Fly for Casualty-Free War', *Jane's Defence Weekly*, 9 June 1999, p. 90. See also John A. Tirpak, 'Send in the UCAVs', *Air Force Magazine*, August 2001, www.infowar.com/mil_c4i/01/mil_c4i_080701a_j.shtml.
153. Lambeth, *NATO's Air War for Kosovo*, pp. 94–7.
154. 'Predator a Lethal Eye in the Sky', www.cnn.com/2002/US/11/04/predator. background/index.html.
155. Keith Somerville, 'US Drones Take Combat Role', news.bbc.co.uk/1/hi/world/2404425.stm.
156. Tirpak, 'Send in the UCAVs'. For further discussion on the roles UCAVs may fulfil, see Col Robert E. Chapman II, 'Unmanned Combat Aerial Vehicles: Dawn of a New Age?', *Aerospace Power Journal*, 16, 2 (2002), www.airpower.maxwell.af.mil/airchronicles/apj/apj02/sum02/chapman.html.
157. Biddle, *Afghanistan and the Future of Warfare*, p. 43.
158. Mr Wolfowitz, quoted in Department of Defense, *Testimony Delivered On Military Transformation* (United States Department of Defense, 9 April 2002), www.defenselink.mil/speeches/2002/s20020409-depsecdef1.html.
159. Brent Stuart Goodwin, 'Don't Techno for an Answer: The False Promise of Information Warfare', Review Article, *Naval War College Review*, 53, 2 (2000), p. 219.
160. Libicki, *Illuminating Tomorrow's War*.
161. Applegate, 'Towards the Future Army', p. 83.
162. Robert H. Scales, Jr, 'Cycles of War: Speed of Maneuver Will Be the Essential Ingredient of an Information-Age Army', *Armed Forces Journal International*, July 1997, p. 41.
163. Biddle, 'Land Warfare', p. 92.
164. Clausewitz, *On War*, p. 83.
165. Libicki, 'Technology and Warfare'.
166. See Christopher Coker, *Humane Warfare* (London, Routledge, 2001), and Ignatieff, *Virtual War*, pp. 168, 186. Indeed, Col Phillip S. Meilinger, USAF, Retired, believes

that airpower has significantly humanised war already. See Col Phillip S. Meilinger, 'Precision Aerospace Power, Discrimination, and the Future of War', *Aerospace Power Journal*, 15, 3 (2001), www.airpower.maxwell.af.mil/airchronicles/apj/apj01/fal01/ meilinger.html.

167. Lambeth, *NATO's Air War for Kosovo*, p. 36.
168. See Sun Tzu, trans. Griffith, pp. 77–9.
169. Arquilla and Ronfeldt, 'A New Epoch', p. 2. Similar ideas are also expressed in Arquilla and Ronfeldt, 'Cyberwar is Coming'.
170. Arquilla, 'The Strategic Implications of Information Dominance', p. 25.
171. See Weeks, 'US Maritime Doctrine and Manoeuvre Warfare'. However, Cebrowski's work doesn't dismiss the act of destruction. Indeed, he focuses some of his attention on the fact that increased battlespace awareness creates more potency in firepower. See Cebrowski, 'Network-Centric Warfare: Its Origin and Future', p. 32.
172. Col Charles M. Borg, *Information Operations: Is the Army Doing Enough?* (Carlisle Barracks, PA, US Army War College, 2001).
173. Donald E. Ryan cited in Ritcheson, 'The Future of "Military Affairs"', p. 35.
174. Campen quoted in Colin S. Gray, *Explorations in Strategy* (Westport, CT, Praeger, 1996), p. 239. See also Campen, 'Introduction', pp. x–xi.
175. Biddle, 'Land Warfare', pp. 104–6.
176. In a similar vein, Lawrence Freedman warns against overplaying the independent role information can play, by reminding us that alone it cannot destroy or move anything. See *The Revolution in Strategic Affairs*, p. 50.
177. Toffler and Toffler, *War and Anti-war*, p. 144, and Casper *et al.*, 'Knowledge-Based Warfare', p. 84.
178. Davis, 'An Information-Based Revolution in Military Affairs', p. 48. Owens, *Lifting the Fog of War*, p. 14. See also Jablonsky, 'US Military Doctrine and the Revolution in Military Affairs', pp. 33–4. Interestingly, Jablonsky regards a more immediate relationship between cause and effect on the battlefield as rendering war more Clausewitzian, in that there is a more direct relationship between war and policy.
179. An example of a war being concluded with just one decisive battle is Alexander's defeat of Porus at the Battle of Hydaspes. For an account of the battle see Fuller, *The Generalship of Alexander the Great*, pp. 180–99.
180. Libicki, *The Mesh and the Net*.
181. In Book 1, Ch. 1, Clausewitz states that to force the enemy to do your will, you must: '*either make him literally defenceless or at least put him in a position that makes this danger probable*'. An acknowledged information dominance is one way to make such a situation probable. Clausewitz, *On War*, p. 85.
182. See Martin C. Libicki, 'The Emerging Primacy of Information', *Orbis*, 40, 2 (1996), pp. 261–74, and Martin C. Libicki, 'Dominant Battlespace Knowledge and its Consequences', in Stuart E. Johnson and Martin C. Libicki (eds), *Dominant Battlespace Knowledge*, Revised Edition (Washington, DC, National Defense University, 1996), pp. 23–49.
183. Arquilla and Ronfeldt, 'Cyberwar is Coming', p. 23.
184. Colonel Owen E. Jensen, 'Information Warfare: Principles of Third-Wave War', *Air Power Journal*, 8, 4 (1994), p. 40.
185. See Richard Szafranski, 'Neocortical Warfare? The Acme of Skill', in John Arquilla and David Ronfeldt (eds), *In Athena's Camp: Preparing for Conflict in the Information Age* (Santa Monica, CA, RAND, 1996), pp. 398–9.
186. Dwight D. Eisenhower, *Crusade in Europe* (London, William Heinemann, 1948), p. 247.
187. Hayden, *Warfighting*, p. 89.
188. Thompson, *Ragged War*, p. 147. James Kiras adds the cautionary note that the

campaign to destroy insurgents is usually a slow and attritional one. Kiras, 'Terrorism and Irregular Warfare', p. 225.

189. Thompson, *Ragged War*, p. 147.
190. Joint Chiefs of Staff, 'Joint Vision 2010', p. 41.
191. Peters, *Fighting for the Future*, p. viii.
192. Hayden, *Warfighting*, p. 89. Although, such an approach may have raised concerns in the Confederacy similar to those directed at Fabius Maximus in the Roman Republic, namely, that the public expected some form of action to be taken against the enemy.
193. Leonhard, *The Principles of War for the Information Age*, p. 222.
194. Clausewitz, *On War*, p. 84.
195. Ibid., p. 273.
196. Hayden, *Warfighting*, p. 68.
197. Clausewitz, *On War*, p. 270. In this context, Parker contends that the plan for the 1588 Armada was too complicated. Parker, *The Grand Strategy of Philip II*, p. 188.
198. Jensen, 'Information Warfare', p. 42.
199. 'Keep your plans simple' is the sound advice from General Bruce C. Clarke, a successful combat commander of World War II. General Bruce C. Clarke, 'Leadership, Commandership, Planning, and Success', *Military Review*, 82, 4 (2002), p. 3.
200. Clausewitz, *On War*, p. 270.
201. Rick Atkinson, *Crusade: The Untold Story of the Persian Gulf War* (Boston, MA, Houghton Mifflin, 1993), p. 299.
202. The concept of a 'force in being' is equivalent to Corbett's notion of a 'fleet in being'. See Corbett, *Some Principles of Maritime Strategy*, p. 201.
203. Timothy L. Thomas, *'Like Adding Wings to a Tiger': Chinese Information War Theory and Practice* (Fort Leavenworth, KS, Foreign Military Studies Office, 2000), www.iwar.org.uk/iwar/ resources/china/iw/chinaiw.htm.
204. Ignatieff, *Virtual War*, p. 5.
205. Coker, *Humane Warfare*, p. 5.
206. Charles J. Dunlap, Jr, '21st-Century Land Warfare: Four Dangerous Myths', *Parameters*, 27, 3 (1997), p. 29. See also Charles J. Dunlap, 'Sometimes the Dragon Wins: A Perspective on Information Age Warfare', in Winn Schwartau (ed.), *Information Warfare: Cyberterrorism: Protecting Your Personal Security in the Electronic Age*, Second Edition (New York, Thunder's Mouth Press, 1996), pp. 436–53.
207. Colin S. Gray, *The Second Nuclear Age* (Boulder, CO, Lynne Rienner Publishers, 1999), p. 8.
208. Mike Moore, 'Unintended Consequences', *Bulletin of Atomic Scientists*, 56, 1 (2000), www.bullatomsci.org/issues/2000/jf00/jf00moore.html.
209. Bennett, *Behind the Battle*, p. 9.
210. Ajay Singh, 'Time: The New Dimension in War', *Joint Force Quarterly*, 10 (1995–96), p. 60.
211. R. L. DiNardo and Daniel J. Hughes, 'Some Cautionary Thoughts on Information Warfare', *Airpower Journal*, 9, 4 (1995), p. 76.
212. In a similar vein, Brent Stuart Goodwin states that 'technology is a poor offset for unsound strategy and policy'. See Goodwin, 'Don't Techno for an Answer', p. 216.
213. Jensen, 'Information Warfare', p. 39.
214. Daniel T. Kuehl, 'Strategic Information Warfare and Comprehensive Situational Awareness', in Alan D. Campen, Douglas H. Dearth and R. Thomas Goodden, *Cyberwar: Security, Strategy, and Conflict in the Information Age* (Fairfax, VA, AFCEA International Press, 1996), p. 185.
215. Clausewitz, *On War*, pp. 138–9.

216. Ibid., p. 138.
217. Watts, *Clausewitzian Friction and Future War*, p. 32.
218. Clausewitz, *On War*, p. 138.
219. Winters *et al.*, *Battling the Elements*, p. 267. See Ch. 5 for discussion on why physical geography will remain central in the conduct of strategy.
220. Winters *et al.*, *Battling the Elements*, p. 270.
221. Van Riper and Scales, 'Preparing for War in the 21st Century', p. 9. As an aside, Marshall indicates that better situational awareness could lead to higher levels of morale, simply because units have the knowledge that their flanks are assured by friendly forces. Marshall, *Men Against Fire*, p. 87.
222. Jacob W. Kipp and Lt-Col Lester W. Grau, 'The Fog and Friction of Technology', *Military Review*, 81, 5 (2001), p. 88.
223. *Joint Vision 2020*, www.dtic.mil/jointvision/jvpub2.htm, pp. 12–13.
224. Adams, *The Next World War*, p. 88.
225. Ibid., p. 115.
226. Watts, *Clausewitzian Friction and Future War*, pp. 126–7.
227. Hayden, *Warfighting*, p. 38.
228. James R. Fitzsimonds, 'The Coming Military Revolution: Opportunities and Risks', *Parameters*, 25, 2 (1995), p. 35.
229. Indeed, Eliot Cohen describes the relationship between policy objectives and the military as the 'unequal dialogue', in which the world of policy dominates. Cohen, *Supreme Command*, p. 207.
230. Thompson, *Ragged War*, p. 135.
231. Wylie, *Military Strategy*, p. 88.
232. The following works provide good analyses of the American War of Independence: John Shy, *A People Numerous and Armed: Reflections on the Military Struggle for American Independence* (New York, Oxford University Press, 1976), Jeremy Black, *War For America: The Fight for Independence 1775–1783* (Stroud, Sutton Publishing, 1991), and Piers Mackesy, *The War For America 1775–1783* (Lincoln, NE, Bison Books, 1993).
233. Van Riper and Scales, 'Preparing for War in the 21st Century', p. 9.
234. Lambeth, *NATO's Air War for Kosovo*, p. 185.
235. Gray, *Modern Strategy*, p. 25.
236. Eliot A. Cohen, 'A Revolution in Warfare', *Foreign Affairs*, 75, 2 (1996), pp. 51–2.
237. See Libicki, 'The Emerging Primacy of Information', and Ignatieff, *Virtual War*, p. 186 for a description of the cultural background to the emphasis on post-heroic warfare.
238. As Ralph Peters notes, 'We have fallen into the old American trap of seeking technological solutions to human problems.' Peters, 'After the Revolution', p. 8.
239. See Ch. 4, for an analysis of SIW.
240. Admiral William A. Owens, 'Introduction', p. 13.
241. Williamson Murray and Mark Grimsley, 'Introduction: On Strategy', in Williamson Murray, MacGregor Knox and Alvin Bernstein (eds), *The Making of Strategy: Rulers, States, and War* (Cambridge, Cambridge University Press, 1994), p. 22. This is also a central tenet of Gray's work.
242. Michael Howard rates this 'social dimension' of strategy as one of the main four dimensions. See Michael Howard, 'The Forgotten Dimensions of Strategy', *Foreign Affairs*, 57 (1979), pp. 976–86. See also Gray, *Modern Strategy*, pp. 27–8.
243. In this context Adam J. Baddeley discusses the relationship between the current RMA and COIN operations. See A. J. Baddeley, 'Insurgency and Counter Insurgency in the Information Age', paper prepared for the BISA Annual Conference, 15–17 December 1997, University of Leeds. Libicki also discusses the wider utility of infor-

mation age capabilities. See Libicki, 'The Emerging Primacy of Information'. These issues are discussed in more detail in Ch. 5. Non-lethal weapons also play a part in this. See Steven Metz, 'Non-Lethal Weapons: A Progress Report', *Joint Force Quarterly*, 28 (2001), pp. 18-22.

244. Leonhard, *The Principles of War for the Information Age*, p. 157.
245. Quoted in DiNardo and Hughes, 'Some Cautionary Thoughts on Information Warfare', p. 76.
246. Libicki, *The Mesh and the Net*.
247. Owens, 'Introduction', pp. 8–10. See also Admiral William Owens, 'The Emerging System-of-Systems', *Strategic Forum*, 63, February 1996, www.ndu.edu/inss/strforum/forum63.html.
248. See Leonhard, *The Principles of War for the Information Age*, Ch. 2.
249. This is partly the result of operational countermeasures, but also the demands of strategy.
250. Bagnall, *The Punic Wars*, pp. 61–2.
251. Luttwak, *Strategy: The Logic of War and Peace*, p. 28.
252. Cook, 'War of Extremes', p. 23.
253. 'US Destroys 6 Iraqi Systems Jamming GPS', *International Herald Tribune*, 26 March 2003, p. 4.
254. Wilson, 'The Transformation of Military Power, 1997–2027', p. 5.
255. See Toffler and Toffler, *War and Anti-war*, p. 144, and Emmett, 'Information Mania', p. 23.
256. See Wilson, 'The Transformation of Military Power, 1997–2027', p. 19, Carlo Kopp, 'The E-Bomb – A Weapon of Electrical Mass Destruction', in Winn Schwartau (ed.), *Information Warfare: Cyberterrorism: Protecting Your Personal Security in the Electronic Age*, Second Edition (New York, Thunder's Mouth Press, 1996), pp. 296–333, and O'Hanlon, *Technological Change*, p. 194.
257. Col M. D. Starry and Lt-Col C. W. Arneson, Jr, 'FM 100-6: Information Operations', *Military Review*, 76, 6 (1996), pp. 3–15.
258. Michael L. Brown, 'The Revolution in Military Affairs: The Information Dimension', in Alan D. Campen, Douglas H. Dearth and R. Thomas Goodden, *Cyberwar: Security, Strategy, and Conflict in the Information Age* (Fairfax, VA, AFCEA International Press, 1996), p. 51.
259. W. Caldwell, Jr, 'Promises, Promises', *Proceedings*, 122, 1 (1996), p. 57.
260. Warner, 'Technology Favours Future Land Forces', p. 52.
261. Libicki, 'Dominant Battlespace Knowledge', p. 31.
262. Bagnall, *The Punic Wars*, p. 186.
263. Bernard Weinraub, 'A Top US Intelligence Officer Admits Army Miscalculations', *International Herald Tribune*, 31 March 2003, p. 5.
264. Paddy Griffith, *Battle Tactics of the Western Front: The British Army's Art of Attack 1916–18* (New Haven, CT, Yale University Press, 1994).
265. Henry C. Bartlett, G. Paul Holman, Jr and Timothy E. Somes, 'Force Planning, Military Revolutions and the Tyranny of Technology', *Strategic Review*, 24, 4 (1996), p. 31.
266. Brown, 'The Revolution in Military Affairs', p. 42.
267. Arquilla, 'The Strategic Implications of Information Dominance'.
268. Holden Reid, 'Enduring Patterns in Modern Warfare', p. 27. This point is also made by Biddle, 'Land Warfare', p. 99, and John Ellis, *Brute Force: Allied Strategy and Tactics in the Second World War* (London, Andre Deutsch, 1990).
269. Krepinevich, 'Cavalry to Computer', p. 37.
270. Gray adopts a similar stance, by arguing that wars usually contain elements of attrition, manoeuvre and control. *Modern Strategy*, pp. 159–62.

271. Cooper, 'Another View of the Revolution in Military Affairs', p. 107. Lamb, 'The Impact of Information Age Technologies', p. 247.
272. On this issue Ralph Peters observes: 'We confront, today, creatively organised enemies employing behaviours and technologies ranging from those of the stone-age to those at the imagination's edge.' Peters, 'After the Revolution', p. 8.
273. *Joint Vision 2020*, p. 6.
274. Lawrence Freedman, 'Conclusion: The Future of Strategic Studies', in John Baylis, James Wirtz, Eliot Cohen and Colin S. Gray (eds), *Strategy in the Contemporary World: An Introduction to Strategic Studies* (Oxford, Oxford University Press, 2002), p. 341.
275. Quoted in *Testimony Delivered on Military Transformation* (United States Department of Defense, 9 April 2002), www.defenselink.mil/speeches/2002/s20020409-depsecdefl.html.
276. Gray, *The Second Nuclear Age*, p. 157. Similarly, Richard Betts suggests that a large conventional foe who stands at a disadvantage in the face of a digitised enemy could escalate up to WMD as an asymmetric form of warfare. Richard Betts, 'The Downside of the Cutting Edge', *National Interest*, 45 (1996), pp. 82–3. See also Fitzsimonds, 'The Coming Military Revolution', p. 34.
277. Colin S. Gray, 'Three Visions of Future War', *Queen's Quarterly*, 103, 1 (1996), pp. 35–48. Another work which considers a future which includes both the RMA and WMD is Wilson, *Preparing for Early 21st Century War: Beyond the Bottom-Up Review*.
278. This is a general point made in Mao's work.
279. Harry G. Summers, 'A War is a War is a War is a War', in Loren B. Thompson (ed), *Low-Intensity Conflict: The Pattern of Warfare in the Modern World* (Lexington, MA, Lexington Books, 1989), pp. 39-40, and Gray, *Modern Strategy*, p. 198.
280. Gray, 'Three Visions of Future War'.
281. Applegate, 'Towards the Future Army', p. 79.
282. Murray and Knox, 'Conclusion: The Future Behind Us', p. 185.
283. Callwell, *Small Wars*, p. 23.
284. Gray, *Modern Strategy*, p. 179, and Callwell, *Small Wars*, p. 27.
285. Lawrence, *Seven Pillars*, p. 182.
286. Cited in Moreman, 'Small Wars and Imperial Policing', p. 109.
287. Callwell, *Small Wars*, p. 85.
288. Moreman, 'Small Wars and Imperial Policing', p. 118.
289. Callwell, *Small Wars*, p. 32.
290. See Edward N. Luttwak, *The Grand Strategy of the Roman Empire: From the First Century AD to the Third* (Baltimore, MD, Johns Hopkins University Press, 1979), p. 42. See also Lawrence Keppie, *The Making of the Roman Army: From Republic to Empire* (London, Routledge, 1984), and John Peddie, *The Roman War Machine* (London, Grange Books, 1997).
291. This thought has been expressed on a number of occasions by Gray during conversations with the author.
292. Baddeley, 'Insurgency and Counter Insurgency in the Information Age', and Libicki, 'The Emerging Primacy of Information'. The application of the RMA in irregular warfare is also discussed in Steven Metz and James Kievit, *The Revolution in Military Affairs and Conflict Short of War*, 25 July 1994, www.cs.virginia.edu/~alb/misc/ rmawarcollege.html.
293. Lamb, 'The Impact of Information Age Technologies', pp. 263–4.
294. For an excellent assessment of just how inescapable geography is see Colin S. Gray, 'Inescapable Geography', in Colin S. Gray and Geoffrey Sloan (eds), *Geopolitics: Geography and Strategy* (London, Frank Cass, 1999), pp. 161–77.

295. Clausewitz, *On War*, p. 416. Of course, weather also can have a significant effect on operations. Just how significant this factor can prove to be is outlined in N. A. M. Rodger, 'Weather, Geography and Naval Power in the Age of Sail', in Colin S. Gray and Geoffrey Sloan (eds), *Geopolitics: Geography and Strategy* (London, Frank Cass, 1999), pp. 178–200.
296. Fuller, *The Generalship of Alexander the Great*, pp. 248–54.
297. Ferrill, *The Origins of War*, pp. 204–5.
298. See Russell F. Weigley, *The Age of Battles: The Quest for Decisive Warfare from Breitenfeld to Waterloo* (London, Pimlico, 1991), p. 59.
299. Winters, *et al.*, *Battling the Elements*.
300. As Wylie notes, to a soldier terrain is everything. Wylie, *Military Strategy*, p. 42. It is equally true to state that warfare in the maritime, air, space and infosphere dimensions is largely dictated by the unique characteristics of each environment.
301. Ashworth, *War and the City*, pp. 116–22.
302. Anatol Lieven, 'The World Turned Upside Down', *Armed Forces Journal International*, August 1998, p. 40.
303. Wilson, *Preparing for Early 21st Century War*, p. 28.
304. Winters, *et al.*, *Battling the Elements*, p. 104.
305. Ibid., p. 122.
306. Williamson Murray, 'Some Thoughts on War and Geography', in Colin S. Gray and Geoffrey Sloan (eds), *Geopolitics: Geography and Strategy* (London, Frank Cass, 1999), p. 204.
307. Ibid., p. 211.
308. Bellamy, *The Evolution of Modern Land Warfare*, pp. 109–12.
309. Winters, *et al.*, *Battling the Elements*, pp. 34–9.
310. Murray, 'Some Thoughts on War and Geography', p. 206, and Meek, 'US Advance Grinds to Halt in Teeth of Storm', p. 1.
311. Winters, *et al.*, *Battling the Elements*, p. 270, and Gray, *Modern Strategy*, pp. 251–2.
312. Emmett, 'Information Mania', p. 19.
313. Leonhard, *The Principles of War for the Information Age*, pp. 70–1, 178.
314. Libicki, *The Mesh and the Net*, p. 21.
315. Hayden, *Warfighting*, p. 180.
316. Thomas P. M. Barnett, 'The Seven Deadly Sins of Network-Centric Warfare', *Proceedings*, 125, 1 (1999), p. 37.
317. Michael Howard quoted in Holden Reid, 'Enduring Patterns in Modern Warfare', p. 17.
318. Paul Harris, 'Radicalism in Military Thought', in Brian Bond and Mungo Melvin (eds), *The Nature of Future Conflict: Implications for Force Development*, The Occasional, 36 (Camberley, Strategic and Combat Studies Institute, Joint Services Staff College, 1998), p. 35, Bellamy, *The Evolution of Modern Land Warfare*, p. 95, and Ellis, *The Sharp End of War*.
319. This is the central message of John Ellis, *Brute Force*.
320. Bender, 'US Weapons Shortages Risked Success in Kosovo', p. 3.
321. Peters, 'The Future of Armoured Warfare', p. 52.
322. Lt Jeff Mustin, 'Future Employment of Unmanned Aerial Vehicles', *Aerospace Power Journal*, 16, 2 (2002), www.airpower.maxwell.af.mil/airchronicles/apj/apj02/sum02/vorsum02.html.
323. See John Arquilla and David Ronfeldt, 'Looking Ahead: Preparing for Information-Age Conflict', in John Arquilla and David Ronfeldt (eds), *In Athena's Camp: Preparing for Conflict in the Information Age* (Santa Monica, CA, RAND, 1996), pp. 492–3, in which they proclaim that warfare will become less destructive and more disruptive. They also identify an 'information dividend', which enables an end to the

    need for large armed forces.
324. Clausewitz, *On War*, p. 161.
325. Dunlap, 'Four Dangerous Myths', p. 35.
326. Richard A. Gabriel and Donald W. Boose, Jr, *The Great Battles of Antiquity: A Strategic and Tactical Guide to the Great Battles that Shaped the Development of War* (Westport, CT, Greenwood Press, 1994).

3

Future Command and the Fate of Military Genius

'[war's] highest solution must be evolved from the eye and brain and soul of a single man ... Nothing but genius, the demon in man, can answer the riddles of war ...'[1]

INTRODUCTION

One cannot fully appreciate Clausewitz's theory of war without understanding the role of the general. The pages of military history are adorned with the exploits of individual human commanders. Men such as Alexander the Great, Napoleon and Field Marshal Slim, to name but three, are credited with displaying the various qualities required to succeed in the art of command. Napoleon himself declared: 'read and meditate upon the wars of the greatest captains'. He continued: 'this is the only means of rightly learning the science of war'.[2] It is because war is a human endeavour, involving the realm of chance, uncertainty, danger and physical exertion, and is the contact point between the military instrument and policy that Clausewitz reserved the accolade of 'military genius' for those who, like the above, excel in the art of command within such an environment.[3]

Of course, command cannot be reduced simply to the attributes of the commander. As Gray postulates, because genius is rare, attention should be paid to the creation of a compensatory command process.[4] In this vein, van Creveld cites the Prussian General Staff as a successful example of this principle.[5] Indeed, Dupuy goes as far as to suggest that the explanation for the success of the Prussian/German General Staff can be found in its institutionalisation of 'military genius'.[6] Nevertheless, even in the absence of a military genius, historically command systems have been based upon the principle of hierarchy, with command responsibility resting ultimately with an individual. It is the combination of the commander's qualities, the command structure and the command ethos that lays the foundation for good command amid the ever-present stresses and chaos of war.

'Military genius' is a term used by Clausewitz to describe those individuals who possess an outstanding 'harmonious combination of elements' required to excel in command.[7] Although the title of this chapter refers to genius, this is not meant to restrict the study of command to the very few individuals who display something extraordinarily special. Rather, the Clausewitzian term 'military genius' can be used as a vehicle for understanding the qualities of good command more generally. The key point to note is that military genius is a human attribute that includes certain cognitive skills, certain moral qualities and an understanding of human issues. Underneath these broad umbrella terms, Clausewitz identifies a number of characteristics which a commander should possess. These include physical and moral courage; incisiveness; presence of mind; strength of will and character; and an ambitious nature. However, Clausewitz gives particular prominence to a general's intuitive ability, his *coup d'œil*, and the determination to see his decisions through to conclusion. He also acknowledges the significance of leadership, as particularly evident in the task of supporting the men through the psychological trauma of battle. Finally, a Clausewitzian general must understand how military force relates to policy.[8] More recently, General Peter de la Billiere has expanded on this latter requirement. Reflecting on his 1991 Gulf War experience, he notes that the commander must give considerable time during a campaign to the post-conflict settlement.[9] To this end, he must consider a range of factors including political, moral, legal, socio-economic and cultural issues. Such concerns surely require a skilled human touch.

In contrast to the 'bold' general in *On War*, Sun Tzu's ideal commander relies less on intuition, and more on caution and measured calculation.[10] This approach reflects Sun Tzu's tendency to regard warfare as more controllable and dominated by the correct manipulation and utilisation of knowledge. In this respect, it is easy to appreciate why the Chinese theorist appeals to the enthusiasts of the contemporary RMA literature. Whereas Clausewitz's military genius relies upon his intuition and determination to make the right decisions in the face of unreliable and contradictory information, Sun Tzu's general seeks to acquire and utilise knowledge as the basis for his actions. This difference between the two theorists is utilised by Ferris and Handel in their call for Clausewitzian generals to be replaced by 'calculating commanders'.[11]

The subject of command is of interest to this study because, indirectly, the RMA literature challenges the continued role of the individual human commander. In particular, two developments of the information age raise questions concerning who, or what, should conduct command,

and what form command structures and ethos should take in the future. The first of these developments is the coming maturation of artificial intelligence.[12] The potential exploitation of AI is not solely a product of increased technological capability in computer processing. Within the RMA literature there is a perceived need for the increased utilisation of computers in decision making. This requirement is driven by the need to process a greater abundance of information more quickly in order to produce higher operational tempo. It has been suggested that computers enable a higher level of performance in war, since their ability to handle and sort large amounts of information means that complex plans can be formed which can then be simplified in their execution.[13] The second feature of the information age that could challenge the role of the individual commander is the rise of the network structure. The digital era permits a high rate of information transfer that facilitates the dissemination of a common picture of the battlespace to every unit. It is this feature, allied to a potential increase in operational tempo, which has raised the possibility that the network structure should replace the hierarchy as the most effective organisational form through which to conduct command.

When considering the fate of the Clausewitzian general, it is not just a question of whether he has become relatively less effective than an information age variant. Ferris and Handel go as far as to suggest that in the age of information plenty the attributes of the military genius may become counterproductive to the exercise of effective command.[14] It is the intention of this chapter to make some initial explorations into assessing the advantages and limitations of integrating the two developments of AI and networks into the art of command, and in particular to discuss the future of the military genius.

THE AGE OF AI AND NETWORKS

In his 1985 work *Command in War,* van Creveld posed some interesting questions concerning the relative strengths of man and machines in the art of command, and in particular he raised the issue of how the burden of work should be divided between them.[15] The development of AI in particular makes these questions even more pertinent for the coming decades. Even the usually sober Eliot Cohen notes, 'the creation of such machines [AI] will mean that humans have gradually begun to cede much of their ability to make decisions to silicon chips. It is a process already well under way in some areas.'[16] Exactly when AI will mature to a point at which a computer can do many of the things a human brain can do, such as produce novel solutions to problems, is disputed and uncertain. Some estimates suggest a wait of 30 to 50 years until the big breakthroughs appear.[17] In contrast, some within the AI community argue that although AI may still be a young discipline it is on the verge of significant progress.[18] We may already be on the path towards these developments through the technique of 'evolutionary computing', which has reportedly rejuvenated the field of AI.[19] Alternatively, it may require the development of 'molecular memory' to produce the processing power required for substantial leaps in AI.[20] Whatever form these developments take, and whatever the timeline, there seems to be general agreement that the advent of AI is inevitable.[21]

Although it may be some time before AI reaches a sophisticated level of development, computers already engage in activities that traditionally have been the preserve of human decision making.[22] The technique of 'knowledge engineering', which involves the uploading of human knowledge about a particular activity into a computer, is already a reality. This technique has enabled the so-called 'Robotrader' to look after $200 million of funds on the world's bonds markets. In fact, the two organisations behind this project, Pareto Partners Ltd and Hughes Research Laboratories, have gone as far as to note that 'in the war for the world's markets, the mechanised divisions are going to win'.[23] Chess is another area in which computer programs are superseding human abilities; in recent years this has occurred even at the grandmaster level.[24]

As computer-based decision making is introduced into an increasing number of human activities, it is unlikely that the art of command will escape this intrusion. Indeed, many of the AI labs in the United States were established and continue to be funded by the Defense Advanced Research Projects Agency (DARPA).[25] However, developing these technologies is only part of the challenge. A more important task is considering whether, and how, AI can be integrated into the art of command, bearing in mind that war is a domain infused by policy, humanity, uncertainty, friction and the existence of an intelligent foe.

In relation to the second development of the current epoch, some analysts regard the rise of the network as a direct challenge to the relative efficacy of the hierarchical command structure. At the forefront of this discourse are Arquilla and Ronfeldt. Arquilla postulates that 'the information age implies generalship by the many, the decentralisation of authority'.[26] Arquilla does temper this thought somewhat by noting that military organisations will always retain an element of hierarchy with someone who has ultimate command responsibility. Taken as a whole, Arquilla and Ronfeldt's ideas are best summed up by their notion that 'cyberwar', a form of warfare which centres around the battle for information, dictates a shift from 'command and control' to 'consultation and coordination'.[27] With these thoughts in mind, the future of the military command organisation may reside in the creation of hybrid organisational structures, which utilise elements of both hierarchies and networks.

Before embarking upon an analysis of AI and networks it is important to reiterate that the main elements that constitute the Clausewitzian nature of war will remain dominant in the battlespace. This establishes the framework within which these two developments must operate. All told, commanders will continue to lead men in circumstances of extreme danger and varied strategic circumstances. These considerations should dictate how AI and networks are integrated into the art of command.

The responsibilities of command can be delineated in a number of ways. Martin van Creveld chose to distinguish between function-related and output-related responsibilities.[28] Whilst recognising the importance of van Creveld's function- and output-related approach, for the purposes of this study the responsibilities of command are perhaps best defined as being concerned with 'internal' and 'external' factors. Internal factors refer to those considerations which relate to the commander's own forces. These concern primarily the maintenance and wellbeing of the forces. In this area, important concerns are the maintenance of morale, the motivation of the troops and general preparation for war. Consequently, the internal role of command is often concerned with factors relating to human participation. Another important element within the internal function is the management of information. In this respect, the US Army's *FM 100-6 Information Operations* is quite right to assert, 'commanders must have information to command'.[29] As information becomes more bountiful, sensible management of this resource becomes more salient in order to avoid the problem of information overload.[30] Therefore, the handling of information is perhaps gaining increased significance in the information age. Nevertheless, Campen's claim that information is the essence of C^2 is erroneous.[31] Although it represents an essential element of the command process, information constitutes just one aspect of the art. Just as important are those issues relating to leadership, strategy and judgment. Montgomery correctly noted that leadership is predominately a battle for the hearts and minds of men.[32]

The external side of the command equation refers to interaction with enemy forces and commanders. To perform well in the external role, a commander must of course make the right decisions in the face of enemy actions, and importantly must retain the initiative. To conceive command in terms of these internal and external considerations presents a useful framework for analysis. Of course, the external and internal factors of command interact with each other considerably. A commander must perform adequately in both of the functions outlined above.

THE AI COMMANDER

In 1969 a senior Soviet army engineer commented: 'the means of automatic control of troops and weapons ... have become a most important form of military equipment'.[33] This observation may have even more pertinence in the information age. Indeed, Libicki postulates that the existence of the Mesh raises serious questions about the continued viability of human command.[34] There are a number of reasons to suggest why conducting command with AI may confer some advantage. The first and most obvious, which relates to the external consideration, is the requirement for speed in decision making relative to the enemy. Of course, a decision has to be correct as well as quick. A quick bad decision is still a bad decision, and may only result in bringing disaster more quickly. Yet, speed is at the heart of many of the great theories of war. In one of his most noted axioms Sun Tzu declares, 'Speed is the essence of war.'[35] Clausewitz more specifically calls for rapid and decisive decisions.[36] The relative speed of decision making is the very essence of Colonel John Boyd's much-praised OODA Loop.[37] At its heart, Boyd's theory is concerned with getting inside the enemy's decision-making cycle, and thereby seizing and retaining the initiative. Similarly, the RMA literature often pays homage to the search for ever-greater levels of operational tempo. For example, Network Centric Warfare places great emphasis on the need for speed in the process of command. To facilitate this, Admiral Cebrowski calls for greater automation in decision making and flattened hierarchies.[38] There is sufficient historical evidence to support such a focus on the speed of the decision-making cycle. Griffith notes that one of the main problems encountered in the offensives of World War I was that the tempo of C^2 was often insufficient to exploit break-ins of the enemy defences. Consequently, the much sought-after breakout could not be achieved.[39]

The requirement for quick decision making may acquire even more saliency in the information age. As the battlespace becomes a place of greater lethality, getting your blow in first could confer a distinct advantage. This is certainly the perspective taken by James Hazlett, who asserts that success or failure in future war will be determined by who gets inside the enemy's decision-making cycle first.[40] The US Army's Mobile Strike Force Advanced Warfighting Experiment (AWE) has reported a significant increase in operational tempo for a digitised force.[41] Such exercises have created certain expectations within the military. 'Joint Vision 2010' asserts that increased operational tempo and greater force integration will probably create a more stressful and faster-moving decision-making environment.[42] Clearly, computers have the ability to process certain forms of information much more quickly than humans, and, although one may shy away from the prospect of giving command authority to a computer, the danger exists that the enemy may not. This latter point can be termed the 'digital imperative', namely, that there is pressure to employ AI in command for fear that the enemy may do so whilst you do not. In such a scenario, a force under human command could have a much slower decision-making cycle relative to one under the command of AI. In this respect, the existence of an intelligent enemy may in this case provide the impetus for radical change in the information age.

An AI commander also has the advantage of not being emotional or susceptible to psychological pressure. Clausewitz identifies a psychological fog of war, a product of man's emotional response to combat.[43] Within this context, Sun Tzu pays a great deal of attention to the art of playing upon the temperament of an opposing commander. For Sun Tzu a commander must be serene and controlled.[44] This is clearly an area of command in which AI can excel. Interestingly enough, although computers cannot be psychologically manipulated, computers do have the ability to psychologically affect human opponents. During his defeat at the hands of IBM's computer Deep Blue, World Chess Champion Gary Kasparov was reportedly put under severe pressure, in part by the enormous calculating power of his opponent. Kasparov, unusually, fell prey to his emotions, lost his objectivity and fell into a well-known trap in the final and decisive sixth game.[45] It is easy to appreciate how the calculating power of Deep Blue could be off-putting when one learns that it can calculate approximately one quarter of a billion chess positions every second.[46] As impressive as this is, the human brain still represents the most powerful processor available.[47] It has been estimated that the average brain can process 20 million billion calculations per second.[48] It should also be noted that chess is an activity that particularly suits AI. As Aaron Sloman notes, 'These sorts of tasks fit more readily into a computer's mechanisms for manipulating large numbers of precisely defined symbols very rapidly, according to precisely defined rules.'[49] AI has traditionally had much more trouble with commonsense tasks such as understanding stories or conversations.[50]

The ability to calculate many options and plan well ahead is another useful attribute for a commander. Brigadier-General Huba Wass de Czege, who has been involved in the US Army's AWE, regards the ability to prepare alternative possible plans with the aid of information technologies as especially valuable.[51] Likewise, General Westmoreland, reflecting upon his command of US forces in Vietnam, comments: 'it was essential for me to plan ahead constantly, to develop contingency plans for any eventuality'.[52] The ability to calculate a quarter of a billion positions every second could be as useful in the conduct of war as it is in the game of chess. However, it must be borne in mind that in many of its aspects chess is a game of known variables. The contest takes place on a known and unchanging board, and the pieces have set attributes. War is a far more complex and uncertain undertaking, not least because it involves humans at all levels.

There are a number of other reasons to indicate that AI could perform well in command. As Napoleon stated, a prerequisite for performing well in command is to study the great commanders of the past, in order to attain a good knowledge of one's art.[53] To refer once again to General Westmoreland's experience in Vietnam, he had at his side a command historian 'to provide historical background and precedent'.[54] Returning to the grandmasters of chess, one of their great assets is the ability to draw upon a thorough memory of great chess games and moves. A computer can obviously hold a great deal of information on past commanders and their campaigns. In this sense, an AI commander can have a comprehensive knowledge of his art, which also could conceivably include a detailed familiarity with the performance parameters of the relevant equipment, and knowledge of the operational procedures and doctrine for all sections of a military organisation. Since an AI commander would have no national or service bias it could serve well as the commander of joint or multinational forces. Such a commander could be programmed to be equally cognisant with the different armed services within, and between, countries.

In the information age it may in fact be necessary to involve AI in the process of command, simply in order to cope with the vast amounts of information produced in modern war. Again, this is particularly pertinent in future conflict in which access to information, and the quick utilisation of that information, may prove increasingly significant. A common complaint from units involved in exercises with advanced information technology is that they sometimes become overwhelmed with information. Every command system has its limitations. As van Creveld notes, Napoleon's Imperial Headquarters, which had previously functioned well, became overwhelmed by the numbers of troops and distances involved in the campaigns of 1812–13.[55] There may come a point when human commanders are unable to cope effectively with the flow of information, and more importantly the requirement for timely decisions based upon that information. To this end, James R. Fitzsimonds is prepared to conclude: 'An information-intensive battlespace may work to our advantage only if humans can be largely removed from the command loop.'[56] In this respect, Colonel Dessert, Jr notes that a commander on an information age battlefield will have the daunting task of keeping track of a significantly extended battlespace.[57] In a similar vein, 'Joint Vision 2010' notes, 'the accelerated operational tempo and greater integration requirements will likely create a more stressful, faster moving decision environment'.[58]

116

An AI commander will not suffer from ill health or fatigue on the battlefield.[59] In contrast 'the [human] mind is subject to adverse effects by environmental factors such as fatigue, stress and hunger'.[60] Jacob W. Kipp and Lt-Col. Lester W. Grau point out an obvious but important observation: 'Technology has changed over the centuries, but man has not. He is still the same basic naked ape who quickly tires, exhibits stress and makes irrational judgements when forced to respond to more than five stimuli.'[61] In theory, an AI commander could conduct a 24-hour battle day after day. In contrast, humans have physical and mental limitations. At Waterloo, Napoleon's deteriorating health forced him to leave the battlefield for a time. It was during this absence from the field that Ney undertook his ill-fated cavalry assault upon the Allied lines. However, computers are not without their weaknesses. Although they do not suffer from pain, flu or fatigue, they do on occasion suffer from viruses and bugs.

Another important element of command in which AI should perform well is familiarity with the terrain. This knowledge could include a familiarity with the ground from any conceivable angle, and the ability to calculate lines of sight. Knowledge of the terrain could be pre-programmed from images collected by satellite and other reconnaissance assets, and could be updated during the battle. Terrain analysis is an area in which computing power already has a role. For example, the 'Athene' system, in use with the French Army, already automates tasks such as terrain analysis.[62] Hazlett postulates that GPS-based 'Automated Terrain Assessment' could perform functions such as the identification of likely choke points.[63] However, the utilisation of computer-based terrain analysis does not facilitate the final subjugation of this source of friction. It has already been noted that Slim warned that the effects of terrain could not be fully known until one is in it. Such advice is not just the musings of a historical figure from a bygone era. In 1991, de la Billiere was just as conscious of this problem, and felt compelled to drive upon the desert terrain on which his forces would operate in order to have a fuller understanding of its effects.[64] Also, physical geography is not necessarily a static phenomenon. Winters makes the important point that geography can change rapidly. A notable example of this is Burnside's aforementioned 'mud march'.

Finally, AI has a particular advantage when it comes to the question of the moral courage required to bear the responsibility of command. The asset of moral courage is regarded by many a writer and practitioner alike as a requisite characteristic for a commander.[65] This is a quality that U. S. Grant is said to have possessed in abundance. It is said that he took decisions easily and without a great deal of agonising.[66] There can be no finer example of an act of moral courage than Arthur 'Bomber' Harris'

'Millennium' raid against Cologne in May 1942. In an effort to prove the value of Bomber Command, Harris brought together virtually his entire bomber force, including reserves, in one attack. This was at a time when Bomber Command was taking significant losses on most big raids. The Official History describes the risks involved: 'such a bold action might produce a great triumph, but, if anything went wrong, the disaster might well be irremediable'.[67] John Terraine's assessment of this decision is undoubtedly correct: 'Harris' calm, deliberate decision to stake his whole force and its future, on the night of May 30/31, showed the true quality of command.'[68] In contrast to these positive examples, some leaders fail to perform effectively under the stress of command. Grant's predecessor as Commanding Officer of Union forces, George B. McClellan, displayed ruinous levels of undue caution in the face of Confederate forces at Manassas despite having a significant superiority in numbers. James McPherson comments: 'Military success could be achieved only by taking risks; McClellan seemed to shrink from the prospect. He lacked the mental and moral courage required of great generals.'[69] In the sixteenth century, Philip II's self-imposed burden of responsibility led him to adopt a style of command that proved to be unmanageable. The argument in favour of AI is that not all human commanders will be as blessed as Grant and Harris in the sphere of moral courage. Therefore, AI eliminates this potential limitation in a commander's abilities. Arguably, AI would not suffer from the opposite human failing of overconfidence. This is an attribute that both Hitler and Napoleon exhibited, and which contributed to their eventual downfall. Arrogance and pride are not problems associated with computers.

There are clearly a number of reasons to suggest that AI rather than humans could conduct certain aspects of command more effectively. Yet, understandably the prospect of handing the command of our armed forces over to computer software programs may seem a fanciful, alien and uncomfortable thought. However, as van Creveld notes, some decision making has already been automated. This is particularly true at the technical level of warfare in areas such as anti-missile operations.[70] As warfare in the information age comes to rely more directly upon information, as it takes place in an increasingly extended battlespace and as the tempo of operations increases significantly, it may be time to spread the automation of decision making further up the levels of war. At the very least, AI may have to play a role as an aide to a human commander.[71] The digital imperative may prove to be a powerful force in the information age. However, there are some fundamental reasons why humans must retain their role in command.

War by its nature is an act in the service of policy.[72] It is this most basic of considerations that raises the first doubts concerning the role AI can play in the art of command. After all, politics is the realm of human inter- actions. Just as war will remain a human activity in the information age, so will politics. It is doubtful whether even highly developed AI would be able to understand the complexities and subtleties of politics, never mind the relationship between policy and the military instrument. Understanding how certain human political actors may respond in certain circumstances may be even more difficult for AI than it is for humans. An AI commander may make a decision which is correct at the tactical level, but which may be inappropriate at the strategic level. One possible method of keeping an AI commander operating within a politi- cal framework is through detailed and extensive rules of engagement (ROE). However, strategy is more complex and subtle than mere ROE. It is questionable whether an AI commander could be flexible enough, or sensitive enough to political considerations, within the varied and uncer- tain environment of war. Military forces are not merely units to be moved around a map, as Mao clearly recognised; they are also political actors.[73] Andy McNab, formerly of the Special Air Service (SAS), reveals an understanding of the relationship between tactical actions and strategic effects when he states: 'we're strategic troops'.[74] The implication of this statement is that the actions of the soldier have effects beyond the tacti- cal and operational arenas. Armed forces are strategic instruments that have an impact on the world of policy, and likewise are influenced by politics.

If we accept that warfare will continue to be characterised by Clausewitz's climate of war, and the man on the scene with a gun, then human attributes and considerations will remain crucial to the successful conduct of command. Although an AI commander will be unaffected by the pressures of battle command, this lack of emotion and the attendant empathy will prevent the same commander from being able to motivate the men it commands. Vegetius, who recognised the prominence of fear on the battlefield, saw the commander's role as critical in response to this: 'an army gains courage and fighting spirit from advice and encour- agement from their general'.[75] Montgomery also notes the significance of the relationship between the leader and the led; for him command is fundamentally about trust.[76] Although one can have great trust in the ability of AI to process information quickly and accurately, will soldiers trust their lives to the decisions of a CPU that can never share their same sense of humanity? Montgomery also stresses the need to address the humanity of the troops in a personal manner.[77] A computer is nothing if not impersonal. One of Alexander the Great's outstanding qualities was the management of his forces. Alexander would endeavour to ensure that his men were well fed and got the required rest. He also took the trouble to visit the wounded in person, often when he was wounded himself.[78] The fact that Alexander was wounded so often in battle is testament to his physical courage and the example he set to his men. At the risk of stating the obvious, an AI commander could never set such an example. Lieutenant-General Horrocks showed that an alternative morale booster was ensuring that the local nurses attended the twice-weekly dances in Tripoli during World War II.[79] The actions of these human commanders, and many like them, reveal a common appreciation of the humanity of the troops under their command. In essence, as Marshall notes, a commander cannot just concern himself with big operational and strategic manoeuvres; he must also deal with the welfare of his men.[80]

Staying with the human element of war, the command literature is awash with references to the need for a commander to meet with his troops face to face.[81] Marshall makes many references to this important aspect of command. In particular, he warns against the general becoming chained to communications technology, and thereby overlooking the value of his presence to the men. He postulates that men at the front gain confidence from the belief that a commander alongside them has a greater understanding of their tactical situation.[82] Being amongst his men provides other benefits for the commander. Marshall argues that information on morale is best gained first-hand from face-to-face contact with the men. In this respect 'there is no substitute for personal reconnaissance'.[83] For Slim, who regarded morale as the key to victory, explaining the rationale of an action to the men face to face, and in terms and language with which they could identify, was vital.[84] In Slim's judgment, the leadership function of command is essentially concerned with the projection of personality.[85] Personality can only really be transmitted through face-to-face communication, during which all of the nuances of human personality can be appreciated. The US Army, at the forefront of efforts to digitise forces, appears to be keeping this human element in mind. *FM 100-6 Information Operations* is undoubtedly correct when it posits that commanders 'will continue to inspire subordinates through face-to-face communications and physical presence'.[86] Brigadier-General Huba Wass de Czege identifies at least three functions which face-to-face communication fulfils: it helps ensure understanding; it allows the commander to gauge morale; and his presence contributes to the leadership role.[87] It has also been noted that putting the commander forward helps reduce uncertainty and the influence of friction.[88] An indication of how significant the presence of the commander is can be demonstrated by General Westmoreland's claim that he committed four out of every seven days to visiting his troops.[89]

When face-to-face contact is not possible, the means of communication chosen still take account of the projection of personality. To this end, forces engaged in Experimental Force (EXFOR), who had at their disposal the latest digital communication technology, often resorted to the use of radio since it enabled the transmission of more information because vocal communication includes tone, stress and nuance.[90] Video teleconferencing (VTC) has, to some degree, enabled a form of face-to-face contact at a distance. Indeed, VTC proved to be a useful tool in Kosovo because it could communicate the commander's intent without the need to gather together the senior officers. This was credited for shortening the decision-making cycle. However, General Clark's daily VTC was criticised because it 'made it extremely difficult for the senior leaders to develop a useful working relationship where they possessed the necessary trust and confidence to issue and execute "mission-type" orders without the need to provide detailed tactical guidance'.[91]

In order to motivate troops one must possess an understanding of the men in question. Major Deborah Reisweber notes that different subordinates require different motivating strategies on the part of the commander.[92] Similarly, Vegetius advises that a general should know the officers under him.[93] It is said that Napoleon displayed a remarkable degree of familiarity with the men under his command.[94] It is questionable whether an AI commander could appreciate and understand his subordinates' personalities. This is just one more example of how focus on AI commanders neglects the human dimension of war. In this sense, Huba Wass de Czege summarises well the limitations of command by AI: 'decision support information technologies can help present and organise information and predict factors in war that are based on the laws of physics, but they are unreliable predictors of moral factors – the human element'.[95] Through the process of evolutionary computing AI can have a great deal of knowledge and even experience of decision making, yet it can never possess the experience of managing men and the art of leadership in its human dimensions. For the many reasons outlined above, it appears that an inability to fulfil many of the internal responsibilities of command would reduce the efficacy of AI in such a role.

The security and wellbeing of a commander is obviously an important consideration. Humans are certainly fragile beings, and yet in many ways they are undoubtedly more robust than silicon-based commanders. Concerns that rightly worry the designers of digitised forces are issues relating to the security and integrity of information systems. Silicon-based systems are vulnerable to EMP and a host of information warfare attacks. Of course, measures can be taken to minimise the chance that information systems and AI-based command can be taken off-line. Yet, even in the face of protective measures, it would seem ill judged to place the burden of command on machines which can, and do, crash at times, or can produce catastrophic failures due to a few lines of incorrect code. A human commander can still function when his supporting silicon-based command structure has gone down. In such a contingency the human commander will be able to rely upon the valuable command assets of intuition and initiative.[96] Of course, intuition is another important human command trait that AI lacks.[97]

In light of the above discussion, it has to be concluded that humans must remain at the centre of command. However, the pressure of the digital imperative remains. As AI develops and becomes more available, those relying solely upon human commanders must fear losing the initiative to an AI foe. How can these two forces be reconciled? One answer would seem to be for humans to retain the final say in command decisions, but to supplement their capabilities with an AI aide.[98] In such an arrangement, AI could fulfil part of the role currently performed by the staff. An AI aide would interpret the mass of information on the modern battlefield, and then present possible courses of action (COA). Commenting upon current developments, including a 1999 experiment in which electronic agents were taught to critique COAs, Bowman, Tecuci and Boicu discuss the role of AI in the command process: 'The agent combines doctrine and tactics with lessons learned throughout military history. It does not replace the commander or make the commander's decisions; it provides concise, relevant and explainable information the commander can consider when making decisions.'[99] The human commander would retain the final say. He would provide the link of humanity to his forces, and also input judgments regarding human factors, such as estimates of morale, into the decision-making process. This arrangement of course creates a situation were decisions are made and acted upon more slowly than if left entirely to AI. However, the political and human dimensions of warfare dictate that humans must retain ultimate command of forces. As Brian Holden Reid accurately asserts, 'Staffs should provide ideas – that is what staffs are for. Yet having a good idea is no guarantee of success.'[100] Victory in war demands much more than good ideas.

In the long term a more developed method by which to garner the benefits of both AI and humans, and yet sacrificing less speed in decision making, may be human augmentation.[101] The direct link-up of humans and computers through silicon implants would supplement human mental capabilities, whilst still retaining the human commander to use his strengths, those of understanding and dealing with the human and political elements of war, and providing leadership. The requirement of trust should be retained by the fact that the final decision is still a human one. The prospect of human augmentation in the way described is obviously some way off, and may never be socially or ethically acceptable.[102] However, it is already occurring at one level with the connection of neural implants into the brains of Parkinson's disease sufferers.[103] It also presents an interesting frontier possibility. Both the 'AI aide' and 'human augmentation' routes recognise the limits of AI and human command, and compensate for these by bringing together the strengths of both into one command process.

However, even when considering just the decision-making function of command, the human and AI commanders should always complement each other. There should not be a strict division of labour in which the AI decides, and the human implements and provides leadership. Such a situation would rob human commanders of their ability to make decisions. Jomini warns of the dangers of a general carrying out someone else's plan. He suggests that those who have not devised a plan can never have a full understanding of it.[104] The human commander must continue to see himself as a decision maker, with the ability to modify or reject the advice of his aide. Failure to retain these abilities could create catastrophic problems should the silicon elements of command go down. Also, because uncertainty will never be removed from the battlespace, Stephen J. Kirin posits that a human commander's *coup d'œil* will enable him to continue to function and make decisions despite this ever-present feature of war.[105] This line of thinking is in direct contrast to the assertion that increasing levels of knowledge are leading to a situation where systematic decision making is eclipsing intuition.[106] Aside from the fact that uncertainty makes systematic decisions problematic, the RMA literature on command commits another error by ignoring the existence of an intelligent foe. Whereas a human commander's intuition may perceive or at least suspect enemy deception, AI may just simply accept the information being fed to it. Paul T. Harig correctly asserts that the intuition of the commander allows him to cut through an overabundance of information and analysis, and focus on feasible solutions. He also notes that too much reliance on hard data can stifle 'hunches' and the scope of different perspectives, in which case decision making may become sterile.[107] Again, we see how decision making includes intangible elements that AI cannot take account of.

HIERARCHIES AND NETWORKS: SHALL THE TWAIN MEET?

Although it has been concluded that AI will aid rather than replace the human commander, generalship by the individual is challenged by another element of the information age: the network. In order to perform proficiently a command process has to adapt to changed circumstances. Napoleon's command system and the organisation of his forces, particularly the corps system, was an adaptation to the level of information available, and to the size and dispersal of the forces he commanded.[108] Today, information technology is facilitating the greater development of networks. In theory, the main challenge posed to traditional concepts of command emanates from the inability of hierarchical command structures to deal effectively with opponents whose C^2 is based upon a network form of organisation.

The RMA literature suggests that a pure network possesses the following characteristics: all individuals are equal and autonomous, and all possible lines of communication can be used. A network has no single commander; rather it has multiple leaders, and decision making is conducted through consultative consensus building.[109] Such an organisational structure is said to be far more adaptive and flexible in the face of changing circumstances than a hierarchical command process.[110] This advantage is enabled by the fact that information and the corresponding decisions do not have to flow up and then down a hierarchical chain. The individual units operate within a common consensus-based vision, but within that unifying objective they are autonomous. In addition, the absence of a head or single decision maker, and the existence of many lines of information flow in theory make a network organisation far more robust and survivable. It is not vulnerable to decapitation, or to friction caused by the loss of communications.[111]

At first glance the network command structure does appear to present an attractive alternative to the hierarchy. Yet there are a number of problems and concerns connected to implementing such a structure into the environment of war. The first problem relates to the nature of humans. The notion of decision making by consensus is optimistic at best, and may in fact be no more than a utopian ideal. Attempting to achieve consensus amongst a group of humans, especially under the duress of a fast-moving battle, would in all likelihood prove a forlorn objective. Jomini actually comments on this dilemma by noting that decision making by consensus often tends towards the lowest common denominator, and therefore creates decisions which are devoid of risk.[112] Conceivably, attempts to reach a consensus could also slow down the decision-making process.

It is also important to remember some of the human qualities required for command. These include moral courage, cognitive complexity and a sufficient understanding of humanity. These traits are clearly not possessed by all.[113] Yet, the pure network structure appears to indirectly imply that everyone can possess these necessary command characteristics. To reiterate an earlier point, warfare will continue to be an activity characterised by men on the ground. Not all of these men will possess the qualities required for leadership and command. Conse-quently, they will need to be led, and this should act as an obstacle to the development of pure network command structures.

By its nature the network command structure is one in which decision making is highly decentralised. Although decentralisation of decision making is generally considered to be a useful command philosophy, decentralisation can be taken to unnecessary and ruinous extremes. Philip Katcher notes that at Gettysburg Jeb Stuart was given too much autonomy. This autonomy, combined with what William C. Davis describes as Jeb Stuart's natural desire for 'flash and dash', meant that his cavalry failed to make any impact upon the decisive battlefield.[114] Similarly, General Schwarzkopf has been criticised for giving his commanders too much leeway in the Gulf War. In particular, concerns have been raised over his 'penchant to allow each service to fight the war as it saw fit'.[115] Equally, the escape of much of the Iraqi Republican Guard is put down to the fact that Schwarzkopf failed to send his Third Army commander, Yeosock, to the front line to directly oversee the advance of XVIII and VII Corps. Gordon and Trainor contend that this was an inappropriate decision since Schwarzkopf knew that General Franks, commander of VII Corps, was known to lack an aggressive style.[116] This example not only highlights the dangers inherent in decentralisation, but in the case of Yeosock also reveals the value in having the commander at the front to supervise and inspire his subordinates. In light of these thoughts, the institutionalisation of a totally decentralised command process would seem inappropriate. Although decentralisation could become even more important in an information age battle, the whole enterprise must still be conducted within the framework of the commander's intent and vision. This vision, to reiterate a point, is the product of a complex cognitive process and the determination and leadership to see it through. A commander must retain the ability to intervene if required to keep everyone in pursuit of his intent. Although, of course, a commander must also be disciplined and resist the temptation to micromanage the battle.

The debate over command structures in the information age does not have to be a strict choice between the hierarchy and the network. In a comparable manner to that in which AI and human commanders can complement each other, so there exists a possible compromise that draws upon the strengths of both hierarchies and networks. The result is a hybrid structure.[117] One such possibility is the 'command network'. The essential ingredients of the command network are: it retains a hierarchical structure, but there is a free flow of information horizontally or vertically, or information can jump echelons as the task at hand requires.

This flow of information enables a more flexible and quicker adaptation to events, because those who need the information can get it, and therefore those who are part of the decision-making process at any time, whatever echelon they are operating at, can retrieve the information they require. Whilst retaining the essence of a hierarchy, the command network is designed to be a flexible structure that changes form as required. The ethos of this particular command structure follows the theory of 'command by negation', in which the higher commanders only intervene when necessary. However, decisions are made in a hierarchical framework due to time pressures.[118] Both van Creveld and Rosen concur on the point that centralised planning enables quicker decision making.[119] This latter point would seem to indicate that there is some disagreement over whether a network or a hierarchy can produce quicker decisions.[120] As is often the case, the answer to this particular quandary may lie somewhere in the middle. The command network, working through a system characterised by the free flow of information and decentralisation of decision making, but retaining the basic hierarchical ethos, can facilitate a process in which decisions are made at the appropriate level. To function correctly such a system relies upon a clear common doctrine of command, and disciplined commanders who are prepared to command by negation.

Those familiar with military history will note that the ethos of the command network has familiar elements to it. Decentralisation of decision making, operating within a commander's broad vision, has been the hallmark of many successful command methods of the past. In particular, both sides in World War I operated such a system later in the war.[121] This command culture is also at the heart of the doctrine of 'Maneuver Warfare' and 'mission tactics'.[122] However, the information age does present some opportunities for change and improvement on this traditional system. The free flow of information potentially empowers lower echelons, and allows them to ensure that their local initiatives stay co-ordinated within the overall effort. A more direct information-sharing relationship between the higher and lower levels of command may induce other changes, including the removal of some of the middle echelons of the command structure.[123]

CONCLUSION

Technological (AI) and organisational (networks) developments of the information age, as well as the character of future war, suggest that command as it is practised today may have to adapt. Certainly, the digital imperative could lead to an increased use of AI as a significant aide to the human commander.[124] However, despite these coming developments, command will still retain many of its essential attributes from the past. Warfare and therefore command will remain essentially human and political activities. In this context, the presence of humans in the art of command, and in particular the requirements for leadership and strategic judgment, will ensure that the future will not be without great individual figures to whom the title 'genius' is attributed. *Warfighting* persuasively argues, 'our philosophy of command must be based on human characteristics rather than on equipment and procedures'.[125] Leaving humans as the primary actors in command will also help insure against possible failures of network information systems or silicon-based commanders. A human commander will still be able to rely upon his initiative and intuition even in the absence, or overabundance, of information.[126] The USMC's doctrine manual *Warfighting* has identified an appropriate balance between humans and computers in the functions of command: 'where judgment is needed you need people; where the rapid retrieval and manipulation of data is needed, you need computers'.[127] Greater transparency in the battlespace may enable more effective C^2 of troops, but it will not ensure inspired leadership.[128]

The RMA literature concerned with command tends to make the same error as that which comments on operations more generally: too much emphasis and expectation is placed upon increased levels of information. This is typified by Leonhard's assertion that command is all about information flow, and that this alone should dictate who makes the decision.[129] As this chapter has argued, command is concerned with much more than simply having the right information. Much of the RMA literature on command regards more information as a panacea for the difficulties of dealing with uncertainty. Greater knowledge can undoubtedly help a commander, but it cannot eliminate uncertainty or guarantee success. In fact, Marshall warns that the desire for more information has often overburdened commanders at the lower echelons.[130] You must be careful what you wish for.

This chapter has concentrated primarily upon battle command. Other military activities, such as those that fall under the rubric of irregular wars and military operations other than war (MOOTW), may well require an even greater degree of human involvement in the art of command. In such operations the political component is often more immediately prominent, and consequently the situation may be far more sensitive.[131] Likewise, a commander may have to consider the human dimension not only in relation to his troops, but conceivably with regard to a civilian population as well.[132] And as the War for Iraq revealed, even during modern regular warfare commanders have to concern themselves with the wellbeing of civilians within the theatre of operations. In Iraq, this ranged from ensuring low civilian casualties to organising and protecting humanitarian aid. In the aftermath of military victory commanders have acquired a role in providing security and rebuilding damaged infrastructure. These roles, and many others, invariably include substantial interaction with the local population.

The increased flow of information will empower lower echelons and facilitate the adoption of a more network-based command structure. This fact, alongside the character of future war, can only enhance the requirement for decentralisation of decision making down to the lowest possible levels, but always operating within the broader vision of the commander. The many attributes required for conducting command effectively, such as the need for leadership, moral courage and cognitive complexity, mean that not everyone can command effectively. This leads to the conclusion that pure networks are ill suited to the demands of battle command. Somebody in the end will have to lead. However, the possibilities inherent in the network structure may enable the stripping away of intermediate echelons. Although the information age has provided the opportunity to exploit a range of developments in the act of command, the RMA literature is again guilty of overplaying their overall significance. In this respect, Arquilla and Ronfeldt's tendency to equate success with the use of certain command systems is an example of reductionism. In response, *Joint Vision 2020* bemoans an overemphasis on information superiority in C^2 at the expense of human factors such as the ability to apply judgment to a situation.[133] To reiterate, strategy is a multidimensional activity, and success requires competence in all of the dimensions.[134]

Keegan is undoubtedly correct when he claims that the requirements of command are different over time and between cultures.[135] This truism could facilitate a different approach to command in the information age. An AI commander could perform well in some aspects of the external functions of command. This relates especially to the requirement for speed in decision making. However, even in the external function of command AI faces some substantial challenges. Faced with acts of deception, as well as an inability to understand the traits of opposing generals, AI may struggle to produce appropriate decisions. Also, AI commanders can only ever be decision makers. An AI general would be rational, calm and able to make quick decisions, and could possess boundless energy. Yet, in the final analysis it is important to remember that good commanders of the past were never just decision makers. They were also, and perhaps more importantly, leaders. Leadership is a key attribute in the internal function of command. When assessing the potential of non-human commanders it is the internal functions that raise the main concerns. It is also important to remember that strategy is about many things aside from just what happens in the battlespace. As noted earlier, commanders have to consider post-conflict settlements during a campaign. This brings them into contact with issues relating to political, moral, legal, socio-economic and cultural factors.

Despite the changes that may characterise the information age, command in war will remain predominately an activity in which the human individual is paramount. The most succinct advice on the art of command once again comes from the USMC: 'our philosophy of command must be based on human characteristics, rather than on equipment or procedures'.[136] The art of command in the future must also reflect the nature of warfare. Therefore, the attributes that constitute a military genius will continue to represent the most important traits for command in the information age, because the nature of war itself will remain the same.

NOTES

1. Winston S. Churchill, quoted in M. Carver, 'Montgomery', in John Keegan (ed.), *Churchill's Generals* (London, Weidenfeld & Nicolson, 1991), p. 148
2. Quoted in Chandler, *The Campaigns of Napoleon*, p. 139.
3. Handel argues this very point when he suggests that the military genius is central to Clausewitz's theory of war because his temperament and intellect are the means with which to deal with the climate of war. See Handel, *Masters of War*, p. 153.
4. Gray, *Modern Strategy*, pp. 53, 108.
5. Martin van Creveld, *Command in War* (Cambridge, MA, Harvard University Press, 1985), p. 143.
6. T. N. Dupuy, *A Genius for War: The German Army and General Staff, 1807–1945* (London, MacDonald and Jane's, 1977), p. 307.
7. Clausewitz, *On War*, p. 115.
8. Ibid., Book One, Ch. Three.
9. De la Billiere, *Storm Command*.
10. See Sun Tzu, *The Art of War*, and Handel, *Masters of War*, p. 153. Despite his preference for a calculating commander, Handel notes that Sun Tzu's insistence on the need for speed and seizing the initiative also suggests that at times the commander must rely on his 'gut feelings'. Handel, *Masters of War*, p. 167.
11. Ferris and Handel, 'Clausewitz, Intelligence, Uncertainty and the Art of Command', p. 45.
12. AI is understood to be the ability for computers to perform many of the functions of the human brain. As noted by Michael Gruber, this could include the facility to solve problems with novel solutions, the ability to learn and the ability to show some common sense. Michael Gruber, 'In Search of the Electronic Brain', *Wired*, 5.05, May 1997, p. 144. David G. Stork posits that real AI is intelligence based on pattern recognition, insight and strategy. See David G. Stork, 'The End of an Era, the Beginning of Another? Hal, Deep Blue and Kasparov', www.chess.ibm.com/learn/html/e.8./c.html.
13. Leonhard, *The Principles of War for the Information Age*, p. 176.
14. Ferris and Handel, 'Clausewitz, Intelligence, Uncertainty and the Art of Command, pp. 44–5.
15. Martin van Creveld discusses how computers could perform the functions of the

human brain. See *Command in War*, p. 3.

16. Cohen, 'Technology and Warfare', p. 251.

17. Simson Garfinkel notes that we will have to wait 30 years for the big breakthroughs in AI. See Simson Garfinkel, '2001 Double Take', www.wired.com/wired/5.01/ features/ ffhal.html. Whereas Professor Paul Churchland, a professor of philosophy and a member of the cognitive science faculty at the University of California, postulates that, although there are neural networks which can already exceed humans in certain abilities, it could take 50 years for neural nets to achieve the capability to write symphonies, for example. Quoted in Max More, 'Thinking About Thinking', www.wired.com/ wired/4.12/features/churchland.html.

18. James F. Allen, *AI Growing Up: The Changes and Opportunities*, American Association for Artificial Intelligence, Winter 1998, www.aaai.org.

19. Gruber, 'In Search of the Electronic Brain', p. 144.

20. Sandy Fritz, 'Introduction', in Sandy Fritz (ed.), *Understanding Artificial Intelligence* (New York, Warner Books, 2002), p. 2.

21. Libicki and Shapiro, 'Conclusion', p. 442.

22. Ibid., p. 437.

23. Robotrader is the product of uploading the expertise of Christine Downton, a star financial analyst at Pareto Partners Ltd. See Clive Davidson, 'Christine Downton's Brain', www.wired.com/wired/4.12/esrobotrader.html.

24. This is of course a reference to the defeat of World Chess Champion Gary Kasparov by IBM's computer, Deep Blue, in May 1997.

25. Davidson, 'Christine Downton's Brain'.

26. Quoted in Craddock, 'Netwar and Peace in the Global Village', p. 226.

27. Arquilla and Ronfeldt, 'Cyberwar is Coming', p. 45.

28. Van Creveld, *Command in War*, p. 6.

29. *FM 100-6*, p. 4-1.

30. For an interesting assessment of the role information plays in the modern battlespace, see Ferris and Handel, 'Clausewitz, Intelligence, Uncertainty and the Art of Command'.

31. Campen, 'Introduction', p. 89.

32. Field Marshal Montgomery, *The Path to Leadership* (London, Collins, 1961), p. 10.

33. Quoted in Hartcup, *The Silent Revolution*, p. 79.

34. Martin C. Libicki, 'The Small and the Many', in John Arquilla and David Ronfeldt, *In Athena's Camp: Preparing for Conflict in the Information Age* (Santa Monica, CA, RAND, 1996), p. 210. See also James Hazlett, 'Just-in-Time Warfare', in Stuart E. Johnson and Martin C. Libicki (eds), *Dominant Battlespace Knowledge*, revised edition (Washington, DC, National Defense University, 1996).

35. Sun Tzu, *The Art of War*, trans. Griffith, p. 134.

36. Clausewitz, *On War*, p. 118. This characteristic is also identified by Edgar F. Puryear, Jr in *Nineteen Stars: A Study in Military Character and Leadership* (Novato, CA, Presidio, 1992), p. 396.

37. OODA stands for observation–orientation–decision–action.

38. Cebrowski, 'Network-Centric Warfare: An Emerging Military Response to the Information Age', p. 4.

39. Griffith, *Battle Tactics of the Western Front*, p. 175.

40. Hazlett, 'Just-in-Time Warfare', p. 116.

41. Col. Rolland A. Dessert, Jr, 'Mobile Strike Force: An Experiment in Future Battle Command', *Military Review*, 76, 4 (1996), p. 35. Blaker also concludes that RMA operational theory results in a higher tempo. See Blaker, *Understanding the Revolution in Military Affairs*, p. 23.

42. See Joint Chiefs of Staff, 'Joint Vision 2010', p. 41.

43. Cited in Van Riper and Scales, 'Preparing for War in the 21st Century', p. 9.
44. Sun Tzu, *The Art of War*, trans. Griffith, p. 136.
45. See 'Kasparov Down – But Not Out', www.chess.ibm.com/home/may11/story_2.html, and Jeff Kisseloff, 'Kasparov's Back Against the Wall', www.chess.ibm.com/home/may10/story_3.html.
46. Stork, 'The End of an Era'.
47. Major Linda C. Jantzen, 'Taking Charge of Technology', *Military Review*, 81, 2 (2001), p. 76.
48. Ray Kurzweil, 'The Coming Merging of Mind and Machine', in Sandy Fritz (ed.), *Understanding Artificial Intelligence* (New York, Warner Books, 2002), p. 94.
49. Aaron Sloman, 'What is Artificial Intelligence?', www.cs.bham.ac.uk/~axs/misc/aiforschools.html.
50. David B. Leake, 'Artificial Intelligence', *Van Nostrand Scientific Encyclopedia* (New York, Wiley, 2002), www.cs.indiana.edu/~leake/papers/p-01-07/p-01-07.html.
51. Brigadier-General Huba Wass de Czege, 'Mobile Strike Force: A 2010 Potential Force', *Military Review*, 76, 4 (1996), p. 72.
52. General William C. Westmoreland, *A Soldier Reports* (New York, Doubleday, 1976), p. 271.
53. This is the advice of Field Marshal Montgomery, who in turn reports that both Napoleon and Machiavelli gave the same counsel. Montgomery, *The Path to Leadership*, p. 28.
54. Westmoreland, *A Soldier Reports*, p. 268.
55. Van Creveld, *Command in War*, p. 97.
56. Fitzsimonds, 'The Coming Military Revolution', p. 33.
57. Dessert, 'Mobile Strike Force', p. 36.
58. Joint Chiefs of Staff, 'Joint Vision 2010', p. 41.
59. Philip Katcher claims that Robert E. Lee's physical ailments left him in significant discomfort, which must have affected his thinking and command performance. Philip Katcher, *The Army of Robert E. Lee* (London, Arms & Armour Press, 1996), pp. 22–3. Rommel also suffered throughout his military career with a severe stomach upset. David Fraser, *Knight's Cross: A Life of Field Marshal Erwin Rommel* (London, HarperCollins, 1994), p. 27. It is impossible to estimate just how severely these afflictions affected the ability of Lee and Rommel. Even though they both performed well in spite of their ailments, it must be assumed that illness reduces the capabilities of a commander to some degree.
60. Lt-Col. Michael Bowman, Gheorghe Tecuci and Mihai Boicu, 'Intelligent Agents in the Command Post', *Military Review*, 81, 2 (2001), p. 46.
61. Kipp and Grau, 'The Fog and Friction of Technology', p. 89.
62. 'Athene Will Put Canadian Army in Command', *Jane's Defence Weekly*, 29, 2, 4 March 1998, p. 7.
63. Hazlett, 'Just-in-Time Warfare', pp. 126–7.
64. De la Billiere, *Storm Command*.
65. For example, see Clausewitz, *On War*, Book One, Ch. Three, Field Marshal Sir William Slim, *Courage and Other Broadcasts* (London, Cassell, 1957), p. 5, and Puryear, *Nineteen Stars*, p. 394.
66. Holden Reid, 'Enduring Patterns in Modern Warfare', p. 28.
67. Quoted in John Terraine, *The Right of the Line: The Royal Air Force in the European War 1939–1945* (Sevenoaks, Sceptre, 1988), p. 484.
68. Ibid., p. 485.
69. James E. McPherson, *Battle Cry of Freedom: The American Civil War* (London, Penguin, 1990), p. 365.
70. Van Creveld, *Command in War*, p. 2.

71. For comments on the role staffs play see Holden Reid, 'Enduring Patterns in Modern Warfare', p. 28 and Vegetius, *Vegetius*, p. 80.
72. Van Creveld, *Command in War*, pp. 186–7.
73. Mao, *Selected Military Writings*.
74. Andy McNab, *Bravo Two Zero* (London, BCA, 1993), p. 8.
75. Vegetius, *Vegetius*, p. 87. Commenting on General Robert Eichelberger, who commanded US forces in New Guinea in 1942, Rosen states: 'Eichelberger himself was always at the front lines, and his example inspired his men.' Stephen P. Rosen, *Winning the Next War: Innovation and the Modern Military* (Ithaca, NY, Cornell University Press ,1991), p. 32.
76. Montgomery, *The Path to Leadership*, p. 9. Likewise, General Frederick M. Franks, Jr, who commanded VII Corps in the 1991 Gulf War, notes that 'Trust, I believe, is the basic bond of leadership.' See General Frederick M. Franks, Jr, 'Battle Command: A Commander's Perspective', *Military Review*, 76, 3 (1996), p. 4.
77. Montgomery, *The Path to Leadership*, p. 18.
78. John Keegan, *The Mask of Command* (London, Penguin, 1988), p. 46.
79. Alan Shepperd, 'Horrocks', in John Keegan (ed.), *Churchill's Generals* (London, Weidenfeld & Nicolson, 1991), p. 236.
80. Marshall, *Men Against Fire*, p. 190.
81. See Puryear, *Nineteen Stars*, p. 401, and Bruce C. Clarke, 'Leadership, Commandership, Planning, and Success', p. 7.
82. Marshall, *Men Against Fire*, pp. 102, 105.
83. Ibid., p. 104, and quote taken from p. 95.
84. Slim, *Courage*, pp. 19–20.
85. Ibid., p. 38. Maj. Scott F. Murray correctly notes that leadership is concerned with the human dimension. See Maj. Scott F. Murray, 'Battle Command, Decisionmaking, and the Battlefield Panopticon', *Military Review*, 82, 4 (2002), p. 51.
86. Captain Joseph S. McLamb, 'The Future of Mission Orders', *Military Review*, 77, 5 (1997), p. 73.
87. Wass de Czege, 'Mobile Strike Force', p. 73.
88. Hayden, *Warfighting*, p. 171.
89. Westmoreland, *A Soldier Reports*, p. 269.
90. Adams, *The Next World War*, p. 114.
91. Wight, quoted in Lambeth, *NATO's Air War for Kosovo*, p. 217.
92. Major Deborah Reisweber, 'Battle Command: Will We Have It When We Need It?', *Military Review*, 77, 5 (1997), p. 57.
93. Vegetius, *Vegetius*, p. 83.
94. Van Creveld, *Command in War*, p. 64.
95. Wass de Czege, 'Mobile Strike Force', p. 74.
96. Paul T. Harig, 'The Digital General: Reflections on Leadership in the Post-Information Age', *Parameters*, 26, 3 (1996), pp. 138–9.
97. Kipp and Grau, 'The Fog and Friction of Technology', p. 89.
98. Holden Reid, 'Enduring Patterns in Modern Warfare', p. 28.
99. Bowman, Tecuci and Boicu, 'Intelligent Agents in the Command Post', pp. 46–7, 52.
100. Holden Reid, 'Enduring Patterns in Modern Warfare', p. 28.
101. Denning, *Information Warfare and Security*, p. 16.
102. Although understandably a controversial issue, human augmentation in the manner described is not beyond the realms of possibility. Paul Churchland is of the opinion that the future will bring the implantation of computers – 'synthetic neurons' – into brains, either to replace damaged brain tissue, or to augment the functions of the brain. See More, 'Thinking About Thinking'. Alvin and Heidi Toffler note that ethical dilemmas will only delay the progress towards a direct link between silicon

chips and the human nervous system. See Alvin and Heidi Toffler, 'The Discontinuous Future: A Bold but Overoptimistic Forecast', Review Essay, *Foreign Affairs*, 77, 2, (1998), p. 139.

103. Kurzweil, 'The Coming Merging of Mind and Machine', p. 91.
104. Jomini, *The Art of War*, p. 58.
105. Kirin, 'Synchronisation', p. 19.
106. See Harig, 'The Digital General', p. 138.
107. Ibid., pp. 138–9.
108. Van Creveld, *Command in War*, p. 72.
109. Arquilla and Ronfeldt, *The Advent of Netwar*, p. 45.
110. Sean J. A. Edwards, *Swarming on the Battlefield* (Santa Monica, CA, RAND, 2000), p. xvii.
111. See Bodnar and Dengler, 'The Emergence of the Command Network', pp. 93–107, Arquilla and Ronfeldt, *The Advent of Netwar* and Edwards, *Swarming on the Battlefield*, p. 74.
112. Handel, *Masters of War*, p. 155. This view is shared by Bruce C. Clarke, 'Leadership, Commandership, Planning, and Success', p. 2.
113. Reisweber highlights the challenge of cognitive complexity in the art of command. See Reisweber, 'Battle Command', pp. 50–1.
114. See Katcher, *The Army of Robert E. Lee*, p. 26, and William C. Davis, *The American Civil War: A Historical Account of America's War of Secession* (London, Salamander, 1996), p. 401.
115. Gordon and Trainor, *The Generals' War*, p. 74.
116. Ibid., p. 431.
117. For a discussion of hybrid command structures see Arquilla and Ronfeldt, 'Looking Ahead: Preparing for Information-Age Conflict', pp. 439–501. Indeed, Arquilla and Ronfeldt suggest that success in future war will depend on learning to interlace hierarchical and network principles. See 'Cyberwar is Coming', p. 27. See also *FM 100-6*, pp. 1–12.
118. The concept of the command network is developed in Bodnar and Dengler, 'The Emergence of the Command Network'.
119. Van Creveld, *Command in War*, p. 98, and Rosen, *Winning the Next War*, p. 39.
120. Westmoreland makes reference to sluggishness of information transfer at times in the hierarchical command chain. Westmoreland, *A Soldier Reports*, p. 269.
121. See Griffith, *Battle Tactics of the Western Front*, and Charles Messenger, *The Art of Blitzkrieg*, Second Edition (London, Ian Allan, 1991), Ch. 1 'Origins'.
122. Hayden, *Warfighting*, pp. 68–9.
123. See 1st Lieutenant Gary A. Vincent, 'A New Approach to Command and Control: The Cybernetic Design', www.cdsar.af.mil/apj/vincent.html. This is a point also made by Arquilla and Ronfeldt in 'Looking Ahead', p. 463.
124. See *FM 100-6*, pp. 1–5.
125. Hayden, *Warfighting*, p. 69.
126. Marshall, *Men Against Fire*, p. 93.
127. Hayden, *Warfighting*, p. 191.
128. *FM 100-6*, pp. 1–14.
129. Leonhard, *The Principles of War for the Information Age*, p. 201.
130. Marshall, *Men Against Fire*, p. 93.
131. Gray, *Modern Strategy*, p. 284.
132. Mao was acutely aware of the need for his troops to treat the local populace with respect.
133. *Joint Vision 2020*, pp. 37–8.
134. Gray, *Modern Strategy*.

135. Keegan, *The Mask of Command*, p. 1.
136. Hayden, *Warfighting*, p. 69.

4

How Strategic is Strategic Information Warfare?

'Our security, economy, way of life, and perhaps even survival, are now dependent on the interrelated trio of electrical energy, communications, and computers.'[1]

INTRODUCTION

Potentially the biggest change to the existing character of warfare, and therefore also the most substantial challenge to the nature of war, is provided by Strategic Information Warfare (SIW). The ability to conclude wars by attacking the National Information Infrastructure (NII) of an enemy through cyberspace would seem to question significant aspects of the nature of warfare as outlined in Chapter 1. Like strategic bombing, SIW seeks to bypass enemy surface forces to strike directly at the perceived centre of gravity. However, whereas airpower still works through the application of destructive firepower and physical force, SIW primarily operates through such non-violent means as 'malicious software' and electromagnetic pulses.[2] In this sense, SIW does not constitute an act of physical violence, nor does it involve any real degree of physical exertion. Although destruction can be the final result of SIW, for example by causing plane crashes through the disruption of air traffic control systems, the instrumental aim of SIW is more often than not to create strategic effect via disruption rather than destruction.[3]

As the opening quotation of this chapter reveals, critical importance is being attached to the security of the NII. The potential vulnerability of the NII to SIW has stimulated much literature and speculation. However, from a strategic perspective merely identifying vulnerability is not enough. As Gray notes: 'The strategic thinker must ask "So what?" and "How?" when presented ... [with] the latest wonder weapon.'[4] SIW will only substantially change the nature of warfare if it proves to be independently strategically effective. As Robert A. Pape notes in relation to coercive air campaigns, measuring success 'is not about assessing *combat* effectiveness but *strategic* effectiveness'.[5] In this respect, Wylie rightly criticises strategic bombing theory for assuming that destruction equals 'control'.[6] If SIW does not prove to have independent strategic decisiveness, then other more conventional (physical and violent) forms of warfare will maintain their role. That being the case, the traditional nature of warfare will remain. However, the fact that SIW exists at all may call for some revision of our perspective on the nature of war. Consequently, when trying to assess whether SIW will change the nature of war, the question that acts as the title of this chapter is central. To restate, 'How strategic is strategic information warfare?'

To answer the above question, this chapter will first define the term 'strategic'. Like 'nature', strategic is a term that is often misused or used loosely in the literature. From this foundation the chapter will proceed to establish what constitutes SIW. This will include an outline of its perceived potential, the various weapons and methods for waging it, target sets and any other pertinent features of this method of warfare. The most glaring problem to be faced when assessing the strategic efficacy of SIW is the absence of any historical examples of a comprehensive campaign. In and of itself this is problematic for SIW as a theory of victory. Greg Rattray raises a salient question when he asks in relation to Kosovo, 'Why did the Serbs not attempt to wage a major strategic information warfare campaign against the United States? Other factors besides the presence of new technological tools must be affecting the perceived utility of strategic information warfare.'[7] This question becomes more pertinent with each conflict that passes without the appearance of SIW. Neither Saddam Hussein's regime nor any of its allies launched an SIW campaign against the United States or the United Kingdom, even when faced with invasion and overthrow.[8] The history books are not completely vacuous of incidents though. There is a substantial history of hacker activities, as well as examples of the insertion of viruses or worms into systems, while exercises such as 'Eligible Receiver' provide us with some sense of the potential of SIW.[9] However, the absence of a comprehensive SIW campaign means that, as a strategic instrument, SIW is untested. One way to overcome this problem is to use the theory and practice of strategic bombing as an instructive case. Such a comparison is justifiable on the grounds that the theory, objectives and target sets of the two forms of warfare are very similar. In 1963 Noble Frankland noted that the British strategic bombing offensive against Nazi Germany was the logical successor to naval blockade.[10] It may be the case that SIW proves to be the next evolutionary step in strategic warfare, and thereby serves as the successor to strategic bombing.[11] In order to facilitate this comparative approach the theory behind strategic bombing will be presented to reveal the similarities with SIW. From this, a brief history of strategic bombing will show how it has thus far failed to act as an independent war-winning strategic instrument. At this juncture, it is worth noting that the vulnerability of societies to strategic bombing has often been overestimated.[12] Even if vulnerability to physical destruction exists, as in the case of Japanese cities to US incendiary attacks in World War II, this vulnerability does not necessarily translate into strategic success. A number of reasons are presented that have reduced the efficacy of strategic bombing. The chapter will then examine whether the factors that have plagued strategic air campaigns will likewise negatively affect SIW, and to what degree they will reduce its strategic efficacy. Of course, SIW is a distinct method of waging war, and therefore it has a number of unique characteristics. Again, these characteristics will be assessed in order to determine whether they reduce or increase the strategic efficacy of this method of waging war.

'STRATEGIC' ERRORS

The following statement by Colonel John A. Warden well illustrates the tendency to misuse the term 'strategic': 'strategic warfare is a different animal than the warfare we have known throughout history'.[13] All warfare, past, present or future, has strategic effect, meaning that the war is merely a *means* to a policy *end*. Mark J. Conversino's article 'The Changed Nature of Strategic Air Attack' illustrates some of the confusion surrounding this issue. Conversino correctly notes that 'strategic' should not be applied, as is often the case, merely on the basis of a weapon's range or the nature of its intended targets. Instead, Conversino offers the following definition of strategic attack:

> The offensive employment of airpower assets to allow the joint force to achieve a decision with minimum contact between opposing military forces, by striking targets that most generally and directly relate to the opponent's ability to maintain military forces in the field as well as his will to resist.[14]

With this interpretation Conversino has correctly moved a considerable distance from some strategic bombing advocates who would not apply the term 'strategic' to attacks against enemy military forces. Rather, they would reserve the term for attacks against enemy centres of gravity within the inner rings of Warden's five-ring model. These inner rings comprise leadership, organic essentials, infrastructure and population.[15] However, the above definition still clings to the notion that strategic attacks are somehow more direct in their application than other forms of attack. Whereas, in fact, a British infantryman attempting to break through German trenches at Neuve Chapelle on 10 March 1915 is still undertaking a strategic attack. His efforts may not be as immediately decisive as other actions, yet he still represents a *means* to an *end*. More direct routes to victory are no more strategic than less direct ones; perhaps they just represent better strategy. Although, as Vegetius notes, in certain circumstances a protracted route to victory can serve as the most appropriate strategy.[16] For example, it can be argued that a more direct North Vietnamese strategy would have been counterproductive during much of the United States' involvement in Vietnam. An overt invasion of South Vietnam would have constituted a clear violation of the Geneva Accords, which conceivably could have solidified US and Western opinion against the North. Had this occurred during the early period of the United States' involvement, the United States' resolve may have proved more robust. Furthermore, a more direct conventional attack would have played to the strengths of US forces and doctrine.

If, as is argued above, 'strategic' refers to all military instruments that serve as means to a policy end, why do certain forms of warfare, such as strategic bombing and SIW, have 'strategic' as an integral part of their designation? In the case of strategic bombing, and potentially in reference to SIW, 'strategic' is used to imply a direct and independent relationship between the means and ends. For example, in reference to strategic airpower, Billy Mitchell, one of the three great theorists of the interwar period (the other two being Giulio Douhet and Hugh Trenchard), was explicit about the independent potential of airpower: 'The old theory that victory meant the destruction of the hostile main army, is untenable. Armies themselves can be disregarded by air power if a rapid strike is made against the opposing centers.'[17] In a similar vein, Douhet predicted that airpower could 'strike mortal blows into the heart of the enemy'.[18] Although such uses of the term 'strategic' as above are inappropriate, this chapter will test the strategic efficacy of SIW on its own terms, namely that it can be independently decisive.[19]

WHAT IS STRATEGIC INFORMATION WARFARE?

Before analysing the potential strategic potency of SIW, it will prove profitable to examine its characteristics. Within the academic literature, government circles and the media, the existence of SIW as a distinct method of waging war has been increasingly legitimised.[20] In the wake of a series of RAND war-gaming exercises, Molander *et al.* were emphatic that SIW should be taken seriously as a strategic concern: 'new strategic threats and new strategic vulnerabilities surface. It is increasingly clear

... that the evolution in strategic warfare will include a dimension of cyberspace threats and vulnerabilities worthy of the label "strategic information warfare".[21] This sentiment is echoed in James Adams' book *The Next World War: The Warriors and Weapons of the New Battlefields in Cyberspace*, in which he declares that SIW could inflict 'strategic' damage on the United States.[22] Just as starkly, Kenneth A. Minihan, the then Director of the National Security Agency, states: 'Dependency on IT has become a clear and compelling threat to our economic well-being, our public safety, and our national security.'[23] At the governmental level, aside from the concern expressed via the creation and findings of the President's Commission on Critical Infrastructure Protection (PCCIP), a number of organisations have been formed to cope with this threat. In the wake of 9/11, these organisations have been consolidated within the 'Information Analysis and Infrastructure Protection' division of the Department of Homeland Security. In October 2001, President Bush signed Executive Order 13231 that established the 'President's Infrastructure Protection Board' to co-ordinate efforts to protect critical infrastructures.[24] Concern over SIW is not restricted to the United States. In March 2001, Robin Cook (then British Foreign Secretary) told the House of Commons: 'A computer-based attack could cripple the nation more quickly than a military strike.'[25] Other countries, such as China, have also expressed concern at the prospect of being attacked with SIW.[26]

There is a considerable body of evidence that justifies the identification of SIW as a new means of waging war. It has been estimated that as far back as 1995 (which is a considerable passage of time in the world of computers, and especially in reference to the development of cyberspace), the Department of Defense's computers were subject to approximately 250,000 hacker attacks in that year. Such figures only represent those attacks that are detected and reported. The actual number of attacks is likely to be significantly greater. A General Accounting Office (GAO) report declared that these attacks could pose a serious threat to the national security of the United States.[27] Exercises designed to simulate an SIW attack have produced some significant results that would seem to tally with the GAO's conclusions. For example, during the June 1997 exercise 'Eligible Receiver', National Security Agency (NSA) computer specialists launched an attack against Pentagon computers, and allegedly could have shut down the C^2 structure of Pacific Command, as well as the entire electrical infrastructure and air traffic control systems of the United States. During 'Eligible Receiver' military logistic operations were also disrupted.[28] Importantly, not only are offensive techniques well established; defensive weaknesses are evident in the critical infrastructures. A 2002 GAO report noted that US federal organisations 'continue to show significant weaknesses that put critical federal operations and assets at risk'.[29] Whilst certain loopholes may be closed, Denning offers a sobering thought, 'There is no silver bullet against information warfare attacks.'[30]

There is also increasing evidence that SIW capabilities can be and are being acquired. The aforementioned GAO report indicates that over 120 countries are developing computer attack capabilities. Likewise, the NSA reports that potential adversaries of the United States are collecting intelligence on US systems and the methods required to attack them.[31] Chinese information warfare theorists have called for the development of a cyber variant of People's War called 'take home battle', in which citizens attack enemy information systems from home using laptops.[32] The proliferation of SIW capabilities is possibly unique, in that the hardware and software required to wage it are readily available, even to individuals.[33] In fact, evidence was found at al Qaeda camps in Afghanistan that the group had gathered information on computerised water systems.[34] A computer is the epitome of dual-use technology, and the software and techniques required are widely available on the Internet.[35] These facts have led Adams to declare that the 'Hacker Chronicles', a CD-ROM of hacker tools and information, is a weapon of war.[36] Winn Schwartau concludes: 'the informed reader now can assume capability'.[37]

The techniques and weapons of SIW are quite varied.[38] They include various forms of 'malicious software', including viruses (which themselves include polymorphic viruses which change appearance in order to complicate the job of anti-viral software), logic bombs and trojan horses. Alternatively, one may wish to resort to 'chipping', or a 'denial of service' attack by flooding an enemy system with e-mail. There is also the increasing threat of EMP devices. Carlo Kopp has described these weapons as the nuclear weapons of the information age in reference to the enormous and wide-scale damage they can inflict on electrical systems. Kopp notes that commercial networked computer systems are particularly vulnerable to this form of attack.[39] SIW techniques can be quite varied and indirect. For example, Adams notes how one might attack the computers underpinning the Stock Exchange by manipulating the air conditioning within the building and thereby create enough heat to impair the functions of the computers.[40]

Like the techniques and tools for waging SIW, the target sets are also varied. The PCCIP categorises five main target sets. These are information and communications; banking and finance; energy and power production; physical distribution; and vital human services.[41] Central to the scale of vulnerability is, as Molander et al. suggest, that post-industrial societies rely upon interconnected network control systems.[42] In this vein,

Frank J. Cilluffo and Curt H. Gergely postulate that 'virtually every facet of an industrial nation's existence depends upon a functioning telecommunications system and the interconnected, networked information systems'.[43] Often highlighted as a key target and vulnerability is the public switched network (PSN).[44] As will be shown later, the overlap in some of these target sets with those of strategic bombing is both evident and quite significant, as is the identification of key node targets such as the PSN. Just as apparent in both methods of waging war is an emphasis placed upon the interconnectedness of modern societies and economies.

There does appear to be enough evidence to support the notion that SIW does indeed constitute a new method of waging war. The capability evidently exists. This has led some commentators to make extravagant pronouncements concerning the strategic impact of SIW. The US Joint Chiefs of Staff (JCS) proclaimed in 1996 that the convergence of vulnerable information infrastructures with traditional critical infrastructures had resulted in a 'tunnel of vulnerability previously unrealised in the history of conflict'.[45] It is interesting to note, in relation to strategic bombing, that in the eyes of the JCS the addition of information infrastructures takes us beyond the vulnerability of strategic bombing theory. Timothy L. Thomas is also guilty of making extraordinary claims concerning the potential of SIW when he claims that the consequences of an attack are comparable to those of a nuclear weapon, but without the physical destruction.[46] Robert L. Ayers, chief at the Centre for Information Systems Security, DISA, concludes, 'we are not prepared for an electronic Pearl Harbor'.[47] Finally, and perhaps most interestingly, a Joint DoD–DCI Security Commission claimed: 'This technology is capable of deciding the outcome of geopolitical crises without the firing of a single weapon.'[48] This last statement in particular may be guilty of equating operational capability with direct and independent strategic effect. As the following section on strategic bombing will show, this link is far from guaranteed.

SIW: RESURRECTING AN OLD FACE OF WAR

The old face of war in question is strategic bombing. Before giving a brief history of strategic bombing, and the many reasons why it has failed to reach the dizzy heights set by some of its proponents, the theory of strategic airpower will be outlined to reveal the similarities between it and SIW.

In the words of John Pimlott, at its simplest strategic bombing is 'the aerial bombardment of the enemy's homeland, hitting industrial and civilian targets in hope of destroying the capacity and willingness to wage war'.[49] Herein lies the core similarity between the two forms of warfare: both rest their hopes of victory on destroying either the will or capability of the enemy to continue fighting by attacking his homeland.[50] In conventional bombing the will of enemy populations is designed to be broken by the death and destruction wrought by high explosives (HE) and incendiary devices. In SIW, it is envisaged that modern information age societies will capitulate once their power-generating systems, banking and finance, food distribution, and air traffic control systems, to name just four targets, cease to function. The potency of SIW rests heavily upon the interconnectedness of information age networked societies. A similar focus can be found in much of strategic bombing theory. For example, in 1938 at the United States' Air Corps Tactical School (ACTS), the 'Air Force' text read:

> the economic structure of a modern highly industrialised nation is characterised by the great degree of interdependence of its various elements. Certain of these elements are vital to the continued functioning of the modern nation. If one of these elements is destroyed the whole of the economic machine ceases to function ...[51]

This notion became known as the 'industrial web' theory.[52] As previously noted, in the information age the key node is often identified as the PSN, whereas in strategic bombing theory the critical target may be oil, transportation or electricity. This belief that certain key nodes exist, and that their destruction will have catastrophic effects on the whole enemy system, is still central to modern airpower thinking. For example, in his article *The Enemy as a System*, John Warden stipulates that, unless very high stakes are involved, an enemy will capitulate when his power-generation system is destroyed or even put under sufficient pressure. For Warden, the more complex a system, the greater the vulnerability of its key nodes.[53] Therefore, we see not only that there exists a striking similarity between classical strategic bombing theory and SIW; contemporary airpower theory also shares similar notions. Indeed, Rattray makes the comparison between SIW and the modern airpower concept of 'parallel warfare'.[54]

Some of the SIW literature itself identifies these similarities. Douglas Waller draws comparisons between the bombing of cities such as Dresden and Tokyo and the methods of SIW. He proclaims that SIW may represent a refinement of the techniques used to destroy those cities.[55] When assessing the potential of an E-bomb attack, Kopp not only draws parallels with strategic airpower theory, but he also utilises Warden's five-ring model of the enemy state in his analysis.[56] Arquilla and Ronfeldt are even more explicit in drawing comparisons. They postulate: 'In many ways, IW in the coming years may resemble the early phases of aerial bombardment.'[57]

The literature on SIW often implies that it represents an independent war-winning instrument. This is also evident in much of strategic bombing theory. Of course, Gray is correct to note that judging airpower solely upon this criterion is inappropriate in that it fails to recognise the many roles airpower can play.[58] Nonetheless, it is a criterion established by some of the airpower theorists themselves. And, as the 1999 war against Yugoslavia reveals, some policy makers have also bought into this idea. In line with the ideas expressed in the writings of theorists such as Warden and Douhet, the practitioners of strategic bombing have expressed faith in airpower's independent war-winning ability. General Spaatz stated in 1945: 'In my opinion we can bring Japan to her knees by B-29 bombing before the ground troops or the navy ever land on the shores of the main island of Japan.'[59] Although it is true that Japan surrendered before an invasion of the main islands became necessary, as will be argued below it is debatable whether this was solely the result of the B-29s and the bomber offensive. Arthur 'Bomber' Harris shared Spaatz's optimism for an independent victory. Harris commented that 'the Lancaster force alone should be sufficient ... to produce in Germany by 1 April 1944 a state of devastation in which surrender is inevitable'.[60]

As the above discussion illustrates, a comparison between the theories of strategic bombing and SIW reveals a number of striking similarities. These include similar target sets, similar objectives, the potential for independent victory and in particular an emphasis on the vulnerability of interdependent societies and economies. Therefore, it will be instructive to analyse the history of strategic bombing as a guide to the potential strategic efficacy of SIW.

A HISTORY OF FAILURE

The 'failure' referred to is not the failure of airpower *per se*, nor is it the failure of strategic bombing to make significant contributions to a war effort. Clearly, both airpower in general and strategic bombing in particular have proved to be valuable strategic instruments. The particular failure in question refers to the inability of strategic bombing campaigns to produce independent war-winning effects. This section of the chapter is designed to show the level of effort expended in various bombing campaigns from World War II to the war over Kosovo. Exploring the levels of effort, operational efficacy and the context of the various campaigns will prove instructive in the following analysis of SIW.

Although urban areas were bombed during World War I, the level of effort was of such a restricted nature that these campaigns do not represent an adequate test of strategic bombing. The significance of these limited raids lies in the conclusions that were drawn by the interwar theorists. The first notable test for strategic bombing came during World War II in both the European and Pacific theatres. The British bomber offensive against Nazi Germany suffered from a number of significant limitations for approximately the first three years of the war. Amongst the most important of these were inadequate equipment in both numbers and quality, and various operational problems mainly associated with navigation, weather and German air defences. However, between March 1943 and March 1944 Bomber Command became operationally mature. Indeed, by 1944 Bomber Command was predominately composed of very capable heavy bombers such as the Lancaster and Halifax III, as well as the Mosquito light bomber.[61] Just as importantly, November 1943 saw the introduction of the P-51 Mustang long-range escort fighter. With the addition of extra fuel tanks, the P-51 could engage German fighters over Germany and thereby significantly reduced Combined Bomber Offensive (CBO) losses.[62] The CBO consisted of attacks against the enemy's morale, primarily through Bomber Command's area bombing campaigns, as well as the US Eighth and Fifth Air Forces' precision attacks that followed the premise of the industrial web theory. One of the most striking examples of the latter was the raids against Germany's ball-bearing industry, concentrated mainly at Schweinfurt. In contrast to more recent wars, the bombing campaigns in World War II did not suffer undue restrictions as a result of political or ethical concerns.[63] In this sense, to a great degree the air commanders were able to conduct the campaigns they desired, albeit within the confines set by operational limitations.

Consequently, in the latter stages of the war against Germany, the CBO had both the instrument and the will to launch enormous raids against German cities and industry that inflicted staggering levels of destruction. In all, the Allies dropped 1.2 million tons of bombs on Germany, destroyed over 40 per cent of the urban areas of its 70 largest cities, and killed roughly 305,000 of its civilians.[64] The intensity of this effort is also worthy of note. Most of the tonnage, 72 per cent, was dropped after 1 July 1944.[65] The levels of destruction that could be inflicted by such an instrument are typified by the firestorm at Hamburg on 27–28 July 1943. This attack, which became the model for future area attacks, killed 50,000 Germans, and destroyed 61 per cent of Hamburg's housing.[66] Of course, this kind of operation was repeated on a larger scale at Dresden in February 1945. Referring to its narrow streets of timber houses, Harris described Dresden as 'built more like a fire-lighter than a human habitation'.[67]

In addition to area attacks designed to break the will of the German population, various key-node targets were also identified and attacked.

There was at the time, and still is amongst historians today, a great deal of debate regarding which, if any, target set represented the Achilles' heel of the German economy and war industry. The debate usually focuses upon oil and the railways.[68] What is certainly true is that both of these target sets were severely crippled towards the end of the war. For example, by April 1945 German oil production stood at 5 per cent of its pre-attack levels.[69]

Although the strategic bombing campaign against Germany contributed significantly to the Allied war effort, it took a crushing land campaign into the heart of the Reich to bring final victory. The area bombing offensive never succeeded in breaking German morale. Also, it is worth noting that, despite the bombing, by March 1945 German armament production was still 50 per cent above its January 1942 level.[70] Just as significantly, Pape notes that German oil shortages resulted from a number of factors aside from the strategic bombing campaign. These included pressure from ground campaigns that compelled German forces to consume oil; the seizure of German oil fields in Rumania by Soviet land forces; and the collapse of the German transport system in February 1945, which was mainly due to tactical airpower flying from air bases liberated by Allied ground forces.[71] In summary, despite the enormity of the bombing campaigns, it took a joint-force, multinational war effort to defeat Germany.

In many respects Japan presented even more favourable conditions for a strategic bombing campaign. Japanese cities were predominately wooden, and therefore represented ideal targets for incendiary raids. Inadequate air defences compounded the vulnerability of urban areas. James Lea Cate and Wesley Frank Craven report that Japan never developed effective defences against night raids.[72] The Japanese also had to contend with the B-29 heavy bomber, which proved a very destructive instrument once many of the problems plaguing the programme were mitigated. In addition, US air commanders had few, if any, significant negative controls placed upon them. It has been noted that Curtis LeMay, the commander of XXI Bomber Command, 'generally did as he pleased'.[73] Again, in contrast to Germany, Japanese responses to the bombing were slow and mostly inadequate. This was particularly the case with efforts to disperse industry, which was enacted too late and was badly organised.[74] Faced with this permissive environment, when the US bomber offensive reached operational maturity, levels of destruction could be inflicted on Japan that equalled, and in some senses surpassed, that inflicted on Germany, and with less expenditure of resources. The B-29 offensives burned 180,000 square miles of Japanese cities; this related to approximately 43 per cent of the 66 largest urban areas. In all, the bombing campaigns killed 330,000, injured 476,000, and destroyed 2.5

million buildings; and 56.3 square miles of Tokyo alone were destroyed.[75]

The strategic impact of the bombing offensive against Japan raises more controversy than the German case. This results primarily from the fact that Japan surrendered before an invasion had to be launched against the mainland. Also, there is some evidence that directly links the decision to surrender to the bombing campaign. For example, Japan's Prince Konoye stated: 'Fundamentally the thing that brought about the determination to make peace was the prolonged bombing by the B-29s.' Japanese Premier Suzuki echoed this opinion.[76] However, to explain the Japanese surrender purely in relation to the efforts of the B-29s falls far short of telling the whole story. For instance, the collapse of the Japanese economy was as much, if not primarily, a result of the sea blockade of the home islands. As Kenneth Werrell notes, the B-29 offensive was bombing an economy already mortally wounded by the blockade.[77] There were other factors that appeared to have influenced the Japanese decision to end the war. A major factor in this respect was the entry of the Soviet Union into the war against Japan, and in particular the defeat of Japan's Kwantung army in Manchuria.[78] Furthermore, it should be remembered that the strategic offensive against the Japanese homeland was conducted from airfields captured by ground and naval forces. Once again, victory in the Pacific war, as in the European theatre, was the result of joint operations.

The US war in Vietnam presents a good example of how strategic airpower can be misused. Many of the issues relating to this misuse will be dealt with in the following section of the chapter. Vietnam is also an interesting case because it throws up a whole range of issues concerning the relationship between airpower and the political and geographic context of a war. At this stage it is sufficient to outline the basic structure of the air campaigns, and in particular to address the issue of whether the 1972–73 Linebacker II campaign coerced North Vietnam into accepting US peace terms.

Vietnam was a complex war, and precisely defining its strategic nature is difficult to achieve with any degree of certainty. However, it is reasonable to assert that between 1965 and 1968 the war in South Vietnam was predominantly a guerrilla-based insurgency. This translated into a low requirement for logistical support for the Communist forces. To this must be added the fact that North Vietnam was principally an agricultural society and economy. Consequently, within the confines of traditional strategic bombing doctrine, the number of strategic targets was limited. Robert McNamara, President Johnson's Secretary of Defense, was apparently aware of this problem.[79] Despite these features of the war, the initial US bombing campaign, 'Rolling Thunder', remained faithful to the industrial web theory.[80] Indeed, the Joint Chiefs of Staff advocated a bombing strategy that followed the traditional objectives of breaking the North's will and capability to support the war in the South.[81] Rolling Thunder, which lasted three years, dropped 643,000 tons of ordnance, and destroyed 65 per cent of the North's oil storage capacity, 59 per cent of its power plants and 55 per cent of its major bridges.[82] A number of factors were involved in limiting the strategic efficacy of the campaign. They include poor strategy, operational problems and political limitations placed on the campaign. However, it appears that even if many of these errors and problems had been avoided the result would have been roughly the same. The character of the war at that time (an insurgency), allied to the will of the North, made it unlikely that strategic bombing could make any decisive impact on the conflict.

By 1972, the year of the Linebacker campaigns, a number of changes had occurred in the war. The North was conducting a more conventional, regular conflict, as typified by the 'Easter Offensive'; President Nixon had shifted US objectives, and importantly he was now engaged on a policy of withdrawal from the war; there was a significant relaxation of the limitations placed on previous campaigns; the external political environment had changed, reflecting a period of détente between the United States and its two main Communist adversaries, the Soviet Union and China; and the United States was able to employ more precise weaponry, with Vietnam seeing the first use of laser-guided bombs (LGBs). Important features of the Linebacker campaigns were greatly increased levels of intensity, and the less restricted nature of the effort. The first campaign helped stop the Easter Offensive, and influenced the North's decision to make concessions during peace negotiations, but ultimately failed to produce a lasting settlement.[83] However, it is the second Linebacker campaign, the so-called 'Christmas bombings', which attract the most controversy. Some commentators believe that Linebacker II had finally fulfilled the promise of strategic airpower. Admiral Moorer (Chairman of the Joint Chiefs of Staff) concluded: 'The 11-day air campaign of December 1972 will, I am certain, go down in history as a testimonial to the efficacy of air power the way it should be used.' [84] In a similar vein, Sir Robert Thompson espoused: 'In my view, on December 30, 1972, after eleven days of those B-52 attacks on the Hanoi area, you had won the war. It was over! ... They would have taken any terms.'[85] In support of Admiral Moorer's perspective, one can argue that Linebacker II was certainly an intensive campaign. During 11 days of bombing, 20,000 tons of bombs were dropped, some of which were precision guided.[86] Also, Hanoi and the principal port of Haiphong were attacked. There are however some important caveats to the enthusiastic assessments above. If one examines the content of the peace accords signed after Linebacker II, it is clear that they were far from being a disaster for the North. In particular, the North was legally permitted to retain troops in the South.[87] Also, the peace agreement did not ensure the sovereignty of South Vietnam for very long, which was conquered by the North in 1975. Indeed, Hawkins declares: 'This apparent victory of air power, however, proved hollow. The Hanoi regime had signed a piece of paper, but it was not fundamentally changed in composition or outlook. It remained committed to its goal of conquering the South.'[88] Overall, it is difficult, if not impossible, to claim that strategic bombing in Vietnam achieved the goals set for it by the early theorists. Aside from the above argument, it has to be remembered that for North Vietnam Linebacker II came at the end of seven years of ground war against the United States and its Southern ally. Strategic airpower had not been the only form of pressure applied on the Communists.

It may be argued that prior to the 1990s a mixture of operational, political, technological and organisational factors had retarded strategic bombing campaigns. From this standpoint, the 1991 Gulf War represents an effective test for this method of waging war. In many respects, the Gulf War presented airpower with a permissive environment. Despite the density of air defences around Baghdad, which were seven times as dense as those around Hanoi during Linebacker II, the coalition air forces quickly attained air supremacy, and in this sense could almost bomb at will.[89] The Iraqi air force hardly contested command of the air throughout the war, and Iraq's Integrated Air Defence System was neutralised on the first night of the campaign.[90] The *Gulf War Air Power Survey* (*GWAPS*) concludes that air superiority was attained by the end of the first night.[91] The US-led coalition had a distinct technological advantage. It is claimed that the F-117A has air superiority built in.[92] Cruise missiles also enabled the Coalition to maintain the pressure of precision strikes on Iraq throughout the hours of daylight.[93] A range of sophisticated surveillance and intelligence assets gave the Coalition what Colin Powell described as the best intelligence in the history of warfare.[94] Although this might be somewhat of an exaggeration, it is not too far from the truth. The desert environment also provided its usual advantages to the employment of airpower. In the political domain, there was very little interference with the campaign, certainly not until the Al Firdos bunker incident on the night of 12–13 February. Before this incident, and unlike Vietnam, there were no sanctuaries for the enemy.[95] The campaign was also well co-ordinated.[96]

These, and other factors, resulted in a strategic campaign that was both of high intensity, and achieved levels of precision and penetration unobtainable in previous wars. The intensity of the campaign is revealed by the fact that approximately 70 per cent of the 'strategic' targets were hit in the first three days.[97] The Iraqi electrical power grid was virtually shut down; 88 per cent of its installed generating capacity was rendered unavailable; and the remaining 12 per cent was isolated to particular localities.[98] Added to this is the fact that within ten days Iraq's refined oil production was totally eliminated.[99]

Nevertheless, despite the range of advantages this campaign enjoyed over previous ones, once again the strategic air campaign failed to produce victory independently. The leadership and C^2 campaigns failed to produce the desired coup against Saddam's regime.[100] Although the Iraqi C^2 was seriously degraded, this part of the air war failed in its aim to cripple the regime's C^2 of its forces. Evidence for this can be found in the fact that the Iraqi leadership was able to redeploy its ground forces once the Coalition ground campaign had begun.[101] The GWAPS similarly indicates that Saddam continued to order the launch of Scud missiles to the end of the war.[102] Even more telling is the undeniable fact that the war had to be concluded by ground forces. This is not to underestimate the role played by airpower as a very significant enabling factor to the ground war, but merely to note that the enemy did not capitulate to air-based coercion; rather his forces were defeated on the ground. There is no more stark appraisal of this fact than General Calvin Waller's statement: 'Let's get real ... ultimately ... you've got to go on the ground and take it back.'[103]

The final air campaign to be assessed is perhaps the most controversial. The NATO bombing campaign against Yugoslavia had a mixture of advantages and disadvantages over its predecessors. On the positive side, NATO had at its disposal levels of precision previously unobtainable. Also, as in the Gulf War, there was never any real challenge to NATO's command of the air from enemy air forces.[104] However, a number of negative factors detracted from the campaign's efficacy. Poor strategy, emanating from poor political judgment at the beginning of the campaign, produced low levels of intensity early on. In this respect, the campaign began to resemble Rolling Thunder with its emphasis on graduated response.[105] This was compounded by the fact that the NATO alliance included a number of countries that had reservations about the conflict. The initial poor strategy included extraordinary announcements by certain NATO leaders ruling out a ground campaign. In his writings, Wylie warns of the dangers of having only one plan, because the enemy will eventually discern it and then counter it.[106] During the Kosovo conflict, NATO not only had just one plan initially, but they also saved the enemy the trouble of identifying it. The weather and terrain in the Balkans also provided serious obstacles. As noted earlier, these frictions were aggravated by an insistence on the part of casualty-averse political leaders that the campaign be waged from 15,000 feet and above. This was a serious restriction in the face of an entrenched enemy who practised a competent campaign of deception.

The controversy surrounding NATO's conflict against Yugoslavia emanates from the fact that the Serbian leadership capitulated before a ground campaign had been launched. This has led some commentators to suggest that airpower had finally achieved an independent victory. For example, Keegan declared that 3 June 1999 was a turning point in the history of warfare 'when the capitulation of President Milosevic proved that a war can be won by air power alone'.[107] Strictly speaking, the Serbs did submit to NATO demands prior to a ground offensive. However, a number of factors aside from the bombing campaign may go some way to explaining this result.

Yugoslavia's decision to withdraw its forces from Kosovo may have had as much to do with the actions of its Russian allies as with the NATO air campaign. As the conflict progressed, Russian support for the Serb effort abated.[108] Indeed, Lieutenant-General Sir Mike Jackson stated in an interview: 'The event of June 3 [when the Russians backed the West's position and urged President Milosevic to surrender] was the single event that appeared to me to have the greatest significance in ending the war.'[109] It is also important to note that Serb units were under mounting pressure from Kosovo Liberation Army (KLA) ground forces.[110] The Serb leadership may also have begun to take more seriously the increased discussion of a NATO ground offensive. This latter point fits with Wylie's assessment that, even if the man on the scene with a gun is not needed, he must be potentially available, and be seen to be so.[111] In this respect, the NATO bombing campaign, although it was not having a great deal of success against Serb forces in Kosovo, perhaps acted as an indicator of NATO's resolve to continue with the conflict. This resolve was substantially reinforced by the Serbian intensification of the ethnic cleansing campaign. Discussing this strategic error, Lambeth goes as far as to suggest, 'it was only because Milosevic made a blunder no less towering than NATO's preclusion of a ground option that the war had the largely positive outcome that it did'.[112] Milosevic may have assumed that it was only a matter of time before a ground offensive would come. Also, Posen reminds us that Serbia actually obtained a better deal than the one they were offered at Rambouillet prior to the conflict.[113] As an assessment of strategic bombing, it should be remembered also that NATO's air campaign was not directed solely against targets that fall within Warden's four inner rings. As the conflict progressed, NATO increasingly attacked Serb forces in Kosovo. This part of the campaign would more easily fit Pape's 'denial' strategy, rather than coercion through punishment. Finally, remembering that NATO's primary strategic objective was the return of the refugees to Kosovo, it is clearly inaccurate to imply that the air campaign was strategically decisive on its own. The primary goal was only obtainable with the deployment of ground forces into the province. Recent reports indicate that the levels of damage inflicted on Serb forces were significantly lower than at first estimated.[114] In addition, it is claimed that, despite the air campaign, Serbian forces in Kosovo retained enough tactical freedom to continue with the expulsions of Albanians.[115] This would appear to suggest that the bombing campaign alone could not have broken either the will or capability of the Serbs. Overall, the campaign against Serbia in some respects is reminiscent of the campaign against Japan. In each case, a ground invasion was not required to achieve victory. However, pressure from sources other than the bombing probably had as much influence in the final outcome.

The function of this section has been to show that, even with the levels of effort, destruction and increasingly precision, attained in the above historical examples, strategic bombing has thus far failed to provide an independent means to achieve strategic decision. This is an important point to bear in mind when we read the SIW literature. The chapter will now examine the reasons for this failure in more detail, and assess whether they could degrade the strategic efficacy of SIW.

LIMITS ON STRATEGIC WARFARE

The practice of strategic bombing has been plagued by a variety of factors that have served to limit its strategic efficacy. Some factors are obviously more damaging than others, but all help to reduce its performance. Many of these factors are usually in play simultaneously, in which case a strategic bombing campaign has many obstacles to overcome. As noted earlier, thus far no campaign has yet managed to overcome these impediments to a point at which it can claim independent strategic victory. It is the intention of this section to assess the significance of these factors, and how much they will impinge upon the performance of SIW. It will be shown that SIW cannot escape from the normal constraints under which all other forms of warfare, and strategic bombing in particular, have to operate.

The first category of restraints is best described by the term *operational difficulties*. This simply refers to the practicalities of a bombing campaign, the act of delivering bombs on target. Within this category some difficulties are plainly more restrictive than others. One area that usually raises problems, particularly in the early stages of a campaign, concerns the instruments of bombing. As noted earlier, it took approximately three years for Bomber Command to become operationally mature. Before that point, the bombing offensive was conducted with aircraft, like the Manchester, which were clearly inadequate.[116] In

Vietnam, the 'Century Series' of fighter-bombers had been designed to deliver nuclear payloads and therefore were not ideally suited for a conventional bombing campaign. For instance, the F-105 suffered from poor manoeuvrability, and lacked the robustness required to engage in hundreds of conventional sorties.[117] Even when the platforms themselves are adequate, problems with munitions can limit efficacy. It has been estimated that 14 per cent of the bombs dropped by US aircraft over Germany were defective.[118] More significantly, Ellis reports that the US bombs that did explode were too small to be effective against machine tools, engineering, construction and transport equipment, except with a direct hit.[119]

During operations the main challenge is finding, hitting and destroying the assigned targets. It is hard to overestimate the difficulties that have historically been encountered in the field of navigation. An extreme but illustrative example is provided by the US 2nd Bombardment Division on 1 April 1944. In particularly bad weather they not only failed to find and hit their target in Germany, but also mistakenly proceeded to bomb the border city of Schaffhousen in Switzerland.[120] Although technologies such as GPS have helped eliminate the perennial problem of navigation, hitting targets with precision still presented a problem until very recently. In World War II, precision could be negatively affected by a host of factors, including poor visibility, malfunction of the bombsight or the lead bombardier being shot down.[121] Although Kosovo, Afghanistan and the War for Iraq suggest that precision is increasingly the norm, hitting the desired target cannot be taken for granted. During the 1991 Gulf War, the bomb-damaged physical environment confused the visual navigation system on some TLAMs.[122] In Kosovo, F-16 fighter-bombers mistakenly bombed an Albanian refugee column near the town of Djakovica.[123] During the War for Iraq there were a number of friendly fire incidents when Coalition forces were targeted by mistake.[124]

Bombing campaigns have continued to be negatively affected by the weather. Terraine describes the weather as the everlasting enemy of Bomber Command.[125] This same enemy still had a high profile in the Gulf War, during which approximately half of all sorties were either cancelled or diverted because of bad weather.[126] The problem has still yet to recede fully as the cancellation of raids over Yugoslavia in 1999 revealed. At one point in the campaign over half of the nightly sorties returned without delivering their munitions because of adverse weather.[127] Within the realms of environmental effects, it is not just weather that retards precision; industrial haze or smoke from bomb damage can also play havoc with dumb bombs and LGBs alike.[128] Technological advances have clearly mitigated many of the problems associated with navigation and precision. In this sense, finding and hitting targets has become more routine. However, as the above examples have shown, the intensity of a campaign can still be affected by the weather, and mistakes in targeting can create political and strategic complications.

Many of these specific operational problems should not prove applicable to SIW in any substantial and direct manner. Many of the weapons of SIW are simple pieces of software, in which case they are relatively easy to produce and use effectively.[129] On the issue of navigation, the nature of cyberspace, which is designed to be navigable, seems to suggest that locating targets should not pose a significant problem. Although a great deal of SIW operates within the distinct geographical environment of cyberspace, some of the techniques of this form of war will suffer from constraints similar to those faced by strategic bombing. For example, Kopp notes that the effects of the atmosphere reduce the lethality of EMP.[130] Because of this, and the problems of estimating the robustness of target equipment in the face of EMP, creating EMP devices with assured effects could prove somewhat problematic. Denning also notes that the effects from these weapons may not be immediately apparent, and therefore assessing their impact can be problematic.[131] However, the issue of operational difficulties is not really concerned with the direct relevance of strategic bombing problems to SIW. Whilst recognising that SIW should not suffer from some of the limitations endured by strategic bombing over the years, the point to be made is that friction will occur and place limits on the operational, and thereby the strategic, efficacy of SIW campaigns. SIW will undoubtedly suffer from its own unique operational difficulties. These will consequently limit the levels of damage that can be inflicted on enemy targets and systems. Also, we should be careful not to overestimate the impact of the above difficulties. After all, even during the relatively primitive days of World War II, enormous levels of destruction were attained. In strategic bombing the difficulties involved in finding and hitting targets have been substantially reduced. However, improvements in the lethality of strategic bombing have not been followed by the realisation of the theories of Douhet and Warden. It would seem that operational problems are not the main reason for the strategic failure of strategic airpower.

Institutions conduct military campaigns. In turn, individuals with varying personas, egos and agendas man these institutions. These *institutional problems*, revolving around intra- and inter-institutional relation- ships, can impact on the efficacy of bombing campaigns, particularly by reducing operational and strategic focus. A classic example of these issues centres on 'Bomber' Harris. Harris had very definite ideas about the role of Bomber Command. To simplify, he saw area bombing as the most promising use of this new instrument, and regarded precision attacks against key nodes as the pointless search for panacea targets. Likewise, he fought hard against the diversion of Bomber Command's assets to other roles, including those in support of the Normandy campaign. Consequently, these views, allied to Harris' stubborn personality, brought him into conflict with both the Air Staff and the Ministry of Economic Warfare. Harris' relationship with the latter has been described as a 'running battle'.[132] These conflicts of interest and opinion amongst those responsible for the bomber offensive resulted in a lack of focus to the campaign.[133] Biddle goes as far as to suggest that had Portal, Chief of Air Staff, been able to dominate Harris the war could have ended sooner.[134] The air campaign in Vietnam is another example where institutional problems afflicted the bombing effort. Mark Clodfelter is of the opinion that the absence of a single air commander produced a chaotic air war.[135] Vietnam also witnessed the negative influence of personalities and bureaucratic arrangements. Reminiscent of the tensions surrounding Harris in Bomber Command, tensions were said to exist between Defense Secretary McNamara and the JCS Chairman, General Wheeler. By respecting the chain of command Wheeler's recommendations had to go through McNamara, a man who at an early stage had lost faith in Rolling Thunder.[136] Similarly, Kosovo presents an enlightening example on this subject. General Clark is forthright in his assessment of the impact, both negative and positive, created by the various interests involved in the war: 'We worked with and worked through the sensitivities of some Allies, the concerns and instincts of diplomats, the self-interests of nations in the region, and the egos, judgements, and experience of some colleagues in uniform, especially in Washington.'[137] When it came to information sharing for the Air Tasking Order (ATO), institutional friction produced a system described as 'cumbersome'.[138] For his part, General Clark is said to have micromanaged the day-to-day conduct of the war.[139]

It is naive to think that SIW would be immune from the kind of personal and institutional tensions described above. Indeed, at present there are many information warfare organisations appearing in the United States. And although some rationalisation has taken place within the Department of Homeland Security, much still needs to be done. The proliferation of organisations has led Peter D. Feaver to declare: 'The IW arena is among the most highly compartmentalised in the entire US defense establishment. The right hand quite simply does not know what the left hand *can do*, let alone what it is in fact doing.'[140] Tensions may be exacerbated as those conducting SIW seek to prove its worth. In these conditions each armed service and institution may attempt to lay claim to be the natural home of SIW, and therefore conflict rather than co-operation of effort could result. After all, proving the efficacy of the strategic bombing instrument was the prime motive for Harris' zealous advocacy of area bombing. However, once again we should avoid laying too much blame at the door of institutional difficulties. Unified command was achieved during the 1991 Gulf War, and yet despite this, and despite solving many of the operational problems of earlier wars, independent strategic victory still proved elusive.

A particular problem that has plagued strategic air campaigns since World War II is concerned with the role of *doctrine*. Doctrine has many sources. These can include a particular strategic or service culture, personal loyalty to particular methods and past experiences. The proclivity within some in the United States towards precision bombing (Curtis LeMay excepted) may be a reflection of the belief in technological answers to strategic dilemmas, as well as a throwback to the marksmanship of the frontier days.[141] Whatever the particular origins of a doctrine, history reveals that loyalty to the established methods can shape a bombing campaign regardless of the specific requirements of the war in question. The Vietnam War presents an obvious case in point. Prior to the war the USAF had prepared to fight a nuclear war against the Soviet Union. As a consequence, the doctrinal manual for 1964, the year before Rolling Thunder began, included no provisions for strategic bombing without nuclear weapons.[142] This was significant because the delivery of conventional munitions required greater accuracy than the delivery of nuclear weapons. Add this to a continued allegiance to the industrial web theory, and the USAF was ill prepared to wage the kind of campaign required in Vietnam. It seems that doctrine had blinded the USAF to the lessons of Korea, which like North Vietnam had few industrial targets.[143] The GWAPS found similar mistakes in the 1991 Gulf War. It complains that target categories were based as much on doctrinal considerations as on intelligence of the Iraqi system.[144] In Kosovo, decisions over which targets to attack were done in a mechanical fashion, in which strategic bombing doctrine was more influential than the extant strategic context.[145]

Although at present there appears to be no official doctrine for waging SIW in the open source material, the literature that has appeared thus far reveals significant similarities with the theory and doctrine of strategic bombing.[146] It is yet to be seen if institutions that acquire responsibility for waging SIW develop the sort of institutional and doctrinal loyalty evident in the other armed services. Based on the history of strategic bombing, the prospects do not look good. The influence of doctrine is important, for if a service is unable to display sufficient flexibility in the face of the varied nature of strategic circumstances then at times it will in all likelihood be condemned to fight the wrong kind of war.

Strategic bombing campaigns rely heavily upon the quality of *intelli-*

gence available on the enemy system. Knowing how the system functions, how much pain it can take and where to inflict that pain are all critical prerequisites. It is ironic, and significant, that the performance of the intelligence function in support of bombing has often been poor. As Sir Charles Webster succinctly notes in relation to the bombing campaign against Germany, poor intelligence can lead to under-bombing of key targets.[147] Poor intelligence can also lead to the bombing of the wrong targets. During the Kosovo conflict, an intelligence failure led to the bombing of the Chinese embassy in Belgrade by NATO aircraft. Failures in intelligence can occur at any of its stages: gathering, analysing or dissemination. It should be noted that, although some of these failings are attributable to bad practice, some are simply the result of the immensity of the task. Pape highlights the size of the task involved in trying to undertake an accurate macrolevel analysis of the German economy in World War II. He notes that the required information was simply not available.[148] The problems associated with the volume of information required is augmented by the fact that in most cases the intelligence acquired is based on a peacetime analysis of the enemy, rather than when they have mobilised their economy for war. The difficulties involved in understanding how a complex interconnected modern economy works are highlighted by the fact that even modern historians, with all the benefits of historical research and hindsight, still disagree over which component of the German economy, at which period in the war, represented its Achilles' heel.

Aside from the enormous amounts of information required for planning and conducting a strategic bombing campaign, the gathering and analysis of the information can be done poorly. For example, in Vietnam the Defense Intelligence Agency (DIA) has been criticised for adopting a numerical and quantifiable approach to intelligence gathering, rather than focusing on the North's strategy.[149] Likewise, Britain's Ministry of Economic Warfare (MEW) is chastised for suffering from intellectual conformity, and hasty analysis of intelligence as a result of strict deadlines.[150] To refer back to the previous section, intelligence organisations also suffer from institutional tensions and difficulties. Such problems were as evident during the 1991 Gulf War as in World War II.[151] Shortcomings in intelligence can lead to spectacular errors. In 1944, the Allies underestimated German aircraft production by a half.[152]

Despite Colin Powell's confident assertion that Coalition forces during the Gulf War had the best intelligence in military history, this conflict still reveals how intelligence difficulties can beset a campaign with such a vast array of intelligence assets. The GWAPS identifies a number of shortcomings in this area. The war had to be waged with an incomplete and out-of-date national database on Iraq, which resulted in significant gaps in the Coalition's understanding of the entire Iraqi system; a rift existed between those organisations responsible for intelligence and those in charge of planning the campaign; dissemination of intelligence was often poor; some targets, such as the 'hide sites' for mobile Scud launchers, were never located; and the significance of certain targets was never appreciated.[153] The GWAPS concludes: 'uncertainties are endemic to intelligence functions'.[154]

Intelligence difficulties do not cease once the war has begun; in fact they often multiply. A particularly difficult area during a war is Bomb Damage Assessment (BDA). The history of strategic bombing is replete with BDA problems and failures. The GWAPS once again provides us with a striking example of BDA-related difficulties, despite the array of assets available for the task. In fact, BDA in the Gulf War has come under particularly heavy levels of criticism. A host of problems afflicted the task, which included: an inadequate number of trained personnel who were swamped by data; the weather; the fact that those responsible for reconnaissance were not involved in campaign planning; a lack of specific training in BDA before the conflict; the speed of the air campaign which hampered analysis; and problems of imagery interpretation. This latter point was particularly evident with penetration munitions, which revealed entry into a structure, but not the damage inflicted inside.[155] Similar failings were evident in World War II, when structural damage to buildings (especially roof coverage) was too readily linked to production losses.[156]

Although much information is available on targets for information attack, intelligence is an area in which SIW could well suffer difficulties similar to those described above.[157] The difficulties of understanding the complex relationships amongst different sectors in an industrial economy have already been noted. An information age economy would appear to present similar, if not greater, difficulties. Matthew G. Devost et al. postulate: 'The sophistication of network analysis necessary to "bring down" a national information infrastructure is substantial.'[158] Aside from the difficulties of comprehending the workings of the enemy's system, predicting the complex interactions instigated by an attack will also stretch intelligence organisations. As Libicki notes, this could well make SIW an uncontrollable activity.[159] BDA also presents some significant problems for SIW. During the 1991 Gulf War, an attack on the Iraqi electrical system with cruise missiles carrying carbon filament warheads was successful but left no obvious damage to the structures; consequently these targets were needlessly attacked again.[160] As this sort of non-destructive form of attack is inherent in certain methods of SIW, it is reasonable to assume that similar difficulties for deciding whether or not a target has been put out of operation will continue.

Libicki highlights this dilemma well when he raises the following questions: 'Did a virus really disable the computer? How can one tell whether a microwave burst really put a tank's electronics out of action?'[161] Kopp notes that similar problems of 'kill assessment' apply to E-bombs.[162] Overall, the significance of intelligence to strategic campaigns cannot be overstated. For either strategic bombing or SIW to prove effective, good intelligence on the enemy system is a crucial prerequisite. The difficulties outlined above are only half of the story. Intelligence must also be collected on the will of the enemy to withstand such attacks. The historical record on this issue is not promising. In this sense, Williamson Murray is undoubtedly correct when he notes that the real measures of success are the intangibles, such as the effect of attacks on the morale of the enemy.[163] The difficulties associated with collecting accurate assessments of these intangibles will be as applicable to SIW as they are to strategic bombing.

A common complaint from the advocates and practitioners of strategic airpower has been the frequent *diversion of their assets* to 'non-strategic' tasks. Terraine identifies 17 significant diversions of Bomber Command's resources during the whole of World War II. These activities included the support of ground offensives, the Battle of the Atlantic and attacks against V-weapons.[164] Likewise, during the Gulf War strategic assets were diverted to engage in 'Scud hunts', to 'dig out' the Iraqi air force hiding in aircraft shelters and to engage in 'tank plinking' against Iraqi armour.[165] Strictly speaking, the activities described above do entail the diversion of air assets from attacking strategic target sets. To assume that resources can, and will, be concentrated in only one direction would be both naive and inadvisable. Modern wars are complex affairs, and tend to be won by prevailing in many areas, in which case placing all your eggs in one basket would be unwise and probably unsuccessful. Also, as writers on both World War II and the Gulf War have stated, we should not overplay the significance of these diversions to the overall results of strategic bombing campaigns. During both of these conflicts enormous damage was inflicted on strategic target sets despite the diversion of resources to other roles.[166]

It is likely that in future conflicts SIW activities will be siphoned off in more direct support of ground operations. One such diversion may entail attacks against information systems that support logistics. This may represent a significant draw on resources because as *FM 100-6* notes, mobilisation is an information-intensive activity.[167] However, as the history of strategic bombing reveals, this should not prove too damaging to the overall SIW campaign. Nor should the practitioners of strategic campaigns complain. Terraine sensibly reminds us that these so-called diversions are nothing of the sort; in fact they 'add up to the war itself'.[168]

War is a political act. That being the case, strategic bombing cannot be conducted in a political vacuum in which only military rationale is in play. This leads us inevitably to the observation, backed by numerous historical examples, that strategic campaigns are limited by *political restraints*. These restraints do not necessarily emanate from a sound balancing of the policy objective and military means; they don't always represent good strategy. Political restraints on bombing can have many sources. These include domestic political considerations, foreign policy concerns and ethical issues. When assessing how significant such restraints can be on the conduct of a campaign, the conclusions reached represent a mixed bag. As will be noted shortly in relation to the Vietnam War, political considerations can greatly influence, one might say dictate, the campaign. However, World War II presents us with an example in which there were few, if any, political constraints on the conduct of strategic bombing. Looking to the future of SIW and strategic bombing, it is wise to assume that such campaigns will rarely be able to operate without such interference from the realm of politics.

Often, bombing campaigns have to contend with various political restrictions operating simultaneously. In the 1991 war against Iraq, the campaign was waged in such a way that casualties on both sides were restricted; little or no damage was inflicted on sites of cultural, religious or historic value; and the Iraqi economy suffered no long-term damage.[169] Raids against the Iraqi regime's administrative support structure were severely curtailed after the Al Firdos bunker incident, in which the families of the Iraqi political elite were mistakenly killed. Murray suggests that this hamstrung the campaign against this particular target set for the rest of the war.[170] Murray may well be right in his assertion, but we have to question whether continuing with this section of the campaign would have produced any decisive results. Limiting target sets provides your enemy with sanctuaries from the bombing. In the Iraqi case, this enabled the Defence Ministry to relocate to the Ministry of Youth building.[171] The much-maligned Rolling Thunder campaign in Vietnam provides us with yet further instances of the kind of political restraints that can be placed upon a bombing campaign. President Johnson had a number of dominant 'negative' objectives that to a large degree dictated how the campaign was waged. The fear of escalating the war, by bringing in China or the Soviet Union, meant that Johnson took no action that appeared to threaten the Hanoi regime, nor seemed likely to threaten Chinese territory or Soviet advisors and technicians operating in the North. In the early stages of the war, Johnson was reluctant to conduct a large-scale conflict for fear of distracting attention away from his domestic political programme. Political sensitivities also ruled out what were arguably the two most promising strategic target sets in North Vietnam, namely the food supply and the population itself.[172] Political restraints can often occur when war is waged by a coalition. General Klaus Nauman, Chairman of NATO's Military Committee during the Kosovo conflict, admitted that the NATO air campaign had been lengthened due to restrictions placed upon the campaign in the interests of alliance political unity.[173] NATO also stopped bombing downtown Belgrade for two weeks after the bombing of the Chinese embassy.[174]

The political objectives of a war can impose limits on the bombing effort for perfectly sound strategic reasoning. In fact, commenting upon Kosovo, Lambeth is persuasive when he argues that the restrictions placed upon NATO for the sake of alliance cohesion were critical for strategic success.[175] In the context of using airpower for colonial control, the doctrine of 'minimum necessary force' was the guiding principle. It was feared that excessive use of force would further alienate colonial subjects. This posture resulted in the dropping of warning leaflets prior to an attack, so as to avoid civilian casualties.[176]

As with the many other factors which have retarded the conduct of strategic bombing, it seems reasonable to speculate that SIW will likewise be susceptible to political restrictions. Many of the above reasons that create political constraints on a strategic campaign will almost certainly be in play in the world of SIW. Diego M. Wendt is correct when he notes: 'As long as there are wars, there will be political restrictions upon actions and targets.'[177] SIW may well display certain unique characteristics, but like all other forms of warfare it will operate in the Clausewitzian world, in which politics informs the military instrument.

SIW does not come with an owner's manual containing detailed instructions on its proper usage. Like all military instruments, even if the technological, tactical and operational levels are adequately well done, the whole project can be dashed by *poor strategy*. There is no guarantee that the decision makers who control the strategic conduct of a war will perform well. The air campaign against Yugoslavia offers an instructive example. NATO had many factors on its side, including better technology, numerical superiority, competent personnel and good performance at the operational and tactical levels of war. However, ineptitude at the strategic level arguably came close to negating these many advantages. Indeed, Lambeth regards strategy as the primary area of weakness in NATO's campaign (Allied Force) for Kosovo: 'The biggest failures of Allied Force likewise occurred in the realm of strategy and execution.'[178]

Mistakes in strategy can take many forms. Identifying the correct strategy is dependent on many factors, including the character of the war, the enemy, policy objectives and the available instruments. The Rolling Thunder campaign in Vietnam was handicapped by poor strategy in a number of ways. When the war was predominantly an insurgency in the South, and the insurgency's sponsor in the North was primarily an agricultural country, an industrial web bombing campaign was unsuited to the task. In conjunction with this, many Vietnamese perceived the war as an anti-imperialist struggle for national unity. The strong will that such a cause engendered was unlikely to be broken by the graduated escalation of Rolling Thunder. Cohen comments, 'To be sure, the second aspect of the centrally controlled bombing of Vietnam – the modulated application of violence – resulted from a theory of strategic signaling and gradual escalation that proved calamitously false.'[179] References to poor strategy assume that the leadership at least has identified an obvious strategy for the bombing campaign. This is not always the case. It has been reported that the 'Tuesday Lunches' at the White House, during which Rolling Thunder was planned, never really dealt with strategy; rather the meetings tended to get bogged down in issues of targeting.[180] War does not always present us with the luxury of taking a form that suits the instruments at our disposal. For example, like Vietnam, North Korea was endowed with few strategic targets for the USAF to attack. The result of this fact was that by 25 September 1950 all the major strategic targets in Korea had been destroyed.[181] In relation to both strategic bombing and SIW, there is no guarantee that all future wars will be waged against well-developed enemies who happen to possess industrial or information age infrastructures. The length of a conflict can also impinge upon the strategic efficacy of strategic warfare. If strategic bombing is to have significant impact on a war, it is more likely to occur in a protracted struggle during which the deprivations wrought by the bombing can take effect.[182] However, as Vietnam reveals, a protracted conflict offers no guarantee of success for strategic bombing campaigns.

Poor strategy can have many negative manifestations. During the British Empire, when faced by the rebellious Sudanese Nuer, Britain identified cattle as the most valuable target to strike. Paradoxically, this particular form of economic destruction merely aggravated the political situation.[183] During both the Gulf War and World War II, strategic bombing advocates failed to realise that, if there were indeed centres of gravity in these cases, the most likely candidates were the armies of Iraq and Germany.[184] The strategies of both these continental powers were centred on their ground forces. Many, if not all, conflicts need to be concluded on the ground, and in this sense both airpower and SIW suffer from their inability to seize and hold territory. Bombing campaigns can also often fail through the absence of continuity, or by falling into the trap of measuring success by quantifiable calculations, for example by gauging progress by acreage destroyed.[185] Operating through such notions tends to be simplistic, as wars are usually complex affairs in which the intangibles play an important part in success. The challenge of strategy is essentially the same whichever form of warfare you have at your disposal. The matching of means to ends will be no easier for SIW than for any other military instrument. As Gray asserts, friction occurs within the relationship between war and politics, and therefore good strategy cannot be guaranteed.[186]

Thus far, the discussion has focused on constraints that are primarily concerned with those who prosecute a strategic campaign. In all wars there is of course another party to the conflict, the other belligerent. The existence of an intelligent foe brings with it the fact of *countermeasures*. Often, the theorists advocating some form of 'strategic' warfare indirectly assume that the enemy will remain passive, or at best will not provide significant obstacles to the success of the campaign. Assumptions that 'the bomber will always get through', and that targets will be identified, hit and destroyed as a matter of course, have been found wanting in the crucible of reality.

An enemy can counter the attacker's activities in a number of ways. Various methods have been designed to limit precision in bombing campaigns. These techniques have included searchlight dazzle of the bomber crews, which has been described as being as significant an obstacle as cloud and haze.[187] An even simpler method is the production of smoke screens over the targets.[188] Aside from offsetting the precision of attacks, target societies have undertaken various means of deception. In Germany, dummy fires were created outside of towns to ape those laid down by the pathfinder bombers.[189] As previously noted, during the Gulf War the Coalition destroyed a substantial number of high-fidelity ballistic missile decoys, which according to United Nations inspectors were only identifiable as fakes 25 yards away on the ground.[190] During the British Empire, tribes under bombardment also displayed a high degree of ingenuity in the face of attack. This would often entail the establishment of an early warning system. In 1925, Zeidi troops in the Aden Protectorate captured British cloth signals that had been designed as a signal to the RAF not to bomb in a particular area.[191] BDA is another area vulnerable to deception. The North Koreans would remove sections of bridges themselves in order to fake bomb damage.[192] Civil defence measures also become routine for those under sustained attack. An enemy can employ very simple man-intensive measures as well. For example, the North Vietnamese employed 500,000 labourers to repair their lines of communication.[193]

The above techniques are but a sample of the various means by which the enemy can attempt to degrade the efficacy of strategic bombing. Perhaps the most effective measures have been achieved in the form of active defence. This is certainly relevant to the Luftwaffe's defence of the

Reich. German night-fighters in particular posed an acute danger to the CBO. Referring to operation 'Pointblank', which had the aim of destroying German fighter production, Frankland declares, 'The German Air Force in being had proved capable of protecting the German Air Force in production.'[194] It has been noted by a number of historians that German defences came close to victory in 1943–44, and that given a freer hand by Hitler they perhaps could have defeated the CBO.[195] It does not take much imagination to conceive that societies under SIW attack will develop equally ingenious ways to offset the efficacy of the information age variant of strategic warfare. Indeed, the threat and activities of hackers have already spawned a myriad of defensive measures. Schwartau declares that the technology and tools already exist to defeat and defend against the information warrior.[196] Similarly, Lawrence Freedman concludes that information systems are not as vulnerable as often assumed, simply because defensive measures are already part of many of those systems.[197] Also, Smith points out that the antivirus industry is well developed and has created a number of good countermeasures.[198] Such measures will not make SIW impotent – the paradoxical logic of strategy will forbid that – but the impact of SIW may be degraded by countermeasures.

In the above paragraph, the dialectic nature of strategy was added to the complexities of waging a strategic campaign. There is, in this sense, another basic problem for those waging either a strategic bombing or SIW campaign. The essence of this problem is best captured in Adam Smith's statement: 'There is a lot of ruin in a country.'[199] Modern industrial societies, and therefore conceivably information age societies, have shown remarkable *resilience* in the face of significant levels of destruction. This presents obvious problems for strategic campaigns that seek to undermine the will and/or capability of the enemy to wage modern war.

The most revealing illustrations of this resilience are to be found amongst the enormous levels of destruction suffered by Germany and Japan in World War II. Despite the aforementioned scale of destruction carried out by the B-29s, the USSBS concludes that in 1945 Japanese worker absenteeism only stood at 8 per cent. Perhaps even more remarkable is the estimation that three-quarters of Hiroshima's industrial plants could have resumed normal operations within 30 days of the atomic attack.[200] The German experience provides equally striking examples. The level of destruction inflicted on Hamburg during the July 1943 firestorm has already been noted; what is just as significant as the physical damage done is the fact that only 1.8 months of industrial production were lost as a result.[201] It has been estimated that direct production losses due to strategic bombing for 1943 and 1944 were only 9 and 17 per cent respectively.[202] These results are not inconsequential, but they certainly fall far short of representing independent war-winning effects. One problem in particular that prohibited more significant results was the fact that German industrial machinery and machine tools often survived an attack even if the factory they were housed in was destroyed.[203] More generally, the German economy simply had much greater capacity and ability to adapt than the airpower enthusiasts had assumed. Resilience was also a feature of certain target sets in the Gulf War. This is particularly true of the Iraqi national telecommunications system, which proved to be more robust and have greater redundancy than at first thought.[204]

Resilience is not just a naturally occurring phenomenon of modern economies, although that certainly appears to be evident to some degree, but it is also facilitated by the enemy's actions. In Germany, in response to attacks on the Schweinfurt ball-bearing plants, a number of steps were taken. These included dispersal of production to other locations, and the redesigning of equipment to reduce ball-bearing requirements. Germany could also offset the impact of attacks on tank production facilities by introducing more effective infantry anti-tank weapons such as the Panzerfaust and Panzerschreck. The North Koreans also displayed some simple but effective countermeasures to offset attacks against their irrigation dams. One such method was to reduce the water level prior to attacks, in which case the raids had to breach a significantly thicker section of the dam structure.[205] These examples would seem to suggest that hitting critical components often proves strategically ineffective simply because they tend to produce responses from the enemy.

The historical record of strategic bombing clearly reveals that modern industrial economies are far more resilient to bombing than the advocates of airpower assume. There is no reason to believe that information age economies should prove any different. Indeed, some of the SIW literature acknowledges this fact. Robert H. Anderson of the RAND Corporation has made a sensible statement to that effect: 'In general, our country's infrastructure is very resilient, as various natural disasters and various incidents to date have shown.'[206] Rattray notes that the complexity of information age infrastructures has created an inadvertent robustness.[207] Like industrial age economies, information age variants surely possess similar levels of capacity and redundancy. Schwartau notes that businesses operate 'Hot Sites', which are backup computer and communication facilities in the event of natural disasters.[208] More specifically, in reference to the capability of E-bombs, Kopp notes that a wider use of fibre optics, hardening and redundancy would all increase the robustness of targets to this form of attack.[209] The principles of strategy do not cease to operate just because we have entered the information age. In all likelihood, modern economies will continue to display high levels of resilience to attack, and certainly those under attack will develop methods to offset the effects of SIW.

The most potent restriction on the efficacy of strategic bombing has been left until last. Since war is essentially a battle of wills, the success or failure of strategic bombing or SIW ultimately rest upon the decisions of the enemy. It is he who must decide whether the pain he has endured outweighs the issues at stake.[210] In this sense, both forms of warfare, especially when they have the *will of the enemy* as their prime target, are somewhat uncontrollable means to an end. Yulin Whitehead is persuasive when he notes, 'The will to fight is an elusive target.'[211] An asymmetry in will appears to lie at the heart of the United States' difficulties during the Vietnam War. The North Vietnamese regime simply cared more about the issues at stake, and consequently was prepared to suffer greater levels of pain than the United States.

The strength of the enemy's will can prove problematic for strategic bombing on a number of levels. First, despite the enormous levels of destruction possible, the target population can simply become accustomed to it. This phenomenon was evident both in Germany, and in British colonies where local tribes would acquire a familiarity which diminished the terror of the early raids.[212] However, even when the population's morale becomes fragile as a result of bombing, the result tends to manifest itself in political apathy, rather than political movements demanding an end to the war. History reveals that people concentrate on their day-to-day survival rather than the greater political issues. This absence of political activity is often compounded by repressive measures on the part of the government.[213] Just as a state's economy achieves greater levels of robustness during a war, so its powers of political control also increase in a time of national emergency.[214] This creates somewhat of a paradox. Just at the time when you are trying to undermine the political stability of the enemy state, you also give it the excuse it requires to shore up that stability. Max Hastings notes how resilient and loyal the German population proved to be. Even in heavily bombed and ruined cities, they still queued to pay their taxes.[215] Attacks against the enemy's population centres and infrastructures can prove counter-productive in other ways. Merely by presenting them with a serious external threat, a bombing campaign often produces a feeling of solidarity between the population and their government. After all, it is the government that provides air defences and relief organisations. It has been extensively reported that those who were opponents of Milosevic prior to the bombing rallied somewhat to support his regime.[216] Indeed, Tom Walker of the *Sunday Times* comments: 'If ever there was a way to unite a troubled people with a history of fierce struggle, General Wesley Clark and his bombers have found it.'[217] Ironically, PGMs have tended to weaken effects on the population's morale and political behaviour. The levels of precision now possible remove some of the terror from being a citizen of a bombed country, and yet the unifying effect of the external aggression still exists.[218] During the War for Iraq, a notable feature of the bombing campaign against Baghdad was the sight of citizens driving around the city during air raid sirens. The context of a bombing campaign can be such that breaking the enemy's will is almost excluded from the realms of possibility. Pape indicates that the political and personal nature of the Nazi regime made surrender a non-option for them.[219]

The notion that a population, or state, would surrender as a result of its electricity or banking system going down in the face of SIW is difficult to accept in light of the experience of strategic bombing. Dunlap correctly identifies a degree of ethnocentrism in these notions, when he stipulates that perceiving these infrastructures of modern life as essential facilities is a very Western perspective.[220] In fact, these sorts of ideas may not even represent Western views. Pape persuasively argues that modern states have very high pain thresholds when important issues are at stake.[221] Likewise, it is difficult to disagree with Pape's observation that having your modern infrastructures rendered unusable is not comparable to being firebombed.[222] If a population's will can withstand Dresden and Tokyo, it can surely hold up in the face of all but the most destructive acts of SIW (perhaps a major nuclear incident). The will of the enemy is likely to prove as difficult a target for SIW as it has for strategic bombing, and for essentially the same reasons.

DISTINCT CHARACTERISTICS OF SIW

An analysis of SIW based solely upon its considerable similarities with strategic bombing would risk selling this new form of warfare short. SIW displays some significant characteristics of its own, which may or may not affect its strategic performance. There would appear to be at least seven such features worthy of note. First, as is noted in a great deal of the literature on this subject, SIW appears to blur traditional boundaries, including those between public and private, crime and war, and peace and war. This notion is typified by the following statement by Lt-Col David Srulowitz, Commander of AFCERT, who asserts, 'We are at war every day trying to detect and defend Air Force networked systems.'[223] There does indeed seem to be enough ambiguity in SIW activities to warrant such concerns as: who is responsible for defending the nation's NII and computers?; do particular hacking and cracking activities represent criminal intent or military and political activities?; and who should respond to such actions and how? The answer to many of these questions probably depends upon the intent of the perpetrators and the scale of their activities. Of course, discerning these two features of an attack may not be possible with any degree of certainty.

The second noteworthy feature, and one that represents a considerable contrast to strategic bombing, is the anonymity and insidious nature of SIW activities. Conventional strategic bombing is always an overt activity, whereas a nation may be under an SIW attack with no knowledge of it until the damage begins to be inflicted. The weapons of such an attack can be placed within enemy systems covertly, waiting for a preprogrammed time or event to trigger the assault. This capability could confer on SIW a level of intensity and simultaneity rarely achieved in conventional bombing. Commenting upon the use of standard protocols across information networks, Denning speculates that 'Vulnerabilities can be pervasive across computer platforms and organizations, allowing thousands of systems to be swept up in a single attack.'[224] This second characteristic also leads to the third. For the victim of the attack, the above characteristic of SIW creates, in the words of Molander *et al.*, formidable warning and attack assessment difficulties.[225] The PCCIP has recognised these dangers, and identified that an SIW campaign requires no detectable logistical preparation. This problem is compounded by the fourth property, the low entry costs required to engage in SIW. All that is really required is a PC with Internet access. Added to this is the wide availability of hacker tools.[226] We are left with a situation in which almost any individual, or group, can acquire SIW capabilities, and then prepare and launch an attack in complete anonymity. The difficulties of responding to such an attack hardly need mentioning.

The fifth notable feature of SIW is that it may have presented attackers with a new target set. In this respect, some commentators have identified the electronic infrastructure, and in particular the financial infrastructure, as new and particularly vulnerable targets. Kopp claims that knocking out these infrastructures would result in significantly more rapid economic dislocation, and produce greater systemic effects, than the more traditional target sets can offer.[227] Without any real examples it is impossible to prove or disprove this assertion. However, in response it is tempting to say that we have heard all this before, particularly in reference to the aforementioned industrial web theory. The sixth point to be made is that SIW appears to offer the disruption of a society without the attendant death and destruction. This could work both to the advantage and disadvantage of SIW as an instrument of strategy. Limiting the physical effects of an attack may help limit the level of retaliation should it come. Alternatively, as was mentioned in reference to strategic bombing with PGMs, this effect may simply diminish the impact on the morale of the target population. Also, as Douglas Waller reminds us, dislocating a society's infrastructure and economy, no matter how non-lethal the weapons themselves, will still inflict casualties in a similar vein to economic blockades.[228] The seventh feature of SIW is that it possesses global reach, and does not require the establishment of overseas bases or platforms to operate from. In this sense, SIW does not require the assistance of the other armed services to function. The global reach of certain bombers, such as the B2, suggests that this is not a unique characteristic. However, it would take a considerable fleet of conventionally armed B2s to hit the same number of targets that just one SIW attack could hit.

These seven characteristics of SIW indicate that this form of warfare has distinct advantages over strategic bombing. This new form of attack, which is low-cost, has global reach, is insidious, is anonymous and has virtually unlimited munitions (you can always write a new virus), does appear to offer the potential for attacks which have an intensity and simultaneity without precedent. However, these advantages only amount to greater operational efficiency. As mentioned earlier, operational efficiency is not the same as strategic efficacy. The distinctive features of SIW do not amount to a magic formula which ensures that this form of warfare will be appropriate for every conflict; be free of friction; be conducted on the basis of good enough intelligence; and not come up against effective enemy defences; or that those responsible for strategy will create a harmonious relationship between means and ends; or that the enemy will capitulate in the face of a devastating SIW assault.

CONCLUSION

Every war is unique. Because of this, it is impossible categorically to declare that neither strategic bombing nor SIW will ever provide strategic success independently. However, the history of strategic bombing thus far reveals that strategic airpower is only a complement to ground forces which provide 'control'. In this sense, Wylie is right to state that strategic bombing theory does not represent a general theory of war. He argues that a general theory must be applicable under any conditions and limitations.[229] Strategic bombing clearly does not fulfil this criterion. This does not mean that strategic bombing plays only a minor role. In fact, it can contribute to victory in a number of ways. Historically, bombing has forced the enemy to divert resources from other activities and fronts; has added pressure on the enemy's morale; has restricted weapons production (in the case of Germany, it propelled the Nazis to shift some production away from CAS bombers and into night-fighters);[230] can serve to maintain morale at home; and can go some way towards satisfying allies of your commitment to the fight. For example, during much of World War II, the only offensive option open to Britain was Bomber Command.[231]

Daniel L. Byman and Matthew C. Waxman's argument that the airpower debate has been distorted by focusing on its independent role can also be applied to SIW. Both airpower and SIW can function as coercive instruments in conjunction with other tools in the strategic toolbox. They should not be dismissed as failures simply on the basis that they have failed to achieve the dizzy heights set by their most ardent enthusiasts.[232] Nonetheless, based on the experience of strategic bombing, and bearing in mind the similarities between it and SIW, it is not unreasonable to suggest that SIW will in most cases fail to reach the heights of independent strategic success. Indeed, Denning concludes: 'At present, however, there is no evidence to support the notion that a country's infrastructures could be so disabled by hacking that a government would surrender to a foreign power or alter its policies.'[233] In this case, the use of traditional ground forces will ensure that the nature of warfare as outlined in Chapter 1 will survive.

It is recognised that this chapter contains much speculation concerning the strategic efficacy of SIW. This is forced upon us by the lack of a comprehensive SIW campaign to date. However, the similarities that exist between SIW and strategic bombing enable us to conclude that many of the factors that have retarded the strategic performance of strategic bombing will in all likelihood have similar, if not directly equivalent, influences on SIW.

Of the factors that have limited the success of strategic bombing, and therefore will likely retard the efficacy of SIW, some are more significant than others. Tactical and operational problems cannot be ignored. Getting the lower levels of strategy right, the practical things, is essential. However, as the history of strategic bombing has revealed, these problems can be overcome and have rarely limited the effects to a significant degree. The levels of destruction provided by Bomber Command from 1943 onwards, starting from such an unpromising beginning, are testament to this. Similarly, the impact of the diversion of resources to other roles should not be overestimated. As with the operational difficulties, these rarely, if ever, significantly retard a strategic campaign *vis-à-vis* attainment of its primary objective.

Of more significance are political restraints on a campaign, which will almost always be present. Although the objectives of policy should direct a campaign, the influence of politics does not always represent wise strategic judgment. Poor strategy can seriously compromise the chances of achieving a successful outcome. Even an excellent technical, tactical and operational military instrument can be rendered strategically impotent if used in the cause of bad strategy. Also worthy of note are institutional problems, which can have serious knock-on effects, such as a lack of operational and strategic focus. Personalities can also play a significant part in the conduct and direction of a campaign. Furthermore, loyalty to a particular doctrine can result in an effective instrument being forced to follow an inappropriate strategy for the war at hand. It can also lead to preparation for a different form of conflict from the one that actually occurs. Difficulties in intelligence should not be underestimated. Not only can these functions be poorly executed, but they may represent insurmountable tasks in the first place. Without good intelligence to identify the key targets and how they interact, a strategic campaign is severely handicapped from the start.

Whilst those conducting a strategic campaign can make a series of mistakes or face a range of internal challenges, the actions of the enemy must also be taken into account. As the example of the German night-fighters reveals, the existence of an intelligent foe can at times put the whole campaign in jeopardy. However, the most significant factors in the failure of strategic bombing are those related to the robustness of the enemy, in terms of both resilience of his capability, and his will to continue the fight. The future practitioners of SIW should take note of the fact that the success or failure of a campaign lies with the target society.

There has been a great deal written on the vulnerability of information age societies to SIW. But vulnerability alone does not lead to strategic success. This is not to say that SIW could not inflict significant levels of disruption; the evidence thus far suggests that it could. The unique characteristics of SIW may improve its operational efficacy relative to conventional bombing campaigns. That being the case, those who are vulnerable should take the appropriate defensive steps. Offensive capabilities should also be developed to operate in the fifth dimension. However, the overriding conclusion of this chapter is that SIW does not work outside of the dialectical nature of strategy, in which case the enemy's actions and his robustness will usually deny a strategic campaign the strategic success it desires, leaving final victory often to be achieved by ground forces. However, the fact that SIW is developing as a form of warfare may compel us to modify our understanding of the nature of warfare. Whether or not this is the case will be discussed later.

NOTES

1. *Critical Foundations: Protecting America's Infrastructures,* Report of the President's Commission on Critical Infrastructure Protection, October 1997, www.pccip.gov.
2. There is an ongoing debate about what actually constitutes 'information warfare'. It is certainly true that NIIs can be attacked by physical acts of destruction. However, Schwartau has defined (pure) information warfare as 'the total absence of bombs,

bullets, or other conventional tools of physical destruction'. See Schwartau, *Information Warfare*, p. 464. Although it is accepted by this work that SIW can be waged with conventional tools of physical destruction, this chapter will test the strategic efficacy of SIW in its 'pure' form. Schwartau's information warfare poses the greatest challenge to the nature of warfare. Also, even if SIW contained some limited instances of conventional physical attacks, the change in the character of warfare would still prove substantial if malicious software and its like comprised the majority of the attacks.

3. Greg Rattray notes, 'Strategic Information Warfare can be conducted in either a physically violent or nonviolent way.' See Greg Rattray, *Strategic Warfare in Cyberspace* (Cambridge, MA, MIT Press, 2001), p. 19.
4. Gray, *War, Peace, and Victory*, p. 23.
5. Robert A. Pape, 'The Limits of Precision-Guided Air Power', *Security Studies*, 7, 2 (1997–98), p. 95.
6. Wylie, *Military Strategy*, p. 61.
7. Rattray, *Strategic Warfare in Cyberspace*, p. 141.
8. The lack of an SIW attack contrasted sharply with some predictions. For example, see John Schwartz, 'Cyberterrorists Sharpening their Tools for Online Warfare', *International Herald Tribune*, 21 March 2003, p. 5.
9. For example, five Dutch hackers obtained sensitive US military information before and during the 1991 Gulf War. They allegedly attempted to sell this information to the Iraqi regime. See Denning, *Information Warfare and Security*, pp. 3–4. There are also many examples in which websites have been defaced for political purposes, although it would be stretching a point to regard them as acts of SIW. See Michael A. Vatis, *Cyber Attacks during the War on Terrorism: A Predictive Analysis* (Hanover, NH, Institute for Security Technology Studies, Dartmouth College, 2001).
10. Quoted in Keaney and Cohen, *Gulf War Air Power Survey*, p. 90.
11. See the discussion below regarding the ambiguities surrounding such terms as 'strategic warfare'.
12. For example, in the official history of Britain's air offensive against Nazi Germany, Charles Webster and Noble Frankland note that the vulnerability of the German economy was overestimated, as was the operational capability of Bomber Command. See Sir Charles Webster and Noble Frankland, *The Strategic Air Offensive against Germany 1939–45*, Vol. III, *Victory, Part 5* (HMSO, London, 1961), p. 285.
13. Colonel John A. Warden III, 'The Enemy as a System', www.airpower.maxwell.af.mil/airchronicles/apj/warden.html.
14. Mark J. Conversino, 'The Changed Nature of Strategic Air Attack', *Parameters*, 27, 4, carlisle-www.army.mil/usawc/Parameters/97winter/conversi.htm.
15. See Warden, 'The Enemy as a System'.
16. Vegetius, *Vegetius*, p. 81.
17. Quoted in Richard P. Hallion, *Storm over Iraq: Air Power and the Gulf War* (Washington, DC, Smithsonian Institution Press, 1992), p. 7.
18. Giulio Douhet, *The Command of the Air* (London, Faber & Faber, 1943), p. 18.
19. For a sensible discussion of the semantics surrounding strategy, and the meaning of 'strategy' in general, see Gray, *War, Peace, and Victory*, especially Ch. 1.
20. For example, see Matthew Campbell, 'US at Mercy of Cyber Terrorists', *Sunday Times*, 17 May 1998, p. 26.
21. Molander *et al.*, 'Strategic Information Warfare'.
22. Adams, *The Next World War*, p. 184. Note once again the loose usage of the term 'strategic'. Within the Strategic Studies literature the appearance of SIW is credited with further complicating the job of the strategist. See Baylis and Wirtz, 'Introduction', p. 2.
23. Kenneth A. Minihan, 'Defending the Nation against Cyber Attack: Information

Assurance in the Global Environment', *CyberThreat: Protecting US Information Networks*, *USIA Electronic Journal*, 3, 4 (1998), usinfo.state.gov/journals/itps/1198/iipe/toc.htm.

24. For details and an appraisal of these government efforts, see Robert F. Dacey (Director, Information Security Issues), *Critical Infrastructure Protection: Significant Homeland Security Challenges Need to Be Addressed*, Testimony before the Subcommittee on Oversight and Investigations, Committee on Energy and Commerce, House of Representatives (Washington, DC, United States General Accounting Office, July 2002).

25. George Jones and Michael Smith, 'Hacking is Now Bigger Threat than Terrorism', *Telegraph*, 30 March 2001, www.telegraph.co.uk/el.

26. Thomas, *Like Adding Wings to a Tiger*, p. 7.

27. GAO Executive Report, B-266140, http://www.infowar.com/civil_de/gaosum.html-ssi. An indication of the growing threat is evident from the fact that computer security incidents reported to the CERT Coordination Centre (a federally funded body) rose from 9,859 in 1999 to 52,658 in 2001. See Dacey, *Critical Infrastructure Protection*, p. 11.

28. Bill Gertz, 'Pentagon Fortifying Computer Networks to Block Hackers', www.washtimes.com/nation/national.html, and Adams, *The Next World War*, pp. 187–8. A comprehensive resource detailing a vast range of hacker activities, as well as general information on computer security issues and information warfare generally, can be found at Infowar.com. As an aside, it is important to note that many of these figures have been questioned. See in particular George Smith, 'An Electronic Pearl Harbor? Not Likely', *Issues in Science and Technology Online*, Fall 1998, 205.130.85.236/issues/15.1/smith.htm.

29. Dacey, *Critical Infrastructure Protection*, p. 29.

30. Denning, *Information Warfare and Security*, p. xiv.

31. See GAO Executive Report, B-266140.

32. Thomas, *Like Adding Wings to a Tiger*, pp. 3–4.

33. Robert Anderson reports that the capabilities required to conduct SIW attacks are quite widespread. See Robert H. Anderson, *Securing the US Defense Information Infrastructure: A Proposed Approach*, www.rand.org/publications/mr/mr993.

34. Dacey, *Critical Infrastructure Protection*, p. 11.

35. The accessibility of SIW capabilities is stressed in the GAO Executive Report, B-266140, as well as by John M. Deutch (former Director of Central Intelligence). See Deutch, 'Foreign Information Warfare Programs and Capabilities'.

36. Adams, *The Next World War*, pp. 162–3.

37. Schwartau, *Information Warfare*, p. 400.

38. It is not the intention of this book to provide a detailed description of each form of SIW weapon. For such details see the following sources: Schwartau, *Information Warfare*, Adams, *The Next World War*, Infowar.com and Waller, 'Onward Cyber Soldiers'.

39. See Kopp, 'The E-Bomb'. A description of the growing availability and capabilities of non-nuclear EMP devices can be found in Adams, *The Next World War*, pp. 149-51.

40. Adams, *The Next World War*, p. 175.

41. See The President's Commission on Critical Infrastructure Protection: Report Summary. Schwartau produces a similar list of targets. He identifies four main categories, which are: the power grid, communications infrastructure, the financial infrastructure and the transportation infrastructure. See Schwartau, *Information Warfare*, p. 43.

42. Molander *et al.*, 'Strategic Information Warfare'.

43. Frank J. Cilluffo and Curt H. Gergely, 'Information Warfare and Strategic Terrorism',

Terrorism and Political Violence, 9, 1 (1997), p. 87.

44. Kevin Soo Hoo, Seymour Goodman and Lawrence Greenberg, 'Information Technology and the Terrorist Threat', *Survival*, 39, 3 (1997), p. 141.

45. Quoted in Andrew Rathmel, 'Cyber-Terrorism: The Shape of Future Conflict?', *RUSI Journal*, 142, 5 (1997), pp. 42–3.

46. Timothy L. Thomas, 'Deterring Information Warfare: A New Strategic Challenge', *Parameters*, 26, 4 (1996–97), p. 90.

47. Quoted in John C. Coale, 'Fighting Cybercrime', *Military Review*, 78, 2 (1998), p. 80.

48. Danial J. Ryan and Julie J. C. H. Ryan, 'Protecting the National Information Infrastructure against Infowar', in Winn Schwartau (ed.), *Information Warfare: Cyberterrorism: Protecting Your Personal Security in the Electronic Age*, Second Edition (New York, Thunder's Mouth Press, 1996), p. 628.

49. John Pimlott, 'The Theory and Practice of Strategic Bombing', in Colin McInnes and G. D. Sheffield (eds), *Warfare in the Twentieth Century: Theory and Practice* (London, Unwin Hyman, 1988), pp. 113–39.

50. Rattray, 'Strategic Warfare in Cyberspace', p. 22.

51. Quoted in Tami Davis Biddle, 'British and American Approaches to Strategic Bombing: Their Origins and Implementation in the World War II Combined Bomber Offensive', *Journal of Strategic Studies*, Special Issue on Airpower: Theory and Practice, John Gooch (ed.), 18, 1 (1995), p. 111.

52. See Daniel T. Kuehl, 'Airpower vs. Electricity: Electric Power as a Target for Strategic Air Operations', *Journal of Strategic Studies*, special issue on Airpower: Theory and Practice, John Gooch (ed.), 18, 1 (March 1995), pp. 237–66, and Robert A. Pape, *Bombing to Win: Air Power and Coercion in War* (Ithaca, NY, Cornell University Press, 1996), especially pp. 62–4.

53. Warden, *The Enemy as a System*.

54. Rattray, 'Strategic Warfare in Cyberspace', p. 118.

55. Waller, 'Onward Cyber Soldiers', p. 32.

56. See Kopp, 'The E-Bomb', p. 323.

57. Arquilla and Ronfeldt, 'A New Epoch', p. 14.

58. Gray, *Explorations in Strategy*, p. 58.

59. Quoted in Kenneth P. Werrell, *Blankets of Fire: United States' Bombers over Japan during WWII* (Washington, DC, Smithsonian Institution Press, 1996), pp. 238–9.

60. Quoted in Ellis, *Brute Force*, p. 185.

61. Terraine, *The Right of the Line*, pp. 513, 605.

62. Richard Overy, *Why the Allies Won* (London, Pimlico, 1996), p. 123.

63. This point is recognised by the official United States Army Air Forces' history, which notes that the air commanders enjoyed great latitude in conducting their campaigns. See John E. Fagg, 'The Climax of Strategic Operations', in Wesley Frank Craven and James Lea Cate (eds), *The Army Air Forces in World War II*, Vol. Three, *Europe: Argument to V-E Day January 1944 to May 1945* (Chicago, IL, University of Chicago Press, 1951), p. 721. The lack of 'negative' objectives in World War II is also noted by Mark Clodfelter, in *The Limits of Air Power: The American Bombing of North Vietnam* (New York, Free Press, 1989), p. 4.

64. Pape, *Bombing to Win*, pp. 254–5.

65. John E. Fagg, 'Mission Accomplished', in Wesley Frank Craven and James Lea Cate (eds), *The Army Air Forces in World War II*, Vol. Three, *Europe: Argument to V-E Day January 1944 to May 1945* (Chicago, IL, University of Chicago Press, 1951), p. 787.

66. Terraine, *The Right of the Line*, pp. 546–7.

67. Ibid., p. 677.

68. For example, Alfred C. Mierzejewski has identified the railways as the key target, whereas Max Hastings regards synthetic oil as the jugular vein. See Alfred C. Mierzejewski, *The Collapse of the German War Economy 1944–45: Allied Air Power and the German National Railway* (Chapel Hill, NC, University of North Carolina Press, 1988), and Max Hastings, *Bomber Command* (London, Michael Joseph, 1979), p. 223.
69. Fagg, 'Mission Accomplished', p. 794.
70. Terraine, *The Right of the Line*, p. 281.
71. Pape, *Bombing to Win*, pp. 278–9, 282.
72. James Lea Cate and Wesley Frank Craven, 'Victory', in James Lea Cate and Wesley Frank Craven (eds), *The Army Air Forces in World War II*, Vol. Five, *The Pacific: Matterhorn to Nagasaki June 1944 to August 1945* (Chicago, IL, University of Chicago Press, 1953), p. 751.
73. Conrad C. Crane, *Bombs, Cities, and Civilians: American Airpower Strategy in World War II* (Kansas, University Press of Kansas, 1993), p. 122.
74. See Werrell, *Blankets of Fire*, p. 230, and Cate and Craven, 'Victory', p. 752.
75. For these and other details of the raids see Crane, *Bombs, Cities, and Civilians*, p. 140, and Werrell, *Blankets of Fire*, p. 227.
76. Quoted in Cate and Craven, 'Victory', p. 756.
77. Werrell, *Blankets of Fire*, p. 233.
78. This is a point made by Barry D. Watts. See Barry D. Watts, 'Ignoring Reality: Problems of Theory and Evidence in Security Studies', *Security Studies*, 7, 2 (1997–98), pp. 152–5.
79. R. F. Futrell, *Ideas, Concepts, Doctrine: Basic Thinking in the United States Air Force 1961–1984*, Vol. 2 (Alabama, Maxwell Air Force Base Air University, 1984), pp. 259–60.
80. Diego M. Wendt, 'Using a Sledgehammer to Kill a Gnat: The Air Force's Failure to Comprehend Insurgent Doctrine during Operation Rolling Thunder', www.airpower.maxwell.af.mil/airchronicles/apj/4sum90.html.
81. Clodfelter, *The Limits of Air Power*, p. 75.
82. Ibid., p. 134.
83. Ibid., especially pp. 167–8.
84. Quoted in Futrell, *Ideas, Concepts, Doctrine*, p. 270.
85. Ibid., p. 271.
86. Clodfelter, *The Limits of Air Power*, pp. ix–x.
87. Ibid., p. 199.
88. Hawkins, 'Imposing Peace', p. 78.
89. For details on the Iraqi air defences, see Hallion, *Storm over Iraq*, p. 163.
90. Williamson Murray, *Air War in the Persian Gulf* (Baltimore, MD, Nautical and Aviation Publishing Company of America, 1995), p. 32.
91. Keaney and Cohen, *Gulf War Air Power Survey*, pp. 56–7.
92. Although, the loss of a Nighthawk over Yugoslavia may somewhat challenge this view. This event underlines the fragility of any technology to countermeasures. Ibid., p. 245.
93. Ibid., p. 14.
94. Ibid., p. 133.
95. Ibid., p. 220.
96. Ibid., p. 145.
97. Pape, *Bombing to Win*, p. 228.
98. Keaney and Cohen, *Gulf War Air Power Survey*, p. 73.
99. Hallion, *Storm over Iraq*, p. 193.
100. This objective is identified by Gordon and Trainor, *The Generals' War*, p. 474.

101. See Yulin Whitehead, 'Information as a Weapon: Reality versus Promises', www.airpower.maxwell.af.mil/airchronicles/apj/apj97/fal97/whitehead.html.
102. Keaney and Cohen, *Gulf War Air Power Survey*, p. 70.
103. Quoted in BBC, 'The Gulf War', Television Broadcast, 9 January 1996.
104. For other NATO advantages see Barry R. Posen, 'The War for Kosovo: Serbia's Political–Military Strategy', *International Security*, 24, 4 (2000), p. 49.
105. Lambeth, *NATO's Air Way for Kosovo*, p. 11.
106. Wylie, *Military Strategy*, p. 71
107. John Keegan, 'Please Mr Blair, Never Take Such a Risk Again', *Sunday Telegraph*, 6 June 1999, www.telegraph.co.uk/et.
108. Posen, 'War for Kosovo', p. 71.
109. Quoted in 'Russia, Not Bombs, Brought End to War in Kosovo, Says Jackson', *Sunday Telegraph*, 1 August 1999, www.telegraph.co.uk/et.
110. See Goulding, 'From Chancellorsville to Kosovo', p. 6, and O'Hanlon, *Technological Change*, p. 129, who also places emphasis on the Russian diplomatic role and the signals coming from NATO about a ground offensive.
111. O'Hanlon, *Technological Change*, p. 72.
112. Lambeth, *NATO's Air War for Kosovo*, p. 246. This point is reiterated by General Clark, *Waging Modern War*, p. 443.
113. Posen, 'War for Kosovo', pp. 79–81.
114. Ibid., p. 64.
115. Ibid., p. 65.
116. The Manchester suffered from a number of inadequacies. These included insufficient engine power, a low ceiling and vulnerability to shrapnel bursts. See Hastings, *Bomber Command*, pp. 148–9.
117. See Hallion, *Storm over Iraq*, pp. 14–15, and Kenneth P. Werrell, 'Did USAF Technology Fail in Vietnam?: Three Case Studies', www.airpower.maxwell.af.mil/ airchronicles/apj/ apj98/spr98/werrell.html.
118. Fagg, 'Mission Accomplished', p. 795.
119. Ellis, *Brute Force*, p. 214.
120. Crane, *Bombs, Cities, and Civilians*, pp. 69–70.
121. Ibid., p. 64.
122. Hallion, *Storm over Iraq*, p. 250.
123. Lambeth, *NATO's Air War for Kosovo*, p. 137.
124. For example, see '18 Die as US Plane Bombs Kurdish Convoy in Worst Friendly Fire Incident', *Guardian*, 7 April 2003, p. 3.
125. Terraine, *The Right of the Line*, p. 459.
126. Crane, *Bombs, Cities, and Civilians*, p. 154.
127. See Michael Evans, 'Weather Holds up the Bombs', *The Times*, 31 March 1999, p. 2, and Lambeth, *NATO's Air War for Kosovo*, p. 27.
128. Terraine notes how Essen was shrouded in an industrial haze. See Terraine, *The Right of the Line*, p. 475. RAF Harrier crews encountered similar problems on their first raids into Kosovo. On this occasion smoke from earlier TLAM raids obscured their targets and interfered with their laser guidance systems. See Michael Evans and James Landale, 'High-Tech Harriers are Blinded by Smoke', *Times*, 26 March 1999, p. 3.
129. This latter point does not take account of SIW defences, the potential of which will be discussed later.
130. Kopp, 'The E-Bomb', p. 318.
131. Denning also raises questions about the current validity of EMP devices. She draws attention to the lack of any substantial evidence of their successful use. Denning, *Information Warfare and Security*, pp. 199–200.

132. Terraine, *The Right of the Line*, p. 493.
133. This is a point made by Webster and Frankland, *Strategic Air Offensive against Germany*, pp. 293–5.
134. Biddle, 'British and American Approaches to Strategic Bombing', p. 124.
135. Clodfelter, *The Limits of Air Power*, p. 128.
136. Ibid., p. 123.
137. Clark, *Waging Modern War*, p. 425.
138. Lambeth, *NATO's Air War for Kosovo*, p. 213.
139. Ibid., p. 192.
140. Quoted in Adams, *The Next World War*, p. 301.
141. See Crane, *Bombs, Cities, and Civilians*, p. 20.
142. Ibid., p. 150.
143. Werrell, 'Did USAF Technology Fail in Vietnam?', p. 7.
144. Keaney and Cohen, *Gulf War Air Power Survey*, pp. 136–7.
145. Lambeth, *NATO's Air War for Kosovo*, pp. xix, 124.
146. For a history of the development of US doctrine on information operations, see Rattray, *Strategic Warfare in Cyberspace*, pp. 311–30.
147. Webster and Frankland, *Strategic Air Offensive against Germany*, p. 304.
148. Pape, *Bombing to Win*, p. 275.
149. Clodfelter, *The Limits of Air Power*, p. 130.
150. Mierzejewski, *Collapse of the German War Economy*, pp. 179–80.
151. Keany and Cohen, *Gulf War Air Power Survey*, and Mierzejewski, *Collapse of the German War Economy*, p. 180.
152. Fagg, 'Mission Accomplished', p. 793.
153. See Keaney and Cohen, *Gulf War Air Power Survey*, pp. 130–8.
154. Ibid., p. 121.
155. Ibid., pp. 138–43.
156. Fagg, 'Mission Accomplished', p. 794.
157. Rattray notes how a great deal of information can be gathered on the vulnerability of certain target sets. Rattray, *Strategic Warfare in Cyberspace*, p. 136.
158. Matthew G. Devost, Brian K. Houghton and Neal Allen Pollard, 'Response to Cilluffo and Gergely', *Terrorism and Political Violence*, 9, 1 (1997), p. 96. This is also noted by Smith, 'Electronic Pearl Harbor?'.
159. Martin C. Libicki, 'Deterring Information Attacks', in Winn Schwartau, (ed.), *Information Warfare: Cuberterrorism: Protecting Your Personal Security in the Electronic Age*, Second Edition (New York, Thunder's Mouth Press, 1996), p. 594.
160. Murray, *Air War in the Persian Gulf*, p. 32.
161. Martin C. Libicki, *Defending Cyberspace and Other Metaphors* (Washington, DC, National Defense University, 1997), p. 4.
162. Kopp, 'The E-Bomb', p. 318.
163. Murray, *Air War in the Persian Gulf* p. 36.
164. Terraine, *The Right of the Line*, p. 691.
165. See Keaney and Cohen, *Gulf War Air Power Survey*.
166. Ibid., pp. 83–4, and Webster and Frankland, *Strategic Air Offensive against Germany*, p. 310.
167. *FM 100-6*.
168. Terraine, *The Right of the Line*, p. 278.
169. See Hallion, *Storm over Iraq*, Keaney and Cohen, *Gulf War Air Power Survey*, and Pape, *Bombing to Win*.
170. Murray, *Air War in the Persian Gulf*, p. 34.
171. William M. Arkin, 'Baghdad: The Urban Sanctuary in Desert Storm?', www.airpower.maxwell.af.mil/airchronicles/apj/spr97/arkin.html.

172. Clodfelter, *The Limits of Air Power*, pp. 43–4, 140.
173. Quoted in 'Europe Politics Hurt NATO Strikes', news.bbc.co.uk/hi/english/world/europe/newsid_334000/334879.stm.
174. Posen, 'War for Kosovo', p. 70.
175. Lambeth, *NATO's Air War for Kosovo*, p. 81. This view is supported by General Clark. See Clark, *Waging Modern War*, p. 426.
176. See David E. Omissi, *Air Power and Colonial Control: The Royal Air Force 1919–1939* (Manchester, Manchester University Press, 1990), pp. 154–9.
177. Wendt, 'Using a Sledgehammer to Kill a Gnat'.
178. Lambeth, *NATO's Air War for Kosovo*, p. 230.
179. Cohen, *Supreme Command*, p. 177.
180. Clodfelter, *The Limits of Air Power*, p. 124.
181. Wendt, 'Using a Sledgehammer to Kill a Gnat', and Crane, *Bombs, Cities, and Civilians*, p. 148.
182. Pape, *Bombing to Win*, p. 75.
183. Omissi, *Air Power and Colonial Control*, pp. 156–7.
184. Keaney and Cohen, *Gulf War Air Power Survey*, p. 57.
185. Fagg, 'Mission Accomplished', and Hastings, *Bomber Command*, p. 46.
186. Gray, *Modern Strategy*, p. 25.
187. Terraine, *The Right of the Line*, p. 516.
188. Crane, *Bombs, Cities, and Civilians*, p. 10. Whilst this may have proved effective in the past, as the War for Iraq reveals technologies such as GPS make the visible identification of the target less important.
189. Ralph Barker, *The Thousand Plan: The Story of the First Thousand Bomber Raid on Cologne* (Shrewsbury, Airlife Publishing, 1992), p. 143.
190. Keaney and Cohen, *Gulf War Air Power Survey*, p. 86.
191. Omissi, *Air Power and Colonial Control*, p. 121.
192. Clodfelter, *The Limits of Air Power*, p. 22.
193. Ibid., p. 132.
194. Quoted in Terraine, *The Right of the Line*, p. 558.
195. Hastings, *Bomber Command*, p. 234, and Overy, *Why the Allies Won*, p. 118.
196. Schwartau, *Information Warfare*, p. 589.
197. Freedman, *Information Warfare: Will Battle Ever Be Joined?*, p. 8.
198. See Smith, 'Electronic Pearl Harbor?'.
199. Quoted in Bernard Brodie, *Strategy in the Missile Age* (Princeton, NJ, Princeton University Press, 1959), p. 6.
200. Pape, *Bombing to Win*, pp. 23, 153.
201. Terraine, *The Right of the Line*, p. 548.
202. Hastings, *Bomber Command*, p. 227.
203. Pape, *Bombing to Win*, p. 271.
204. Keaney and Cohen, *Gulf War Air Power Survey*, pp. 69–70.
205. See Pape, *Bombing to Win*, pp. 76, 163–4, 274.
206. Robert H. Anderson, 'Risks to the US Infrastructure from Cyberspace', Verbal Testimony to the Permanent Subcommittee on Investigations, 25 June 1996.
207. Rattray, *Strategic Warfare in Cyberspace*, p. 133.
208. Schwartau, *Information Warfare*, p. 528.
209. Kopp, 'The E-Bomb', pp. 304–19.
210. Pape, *Bombing to Win*, p. 13.
211. Whitehead, 'Information as a Weapon'.
212. See Crane, *Bombs, Cities, and Civilians*, p. 100, and Omissi, *Air Power and Colonial Control*, p. 132.
213. Pape, *Bombing to Win*, p. 272.

214. Ibid., p. 33.
215. Hastings, *Bomber Command*, p. 232.
216. See Pape, *Bombing to Win*, p. 272, and Roger Boyes, 'Serb Unity is the Deadliest Weapon Confronting NATO Alliance', *Times*, 30 March 1999, p. 6.
217. Tom Walker, 'Outgunned Underdogs Await Day of Revenge in a "Man-to-Man" Battle', *Sunday Times*, 28 March 1999, p. 2.
218. Arkin, 'Baghdad', p. 10.
219. Pape, *Bombing to Win*, p. 296.
220. Dunlap, 'Sometimes the Dragon Wins', p. 447.
221. Pape, *Bombing to Win*, p. 316.
222. Pape, 'The Limits of Precision-Guided Air Power', p. 103.
223. Quoted in Adams, *The Next World War*, p. 203.
224. Denning, *Information Warfare and Security*, p. 16.
225. Molander *et al.*, 'Strategic Information Warfare'.
226. See Molander *et al.*, 'Strategic Information Warfare', *Critical Foundations*, and Rattray, *Strategic Warfare in Cyberspace*, pp. 137, 141, 148.
227. Kopp, 'The E-Bomb', pp. 323–4.
228. Waller, 'Onward Cyber Soldiers', p. 32.
229. Wylie, *Military Strategy*, p. 57.
230. Overy, *Why the Allies Won*, p. 129.
231. Terraine, *The Right of the Line*, p. 259, and Hastings, *Bomber Command*, p. 348.
232. Daniel L. Byman and Matthew C. Waxman, 'Kosovo and the Great Air Power Debate', *International Security*, 24, 4 (2000), pp. 5–38.
233. Denning, *Information Warfare and Security*, p. 65. Denning also provides a useful service by dispelling some of the myths surrounding the damage certain types of SIW attacks may inflict. See pp. 70–1.

5

Information Power: Strategy, Geopolitics and the Fifth Dimension

'Now, as in revolutions past, technology is profoundly affecting the sovereignty of governments, the world economy, and military strategy.'[1]

INTRODUCTION

Thus far, this work has postulated that the fundamental nature of war will not change with the coming of the information age. Yet, it has also been suggested that important changes will occur. Particularly worthy of note are: the development of SIW as a new instrument of strategy; the general rise in the importance of information in the battlespace; and greater levels of flexibility offered by information power to those practising strategy. Not surprisingly, some analysts foresee profound geopolitical consequences resulting from the information revolution. The above quotation is illustrative of a growing literature that attributes revolutionary implications to the development and spread of IT. Typically these works predict the empowerment of small and/or non-state actors; the decline of the nation-state; a decreasing relevance for the physical world and its relationships; and the rising importance of information in the strategic world at the expense of traditional military capabilities.[2]

Technological developments that facilitate a more effective exploitation of a particular dimension of strategy can have important consequences. For example, the utilisation of the air and space environments in the twentieth century (the third and fourth dimensions respectively) has further complicated the strategic world, and has presented new vulnerabilities and opportunities. In response, many actors have had to develop an understanding of these environments and how to operate within them. Some technologies, such as nuclear-armed intercontinental ballistic missiles (ICBMs), may also have consequences for geopolitics and the continued relevance of geographical factors in international politics and strategy. The development of Soviet ICBMs made the United States vulnerable to attack in a manner that negated the defensive attributes of the Atlantic and Pacific oceans. However, the geopolitical ramifications of nuclear weapons have not been as dramatic as some authors speculated. For example, in 1957, Hertz speculated that nuclear weapons would signal the demise of the nation-state, since it had seemingly become unable to fulfil the primary function of protecting its citizens.[3]

When considering the relationship between technology and geopolitics, it is important to remember that geopolitical theory has often rested on the premise that technology can help shape the geopolitical world. After all, Sir Halford Mackinder regarded the development of railways as the key to unlocking the potential of the Heartland, thereby signalling the rise of continental powers at the expense of the maritime countries.[4] It is therefore not implausible that the continued development of IT could have significant consequences for strategy and geopolitics. However, we must not overplay the significance of the information revolution. To do so could lead to a form of technological determinism. Mackinder avoided this particular pitfall by suggesting in his later work that the Heartland power could be offset by the Midland Ocean coalition.[5]

Other theorists have been less restrained than Mackinder and have tended to overemphasise the significance of a new technology or dimension of strategy. As indicated in the previous chapter, this occurred in the early years of airpower during the interwar period. Despite a number of comprehensive strategic bombing campaigns, most notably in World War II, Vietnam and the 1991 Gulf War, the claims of theorists like Douhet have yet to be fully realised. However, this failure does not mean that the third dimension is unimportant. Airpower has for some time been regarded as the equal of the other forms of strategic power, and in certain quarters and/or certain circumstances is considered to be the leading edge of military power.[6] In this respect a new technology or particular dimension of strategy may not become independently dominant, but may still attain a significant level of importance. In reference to IT, the fifth dimension is likely to become even more significant in the practice of strategy. But it would be a mistake to overlook the continued importance of physical geography and the military forces that operate in the traditional physical environment.

In light of these thoughts, the objective of this chapter is to provide a framework that promotes a better understanding of the role information activities can play in the means–ends world of strategy. To this end, this chapter will demonstrate that a fifth dimension (the infosphere) of strategy does exist. From this, the chapter will explore the nature of this new dimension and analyse how this affects the practice of strategy within it. Analysing the advantages and limitations of 'information power' is crucial in any attempt to understand the long-term implications of the fifth dimension. It will be shown that these limitations indicate that physical expressions of strategic power, and the geography in which they operate, will remain relevant. With these foundations in place we can begin to understand the significance the information revolution has for geopolitics.

INFOSPHERE: THE FIFTH DIMENSION OF STRATEGY

As noted above, a considerable step in appreciating the significance of the information environment and its attendant power is to understand the nature of the fifth dimension. The other forms of strategic power: sea, land, air and space, all have their own physical environments that have unique characteristics.[7] The nature of each environment determines to a degree how the corresponding power can be utilised. Information power operates within an environment that is best defined as the 'infosphere'. Due to its ethereal nature the infosphere does not take easily to any concrete definition. In fact, the infosphere is best thought of as an amorphous entity where information exists and flows. Although clearly not a physical medium in the same vein as the other dimensions of strategy, an information dimension can be identified. Weapons, in the form of malicious software, can flow through the infosphere, and in this sense the fifth dimension acts as a medium for strategic power. In a similar vein, conflict occurs within the infosphere. The World War II activities of the Royal Air Force's No. 80 (Signals) Wing, the so-called 'Beam Benders', present an interesting case study of conflict in the fifth dimension.[8] Like the sea, one of the functions of the infosphere is to act as a highway, through which information and weapons can flow.[9] The sea is also a place where large deposits of natural resources are to be found. Having secure access to the sea helps to ensure that these resources can be exploited. Likewise, deposits of information reside within the infosphere. In an age in which information is increasingly regarded as vital to the effective functioning of society,[10] ensuring access to this resource will be critical. These characteristics seem to imply that the infosphere does indeed constitute a medium of strategy, which has enormous economic, social, political and military relevance. Ultimately, the defining characteristic that identifies the infosphere as a dimension of strategy is that various forms of strategic power can be projected through and within this distinct environment. Therefore, like the other environments, operating in the fifth dimension requires distinct skills and doctrine.

The above description of the infosphere requires some important qualifications. Parts of the infosphere actually exist in the physical world. Rattray explains this effectively in some detail:

> Cyberspace, however, is actually a *physical domain* [emphasis in the original] resulting from the creation of information systems and networks that enable electronic interactions to take place. The 1s and 0s of bits have physical manifestations in the state of electrons in a semiconductor gate or the waveforms of light passing through a fiber-optic cable.[11]

The electromagnetic spectrum, which acts as the substantial under-pinning to the infosphere, is also a physical reality. This also applies to the many physical assets that form part of the infosphere, such as satellites, cables, computers and humans. In this respect, *Joint Vision 2020* provides a useful definition of the information environment: 'the aggregate of individuals, organizations, and systems that collect, process, or disseminate information, including the information itself'.[12] In this way, there exists a significant overlap between the fifth dimension and the physical world. Libicki describes cyberspace (an important part of the infosphere) as being characterised by 'placelessness'.[13] This point is generally true, although not entirely, and may become less true as time progresses. Increasingly parts of cyberspace, and indeed information itself, are being territorialised, in that businesses, individuals and states are claiming ownership. There is a sense that this is 'our' information, or these are 'our' computers, and we will choose whether to let you in or not. Of course, with the right skills access can be gained to some restricted systems and information. However, it would be questionable to conclude that boundaries in cyberspace are an illusion simply because computer systems and information can be accessed by unauthorised users. The fact that people can gain illegal access across a state's borders does not invalidate the geopolitical reality of nation-states. These thoughts have important implications for those who claim that a new geopolitical reality is on the horizon because the infosphere is without boundaries. As Robert O. Keohane and Joseph S. Nye, Jr note, 'information does not flow in a vacuum but in political space already occupied'.[14]

Whether or not the infosphere is strictly speaking a physical reality is perhaps no more than a problem of definition. In the practical world of strategy what really matters is to perceive the infosphere as a place that exists, understand the nature of it and regard it as something that can be manipulated and used for strategic advantage.

As noted, the nature of the infosphere has important implications for those operating within it. One of the most prominent characteristics of the fifth dimension is that relative to the other dimensions of strategy it can be expanded or contracted far more easily, and to a much greater degree, by man's actions.[15] The fifth dimension is malleable; to some extent it can be moulded and shaped. For example, the launch of a new satellite and the connection of a computer to the Internet are two ways of expanding the fifth dimension. A new satellite produces new information, or a new conduit through which information can flow, and thereby the infosphere is expanded. The converse methods to achieve contraction should be obvious. Thus we have a situation in which some assets of information power, such as satellites and computers, are also simultaneously elements of the infosphere. The infosphere can also be manipulated through the art of deception. These truisms have implications for those wishing to contest command or control of the fifth dimension.

Within the infosphere a dynamic relationship exists between those wishing to protect their information activities and those attempting to undermine them. Protecting and securing information flow and integrity will require constant vigilance.[16] This is an important point to note. There are few absolutes in the infosphere. As elsewhere in the strategic world, the existence of an intelligent foe means that those practising information power will face counters to their activities. Again, this affects the degree of revolutionary change that the fifth dimension may produce. If information power is offset or abated, its strategic efficacy may be diminished.

Terms other than the 'infosphere' may be put forward to describe the fifth dimension. Another candidate that may be championed is 'cyberspace'. However, cyberspace connotes a modern construction. To cite Libicki's definition, cyberspace is 'the sum of the globe's communications links and computational nodes'.[17] Cyberspace is only part of the infosphere. Like information warfare itself, the infosphere is an ancient component of strategy. As noted in the Introduction to this book, Napoleon's use of a cavalry screen to hide the movement of forces is a classic example of information warfare.[18] By definition, Napoleon was also manipulating the infosphere. The assets of information power need not be high-tech, or dedicated solely to information tasks. A simple hilltop represents an asset of information power. The significance of physical high ground as an asset of information power has many historical examples. The battle for the Falkland Islands presents one relatively modern case. The capture of Mount Kent by British forces established a useful observation post over Port Stanley, and prevented the Argentinians using this ground to rain down observed artillery fire on 3 Commando Brigade.[19]

When considering the fifth dimension, a reasonable question to ask is why existence of the infosphere and the concept of information power have not been noted until the information age. The most compelling response to this is that the information age has raised our awareness of information. In addition, the developments of cyberspace and SIW have given the fifth dimension a more distinct strategic function. Consequently, we are adopting a mindset that sees information as a tangible resource. Long-established beliefs can be reassessed. For much of history it was taken for granted that time was absolute. It now transpires that time is relative.[20] As the information age develops, and with it the growing significance of information, the infosphere may be attaining a greater prominence in many sectors of our economic, social, cultural and military life. It is the developing salience of information that has raised the profile of the infosphere.

Of course, as noted in the Introduction to this work, mankind has always been aware of the existence and value of information. Information has always been an important resource. In many ways, the greater exploitation of the infosphere is analogous to the exploitation of the air dimension in the twentieth century. The third dimension has always played a role in warfare, mainly through the transmission of vocal or percussion commands, or as the medium through which projectiles travel.[21] However, it took the invention of heavier-than-air machines to lead to a far greater exploitation of this dimension of strategy. Similarly, it may have taken the broader exploitation of the electromagnetic spectrum, and in particular the emergence of cyberspace, to realise fully the potential of information power.

CONTROL OF THE INFOSPHERE

The principal operational concept in both the air and sea environments is concerned with gaining command or control of the environment in question. Douhet defines command of the air as: '[to] have the ability to fly against an enemy so as to injure him, while he has been deprived of the power to do likewise'.[22] Most of the airpower theorists stress that command of the air is a vital prerequisite to other operations. Douhet theorised that complete command could be obtained through the destruction of enemy air assets, preferably whilst they were still on the ground.[23] Gaining 'total' command of the global infosphere, in accordance with Douhet's theory, is an impossible and even undesirable objective. To reach such a state, all potential enemies would have to be denied effective use of their information assets. Whereas an enemy has a relatively limited quantity of physical assets upon which his airpower is based, the assets required to operate a form of information power are numerous. Also, because some of these assets come under the ownership of the civilian sector, and many are shared, excluding an adversary from the global infosphere is extremely difficult. The communication infrastructure that forms the basis of the Internet is a prime example of how some information power assets are shared.

Echoing Sir Julian Corbett's theory on sea power, at the global level the infosphere will commonly remain in an uncommanded state.[24] In fact it may prove disadvantageous to completely deny an enemy the use of his information assets. Certain information power activities require the existence of a functioning enemy information infrastructure. The more insidious acts of information power, such as semantic attacks (which degrade the integrity of enemy information), intelligence gathering and deception, all require a functioning enemy information infrastructure. The same applies to some of the methods used in SIW. In this sense, to facilitate an effective information power campaign for oneself, and deny the same to the adversary, an actor may want selectively to destroy some of the enemy's assets, or none at all. Such considerations are circumstantial and depend upon the campaign's objective. Even in the battlespace, certain actions, such as deception, will require the existence of enemy information assets. In this way, an information campaign is less about attaining command through the destruction of enemy assets, and is more about *control* of the infosphere. Control of the infosphere can be defined as *the ability to use the infosphere for the furtherance of strategic objectives, whilst denying the enemy from doing the same.* When considering 'control of the infosphere' it is important to recognise the difficulties of completely preventing the enemy from utilising his information assets. In this respect the best that can be hoped for is to limit the strategic efficacy of his information power. 'Control of the infosphere' denotes a situation in which an actor is able to control information and its flow, and bend the infosphere to serve his strategic objectives. In this vein, one may not wish to destroy an enemy's information assets, but rather control what information can flow through, from or into them, manipulate that information or simply gain access to it.

As noted, with the difficulties of securing global command of the infosphere in mind, it is useful to look to the work of Sir Julian Corbett and John Warden III. Both of these theorists refine the concept of command. They both recognise that command does not have to be either 'total' or 'permanent'.[25] As already noted, to achieve command of the infosphere will prove impossible, even on a temporary basis.[26] The challenges of operating in the infosphere are further illustrated by the fact that even the level of 'control' possible may be moderated by the increasing availability of personal information assets such as mobile phones, and civilian sources of information such as satellite images.[27] Nonetheless, being able to report back enemy positions via a mobile phone is a far less potent use of information power than a real-time sensor-to-shooter relationship. As Nye and Owens note, 'some kinds of information – the accurate, timely, and comprehensive sort – are more valuable than others'. Having an information edge can matter.[28] In this sense, an actor operating with the more potent form of information power has an advantage when trying to get inside the enemy's decision-making cycle.

The 1991 Gulf War illustrates the value of having 'control' of the fifth dimension. The Coalition forces possessed information dominance, and were able to wage acts of political and psychological warfare, as well as acts of deception against the Iraqis. The Coalition forces selectively destroyed Iraqi communications architecture, leaving some nodes intact. As the Republican Guard forces began to move, their landline communications became less useful, and so they resorted to transmitting through radio communications. This latter form of communication is far easier to intercept. Leaving some enemy information assets intact paid dividends for the Coalition.[29] The level of military victory attained by Coalition forces emphasises that an asymmetry of information power confers significant advantages, particularly if it results in control of the infosphere.[30] However, as noted throughout this book, strategy is a complex, multidimensional activity that requires competence in a number of spheres. Consequently, mastery of the information environment will not alone guarantee victory.

The most important point to come from the above discussion is that the term 'command' is perhaps inappropriate to describe strategic relationships within the infosphere. The complexities of ensuring one's own use of the infosphere and denying the same to an adversary, allied to the requirement of a functioning enemy information infrastructure to facilitate certain information operations, suggests that *control* of the infosphere may be a more appropriate concept. Like command, control of the infosphere is never likely to be either total or permanent. But as already noted by Nye and Owens, having an information edge can confer significant advantages.

THE ACCESSIBILITY OF INFORMATION POWER

Information power is that form of strategic power that operates in or through the infosphere. The primary characteristics of information power are its accessibility and flexibility. The combination of these two characteristics endows information power with a great deal of potential in the strategic world. Information power can be used in many operations including: intelligence gathering; terrorism; strategic warfare; raids; political warfare; economic warfare; logistic support; interdiction; and the direct support of conventional military operations.

Sub-state actors are not omitted from engaging in information power activities. Terrorists are no exception.[31] Barry Collin postulates that in the near future the terrorists of today will seem primitive by their use of bombs and bullets. Collin suggests that to highlight their cause terrorists are more likely to target information infrastructures with the weapons and techniques of the information warrior.[32] This view is challenged by Richard Forno who regards 9/11 acting as 'a stark reminder that the method of attack for terrorists will be a high-visibility, high body-count target; not hacking, cracking, or conducting a so-called "cyber war"'.[33] Nonetheless, cyberterrorism does have some distinct advantages for the terrorists. It offers global reach at low entry costs.[34] And as Arquilla and Ronfeldt note, it can achieve all of this without raising the ire associated with the death and destruction of more traditional acts of terror.[35] Walter Laqueur is unequivocal about the inherent potential of cyberterror: 'If the new terrorism directs its energies toward information warfare, its destructive power will be exponentially greater than any it wielded in the past.'[36]

It has been postulated in some of the literature that there are cultural and technical obstacles that might prevent terrorist groups from adopting wholesale the methods of cyberterror. These include the cultural glorification of violence and heroic acts, and the enormous intelligence challenges involved in understanding the complexities of information age infrastructures.[37] In this sense, more traditional acts of violence may remain an important instrument in the terrorist's tool kit. However, any cultural or technical impediments to the adoption of cyberterror that may exist today will undoubtedly diminish as the information age matures further. And as Kevin Soo Hoo et al. assert, the arrival of cyberterror lowers the threshold for engaging in acts of terror. This latter point, combined with the growth of political groupings over the Internet, would seem to indicate that acts of cyberterror will increase.[38] Indeed, acts of cyberterror may have already occurred. Denning draws attention to attacks in the 1970s against computer systems by the Italian Red Brigades, in what may be described as the forerunner of modern cyberterror. More recently, the Internet Black Tigers (an offshoot of the Liberation Tigers of Tamil) attacked Sri Lankan embassies with e-mail bombing.[39] It has also been alleged that Japanese groups have attacked the computerised control systems of trains.[40] Overall, it is reasonable to assert that terrorism will undoubtedly acquire an information face. Yet, as 9/11 and suicide bombings in Israel graphically illustrate, the more physical destructive outpourings of terrorism will continue to pose a serious threat. This area of strategy is illustrative of the fact that the more traditional physical forms of conflict will not disappear; rather they will merely exist alongside those in the fifth dimension.

The accessibility of information power is predominately the result of the very low entry costs required to engage in certain activities within the infosphere. These low costs enable small actors to operate reasonably effectively in the fifth dimension. This is not an entirely unique characteristic. Smaller actors can also operate significantly in the other dimensions of strategy. Terrorists or insurgents can of course operate with varying degrees of success in the physical world. Furthermore, relatively smaller powers can also employ sea power. As Gray notes, a *guerre de course* can make a mockery of maritime surface command.[41] Privateers operating against the shipping and interests of Philip II of Spain, at times with the financial backing of Elizabeth I, had a psychological impact on the Spanish sovereign quite out of proportion to the damage they inflicted. It is argued that the activities of men such as Sir Francis Drake contributed significantly to Philip's decision to seek the overthrow of Elizabeth, which in turn led to the ill-fated 'Enterprise of England' in 1588.[42] Also, it is worth noting that in the contemporary world, groups such as the Tamil Tigers have been able to utilise sea power.[43] However, it is generally fair to say that a smaller actor exercising information power effectively can exert leverage more potently than is often the case in the other dimensions.

Certain non-state actors are defined and exist as strategic players almost entirely due to cyberspace. Often these groupings can only function effectively within the realms of the infosphere. Certain collections of hackers fall into this category. Groups such as these operate predominantly in the Global Information Environment (GIE). However, the interaction between the GIE and the Military Information Environment (MIE) is such that they could potentially influence matters on the battlefield to some degree.[44] An important point to note is that *a little information power can go a long way*. This maxim emanates from the level of global interconnections in cyberspace, and the dependence of some actors upon these connections and the information flow they facilitate. This means that a small actor using information power has both global reach and the opportunity to engage in various kinds of information power activities, including political warfare, interdiction and SIW, to name just three. The information age produces a reach and power almost unparalleled for sub-state actors.[45] Yet, information power does not guarantee strategic success.

Importantly, these smaller actors do not possess many of the assets specific to an information campaign in the MIE. In this sense, we can distinguish between those who operate and are competent in the GIE, and those powers that are also competent in the MIE. And yet, the use of information power in the MIE is not restricted to developed countries such as the United States. General Aideed's forces in Somalia are noted to have displayed a high degree of competence in using information assets (including mobile phones), which kept them apprised of the movement of US forces. The US experience in Somalia reveals that, although having a plethora of advanced information assets is generally a good thing, they do not automatically endow you with an overwhelming information advantage. More importantly, Somalia also reveals that successful strategic performance relies on far more than just information power. This campaign also highlights the fact that information assets cannot always provide the required information. Expensive technological systems cannot easily identify a guerrilla from amongst the general population.[46]

THE ADVANTAGES AND LIMITATIONS OF INFORMATION POWER

When assessing the significance of the infosphere for geopolitics and the fate of the physical dimensions, it is important to consider that, like the other forms of strategic power, information power has both advantages and limitations. The overall significance of information power is directly related to its strategic efficacy. If the limits of its strategic potential are too pronounced, it will in all likelihood fail to bring about radical change.

One of the most important advantages offered by information power is that some of the assets required to operate in the infosphere are relatively cheap to acquire. Internet-ready computers are a case in point. Computers are not only inexpensive; they are also multi-role items. Other noteworthy advantages are that information power can be projected globally far more easily than other forms of power, and that it is particularly good for covert activities.

In relation to the battlespace, information power acts as a force multiplier across the spectrum of military activities. It has evolved into an essential companion to modern combat forces. Securing some level of control of the infosphere will help enable fast and effective C^2, accurate and timely logistics and good reconnaissance of the battlefield; and in a more direct relationship, information power can vastly enhance the effectiveness of firepower with real-time target information and precision strikes. By degrading an enemy's information power to a point where information dominance is achieved, offensive information operations can give friendly forces a significant edge. Control also paves the way for acts of political and psychological warfare, as well as acts of deception.

For an actor facing a conventionally superior force, information power may provide the means to engage in asymmetric strategies. These may include information denial, political warfare campaigns or cyberterror. Whereas, for a major military actor, information power offers a range of less lethal and less direct options that may prove less contentious in certain contingencies. In this context, information power could take the form of information aid to an ally, as an alternative to sending military forces. This could prove useful in certain interventions, and also suits the requirements for post-heroic warfare when such an approach is both justified and effective. In those circumstances in which military force is required, information power may provide greater accuracy and therefore less collateral damage.[47] In essence, possessing information power endows an actor with greater flexibility and an increased range of instruments through which to pursue strategic objectives.

However, information power offers no panacea. Its limitations must be kept in mind. For instance, some of the assets that form the basis of modern information power in the battlespace are potentially vulnerable. Wargames have highlighted possible future vulnerabilities of US space systems.[48] Some commentators have also noted how vulnerable some key airborne platforms may become.[49] And EMP, a candidate bogeyman of the information age, poses a general threat to many of the modern assets of information power.

To return to the issue of uncertainty in the battlespace, Major-General W. J. P. Robins notes that no information is ever complete and up to date, and therefore it is important to be aware of its limitations.[50] There are times when of course information will be up to date and complete, but General Robins' point is well taken, and is in line with the conclusion reached in Chapter 2 that uncertainty will never be totally removed from the battlespace. It is also worth reiterating the point that deception by the enemy will often degrade the utility of information. Again, being aware of these limitations of information is wise counsel.

The use of information power is complicated by the civilian owner-ship and shared nature of some of its assets. This produces a degree of unpredictability in information operations. However, such complications can be an advantage for certain users. An information warrior operating in cyberspace may welcome the complexity of interconnections to hide his presence and activities. Nonetheless, being so deeply interconnected produces other possible pitfalls. There is a real danger that certain forms of information attack could produce cascading effects. For example, an ill-conceived worm attack against enemy information systems may return to one's own systems over the global network. In this way, infor-mation power can be misused, and it can bite back.

A FUTURE FOR PHYSICAL FORCES

There are some more fundamental limitations to the strategic efficacy of information power. If the information revolution is to make physical geography and its relationships increasingly unimportant, then by implication it must make traditional forms of military power irrelevant. Otherwise, if strategic objectives are still pursued through the use of traditional military forces, then physical geography will still be relevant. Troops and equipment will need to be transported, in which case physical geography and distance will continue to matter. Also, the effects of terrain and the weather will still influence the conduct of operations.

At this juncture it is profitable to return to the debates outlined in Chapter 2 and Chapter 4. There are two main ways in which the information revolution may render traditional forms of military power and geography obsolete. Firstly, information may become the dominant factor in warfare, to the point at which information dominance may be the defining war-winning characteristic. To reiterate the premise of this thought: one belligerent in a conflict may have such obvious information dominance, allied to PGMs, that victory becomes inevitable. As was concluded earlier, it is not inconceivable, in permissive conditions, for a conflict to end once information dominance has been achieved. Alternatively, as noted, Libicki postulates that information assets will create such visibility that offensive operations cease to be practicable.[51] In this way information power attains such dominance as to make physical expressions of power all but obsolete. A host of reasons were identified in Chapter 2 to suggest why such visions will not come to pass. Further to this, when considering the role of the infosphere it is important not to detach information power from the physical expressions of military force. Certain elements of information power emanate from the deployment of physical assets that at times require combat either to enable their deployment or to protect them. More often than not information power will act in concert with the other expressions of strategic power. Information power still needs air, land or sea forces to destroy the targets it has identified, or to move supplies and troop deployments. In the Gulf War of 1991 it took the physical destruction and removal of ground forces to achieve the Coalition's objectives. Iraq's forces did not capitulate in the face of the Coalition's obvious information dominance. Also, the attainment of information dominance may require the destruction of enemy information assets. This will more often than not require the utilisation of traditional forces. Similarly, Keohane and Nye note that at times 'soft power', for which information power is ideally suited, may require the application of 'hard power'. The example they provide is that of military force being required to seize a radio station from which soft power can be generated.[52] These thoughts are not designed to underestimate the utility of information power, but merely to note that it is but one instrument of strategy alongside the others. Most often, the best results will come from a combination of these instruments.

The requirement to combine information power with the other instruments of strategy is nowhere better illustrated than in holding the high ground. The exploitation of the third and fourth dimensions in the twentieth century created a situation in which the high ground was most potently composed of the air and space environments. Richard Szafranski and Libicki contend that the infosphere must now be regarded as the high ground.[53] It may be more appropriate for the fifth dimension to be seen as the third part of the high ground equation. As a consequence, ensuring command of the high ground is an increasingly complicated task, which involves a synergistic relationship between these three dimensions.

Within the context of a military campaign these three dimensions of warfare (infosphere, air and space) are so inextricably linked that for regular armed forces command or control must be ensured in all of them simultaneously. To lose command or control of space would seriously compromise information power due to the inability to utilise space-based information assets. Of course, this does not relate to all actors in all circumstances. For example, a lack of space assets does not automatically equate with ineffective information power. An irregular enemy can often compensate for the absence of advanced information assets through the utilisation of HUMINT. However, returning to the needs of a regular force, losing control of the air would create a similar situation to that faced with the loss of space control, due to the inability safely to deploy air-based information assets such as JSTARS, AWACS (Airborne Warning and Control System) and UAVs. Likewise, to lose control of the infosphere could undermine both space power and airpower. An adversary with some degree of control of the infosphere could potentially interfere with satellites, airborne platforms and the attendant communications. In addition, the integrity of information provided by air and space assets could be challenged. From these thoughts we see how a trinity develops, requiring protection for all three of its dimensions to ensure some form of command or control in each of them. In this sense, information power relies on more traditional forms of military power just as much as they rely on it. This thought is further complicated by the fact that space, air and information power all rely upon ground installations to function, which in turn require protection. In this sense, the interconnected relationships amongst the different dimensions are further enhanced. In the words of Cohen, 'The real and the virtual battlefields [have] become a complex inextricable whole.'[54]

The second means by which information power may render physically based forces and environments obsolete is through strategically successful attacks against the National Information Infrastructure (NII) of an opponent. In such a context, distance and geography would begin to take more of a back seat in strategy, and wars could well be waged solely through the infosphere. However, as discussed in the previous chapter, it is unlikely that SIW will provide an independent theory of victory. Within the SIW literature there is often reference to a potential electronic Pearl Harbor. In response, it is worth remembering that the United States recovered from the Japanese attack in 1941, and went on to win the Pacific war.

From the above discussion it has been suggested that information power is unlikely to provide an independently successful tool of strategy, in which case the more traditional instruments of strategy will still play an important role. However, it has also been shown that by utilising the infosphere a wide variety of actors, both big and small, can project power globally without reference to established geographic realities. So what does this all mean for geopolitics?

GEOPOLITICS AND THE FIFTH DIMENSION

As noted in the introduction to this chapter, a number of writers foresee revolutionary change occurring in geopolitics. Walter B. Wriston unequivocally states, 'Information technology has demolished time and distance.'[55] Likewise, Jessica T. Mathews argues that the information revolution is bringing a novel redistribution of power, which reduces the importance of proximity and endows non-state actors with unprecedented levels of power.[56] Some of these observations seem to have a certain validity. For example, information power is extremely accessible, and, to reiterate, a *little information power can go a long way*. In relation to acts of SIW, interdiction, economic warfare and political warfare, small actors and even individuals have seldom had such readily available capabilities. Overall it seems credible to suggest that these characteristics of information power will have geopolitical implications. The important questions are how significant these implications will be, and how will they be manifested?

Geopolitically the information age may create somewhat of a paradox. On the one hand it may encourage states to become involved more readily in issues and crises regardless of their relative geographic position. Alternatively it may lead to a more isolationist stance. In 1968 Albert Wohlstetter argued that technological advances in transportation and telecommunications result in an extension of the neighbourhood, which brings increased chances for both co-operation and conflict. A state's interests become more global as cultural, capital and economic exchanges increase.[57] Aside from the fact that a state may have greater interest in events that are not geographically contiguous to it, informa-

193

tion power may also present an actor with a greater capacity to become involved in external matters. Sending military forces into a crisis zone is often an expensive and risky undertaking, and can prove politically controversial. Information power presents opportunities to influence events without direct presence and in a more discreet manner.

In contrast, being vulnerable to certain information power activities may make states more wary of becoming involved. The vulnerability of a state's NII to information attack, or the prospect of widespread political warfare campaigns against the involvement of the state in an external matter, could propel foreign policy towards isolationism. Such considerations are heavily influenced by the context in which they take place. The issue involved may be of such import that a state is willing to accept the adverse effects of an information power campaign. Also, a state may have developed effective countermeasures or counter-information campaigns in order to limit the damage.

Ultimately, when considering the broad implications of technological developments on geopolitics, it is crucial to remember Luttwak's theory that countermeasures will be developed which limit the long-term influence of any successful strategy or instrument. Desmond Ball regards the development of these countermeasures as inevitable, in which case the conclusions of any technological development have only passing relevance.[58] Libicki has suggested that each new medium of strategic power brings with it a new geographical logic that dominates and transforms the old media. He cites the exploitation of the air environment as an example of this. In particular, he uses the example of the British Isles, which could now be attacked through the air regardless of the fleet that had traditionally acted as the ultimate homeland defence force.[59] There are three obvious responses to Libicki's argument. First, we can reiterate the conclusions of the previous discussion regarding the failure of airpower to effect an independent strategic victory. Second, it is important to note that the fleet still played a critical role by helping to prevent the Germans from mounting an invasion of Britain during World War II. In this sense, the logic of the old medium (the sea) still mattered. Finally, the British development of a countermeasure, in the form of an integrated air defence system, helped limit the ability of the air environment to change the geopolitical logic of Europe.

Historically, technologies that might at first appear to offer radical change have often failed to render the prevailing geopolitical environment irrelevant. Even under the Cold War nuclear shadow, which seemed ambivalent of some established geopolitical realities, traditional geographical concerns were still significant. Again, this reveals that although certain technological developments can affect the geopolitical world they do not necessarily make all aspects of the previous environ-

194

ment obsolete. For example, distance and geographical features still pervade nuclear matters. Desmond Ball observes that the lack of suitable bases for the Soviet ballistic missile nuclear submarine (SSBN) force meant they had to pass through choke points *en route* to the open seas, which made NATO's job of tracking them much easier.[60] Geography pervades nuclear issues in other ways. For example, where an enemy missile is launched from has significant implications for the command and control of nuclear forces. Shorter flight times for delivery systems can make quite a difference. As Ashton B. Carter has noted, Soviet submarine-launched ballistic missiles (SLBMs) reduced the time scale for nuclear operations to 15 minutes or less. This increased the likelihood of US nuclear forces, especially its bombers, being caught on the ground in a Soviet first strike.[61] In these examples, although ICBMs and SLBMs made geographic distance less of an obstacle to the projection of force, they did not make distance or geography irrelevant. Far from it, these factors were critical in nuclear operations.

During the Cold War, geopolitical concerns unrelated to nuclear-armed ICBMs or SLBMs were still influential. The US involvement in Vietnam was an expression of a containment policy that owed much to Mackinder's theories on the Heartland. In this sense, some conflicts are fought for reasons unrelated to the dominant technology of the period. Although the shadow of nuclear weapons influenced how the United States conducted the war, nuclear issues did not cause the conflict, as they nearly did in Cuba in 1962. Also, because the forces used were conventional, traditional geographical issues such as lines of communication still mattered. Further to this, as previously mentioned, the pre-war assumption that nuclear weapons would dominate future conflicts distorted USAF operations during the early stages of the war. This latter point is a warning to those who focus almost entirely on the latest technological development.

It is also important to bear in mind the broader strategic limitations of any particular dimension of strategy. For example, the maritime environment is certainly critically important to many actors, and plays a central role in the world's transportation and trading activities. Yet, Gray and Corbett are undoubtedly right when they note that sea power is only relevant to how it affects the main area of human dwelling: the land.[62] Gray extends this logic to the information age, and, in response to Libicki's claim that cyberspace is placeless, Gray claims that humans are not placeless because they exist in a geographic reality.[63] The same can be said for the natural resources humans rely upon. To produce strategic leverage, information power must significantly influence the physical world. As has been argued throughout this work, to achieve such influence will more often than not require the aid of traditional forms of power, and specifically the man on the scene with a gun.

Finally, it is important not to become deterministic with regard to geopolitics and technology. Wohlstetter wisely points out that being able to project power does not automatically mean that you will.[64] When thinking about geopolitics we should not forget the 'politics' side of the equation. There has to be some policy rationale for utilising information power against, or in support of, someone. Simply being able to project power in real time and on a global scale does not mean that you will do so in every case

CONCLUSIONS

Although not wholly recognisable as a physical environment, the infosphere does constitute a fifth dimension of strategy. Ultimately, a form of strategic power can be projected within and through it. Information power is an extremely flexible instrument. Also, the information age empowers non-state actors in ways we have not seen before. As a consequence of its flexibility, ubiquity and accessibility, it is hard to imagine a strategic actor performing well in the twenty-first century without understanding and taking account of information power. Again, Cohen is persuasive when he argues: 'As with the opening up of space, the realization of the potential for war in cyberspace would elicit an efflorescence of organizations, concepts, and patterns of conflict parallel to, but very different from, those of conventional warfare.'[65]

The broader geopolitical implications of the fifth dimension are directly dependent on how effective information power can be in the means–ends world of strategy. At times, and in certain cases, information power may prove to be independently sufficient to achieve policy objectives. This may be the case in the transfer of reconnaissance information to an ally. But in many instances information power will have to act in concert with the other physical instruments of strategy. This results primarily from the fact that humans exist and operate in the physical world. As a result, physical geography continues to matter in both military and geopolitical terms. Because geography matters, distance and proximity will also continue to play an important role. In addition, it is worth remembering that the infosphere and information are being territorialised. Rather than being an environment that is ambivalent to the traditional geopolitical reality, the infosphere will partially reflect it.

Also, as Keohane and Nye remind us, rather than just empowering sub-state actors, the information revolution can enhance the potency of a state's conventional military power. In fact, Keohane and Nye go further, and correctly note that the geographically based nation-states will continue to structure politics in the information age. They may be less accurate however when they suggest that nation-states will rely more on information and less on material resources.[66] It is a mistake to raise the significance of information above the other instruments of power. States in general will base their power in all the dimensions of strategy as befits their particular situation and the circumstances of the time.

Strategy is a complex beast. The twenty-first-century strategic and geopolitical environments will not be solely determined by any one dimension or form of power. However, if any dimension can make a claim to primacy it is the land environment on which humans live. In the end, the expressions of power in the other dimensions must be able to exert leverage into this most basic of environments. Yet, the geopolitical landscape will change, because a form of strategic power (information power) can be projected globally without recourse to physical geography. However, the limitations of information power, allied to the basic dominance of physical geography, suggest that the new geopolitical reality will reflect physical geography at least as much as it will reflect the infosphere.

NOTES

1. Walter B. Wriston, 'Bits, Bytes, and Diplomacy', *Foreign Affairs*, 76, 5 (1997), p. 172.
2. The following works variously include some of these ideas. Libicki, 'The Emerging Primacy of Information', Vlahos, 'The War after Byte City', and Mathews, 'Power Shift'.
3. Quoted in Paul F. Herman, Jr, 'The Revolution in "Military" Affairs', *Strategic Review*, 24, 2 (1996), p. 26.
4. Halford J. Mackinder, *Democratic Ideals and Reality* (New York, W. W. Norton, 1962). Ciro Zoppo also notes that geography, technology and power politics are intrinsically related. See Ciro E. Zoppo, 'Classical Geopolitics and Beyond', in Ciro E. Zoppo and Charles Zorgbibe (eds), *On Geopolitics: Classical and Nuclear*, NATO ASI Series (Dordrecht, Martinus Nijhoff Publishers, 1985).
5. The Midland Ocean was to comprise a strategic reserve in North America, an aerodrome in Britain and a beachhead in France. The similarity of this concept to NATO is noteworthy.
6. See Gray, *Modern Strategy*, p. 232.
7. For example, for an assessment of the space environment see Everett C. Dolman, 'Geostrategy in the Space Age: An Astropolitical Analysis', in Colin S. Gray and Geoffrey Sloan (eds), *Geopolitics: Geography and Strategy* (London, Frank Cass, 1999), pp. 83–106.
8. Laurie Brettingham, *Royal Air Force Beam Benders No.80 (Signals) Wing 1940–1945* (Leicester, Midland Publishing, 1997).
9. Sam J. Tangredi argues that, 'cyberspace, too, operates as a medium of exchange. Is it not logical that sea power concepts apply there?' See Sam J. Tangredi, 'Sea Power: Theory and Practice', in John Baylis, James Wirtz, Eliot Cohen and Colin S. Gray (eds), *Strategy in the Contemporary World: An Introduction to Strategic Studies* (Oxford, Oxford University Press, 2002), p. 133.

10. Toffler and Toffler, *War and Anti-war.*
11. Rattray, *Strategic Warfare in Cyberspace*, p. 17.
12. *Joint Vision 2020*, p. 10.
13. Libicki, 'The Emerging Primacy of Information', p. 274.
14. Robert O. Keohane and Joseph S. Nye, Jr, 'Power and Interdependence in the Information Age', *Foreign Affairs*, 77, 5 (1998), p. 84.
15. Both Rattray and Libicki concur that the infosphere is essentially man-made. See Rattray, *Strategic Warfare in Cyberspace*, p. 65, and Libicki, *Defending Cyberspace*, p. 5. History reveals a number of cases in which the other dimensions have been expanded or contracted. To take land as an example, cases can be found which show limited examples of both expansion and contraction of this dimension. During the aforementioned siege of the island city Tyre in 333–332 BC, Alexander the Great constructed a 200-foot-wide mole between the coast and the city. This enabled Alexander's land forces to attack the city directly. See Ferrill, *The Origins of War*, pp. 204–5. In 1672, the Dutch responded to the French invasion by opening the dikes to flood the land, and thereby hold back the invaders. See Weigley, *The Age of Battles*, p. 59. These two examples show an expansion and contraction of the land environment respectively. In a less direct sense, the submarine environment could be expanded – in a strategically useful manner – through the development of vessels which can withstand higher hull pressures. This of course is not an expansion of the environment itself, but is rather an expansion of man's exploitation of it. Nevertheless, it is an expansion.
16. As Georgetown University computer science professor Dorothy Denning notes, 'The problem is that the technology leaps ahead of the security, and that's going to be with us forever.' Quoted in Carlin, 'The Netizen'.
17. Libicki, 'The Emerging Primacy of Information'.
18. Chandler, *The Campaigns of Napoleon*, p. 165.
19. Max Hastings and Simon Jenkins, *The Battle for the Falklands* (London, Pan Books, 1997). pp. 300–1. See also Vegetius, *Vegetius*, p. 70.
20. See Stephen Hawking, *A Brief History of Time: From the Big Bang to Black Holes* (London, Bantam Books, 1995).
21. E. J. Kingston-McCloughry notes that '[a]ll projectiles, admittedly, except the torpedo, travel to their targets through the medium of air'. E. J. Kingston-McCloughry, *War in Three Dimensions: The Impact of Air-Power upon the Classical Principles of War* (London, Jonathan Cape, 1949), p. 22.
22. Douhet, *The Command of the Air*, p. 83.
23. Ibid., p. 34.
24. Corbett, *Some Principles of Maritime Strategy*, p. 77
25. See Corbett, *Some Principles of Maritime Strategy*, p. 89, and Colonel John A. Warden III, *The Air Campaign: Planning for Combat*, Future Warfare Series, Vol. 3., (Washington, DC, Pergamon-Brassey's, 1989), p. 130. A good analysis regarding the refinement of the command of the sea concept can be found in Eric Grove, *The Future of Sea Power* (Annapolis, MD, Naval Institute Press, 1990), especially pp. 12–13.
26. A useful distinction between the Global Information Environment (GIE) and the Military Information Environment (MIE) is outlined in *FM 100-6*. See also Starry and Arneson, 'FM 100-6'.
27. Satellite images can now be downloaded from the Internet. See George I. Seffers, 'Army War Game Reveals Power of Commercial Data', *Defense News*, 22–28 September 1997, p. 44. See also Starry and Arneson, 'FM 100-6'.
28. Joseph S. Nye, Jr and William A. Owens, 'America's Information Edge', *Foreign Affairs* 75, 2 (1996), p. 24.
29. See Atkinson, *Crusade*, p. 439.

30. This last point is not designed to suggest that information was the decisive factor in the conflict. Although it was an important element of the victory, other factors played their part. War is a very complex activity, and to succeed in war requires competence in many areas.

31. For a useful definition of terrorism see Kiras, 'Terrorism and Irregular Warfare', p. 211.

32. 'New Security Threats Rest in "Cyber Terrorism"', www.infowar.com/CIVIL_DE/ civil_c.html-ssi.

33. Richard Forno, 'September 11th Does Not Mean Cyberwar is Coming', www.infowar.com/mil_c4i_091401b_j.shtml.

34. These points are made in an interesting assessment of the value of IT to terrorists, in Soo Hoo et al., 'Information Technology and the Terrorist Threat'.

35. Arquilla and Ronfeldt, The Advent of Netwar.

36. Walter Laqueur, 'Postmodern Terrorism', Foreign Affairs, 75, 5 (1996), p. 35.

37. Rathmell, 'Cyber-Terrorism'. Brian Jenkins expresses similar reservations about the use of cyberterror; see Soo Hoo et al., 'Information Technology and the Terrorist Threat', pp. 145–6.

38. Soo Hoo et al., 'Information Technology and the Terrorist Threat', p. 144.

39. Denning, Information Warfare and Security, pp. 68–9.

40. Michele Zanini and Sean J. A. Edwards, 'The Networking of Terror in the Information Age', in John Arquilla and David Ronfeldt (eds), Networks and Netwars: The Future of Terror, Crime, and Militancy (Santa Monica, CA, RAND, 2001), p. 44.

41. Gray, The Leverage of Sea Power, p. 12.

42. Don Diego Pimentel, a senior Armada commander, declared to his English interrogators: 'The Reason why the king undertook this war [against England] was that he could not tolerate the fact that Drake, with two or three rotten ships, should come to infest the harbours of Spain whenever it pleased him, and to capture its best towns in order to plunder them.' Quoted in Parker, The Grand Strategy of Philip II, p. 176. This argument is also made in Colin Martin and Geoffrey Parker, The Spanish Armada, Revised Edition (Manchester, Mandolin, 1999), p. 80, Roger Whiting, The Enterprise of England: The Spanish Armada (Stroud, Alan Sutton Publishing, 1995), and John Sugden, Sir Francis Drake (London, Pimlico, 1996), p. 201.

43. This exploitation of sea power by the Tamil separatists led Sri Lankan President Chandrika Kumaratunga to announce an upgrade of the Sri Lankan navy. See 'Sri Lanka Says Navy Will Be Upgraded to Combat Tigers', Jane's Defence Weekly, 12 November 1997, p. 5.

44. For a description of the MIE and GIE see FM 100-6.

45. See Fuller, Armament and History, p. 144, for comments on global reach and speed of radio.

46. O'Hanlon, Technological Change, pp. 118–19.

47. For a discussion of counterinsurgency in the information age, see Baddeley, 'Insurgency and Counter Insurgency in the Information Age'. Libicki also discusses the potential of providing allies with information as a means of intervention. See Libicki, 'The Emerging Primacy of Information', especially pp. 266–8. However, he does recognise that at times information alone will not be enough, and that a virtual presence may reduce US leverage. See Illuminating Tomorrow's War.

48. Barbara Starr, 'Wargames highlight US vulnerability in space', Jane's Defence Weekly, 8 October 1997, p. 17.

49. In particular, Libicki has raised concerns about AWACS and JSTAR aircraft. See Libicki, 'The Emerging Primacy of Information', p. 268.

50. W. J. P. Robins, 'Information Age Operations', RUSI Journal, 142, 3 (1997), p. 40.

51. Libicki, 'The Emerging Primacy of Information', and Illuminating Tomorrow's War.

52. Keohane and Nye, 'Power and Interdependence in the Information Age', p. 90.
53. This is a point stressed in Richard Szafranski and Martin C. Libicki, '... Or Go Down in Flame? Toward an Airpower Manifesto for the Twenty-first Century', *Airpower Journal*, 10, 3 (1996), pp. 65–77.
54. Cohen, 'Technology and Warfare', p. 250.
55. Wriston, 'Bits, Bytes, and Diplomacy', p. 172.
56. See Mathews, 'Power Shift'. Goodwin also notes that a common theme in some of the RMA literature is the notion that information warfare represents the rise of a new political-economic order, in which non-state actors do better than the Westphalian states. See Goodwin, 'Don't Techno for an Answer', p. 216.
57. Albert Wohlstetter, 'Illusions of Distance', *Foreign Affairs*, 46, 2 (1968), pp. 242–5.
58. Desmond Ball, 'Modern Technology and Geopolitics', in Ciro E. Zoppo and Charles Zorgbibe (eds), *On Geopolitics: Classical and Nuclear*, NATO ASI Series (Dordrecht, Martinus Nijhoff Publishers, 1985), p. 175.
59. Libicki, 'The Emerging Primacy of Information, p. 261.
60. Ball, 'Modern Technology and Geopolitics', p. 187.
61. See Ashton B. Carter, 'Assessing Command System Vulnerability', and 'Sources of Error and Uncertainty', in Ashton B. Carter, John D. Steinbruner and Charles A. Zraket (eds), *Managing Nuclear Operations* (Washington, DC, Brookings Institution, 1987), pp. 555–610, 611–39.
62. Gray, *Leverage of Sea Power*, p. 4.
63. See Colin S. Gray, 'A Rejoinder by Colin S. Gray', *Orbis*, 40, 2 (1996), p. 276.
64. Wohlstetter, 'Illusions of Distance', p. 246.
65. Cohen, 'Technology and Warfare', p. 250.
66. See Keohane and Nye, 'Power and Interdependence in the Information Age', pp. 88, 94.

6

Concluding Thoughts:
A Clausewitzian Future

'Sun Tzu's notions of victory with minimal violence may displace
Clausewitz's emphasis on the deadly clash of armies amid fog and friction.'[1]

INTRODUCTION

The above statement by Arquilla and Ronfeldt, two of the most prominent
writers on information age warfare, represents the explicit declaration of an
often implicit, even unintentional, notion prevalent in much of the RMA
literature. In this respect, the statement identifies the central assumptions
that this book has set out to challenge, namely, that the nature of warfare
has changed in that it will become a less violent, less uncertain and more
controllable activity. If this proved to be the case, then the dominant
Clausewitzian paradigm would have become anachronistic and should be
replaced by theoretical works more fitting to the information age. Arquilla
and Ronfeldt propose the work of Sun Tzu as an alternative to Clausewitz,
yet it is also worth exploring works written in the information age to test
their utility as general theories of war. To the Clausewitzian faithful this
exercise may appear to be verging on the sacrilegious. However, as noted in
Chapter 1, the influence of certain works of strategic theory is such, and the
subject they are concerned with of such import, that retaining a work of
theory merely on the grounds of loyalty is unhelpful, and may even be
counterproductive to the pursuit of better strategic performance. It is
worth returning to Brodie's question in relation to the opportunity costs
involved in reading *On War*: 'Is the reading of this book at this time worth
more to me than the reading of any other works that I could read with the
same time?'[2] Moreover, Gray, who describes *On War* as 'my constant
companion',[3] declares that strategic theory is a living tradition; hence
Clausewitz's work requires amendment.[4]

To this end, this chapter will assess whether the various changes to the
character of warfare, as outlined in Chapters 2 to 5, will be sufficient to

merit a change to the nature of war. Although it will be established that both Clausewitz's 'climate of war' and his 'trinity' remain fundamentally intact, some significant changes have occurred in the information age, potentially with more to come. This blend of continuity and change forms the basis for the evaluation of whether the various works of theory retain their validity for the future. It is the conclusion of this work that, despite further changes to the character of war wrought by the information age, Clausewitz's *On War* is still worthy of Brodie's assessment as 'not simply the greatest but the only truly great book on war'.[5] Yet, and in line with Brodie's own balanced examination of Clausewitz, the Prussian's work needs some reassessment and supplementation in the modern world.[6] The two other great classic works of strategic theory enjoy mixed fortunes in the information age. It will be argued that, despite many claims akin to that expressed in this chapter's opening quotation by Arquilla and Ronfeldt, aside from his emphasis on the role of knowledge in warfare, Sun Tzu's reputation should not be greatly enhanced by recent changes. In contrast, a reinvigoration of Jomini's work may be justified, although his dogmatic emphasis on certain principles, and his fixation primarily on the operational level, ultimately leaves him lagging behind Clausewitz as a general theorist of war.

Finally, there is the issue of works of theory written in the information age. Amidst the glut of RMA literature three bodies of work stand out for recognition as prospective general theories of war. These are the Tofflers' *War and Anti-war*; the collective works of Libicki; and Arquilla and Ronfeldt's writings, most of which can be found in the one volume *In Athena's Camp*. That these three have been chosen above all others does not necessarily indicate that they have produced the most competent modern writing on the subject. Neither have they been the only significant contributors to the current RMA debate. In this respect, Admiral Owens, Andrew Marshall and James Blaker are important figures. The three chosen bodies of work have been singled out on the basis that they transcend a narrow focus on the battlespace and extrapolate on the wider implications of the information revolution. Their work has a broad, encompassing perspective. These authors can also claim to have been significantly influential in various important quarters. Indeed, David Silverberg comments that 'the Tofflers are everywhere – at least everywhere in the defensive universe'.[7] Similarly, Coker describes how the Tofflers' *War and Anti-war* 'has become a revered text in the US military since its publication in 1991'.[8] The aforementioned works are also representative of many other writings to be found in the RMA debate, in the sense that their central themes are evident in much of the RMA literature. Consequently, to examine these authors is also to examine much of the wider writings in the RMA literature. Therefore, these three works will be evaluated to assess whether they represent general theories of war, and are worth the opportunity costs involved in reading them.

The chapter will conclude by identifying certain basic factors that determine the enduring nature of warfare, regardless of historical, political or technological context. As noted, this nature of warfare is exemplified in Clausewitz's 'climate' and 'trinity'. Although it will be shown that certain elements of the climate of war are not always directly in play during any particular conflict, they are always waiting on the sidelines ready to be reintroduced. This latter comment is of particular relevance to violence as an element in the nature of war. Violence is not always evident in conflict (for example in electronic warfare or 'pure' SIW), yet the dialectic nature of strategy makes its reintroduction an ever-present possibility. This explains why Clausewitz's emphasis on battle is at times inappropriate, but ultimately correct.[9] It is the abiding factors of policy demands; geography; the dialectic nature of strategy; the adaptability of war (its polymorphous character); and the fact that war is an activity waged by humans, which ensure the resonance of Clausewitz's nature of warfare in the information age. In this sense, any analysis of the nature of war, and therefore the suitability of a particular work of theory, cannot be performed without recourse to these five essential features of strategy.

When examining the relevance of various works of strategic theory two prominent questions come to mind. Why is theory important? What characteristics should a general theory of strategy possess? As a general proposition, Wylie's assertion that no general theory can guarantee success should be treated as the first and most important thought on this issue.[10] It is important to recognise the limits of theory within the practical world of strategy. Clausewitz recognised that theory could only ever be second best to what military genius does: 'What genius does is the best rule, and theory can do no better than show how and why this should be the case.'[11] And yet, theory is important. As Wylie himself stipulates, one of the most significant roles of a general theory of war is that it enables each of the armed services to see beyond its own environmentally restricted perceptions.[12] Similarly, a general theory may also help guard against the tendency to view strategic issues from a purely contemporary perspective, and therefore avoid the error of mistaking a fad for the enduring truth. Of course, theory can, and does, influence behaviour.[13] One of the most obvious and direct examples of this phenomenon is the relationship between the theory and practice of strategic bombing, particularly in the interwar years when the central theoretical tenets of both precision and area/morale bombing were formulated in the works of Douhet, Trenchard and Mitchell. As Murray notes, the influence of theory can reach into many areas including doctrine and force composition: 'The theories of Douhet and other early airpower advocates ... have exercised a great influence on the development of air forces since that time.'[14] Likewise, the theorists of nuclear strategy during the Cold War were said to have 'wielded enormous influence, not only over the way an entire generation's thoughts about military issues were shaped but also over the formulation of defence policy in the nuclear-weapon states'.[15] Returning to the information age, the Tofflers' *War and Anti-war*, which, as will be argued later, is the weakest of the three bodies of work considered here, has 'influenced many in the military'.[16] It appears that strategic theory can have both positive and negative influences on strategic behaviour. For example, strategic bombing theory has distracted attention and resources away from the other roles of airpower. For the practitioner, the key challenge in this respect is to differentiate the good from the bad in a general sense, and to extract the useful elements from each work of theory. Good theory can be a useful ally to the practitioner, whereas unsound theory can mislead.

There are at least five main characteristics which a general theory must posses so that it acts more as an aid than as a hindrance. Firstly, it should be universal, and inclusive of all the different forms warfare can take.[17] This is of particular importance when considering much of the RMA literature that often tends to focus on the regular battlespace. Just as important as this first feature, any theory must coincide with reality.[18] To this end, Murray and Grimsley's declaration that strategy is the art of the possible can be taken as a warning to those who would construct complex or naively optimistic plans or theories.[19] In this context Clausewitz provides an important warning to the RMA enthusiasts: '[Theory's] purpose is to demonstrate what war is in practice, not what its ideal nature ought to be.'[20] Thirdly, any theory must be of use to the practitioners of strategy. On this issue, Brodie is once again very persuasive: 'Above all, strategic theory is a theory for action.'[21] Echoing Brodie's wise counsel, Moran argues, 'The goal of theory in any field is to improve our understanding of reality, and our ability to act effectively.'[22] The fourth element for a general theory is that, in Gray's words, it should not be affected by technology, geography or tactical details.[23] The fifth and final characteristic is again taken from the outstanding work of Wylie, and concerns his superior concept of 'control'. Wylie argues that any general theory should have woven into it the notion that the objective of strategy is 'control'.[24] This final characteristic is perhaps the most controversial of the five outlined above. The controversy emanates from the fact that by advocating a guiding principle the theory is edging towards a prescriptive tone. However, because the aim of any strategy is control, and the concept of control is so embracing, this final feature of theory does not become restrictive in the same manner by which Jomini's principles often do. It is also important to return to the essence of the third characteristic, and to note that, by highlighting the constructive nature of theory's role in the attainment of control, Wylie is merely placing the needs of the practitioner at the heart of his ideas. Strategic theory cannot afford to be an abstract pursuit.

In the final analysis it is appropriate that the wisest words written on the role of strategic theory are to be found in *On War*. Clausewitz succinctly identifies both the value and limits of theory: '[Theory] is meant to educate the mind of the future commander, or, more accurately, to guide him in his self-education, not to accompany him to the battle-field.'[25] Later on in the work he elaborates on these thoughts:

> Theory cannot equip the mind with formulas for solving problems, nor can it mark the narrow path on which the sole solution is supposed to lie by planting a hedge of principles on either side. But it can give the mind insight into the great mass of phenomena and of their relationships, then leave it free to rise into the higher realms of action.[26]

Theory should be an aid to judgment,[27] whilst at the same time accepting the chaotic and varied nature of war, and thereby forgo rigid principles for victory, leaving the human element as the final arbiter of success or failure.

THE UNCHANGING CLIMATE OF WAR

Clausewitz's 'climate of war' can be perceived as a framework to understand much of the nature of warfare. In this respect, preparation for war, and indeed its conduct once hostilities have begun, should be undertaken with the expectation that the four elements of the climate have to be faced and dealt with. Consequently, military culture should reflect this reality. It is therefore important to identify whether or not the climate of war has been altered by the information age. Physical violence is one of the primary characteristics that distinguishes war from other activities in grand strategy. It is telling that Hedley Bull identifies violence as one of the three attributes that define war as: 'organised violence carried on by political units against each other'.[28] Although Clausewitz recognised that strategic success did not always require battle, and therefore violence did not invariably take place, he recognised that battle was constantly possible and always present in the calculations of the belligerents. It is therefore significant that this basic aspect of the nature of warfare has been challenged within the RMA literature. The challenge takes various forms with differing degrees of severity. At the more reasonable end of the spectrum is a greater emphasis on disruption, as opposed to destruction, as a means to victory. Such claims do not necessarily dictate an absolute end to violence, although they do seek to diminish its occurrence and severity. The more extreme comments in this argument can be found in Libicki's notion of information dominance and information-provided transparency rendering physical expressions of force redundant. Of equal significance is the potential professed for SIW. SIW represents an interesting compromise, although one that ultimately can lead to the end of physical violence in warfare. SIW is still an act of force to compel an enemy to one's will, and therefore still lies within the realms of warfare, yet it does not necessarily represent an act of physical force. Within the RMA literature there exists a tendency to reduce the complex activity of war to a point at which information becomes the decisive element. This proclivity is exemplified by Leonhard's *The Principles of War for the Information Age*, and similarly can be found at the heart of the works of Libicki and Arquilla and Ronfeldt.[29] Taking these views too seriously could result in an undue emphasis on information assets and operations in procurement and doctrine, as well as having significant effects on military culture.

There are four main reasons why violence cannot be removed from the act of war. First, strategy may require the physical destruction of enemy forces and assets. As noted earlier, this was an expressed objective both in the post-D-Day campaign against the Wehrmacht, and against Iraq's Republican Guard in 1991. In a more extreme example, sections within the Roman Republic viewed the destruction of the Carthaginian civilisation as the final goal of the protracted Punic Wars. This is not to suggest that such objectives will always be appropriate. On this point Wylie is generally correct when he notes that control should usually be achieved somewhere between extermination and not solving the problem.[30] The key to strategic judgment is identifying where that point lies and if it has been reached. Second, in some instances violent destruction of enemy forces will prove much simpler and therefore easier to execute than a finely tuned disruption campaign. The former approach has the advantage of having a greater sense of finality about it. In many instances a disrupted foe can regain cohesion much more rapidly than a destroyed foe can reform itself. Third, control will often require the physical presence of ground forces, in which case the enemy will probably need to be physically removed from the territory in question. Although at times an enemy on the wrong side of information dominance will cede control, there will surely be many occasions in which the enemy will have to be physically, and violently, removed. An example of such a situation is the 1991 Gulf War, in which it took the violently executed

Coalition offensive to compel Iraqi forces to withdraw from Kuwait. Finally, because war is an interaction between at least two intelligent actors, an enemy can always reintroduce violence into a non-violent conflict. Reflecting his emphasis on the pre-eminence of battle, Clausewitz persuasively argues, 'the enemy can *frustrate everything through a successful battle* ... Thus it is evident that destruction of the enemy forces is always the superior, more effective means, with which others cannot compete' (emphasis in the original).[31] In the modern world violence can be reintroduced in the extreme form of WMD. We should also keep in mind Dunlap's idea that an enemy may feel that strategic advantage can be obtained by pursuing especially violent forms of conflict.[32] This was one of Iraq's ultimately futile strategies used against the invading Coalition forces, and was particularly evident in their use of suicide bombers. It seems appropriate at this juncture to reiterate once again Clausewitz's warning concerning the dangers inherent in blunting one's own ability to prosecute violent forms of warfare for fear that an enemy so endowed would hold an advantage.[33]

In the final analysis, it is important to note that warfare has always contained elements that are non-violent. From Clausewitz's own period the Battle of Ulm is a prominent example, and electronic warfare (EW) suggests itself as a noticeable non-violent feature of the modern era. However, both of these illustrations still fit into the Clausewitzian notion concerning the overarching presence of violent battle. Indeed, EW and psychological operations can be perceived primarily as activities that are mutually supportive of the violent application of force. This can also apply to SIW and/or acts of IW in the battlespace under certain circumstances. For instance, IW attacks against logistic systems or the informational/industrial infrastructure of a foe can be regarded as supporting operations to the main military campaign that is conducted by physical military forces. In this sense, SIW and IW more broadly resemble the supporting roles often played by airpower. However, it is when SIW performs a similar role to strategic bombing in the pursuit of an independent theory of victory that cracks appear in the view that war is always potentially an act of physical violence. Under these circumstances SIW represents an act of force, but not necessarily an act of physical force. And, although SIW can lead to violence, destruction and loss of life, if carefully targeted it can act as a coercive tool without these effects. As noted in the previous chapter, this is one of the alleged advantages of cyberterror. The arrival of SIW would therefore seem to question the absolute validity of one aspect of the nature of warfare as outlined in Chapter 1. In fact, SIW goes even further, through its ability to wage war without recourse to any real physical exertion or direct involvement of humans at a physical level. However, as a caveat it is important to note that humans are still intimately involved as both the instigators of the attack and the intended target (the mind of the opponent). Nonetheless, the discussion of the strategic potential of SIW in Chapter 4 indicates that this challenge to the nature of warfare is less apparent than first seems to be the case. The inability to convert SIW into a strategic theory of victory indicates that, although SIW does represent a new form of warfare, in most circumstances it will merely act as a supporting element to traditional forces.

The dominant factors in the above deliberations are the requirements of strategy and its dialectic nature. It is strategy that largely dictates whether and how much violence is required. War is usually violent, but strategy requires more than just the application of violence and destructive force. Indeed, a large part of the art of strategy involves making a judgment on when to apply violent and destructive force, how much, in what form and against which targets. At times, such as in the context of a nuclear deterrence strategy, the mere threat of the use of force may suffice. Nonetheless, even in these circumstances the possibility of battle is the key. This latter point works on two levels. First, it is the potential destructive power of nuclear forces (or conventional forces in conventional deterrence) that acts as the prime mover for a deterrence strategy. Second, being prepared to fight a nuclear 'battle' (having a warfighting doctrine), as opposed to existential deterrence, enhances the credibility of a deterrence posture.[34] Another case in which military force was often indirectly threatened rather than used directly was the Roman legions in the early Empire. Although always ready to be deployed and used, the legions often achieved their objectives by the mere fact of their presence.[35] In certain contingencies, such as COIN, counterterrorism or colonial policing, a more minimal use of force may be judicious.[36] It is within these contingencies that non-violent forms of information power may have particular relevance. Whereas, in the face of a regular and substantial enemy such as the Third Reich, the strategy of unconditional surrender was translated into the direct application of large levels of destructive and violent force. The great practitioners of strategy have usually been adept at balancing the use and non-use of destructive force, and its relationship to the other instruments of grand strategy. This is true of T. E. Lawrence and Alexander the Great, to name just two. To take the latter as an example, Alexander's campaign against Darius III of Persia was constructed of a balance between successful battles and cruel punishments (Tyre) on the one hand, and leniency and constructive relationships with his conquered enemies on the other.[37] In Alexander's strategy can be seen a superior synthesis of Clausewitz and Sun Tzu's paradigms. However, ultimately those elements of his campaign with which Sun Tzu would have been most content were only possible as a result of his battlefield victories over the Persian army.

The optimism in the RMA literature's claim to be able to significantly reduce or eliminate violence from war is equalled by its visions concerning the reduction of uncertainty in conflict. Again, the significance of this issue relates to both the preparation and conduct of war. The inherent dangers in all too readily accepting the conclusions of those who profess the coming dominance of concepts such as DBK are persuasively expressed in Wylie's assertion that 'planning for certitude is the greatest of all military mistakes'.[38] Of particular concern is the notion that an RMA force requires fewer, if any, reserves. This conclusion is reached by two different, but related, routes. The first perceives reserves as purely a mechanism to deal with uncertainties. Consequently, if information systems can eliminate the fog of war then reserves become redundant. Second, this same level of certainty enables warfare to be successfully concluded by a single decisive action, in which case reserves will never have an opportunity to play a part. In response to these thoughts we can turn to the work of T. E. Lawrence, who penned these lines in his discussion of the intangible elements of war and in response to earlier theories relating to the demise of the reserve:

> There was a line of variability (man) running through all its estimates. Its components were sensitive and illogical, and generals guarded themselves by the device of reserves ... Goltz has said that when you know the enemy's strength, and he is fully deployed, then you know enough to dispense with a reserve. But this is never. There is always the possibility of accident, of some flaws in materials, present in the general's mind: and the reserve is unconsciously held to meet it ... Nine-tenths of tactics are certain, and taught in books: but the irrational tenth is like the kingfisher flashing across the pool and that is the test of generals.[39]

Lawrence summarises well some of the many reasons why war will remain an uncertain activity. However, the increased levels of certainty envisaged in the RMA literature cannot be dismissed out of hand. All things being equal, information systems and better information operations should ensure that certain elements of warfare will become less uncertain for certain periods of time. This is particularly true in relation to the disposition of forces in the battlespace. To this end, 'Joint Vision 2010' is right to expect 'increased transparency'.[40] The significance of this should not be underestimated. Historically, many battles have been heavily influenced by uncertainties in the whereabouts and status of forces. The Battle of Waterloo provides just one example from Clausewitz's own time, and is typified by the concerns and uncertainty about 'Where is Blucher?' This potential for increased transparency, allied to the increased reliance on information in certain weapon systems, and the greater assurity of destruction in the battlespace, implies that Libicki is correct to emphasise the significance of the conflict over information. Likewise, Leonhard is right to call for information operations to be regarded as an equal in combined-arms operations and joint warfare.

Whilst accepting the potential for increased transparency, it is important to correct the error in the RMA literature that too readily links success in the infosphere to a theory of victory. Aside from the fact that strategy requires competence across a whole range of dimensions,[41] it is also important to note that certainty will in all likelihood never be achieved. This is due to at least seven main reasons. First, because war is an interaction with an intelligent enemy, certainty is reduced by the non-linear results of the interaction itself, and also by the deliberate actions of the enemy. This latter category includes acts of deception and attacks to degrade information systems. Second, as Lawrence notes in the above quotation, war is infused by intangible elements, many of them relating to humans and therefore of an unquantifiable nature. The third element of uncertainty is 'intent'. Seeing the disposition of enemy forces is not the same as understanding what he will do with them, although dispositions can give an idea of intent. In his piece *What is Information Warfare?* Libicki notes that stronger encryption, ironically a product of the information age, will make it significantly more difficult to uncover enemy intentions from his transmissions as was done with Ultra in World War II.[42] Fourth, information overload will complicate the task of identifying certainty. In this respect, there is an important distinction between having information and knowing the true state of affairs. We can extrapolate from the case of Pearl Harbor that the increase in information in the twenty-first century will not only see an increased production of useful information, but will also witness a growth in noise. The fifth factor that maintains uncertainty relates to the geography of any particular battlespace. This is particularly relevant in the increasingly prevalent urban battlespace. Uncertainty in this instance is not just a product of the physical structure of an urban area, but can also be produced by an enemy mingling with the civilian population. This was a particular problem for Coalition forces in Iraq during the 2003 war. The system of systems will not solve the age-old problem of distinguishing a guerrilla from a civilian. This suggests another related problem for acquiring greater certainty, and is concerned with the many forms war can take. As noted, some of these forms do not include regular identifiable forces. The sixth problem is that of human error or bias. Ultimately, information has to be handled and used by humans. Also, returning to the discussion of military genius, certain commanders may not have the cognitive abilities to make effective use of the information they receive. Judgment in war is still very much an art, not a science. Finally, the level of certainty attainable will be affected by the play of chance. Warfare in the information age will not run like clockwork, in which case a plan based on perfect and complete information can still fail because of some unforeseeable incident. In conclusion, these seven main factors that reduce certainty mean that warfare still lies in the realms of the unpredictable. Therefore, war is still an environment in which, as Clausewitz notes, the judgment of the commander is paramount.[43]

In many respects the current RMA reflects the strategic culture of elements within the United States. This translates into a tendency to seek technological fixes to strategic problems, and the increasing removal of humans from the sharp end of war. The former of these traits could result in poor strategic performance, whereas there is some, albeit limited, rationale for the latter. There is a certain operational logic in the increased utilisation of UCAVs, stand-off munitions and artificial intelligence. These developments offer the potential for higher operational tempo. As with many of the proposals and visions of the RMA, problems with these concepts arise if they are not considered within a strategic framework. Often, desires for less direct human involvement in conflict emanate from two sources. The first relates to an alleged sensitivity to casualties, whereas the second is based on an overly optimistic appraisal of the strategic efficacy of bombardment. It is interesting that various strands of the RMA literature exhibit two contradictory errors of analysis. Certain works place too little emphasis on the strategic value of battle and firepower, often because of an undue confidence in the efficacy of information operations. Alternatively, too much faith is placed in the strategic efficacy of stand-off bombardment. However, although these two approaches represent contradictory errors they both have an identical inadequacy: an astrategic outlook.

To understand why humans must remain directly involved in the prosecution of war, we need look no further then the requirements of strategy, war's varied forms and strategy's dialectic nature. Wylie's concept of control once again serves as the most useful frame of reference in relation to strategic needs. Wylie helpfully concludes that control is about people.[44] From this perspective we can begin to recognise the value of infantry and ground forces more generally. To reiterate, it is only these forms of military power that can provide prolonged, durable presence and exert control over the key issue, whether that be a population or some other resource. This is of particular importance in irregular conflicts, in which the direct protection of the population is often paramount, and when the political dimension is more pronounced.[45] The flexibility of the man on the scene with a gun is also of merit when we consider the geography of certain battlespaces. In this respect, urban, heavily forested and mountainous regions are obvious candidates. In conclusion, certain strategic requirements, allied to specific geographical environments, make it almost imperative that ground forces, and infantry especially, be the leading edge in a campaign.

Once it is accepted that ground forces must be available to meet the needs of strategy, it is a logical step to defend the continued existence of manned platforms in the face of Libicki's assault by 'the small and the many'.[46] Although flexible, infantry forces invariably are both vulnerable and relatively slow moving. The traditional answer to these two problems has been manned platforms that provide protected firepower and mobility. These appear to be as relevant in the information age as they have been previously. During the War for Iraq, MBTs and APCs continued to provide this vital role. Organic firepower would also serve as a guarantee should the networks upon which distant firesupport relies be attacked or go down for other reasons. It is worth making the point again that the advocates of concepts such as the Mesh and SOS do not pay enough serious attention to the paradoxical logic of strategy. If information networks prove to be a significant force multiplier, then these same networks may become the prime target of enemy efforts. This is not to undermine the valuable and increasing role that stand-off firepower will play, but merely to note that organic firepower is a sensible and complementary element. This combination of distant and organic firepower was at the heart of improvements in operational and tactical art during World War I. In that particular case indirect artillery certainly had a leading role, and yet infantry platoons also required and benefited from innovations such as the Lewis gun.[47] Further, as Applegate correctly notes, organic firepower also provides punch should the other armed services which contribute firesupport not be available.[48] This is particularly important in urban operations. Although as the War for Iraq showed, airpower can still fulfil a very significant function in such a context. Returning to the needs of strategy, the lessons of Bosnia are also worthy of attention. Although heavy armour does not appear to have an obvious role in such peace support operations as in the Balkans, British Challenger tanks performed a useful psychological, deterrent function, and aided efforts to limit the escalatory tendency of the conflict. This latter example merely serves to highlight the varied and flexible roles manned platforms can perform.

The continued requirement to put ground forces into harm's way does not mean that some of the innovations of the information age will not have a role. For certain missions, and in certain circumstances, unmanned platforms and/or stand-off munitions will represent the leading edge. Yet, it is difficult to perceive how these same technologies can perform the many varied tasks strategy and the variability of war, including variable geography, call for. Consequently, because humans will continue to wage war directly, the individual human commander, perhaps aided by AI, also has a safe future. In this respect, the commander fulfils two primary functions. First, he deals with the humanity of the men under his command, and second, he plays a vital role by making strategically important judgments. A fundamental point that much of the RMA literature, with its emphasis on technology and/or information operations, misses or undervalues is Gray's assertion that strategy is about, and is done by, people.[49] Since war will continue to be characterised by violence; human involvement; uncertainty; strategic needs; and interaction with an intelligent enemy; friction and chance will invariably continue to operate as well.[50] It can therefore be concluded that the information age has not de-legitimised the Clausewitzian climate and nature of war. Nevertheless, the information age has introduced some significant changes to the character of war.

COMING CHANGES

Although the foundations that constitute the nature of warfare remain fundamentally intact, the information age does appear to have brought about some important changes which impact on the practice of strategy. With the maturation of the infosphere as a dimension of strategy in mind, it is appropriate to regard the current epoch as of equal importance to the changes wrought by both the air and nuclear revolutions in the twentieth century. Whether these moments of change represent RMAs is somewhat of a mute point. It is of no real importance whether any particular change can be classified as an RMA in some academic script; instead, what matters is how these changes can be exploited in the reality of strategic practice. What follows is an analysis of the main changes and their implications.

The first notable feature of warfare in the information age is that information may have become more directly relevant to the outcome of military operations. The key words in this last sentence are 'more' and 'directly'. Information has always played an important role in warfare, as Slim's comment and Hannibal's success at Lake Trasimene testify.[51] Yet, there is some validity in Libicki's assertion that war may increasingly take the form of hide-and-seek. This results from the increased omnipotence and efficacy of sensors, the increasingly rapid dissemination of information to shooters, and the growing levels of precision and guarantee of kill.

Libicki's thesis loses its persuasiveness when it concludes from these findings that war will cease to be a force-on-force experience. In this respect Libicki has committed a number of errors. The first is to underestimate the paradoxical logic of strategy. Superior information and weapon systems will not be permitted to rule the battlespace indefinitely and unmolested. Responses to these systems can take either a symmetrical or asymmetrical form. The Pacific war reveals how simple fortification measures by the Japanese offset US distant firepower. Japanese bunkers were notoriously difficult to knock out.[52] Libicki's notions also rest upon the false belief that information has become the dominant dimension in warfare. Consequently, due to the recognised potency of the sensor-to-shooter relationship the battle over information becomes the decisive and possibly only element of the war. In contrast, although still recognising the advantages to be gained from information superiority, it is plausible that a force can still function without substantial information support. Admittedly, the force may operate less effectively, and may be more vulnerable, but to expect it to capitulate immediately upon losing the information battle is an act of reductionism. In fact, it is likely that a force deprived of physical supplies will operate less effectively than if it had been deprived of its information assets. An infantryman or tank can still function without being connected to an information net, but both will not operate effectively for long without food, water and fuel respectively. Nevertheless, to reiterate, information has become a more prominent, and perhaps a more significant, dimension in warfare. This fact should be recognised by the acceptance of Leonhard's notion that information operations be regarded as an equal part of combined warfare. Further to this, success in information operations may increasingly require the realisation of Libicki's call for an info corps to operate in this fifth dimension of strategy.[53]

The encompassing term 'digitisation' constitutes the second significant change. In particular, attention should be focused on the C^2 implications. Again, it is worth noting that digitisation does not achieve anything definitively new; C^2 still functions when using semaphore, drums or wireless radio. Yet, the relative advantages of digitisation should be exploited. In particular, command structures are affected. To this extent, the advocates of the organisational implications of the information age are worthy of note.[54] Chapter 3 noted that distinct advantages could be obtained from a hybrid command structure that utilises the best features of both hierarchies and networks. In theory, such a structure would benefit from the flexibility, adaptability, information flow and robustness of a network, while at the same time retaining the concept of the commander's 'intent' as the overarching guide to action. Discussions of C^2 in the information age invariably raise the prospect of command by AI. Chapter 3 suggested that, although possessing some advantages, AI should only ever be regarded as an aide to the irreplaceable human commander. All told, digitisation and its organisational implications warrant exploitation, but we should not fall into the trap of elevating these elements of strategy to the point at which they are claimed to be the dominant and decisive dimensions. A digitised force, operating with information age organisational structures and ethos, should provide a number of relative advantages over its industrial age counterpart, but it will not ensure strategic success.

The third new element of the current epoch in warfare has a more genuine originality than the previous two. SIW, with its non-violent, non-physical, real-time, global reach, does represent a new means of waging war. However, as discussed earlier, it shares some significant similarities with strategic bombing. It is the conclusions drawn from this comparison that suggest that SIW will rarely, if ever, represent an independent theory of victory. Consequently, SIW will not fundamentally alter the nature of war. However, this limitation in its strategic efficacy does not significantly detract from its importance. Precisely because this form of warfare is so readily accessible, and so potentially damaging to an information age society, any defence community must take it seriously. Taking it seriously entails the development of both offensive and defensive capabilities.

SIW represents just one element in the grand strategic instrument of 'information power'. As an overall concept this fourth change is not new to the information age. Yet like many of the other changes, it may be enjoying increased potential. This heightened promise is related to the growing significance of information generally and the growth and development of cyberspace in particular, which has endowed information power with a greater range of outlets, operations and more direct impact.

The final change worthy of note is a result of a culmination of the previous four, and therefore represents the most significant development of the information age. The rise in the significance of the infosphere, the fifth dimension of strategy, cannot be ignored. Like the other dimensions, strategy in the infosphere has its own character, and requires operations, organisations and career paths that are specific to its unique nature.[55] The dominant operational and strategic concept in this fifth dimension is 'control of the infosphere'. Control, as opposed to command, not only reflects the complex reality of the infosphere, but also facilitates greater levels of flexibility for operations in this unique environment. However, the essential point to make about the infosphere is that it represents only one, and not the decisive or dominant, dimension of strategy. In this respect, Corbett's realistic assessment of the potential for sea power is equally applicable to information power. Information power only has relevance in how it exerts leverage on to the land where people live. For this reason, the infosphere will add an extra dimension to geopolitics; it will not render traditional geopolitical concerns irrelevant.

It was Clausewitz himself who acknowledged that each age had its own particular character of war, but that there also existed certain universal elements that should always be considered.[56] This book has demonstrated that warfare in the information age exhibits its own characteristics, and even presents some significant changes. Yet, the essential nature of warfare, as exemplified in Clausewitz's climate and trinity, remains unchanged. Therefore, at minimum, *On War* remains a great, and relevant, work of strategic theory. The question then is, does it remain the 'only truly great book on war', and does it need supplementing with the reinvigorated works of Sun Tzu and Jomini? Alternatively, are the changes wrought by the information age of such seismic proportions that the nature of war can now only be understood with reference to new works of strategic theory as well?

Arquilla and Ronfeldt argue that Sun Tzu now represents a more accurate reflection of war than does the work of Clausewitz. Their interpretation is in agreement with B. H. Liddell Hart's assessment in the 'Foreword' to Samuel Griffith's 1963 translation of the Chinese general's work. Whilst accepting the status of Clausewitz, Liddell Hart considers his work dated in comparison to Sun Tzu's.[57] It is fitting therefore to begin this assessment with the work of this Chinese doyen of the information age. Sun Tzu has much to offer those wishing to understand war. Yet, in many important respects his work represents more of an ideal than a reality, and at times engages in reductionism. The most prominent positive feature of *The Art of War*, and the one which receives most attention in the current epoch, is the central role attributed to knowledge in the conduct of strategy. Sun Tzu is right to promote the value of gathering knowledge on the enemy, oneself and the terrain. And yet, like many of his information age counterparts he makes too direct a link between knowledge and success. Acting as a balance to all such theories that distil the art of strategy down to one or two dimensions is Gray's assertion that success requires a level of competence in most of the dimensions.[58] In this respect, Sun Tzu proffers sound advice, but do not take his assertions too literally. Although not often noted by the RMA enthusiasts, Sun Tzu's statement concerning deception in warfare is of particular relevance in the current age. There is a certain irony for those writers who put faith in the potency of information, because quite naturally the goal of deception is to reduce the efficacy of information and knowledge. Therefore, the same theorist (Sun Tzu) who promotes the value of information gathering also values one of the primary methods to render that same information less effective. This is to Sun Tzu's credit. By creating juxtaposition between knowledge and deception, he captures the dynamic nature of the conflict over information. Indeed, *The Art of War* is primarily concerned with the manipulation of information, and in this respect exemplifies the concept of control of the infosphere.

On the subject of information Clausewitz is far too negative. However, Gray is undoubtedly right that Clausewitz's concept of the fog of war is a healthy corrective to those writings that promise total situational awareness or DBK.[59] In agreement this book has somewhat laboured the point that various factors will ensure the continued primacy of uncertainty. Similarly, Clausewitz is correct to stress the role of the commander in dealing with this inevitable uncertainty. However, the Prussian unduly downplays the role information gathering can have in dealing with uncertainty. Clausewitz's attitude to the role of information is exemplified by the mere one-and-a-half pages he devotes explicitly to the subject, and the negative influence he believes information has by creating doubts in the commander's mind. On the issue of information it seems that the most balanced approach lies within a synthesis of Clausewitz and Sun Tzu's work. Interestingly, this synthesis is evident in Jomini's *Art of War*. Jomini accepts the inherent uncertainties in warfare, acknowledges the fact that information may be inaccurate and concedes that perfect information is not attainable. Like his Prussian contemporary, he sees part of the answer to this problem lying in the qualities of the general. However, within his work Jomini also espouses the value of collecting information, discusses relevant issues such as information security and encryption, and by his ideas concerning decisive points suggests that useful, perhaps decisive, knowledge is attainable. On this subject, Jomini presents perhaps the most balanced perspective of the three great theorists.

Sun Tzu's unfortunate tendency for reductionism is nowhere better exemplified than in his axiom, 'For to win one hundred victories in one hundred battles is not the acme of skill. To subdue the enemy without fighting is the acme of skill.'[60] The broad scope of strategy does not tolerate such a one-dimensional approach. As mentioned repeatedly throughout this work, destruction of the enemy and/or his forces can be a requisite for the attainment of one's strategic objectives. In the case of the 1991 Gulf War, had the Coalition somehow been able to force the withdrawal of Iraqi forces without the need for battle, it is unlikely that an unscathed Iraqi army would have ceased to pose a threat to Kuwait, and therefore the attainment of the Coalition's objectives would have been even less complete than they were. Upon close examination of Sun Tzu's work it becomes clear why his theories are popular amongst some of the RMA advocates. In certain respects he espouses ideas that have a very contemporary ring to them. To summarise: he proclaims the desirability of short wars, economy of force, the decisive role of information and the minimisation of enemy casualties. A quick assessment of these notions might lead to the following conclusions: a protracted conflict can promote an actor's goals in certain cases (North Vietnam); preserving one's forces is generally a useful principle; information is an important feature of warfare, but rarely decisive; and the level of violence/destruction inflicted on the enemy should be dictated by strategic requirements. This is not to say that Sun Tzu's work does not encompass some subtle and balanced appraisals. For example, see the above discussion concerning Sun Tzu's appreciation of the need to 'control' the infosphere. Also, his discussion of ordinary and extraordinary forces suggests that he understands the complex character that war can take.[61] However, these thoughts do suggest that Sun Tzu's analysis, although containing useful and sometimes insightful perceptions, is generally too restrictive to encompass the breadth of strategic requirements and circumstances.

Jomini goes some way towards rectifying these deficiencies, and in this respect his work reflects a more nuanced approach than he is often given credit for. Being a good Napoleonic thinker, Jomini regards the destruction of the hostile army as the most effective means to produce decisive results 'since states and provinces fall of themselves when there is no organised force to protect them'.[62] However, he also concedes that results can be gained by outmanoeuvring the enemy to fall upon his flanks and thereby demoralise him. Although, interestingly Jomini regards such victories as less decisive than those obtained through destruction of the enemy's force.[63] Finally, and perhaps reflecting a recognition of the political and human elements in strategy, and also Napoleon's experiences in the Iberian Peninsula, Jomini describes the application of physical military force to quash a 'war of opinion' as 'inappropriate measures for arresting an evil which lies wholly in the human passions'.[64] On this issue, as is the case with the role of information in war, Jomini benefits from a re-evaluation of his work inspired by the information age.

Despite the quality of Jomini's ideas, Clausewitz's thoughts on the function of violence in war are undoubtedly the superior analysis. The essence of his thoughts is to be found in Book One Chapter Two, and Book Eight. In these sections of *On War* Clausewitz reveals that he does not subscribe to a blind fixation on physical destruction of the enemy. His range of thoughts on this issue includes the acceptance that many roads lead to success, and whether violence is required depends on the particular circumstance.[65] He also correctly identifies the destruction of the enemy's force as merely a means to an end rather than being an end in itself.[66] Importantly, Clausewitz is cognisant that under certain conditions defeat of the enemy forces is not possible, for example if one side has a marked relative weakness.[67] Furthermore, Clausewitz's own definition of destruction of the enemy does not rest solely upon acts of physical violence: 'The fighting forces must be *destroyed*: that is, they must be *put in such a condition that they can no longer carry on the fight.* Whenever we use the phrase "destruction of the enemy's forces" this alone is what we mean' (emphasis in the original).[68] This is an important statement by the Prussian theorist, because it demonstrates that his work is in harmony with those instances in which the enemy can be defeated with little or no acts of physical violence. In this respect, Clausewitz retains his validity on those rare occasions when disruption or manoeuvre is decisive. Although, as noted in Chapter 1, this does not detract substantially from his perspective that war is usually an act of bloodshed: '*violent resolution of the crisis, the wish to annihilate the enemy's forces,* is the first-born son of war' (emphasis in the original).[69]

These thoughts reveal that Clausewitz perceived war as a varied activity in which violence had a more muted role at times. Yet, it is when he links these thoughts to the role of combat and fighting that his superior analysis becomes most evident. Whist recognising that war does not always include physical fighting, and that strategy does not always require it, two factors ensure that physical combat and violence have central and dominant roles in warfare. It is this reality that must underpin any preparation for future war. First:

> Combat is the only effective force in war; its aim is to destroy the enemy's forces as a means to a further end. That holds good even if no actual fighting occurs, because the outcome rests on the assumption that if it came to fighting, the enemy would be destroyed. It follows that the destruction of the enemy's force underlies all military actions.[70]

As previously accepted, destruction of the enemy can in theory be achieved by disruption. However, the rarity of such a decisive non-violent, non-attritional act is such that war preparation must have at its heart the expectation that violent combat will occur. Secondly, Clausewitz reminds us that, because war is conducted amongst competing belligerents, the natural tendency is for war to escalate to its extremes. This translates into the possibility that the enemy can reintroduce combat and violence. By reintroducing violence against an enemy unprepared for such an eventuality, the belligerent who raises the ante may gain an advantage. Although overselling the point somewhat, Clausewitz is still ultimately correct to stress the superiority of combat in war when he states, 'the enemy *can frustrate everything through a successful battle*' (emphasis in the original).[71] The superiority of Clausewitz's analysis emanates from the fact that it encompasses the role of an intelligent enemy; the fact that war is ultimately a battle of the wills conducted primarily through physical expressions of force; and the emphasis placed on the dominant role of strategy. It is this latter point that the RMA literature so often overlooks. Although recognising that each age and culture will have its own peculiar preconceptions of war, and therefore its own limiting conditions,[72] Clausewitz rightly notes that policy, amongst other things, will (one can say 'should') determine the character of a war.[73] This would suggest that post-heroic warfare has some recognised validity from a Clausewitzian perspective. However, as Clausewitz himself recognises, although certain conditions are unique to each age, there are universal truths that every theorist, regardless of context, must include.[74] These ubiquitous elements must be given priority over current political or social inclinations. Otherwise, an enemy operating within the universal elements would invariably gain an advantage over those who neglect these truths.

Of the three classic works of theory, Clausewitz and Sun Tzu embody the human element of warfare most convincingly. Although all three works place great emphasis on the role of the human traits of the commander, Jomini's thesis suffers from his overly deterministic discussion of operational and geometric principles, which seem to leave insufficient room for discussions of the human and therefore political aspects of strategy. Gray correctly includes the human element as one of his main dimensions of strategy. Although it represents an obvious dimension, the human role in strategy requires attention because war is conducted ultimately by humans. Again, this work has shown how the RMA literature has a tendency to regard warfare as being composed solely of quantifiable units that can be translated by the system of systems into information to be displayed on a computer monitor. This approach commits two significant errors. First, since politics is concerned with the interaction of humans, it ignores the fundamental role played by politics and the affairs of humans in strategy. Just as erroneous, the RMA literature underestimates the moral forces at play in war. As *Warfighting* recognises, these intangible elements play at least an equal part in deciding the outcome of any particular conflict.

Sun Tzu's work contains a number of dominant themes. The role of knowledge in war has already been identified. However, another thread running through *The Art of War* is the recognition that war is conducted against an opposing human mind. This may be a result of Sun Tzu's Confucian tradition which regards war as partly a cerebral activity. Although he is sometimes rightly criticised for giving insufficient attention to the paradoxical logic of strategy, and thereby does not fully explain the significance of an opposing human belligerent, Sun Tzu is acutely aware of the fact that war is far more than just force dispositions.

In this respect he discusses a number of factors, including the advantages to be gained from playing on the temperament of the enemy commander, and the relationship between commander and population; he even notes that human frailties can be exploited when he discusses cultural warfare waged via the introduction of licentious dancers.[75] History is in accordance with Sun Tzu's emphasis on the significance of human traits in war. Whether it is Hitler's ideological fervour, Napoleon's egocentric visions of grandeur or Hannibal's thirst for revenge, individual human characteristics can have both positive and negative effects on strategic performance.

Similarly, for Clausewitz the organic whole of war is constructed of a mix of physical and psychological/human factors. This is evident in the trinity, which contains the human elements of passion, politics and the play of chance. Akin to Sun Tzu, Clausewitz places great emphasis on the traits of the commander. Aside from recognising the human traits required for *coup d'œil* (the essence of military genius), much of the dominant concept of friction emanates from human involvement in the art of war. It is within the unified concept of friction that the effects of the nature of warfare can be felt. As is often cited, friction distinguishes war in theory from war in reality. Importantly, the broader concept of friction includes not only chance events such as mechanical failure or the weather, but also includes the mismatch between means and ends, as well as a number of human-related difficulties such as danger, physical exertion, physical and political limits on the use of force, and unpredictability resulting from interaction with the enemy.[76] Admittedly, the delivery of firepower by PGMs, or the application of power through SIW, should exhibit different and less obvious forms of friction than the conveyance of power by foot soldiers who have to contend more directly with the enemy's forces and terrain. However, the two former methods of war both have their own forms of friction, and their inability to produce decisive strategic results will ensure that the more friction-prone expressions of power will continue. The role of friction is critical because it largely determines whether or not war is a controllable activity. Sun Tzu tends towards regarding war as a controllable phenomenon, so long as one can acquire good knowledge and have effective command and control of one's forces. Clausewitz perceives war as being more manageable as opposed to controllable. The military genius can achieve policy ends by the use of military means. However, this positive control of war does not represent an act of reductionism, or a one-dimensional perspective that rests its assumptions on the advantage to be gained from good C⁴I. Instead, Clausewitz focuses upon the military genius's ability to cope with friction through his cognitive abilities and strength of determination. On this point, a synthesis of these two theorists' work is perhaps most appropriate. Better knowledge and C^2 should in theory reduce the chaos of war. And yet the intangibles, many the result of human involvement, are best dealt with by human actors. To this synthesis, one should also add the value of factors such as training and quantity, which also help reduce the influence of friction.[77]

THE NEW THEORISTS

Evidently, the information age has brought mixed, but generally favourable, fortunes for the three great classical works of strategic theory. In the final analysis, Clausewitz still retains his pre-eminence because the core of his work has proven to be universally applicable, and his approach reveals a subtle balance that reflects the complex nature of war and strategy. Interestingly, although his views on the role and value of information clearly do not do sufficient justice to this important dimension of strategy, his general appreciation of the prominence of uncertainty remains valid. Information is the one significant area in which *On War* needs supplementation. On this issue, both Sun Tzu and Jomini are useful. The Swiss theorist offers a more balanced appraisal of information by valuing its contribution, but at the same time does not propel it to a dominant and decisive place in the outcome of strategy. Whereas, Sun Tzu provides a useful antidote to Clausewitz's pessimism, but ultimately assumes that too much certainty is achievable. The real value of the Chinese theorist's work comes from his implicit understanding of how information can be manipulated, and therefore *The Art of War* is useful reading for those contemplating 'control of the infosphere'.

Due to the growing and more direct significance of the infosphere it seems at least possible that some of the theory written during, and reflecting, the information age will prove useful in a supplementary role to the three great works. Therefore, we shall examine the works of Libicki, Arquilla and Ronfeldt, and the Tofflers, to decide whether they contain enough practical value to offset the opportunity costs of reading them.

As previously mentioned, the Tofflers have produced some of the most influential work of the information age. It is therefore of concern for those interested in sound strategic practice that their theory represents the weakest of the three works reviewed here. Frank C. Mahncke bemoans their anecdotal style that presents little evidence or substantive analysis.[78] Generally, the Tofflers display an ignorance of strategic thought. This lack of strategic understanding is manifestly evident in their claim that the future is 'post-Clausewitzian'.[79] At the heart of the Tofflers' thinking on future warfare is 'knowledge'. Their mindset is exemplified by the comment that we are witnessing a transformation from brute-force to 'brain-force' in warfare.[80] The similarity to Sun Tzu's perception of war as a cerebral activity is both striking and revealing. In particular, it leads to the first and most obvious response to the Tofflers' statement. Are they suggesting that warfare prior to the information age did not have a substantial cognitive element? Warfare has always been an activity in which mental acuity has played a central role. It is also erroneous to distinguish between the physical and mental dimensions of warfare.

Whilst information enables a more effective use of munitions at the technical and tactical levels, it does not represent the 'leading edge' in all contexts. Herein lies one of the fundamental failings and dangers of the RMA literature, and the Tofflers' work in particular: reductionism. By concentrating on just one of the many dimensions of strategy, these works implicitly, sometimes explicitly, suggest that success can be gained through superior performance in just one particular dimension. Gray's notion of strategy as a complex, unified activity is the perfect counter to such ideas. Like many of the RMA enthusiasts the Tofflers base their ideas on a perceived revolutionary increase in the importance of the knowledge dimension to strategy. However, unlike those elements of the RMA literature that focus primarily upon the battlespace, the Tofflers draw wider conclusions concerning the role of information in grand strategy. In his review of *War and Anti-war*, Krisinger suggests that the Tofflers' theory, like that of post-heroic warfare, is underpinned unduly by ethical considerations.[81] In this respect, they exhibit similar thoughts to those expressed by Libicki, namely, that increased transparency and greater potency of information power offer the opportunity to prevent violent conflict before it begins.[82] Drawing attention to the various functions information power can fulfil is an important and creditable undertaking. However, once again an overly optimistic appraisal of its potential is the result of insufficient attention being paid to strategic considerations.

These two errors, lack of strategic perspective, and optimistic reductionism, underpin much of the limitations in the Tofflers' theory. For example, their focus on the knowledge terrain, again echoing Sun Tzu's thoughts, represents judicious advice and practice.[83] Yet, they again fail to recognise that knowledge is just one dimension of strategy. Likewise, it is hard to criticise the Tofflers on their comment that the outcomes of war often depend heavily on intangible factors rather than more quantifiable elements such as numerical superiority.[84] Nevertheless, history reveals that a significant resource imbalance can prove influential to the outcome of particular conflicts. Once Germany and Japan had failed to achieve decisive quick victories over the Allied powers, it is difficult to see how the resource-rich Allies could not ultimately prevail given reasonable competence in the other dimensions.[85] The Tofflers escape the regular war fixation of much of the RMA literature. In this sense, they are correct to discuss the diversity of wars, and the difficulties of creating omni-capable forces.[86] The limitation in their theory on this issue comes from the reduction of the complex activities of wealth creation and warfare to the three-wave hypothesis of civilisation. War is certainly a diverse and adaptable activity, but this is more than just the product of which wave of civilisation the belligerents belong to. The character of each war is dependent on many factors, including policy goals, geography, individual preferences and interaction between the opponents. Overall, it has to be concluded that the opportunity costs of reading the Tofflers' work are simply too high to justify the effort required. Also, anything of value they do discuss, such as the value of the knowledge terrain, is more competently addressed in Sun Tzu's *The Art of War*. Taking the Tofflers too seriously has the potential to negatively affect strategic performance. Such a one-dimensional approach to the complex and unified pursuit of strategy will likely leave those who follow such a path ill equipped to deal with the varied demands of strategy, and an ever-present intelligent enemy.

Libicki is one of the most prolific writers on information age warfare. His work exhibits a host of useful observations, many of which should be considered as having serious practical application and merit. In particular, his discussions of information power and the information environment are helpful, but ultimately too radical and too prone to reductionism. Unfortunately, and much like the Tofflers, generally his work lacks strategic context, and therefore much of his work suffers from a lack of universal relevance. As befits a theorist of the RMA, information is firmly at the heart of Libicki's vision of future warfare. Two related concepts dominate his work. First, he regards the 'Mesh' to be of such significance that he declares that it represents a change in the nature of warfare, and equally poses a challenge to the role of human command in war.[87] Alongside the Mesh stand Libicki's thoughts on information power. Together, these two changes elevate information, and the information environment, to positions of prominence in the conduct of strategy. As noted earlier, in the battlespace this translates into 'hide-and-seek' warfare, in which information dominance becomes the deciding factor. Whereas, on the bigger stage the global reach of information renders physical geography less important, and enables effective military intervention without the deployment of forces. Taken together, these visions offer the promise of waging war with significantly less bloodshed.[88] For someone who places information at the core of future warfare, Libicki is surprisingly negative on the potential offered by SIW and very optimistic about the ability to defend cyberspace.[89] This complacency, although somewhat of a welcome relief in comparison to those who overplay the potential of SIW, derives from a general overconfidence in the robustness of information systems.

On this latter point, Libicki does go some way towards recognising the paradoxical logic, in that he accepts that an enemy facing the Mesh will undertake measures to offset its potency. To this end, he discusses acts of deception, the challenge posed by stealth, and the difficulties encountered by the Mesh in certain irregular conflicts and environments.[90] However, ultimately Libicki foresees that the answer to these problems lies in better detection technology, such as face recognition software to identify terrorists or guerrillas in densely populated urban environments. His answer is always technological, rather than strategic in nature. In this context, whilst acknowledging that irregular conflict in a dense environment represents a possible asymmetric response to the RMA, he optimistically concludes that the information 'Grid', through the proliferation of sensors and networked electronics, can negate the potency of this challenge.[91] Once again, the absence of any strategic context to his discussion is notable. He even addresses the asymmetrical responses of WMD and EMP, but ultimately concludes that the Mesh will be able to neutralise this threat by targeting the means of delivery and/or production sites. Alternatively, by removing tempting targets from the battlespace and by encouraging a more discriminating use of force, the Grid reduces the impetus to use WMD.[92] These examples are revealing in that they highlight Libicki's overemphasis on the technical and tactical levels of strategy; whereas, a successful method of waging war can conceivably be offset at any of the levels of strategy.

Libicki's work contains some very useful comments on the strategic role of information power. In particular, he is convincing when he discusses its strategic flexibility; the importance of attaining some form of information superiority; the related difficulties in gaining command of the information environment; and the requirement for an information force with its own doctrine and culture. On occasions, he acknowledges the strategic limitations to information operations. In particular, he acknowledges that they cannot usually translate into a theory of victory if they operate in the service of poor strategy.[93] All told, these positive contributions by Libicki, especially his work on information power, make his work worthy of attention. However, certain significant failings ensure that his work cannot be regarded as universal and therefore comparable to the great classical theories. In particular, there are too few occasions in which he exhibits an interest in the relationship between policy and the use of force. For example, Libicki describes how precision bombardment facilitated by the Mesh can enable the United States to 'control' the battlespace.[94] Contrast this perception of control with that of

Wylie's. The difference is clearly one of appreciation of strategic requirements. In this example Libicki has fallen into the trap of equating bombardment with a theory of war. He does this partly because one of his main guiding points seems to be an emphasis on post-heroic warfare. Libicki exhibits a similar insufficient appreciation of strategy in his limited discussions of irregular conflict. As Gray states, in these forms of war politics is more pronounced.[95] For Libicki, the challenges of these conflicts do not lie in the careful matching of means to ends, but rather in better surveillance techniques. In a similar vein to the Tofflers, Libicki's ideas have an air of reductionism about them. Information is far too central and dominant in his conception of strategy. Finally, he underestimates the significance of the paradoxical logic. Accordingly, Libicki's information systems are too robust in the face of enemy actions. Even if this was possible, he still does not convincingly explain how a dominant Mesh will translate into a theory of strategic victory. In the final assessment, Libicki's work is akin to that of Douhet. Both of these theorists introduce some important concepts and issues that require careful consideration and even action. However, basing your strategy around the ideas of Libicki is as unlikely to result in strategic success as for those who have sought a theory of victory by following Douhet's work.

The work of Arquilla and Ronfeldt displays a confusing mixture of radical claims concerning the revolutionary potential of the information age, and a more balanced, broader perspective on the future of warfare. Invariably, information is the instrument of change in Arquilla and Ronfeldt's theories. 'Cyberwar', which acts as the organising concept for the future battlespace, is defined as 'conducting, and preparing to conduct, military operations according to information-related principles'.[96] More fundamentally, information flow facilitates powerful organisational change, resulting in the empowerment and rise of the network form of organisation. To support their claims, the authors cite a number of historical cases in which success went to those operating along lines similar to cyberwar and netwar principles. The examples they rely upon include the Mongols in the thirteenth century, the Chechen rebels fighting post-Soviet Russia in the 1990s, and the Communist forces waging war against the United States and its South Vietnam ally. In relation to Vietnam they claim:

> The networked organisational style of guerilla fighters ... suggests the tremendous robustness of these fighters in the face of even the sternest countermeasures. The Vietnam War provides *the best example* of a networked insurgency withstanding everything the American hierarchy threw at it. [emphasis added][97]

This example, which reduces the complex conflict in Vietnam to differences in organisational structures, is an unfortunate choice. The insurgent force (Viet Cong) in South Vietnam had been defeated by its 'hierarchical' opponents by 1968. The force that conquered South Vietnam in 1975 was the regular, and hierarchical, NVA.

Nevertheless, their discussions concerning networks lead Arquilla and Ronfeldt into a welcome consideration of the broader spectrum of war. Unlike many of their contemporary RMA colleagues, they are prepared to give serious attention to irregular warfare in the information age. Indeed, they confidently claim that information-related principles are just as applicable at the lower end of the spectrum as at the higher 'regular' extremity. However, Arquilla and Ronfeldt unfortunately reveal too much enthusiasm for van Creveld's notion concerning the irregularisation of warfare. Indeed, 'netwar', described as 'an emerging mode of conflict (and crime) at societal levels, involving measures short of war',[98] can be perceived as being a 'virtual transformation of war'.

For Arquilla and Ronfeldt, the consequence of these changes is in an increasing emphasis on network forms, in which information becomes a critical commodity. Therefore, this leads to the claim that 'decisive duels for the control of information flows will take the place of drawn-out battles of attrition or annihilation; the requirement to destroy will recede as the ability to disrupt is enhanced'.[99] A reasonable question to pose in response to these thoughts is: why do many of the RMA theorists believe that the new must necessarily replace the old? Is it not plausible that the new will take its place alongside the old? Due to the basic requirements of 'strategic control', and the paradoxical logic, the airpower revolution has not rendered the older expressions of military power irrelevant. Rather, it has taken an important place in joint warfare. In a similar vein, it is likely that the conflict over control of the infosphere will not prove decisive, but instead will be an important component of joint operations. Similarly, since truly decisive manoeuvre is rarely achieved, to declare the end of attrition and annihilation is highly questionable. To reiterate, Gray rightly asserts that attrition, manoeuvre and control are not mutually exclusive; in fact they are interrelated.[100] Nevertheless, Arquilla and Ronfeldt take a further optimistic step and declare that cyberwar offers the potential to make war less bloody for both sides in a conflict, and therefore more humane.[101] Moving even further from the Clausewitzian paradigm, they postulate that in the information age friction ceases to be the main concern; instead limiting entropy will be the key.[102] This comment clearly reveals a misunderstanding of what friction entails. If we accept Barry Watts' explanation of the range of factors that make up the unified concept of friction, it is hard to understand how these difficulties, including the mismatch between means and ends and interaction with the enemy, can cease to be of concern. The coming of the information age does not merit the replacement of friction as the overarching and yet simple explanation of why war in practice differs from war in theory.

From the above comments it is clear that this work has identified a number of substantial problems with Arquilla and Ronfeldt's theories. Yet, these should not detract entirely from the positive contributions their work can make. For example, like Libicki, they correctly discuss information as another dimension of strategy that may act as the first choice for decision makers in certain circumstances.[103] They are also right to highlight the role of information by defining it as a strategic resource.[104] Also, their aforementioned discussion of how irregular conflicts may be affected by the information age at least opens the debate on this much-neglected subject in the RMA literature. However, it is noteworthy that they fail to expand their broader discussion of future warfare to discuss how WMD fits into their visions.

One of the most useful aspects of their work is that concerned with hybrid command structures. They provide a balanced appraisal of the advantages to be gained from both network and hierarchical models, and through this reveal that they have some understanding of the needs of battle command. Another important aspect of their work is that they move away from much of the RMA literature's obsession with stand-off high-tempo operations. In contrast, they acknowledge that cyberwar is just as applicable slow and close-in. However, their inability to move beyond the information-centric concept of cyberwar still poses a problem. At one stage they appear to come close to accepting an attritional element to future war when they note that, in a state of near-parity, cyberwarfighting proficiency will result in the need for 'big battalions'.[105] Their call for the need to construct an enemy information order of battle is also an important recognition of the increasing importance of information operations to success in joint warfare.[106] Finally, and most importantly, Arquilla and Ronfeldt, very much akin to Corbett's notions of sea power, declare that, important though the conflict in cyberspace (infosphere) may be, the outcome of any conflict will be decided by what happens in the 'real' world.[107] This may be their most important contribution to the debate on warfare in the information age.

Of the three theorists of the information age considered here, the work of Arquilla and Ronfeldt is undoubtedly the most useful in the practical world of strategy. Their broader outlook, encompassing a greater range of the spectrum of conflict and stretching into the realms of grand strategy, results in a more balanced appraisal. Likewise, their discussion of command structures is a judicious attempt to harness the benefits of both hierarchies and networks. In these respects it is difficult to disagree with Goodwin's assessment of *In Athena's Camp* as the most sober analysis of information warfare.[108] However, in the final analysis their work also exhibits reductionism, and would benefit from perceiving information as just one dimension amongst equals rather than as *the* dimension of the future. Due to this undue fixation on information, they consequently suffer from the fallacy of the decisive manoeuvre. In this sense they fail to appreciate the varied and complex nature of warfare. This is exemplified by their claim that cyberwar represents as big a change as blitzkrieg.[109] Again, their choice of example is both instructive and unfortunate. Despite the undoubted advantages this German operational innovation produced during the early years of World War II, these were offset by Allied competence, and German incompetence, in many of the other dimensions of strategy. The fact that Germany was defeated despite its operational and tactical prowess reveals the complex unified nature of strategy.

CONCLUSION

In the practical realms of strategy any theory that endeavours to be universal must reflect the true nature of war. If a theory fails to achieve this then the theory itself, as well as those whose military culture is based upon it, will receive a rude awakening in the crucible of war. It also seems that the more prescriptive a theory, the less universal it is. Prescription is a trait much of the RMA literature exhibits, primarily through its advocacy of attaining victory through information-related concepts such as information dominance. Sun Tzu also exhibits this tendency for prescription at times, especially in his maxims concerning the value of speed in warfare, and the desirability of achieving victory without battle. Wylie correctly notes that principles, which prescriptive theories often include, only reflect the specific time, place and need of writing.[110]

Historical experience suggests that the nature of war is moulded by five dominant factors. These are the policy objective, geography, the polymorphous character of war, the paradoxical logic and the fact that war is an activity waged by humans. The first of these, the influence of policy, is what strategy is all about. The challenge of matching military means to policy ends dictates the type and level of force required, and whether, and how much, violence and destruction are needed. The capabilities and will of the enemy must also form part of this equation. The policy objective also decides the relationship between military force and the other instruments of grand strategy,[111] and of course identifies the military objectives to be attained. The variety of military objectives that may be sought includes: the destruction of enemy forces, the capture of territory and the protection and allegiance of populations, to name just three. This variety of objectives also partially accounts for the polymorphous character of war. However, the polymorphous character of war is also a product of the characteristics of the enemy, and the geography in which the conflict is waged.

Luttwak's identification of the paradoxical logic, and Clausewitz's emphasis on the fact that war is waged against an intelligent foe are essential when considering the nature of war. Unfortunately, most of the RMA literature fails to take sufficient account of this core feature of strategy. The existence of an intelligent enemy has two significant effects. Firstly, an intelligent foe can endeavour to offset an enemy's strong suit. In this sense, tactical or operational proficiency based on the exploitation of the RMA, or a theory of war centred on SIW, may not translate into strategic success. The advantages to be gained from the RMA can be offset at all the levels of strategy. A second consequence of the paradoxical logic, which is of particular significance to the RMA literature, is the fact that an enemy can introduce into a conflict a level of violence for which a post-heroic military is unprepared. All those who espouse and encourage a less violent approach to warfare should take heed of Clausewitz's warning, which is worthy of repetition:

> The fact that slaughter is a horrifying spectacle must make us take war more seriously, but not provide an excuse for gradually blunting our swords in the name of humanity. Sooner or later someone will come along with a sharp sword and hack off our arms.[112]

Violence is an integral part of the nature of warfare, and an enemy can often reintroduce it regardless of one's efforts. Therefore, military culture should reflect the violence inherent in war. In fact, an enemy may adopt the extreme levels of violence offered by WMD as an asymmetrical response to RMA competence. Alternatively, he may opt for the more sporadic, unpredictable violence associated with various forms of irregular conflict, such as terrorism, and thereby deny a regular RMA force its preferred operational environment.

Much of the RMA literature undervalues the fifth significant element that helps shape the nature of war: its human dimension. War is a human undertaking at both the physical and psychological levels. The direct role played by humans in the conduct of war is ensured by Wylie's correct assertion that the man on the scene with a gun represents control. This concept embodies Corbett's balanced appraisal that every expression of strategic power must exert leverage into the land dimension. Any theory that underestimates the human element and focuses primarily upon the technological dimension will prove inadequate because it ignores the intangibles of warfare. By ignoring these intangibles one is invariably overlooking a significant aspect of strategy, and one that plays a major role in deciding the outcome of any particular conflict.

One example of how significant human factors can be in strategy is that of Philip II of Spain in the sixteenth century. Philip's personality, and more precisely his over-centralised style of decision making, which itself was born of his overwhelming feeling of responsibility for the defence of the Catholic faith during the Reformation, was a major factor in his failure to achieve policy objectives. Indeed, Philip is of particular relevance because he possessed an information advantage over many of his opponents, and himself placed much belief in the fact that this information would bring him success. However, his information advantage was offset by a number of factors. These included his cognitive rigidity which meant that he ignored information that contradicted his established ideas; an over-centralised command style which prevented initiative by his subordinates and created information overload for himself; the imperial overstretch of the Spanish Empire; the competence of his main adversaries, in particular Elizabeth I; and poor operational planning and performance, which was exacerbated by poor luck, such as the weather at the time of the 1588 Armada.[113] Because strategy is a human activity, infused by politics, it remains an art, and therefore requires human acts of judgment to succeed.

Despite the many changes to the character of warfare that have occurred since the early nineteenth century, and in spite of the changes yet to come in the information age, Clausewitz's *On War* still reflects the true nature of war most accurately. This is primarily the result of his superior concepts of the trinity and climate of war. Within these ideas lies an understanding of the subtle yet complex nature of war. In particular, Clausewitz's theory encompasses the relationship between means and ends, and the universal concept of friction: that which distinguishes war on paper from war in reality. Therefore, when thinking about and preparing for future war, our starting point should be the work of Clausewitz. However, Gray is right in his assertion that we need more than just *On War*. The greatest and only true great book on war, to paraphrase Brodie, should be supplemented. At the level of general theory, three works suggest themselves. These are: Luttwak's *Strategy: The Logic of War and Peace*, primarily for its identification of the paradoxical logic of strategy, although its discussion on the harmony of the levels of strategy is also a worthwhile and beneficial read; Wylie's *Military Strategy: A General Theory of Power Control*, which is distinguished for its universally useful concept of control, and the related ideas concerning the man on the scene with a gun; and Gray's *Modern Strategy*, which is chosen for its identification of the many dimensions of strategy, its broad scope covering the whole spectrum of strategic matters, and its concept that strategy represents a unified, practical undertaking.

Despite Clausewitz's universal applicability, his work does suffer from an underestimation of the role information can play in reducing uncertainty and aiding strategic performance. It should be noted that this is not a criticism of his concept of uncertainty in warfare, which as was argued in Chapter 2 remains an ever-present feature of conflict. However, because information has become more directly relevant in the practice of strategy, and for the same reasons that we benefit from a familiarity with the work of Corbett and Kahn, who provide deeper insight into the subsets of Strategic Studies, we require works that explore information power and the nature of the infosphere. To this end, Sun Tzu, Libicki, and Arquilla and Ronfeldt all express interesting ideas that illuminate thinking on information power. In this context, control of the infosphere provides a valuable theoretical construct to inform operations within this unique environment. When considering the overall value of information at a more general level, a synthesis of the theories of Sun Tzu and Clausewitz displays the most balanced appraisal. As noted earlier in this chapter, elements of such a synthesis can be found in the work of Jomini.

In conclusion, it is important to emphasise that information is just one dimension of strategy. Gray notes that deficiencies in the technological dimension can be compensated for by other means.[114] So it is with information. A force without information dominance can still operate, although it may be more vulnerable and less effective at the tactical and operational levels. In contrast, a force without supplies will soon cease to function at all. This comment is designed to show the relative importance of the information environment. Similarly, in his work Bennett draws attention to the limitations of intelligence. He notes that good intelligence is virtually useless without sufficient force to exploit it, although it does represent a significant force multiplier.[115] He also makes the vital point that during World War II the true value of Ultra could only be appreciated by recognising its limits.[116] So it is with information. Having some form of control of the infosphere, or at least denying it to your enemy, is beneficial in the same way in which it is useful to have air superiority. Yet, having control of the fifth dimension, or not, will guarantee neither success nor failure at the strategic level.

The current RMA will instigate many changes to the character of warfare, and many of these, such as digitisation, hybrid command structures and SIW, should be exploited. However, we should not expect these changes to alter the nature of war. In this respect, it appears that much of the theory which has been produced during the information age does not reflect the true nature of war; rather it represents a philosophical fad which reflects political and social desires for post-heroic warfare, and which has an undue emphasis on information as the decisive dimension of strategy. Consequently, military culture, doctrine and innovation should be based upon the Clausewitzian paradigm that still represents the closest manifestation of the true nature of war.[117] It is therefore fitting to end with a quotation from *On War* that provides a superior understanding of the need to balance the requirements of the day with the universal nature of war. How this fine balance is achieved lies at the heart of strategy.

> We can thus only say that the aims a belligerent adopts, and the resources he employs, must be governed by the particular characteristics of his own position; but they will also conform to the spirit of the age and to its general character. Finally, they must always be governed by the general conclusions to be drawn from the nature of war itself.[118]

NOTES

1. Arquilla and Ronfeldt, *A New Epoch*, p. 18.
2. Brodie, 'The Continuing Relevance of *On War*', p. 55.
3. Gray, *Modern Strategy*, p. xi.
4. Ibid., p. 76.
5. Brodie, 'The Continuing Relevance of *On War*', p. 58.
6. For his part, Brodie argued that Herman Kahn's work on nuclear strategy was a useful supplement to Clausewitz, although only in a limited manner. Ibid., p. 57.
7. David Silverberg, 'Tofflermania', *Armed Forces Journal International*, June 1995, p. 60.
8. Coker, *Humane Warfare*, p. 15.
9. On this point Gray perceptively comments, 'modern scholars have struggled in vain to sidestep the logic in Clausewitz's insistence upon the permanent salience of the possibility of combat'. Gray, *Modern Strategy*, p. 97.
10. Wylie, *Military Strategy*, p. 2.
11. Clausewitz, *On War*, p. 157.
12. Ibid., p. 29.
13. Gray, *Modern Strategy*, pp. 4, 35, and Moran, 'Strategic Theory and the History of War', p. 19.
14. Williamson Murray, *The Luftwaffe 1933–45: Strategy for Defeat* (Washington, DC, Brassey's, 1996), p. xxiv.
15. John Baylis and John Garnett, 'Introduction', in John Baylis and John Garnett (eds), *Makers of Nuclear Strategy* (New York, St Martin's Press, 1991), pp. 1–2.
16. Lt-Col Chris J. Krisinger, 'War and Anti-war: *Caveat Emptor*', Review Essay, *Strategic Review*, 24, 2 (1996), p. 67.
17. See Wylie, *Military Strategy*.
18. Ibid., pp. 62–3.
19. Murray and Grimsley, 'Introduction', p. 22.
20. Clausewitz, *On War*, p. 718.
21. Cited in Gray, *Modern Strategy*, p. 3.
22. Moran, 'Strategic Theory and the History of War', p. 17. Gray makes a similar point. See Gray, *Modern Strategy*, p. 82. Clausewitz also contends that harmony must exist between theory and practice. Clausewitz, *On War*, p. 164.
23. Gray, *Modern Strategy*, p. 110.

24. Wylie, *Military Strategy*, p. 77.
25. Clausewitz, *On War*, p. 163.
26. Ibid., p. 698.
27. Ibid., p. 183.
28. Bull, *The Anarchical Society*, p. 184.
29. In the case of the latter, 'Cyberwar is Coming' is particularly guilty of this sin.
30. Wylie, *Military Strategy*, p. 70.
31. Clausewitz, *On War*, p. 111.
32. Dunlap, 'Sometimes the Dragon Wins'.
33. Clausewitz, *On War*, p. 309.
34. For a discussion of these issues see Colin S. Gray, 'War-Fighting for Deterrence', *Journal of Strategic Studies*, 7, 2 (1984).
35. Luttwak, *The Grand Strategy of the Roman Empire*, p. 125.
36. See Omissi, *Air Power and Colonial Control*.
37. For details of Alexander's campaigns, see Fuller, *The Generalship of Alexander the Great*, Hammond, *The Genius of Alexander the Great*, and Lane Fox, *Alexander the Great*.
38. Wylie, *Military Strategy*, p. 72.
39. Lawrence, 'Guerrilla Warfare', p. 884.
40. Joint Chiefs of Staff, 'Joint Vision 2010', p. 39.
41. Gray, *Modern Strategy*.
42. Libicki, *What is Information Warfare?*
43. Clausewitz, *On War*, p. 97.
44. Wylie, *Military Strategy*, p. 89.
45. Gray, *Modern Strategy*, p. 284.
46. Libicki, 'The Small and the Many'.
47. See P. Griffith, *Battle Tactics of the Western Front*.
48. Applegate, 'Towards the Future Army', p. 81.
49. Gray, *Modern Strategy*, p. 26.
50. These characteristics of war provide the majority of the ingredients of Clausewitz's 'unified concept of a general friction'. See Watts, *Clausewitzian Friction and Future War*, p. 32.
51. See 'Introduction', p. 2, for Slim's comment. Gray also correctly identifies information as a permanent dimension of war. *Modern Strategy*, p. 252. See also Lawrence, 'Guerrilla Warfare', p. 885.
52. See Ronald H. Spector, *Eagle against the Sun: The American War with Japan* (New York, Free Press, 1985), p. 262.
53. Libicki, *The Mesh and the Net*.
54. This is a central component of Arquilla and Ronfeldt's work.
55. *Joint Vision 2020*, p. 19.
56. Clausewitz, *On War*, pp. 717–18.
57. B. H. Liddell Hart, 'Foreword', in Sun Tzu, *The Art of War*, trans. Samuel B. Griffith (London, Oxford University Press, 1971), p. v.
58. Gray, *Modern Strategy*, p. 358.
59. Ibid., p. 96.
60. Sun Tzu, trans. Griffith, p. 77.
61. Ibid., pp. 91–2.
62. Jomini, *The Art of War*, p. 89.
63. Ibid., p. 201.
64. Ibid., p. 26.
65. Clausewitz, *On War*, p. 107.
66. Ibid., p. 110.

67. Ibid., p. 103.
68. Ibid., p. 102.
69. Ibid., p. 113.
70. Ibid, pp. 110–11.
71. Ibid., p. 111.
72. Ibid., p. 717.
73. Ibid., p. 732.
74. Ibid., p. 718.
75. Sun Tzu, trans. Griffith, p. 114.
76. Watts, *Clausewitzian Friction*, p. 32.
77. Gray, *War, Peace and Victory*, pp. 107–8.
78. Frank C. Mahncke, 'Information Warriors', Book Review, *Naval War College Review*, 47, 3 (1994), p. 133.
79. Alvin and Heidi Toffler, 'Foreword: The New Intangibles', in John Arquilla and David Ronfeldt (eds), *In Athena's Camp: Preparing for Conflict in the Information Age* (Santa Monica, CA, RAND, 1996), p. xx.
80. Toffler and Toffler, *War and Anti-war*, pp. 10–11.
81. Krisinger, 'War and Anti-war: *Caveat Emptor*', p. 128.
82. See Toffler and Toffler, *War and Anti-war*, pp. 230–1.
83. Ibid., p. 158.
84. Ibid., pp. 71, xiv.
85. For an account of the resource inequalities between the two sides, see Ellis, *Brute Force*.
86. Toffler and Toffler, *War and Anti-war*, pp. 81, 84.
87. Libicki, 'The Small and the Many', p. 210.
88. Ibid., p. 197, and Libicki, 'Dominant Battlespace Knowledge and its Consequences', p. 40.
89. Libicki, 'The Small and the Many', p. 274, and *Defending Cyberspace*.
90. Libicki, 'Dominant Battlespace Knowledge and its Consequences'.
91. Libicki, *Illuminating Tomorrow's War*.
92. Libicki, *The Mesh and the Net*, and *Illuminating Tomorrow's War*.
93. Martin C. Libicki, 'Information Dominance', *Strategic Forum*, 132, November 1997, http://www.ndu.edu/inss/strforum/SF132/forum132.html.
94. Libicki, 'The Small and the Many', p. 195.
95. Gray, *Modern Strategy*, p. 284.
96. Arquilla and Ronfeldt, 'Cyberwar is Coming', p. 30.
97. John Arquilla and David Ronfeldt, 'Information, Power, and Grand Strategy: In Athena's Camp – Section 1', in John Arquilla and David Ronfeldt, *In Athena's Camp: Preparing for Conflict in the Information Age* (Santa Monica, CA, RAND, 1996),
    p. 157.
98. Arquilla and Ronfeldt, 'The Advent of Netwar', p. 277.
99. Arquilla and Ronfeldt, *A New Epoch*, p. 2.
100. Gray, *Modern Strategy*, pp. 159, 177.
101. Arquilla and Ronfeldt, 'Cyberwar is Coming', pp. 44–5.
102. Arquilla and Ronfeldt, 'Information, Power, and Grand Strategy: In Athena's Camp – Section 1', p. 157.
103. John Arquilla and David Ronfeldt, 'Information, Power, and Grand Strategy: In Athena's Camp – Section 2', in John Arquilla and David Ronfeldt, *In Athena's Camp: Preparing for Conflict in the Information Age* (Santa Monica, CA, RAND, 1996),
    pp. 419–20.
104. Arquilla and Ronfeldt, 'Cyberwar is Coming', p. 25.

105. Ibid., p. 47.
106. Arquilla and Ronfeldt, 'Information, Power, and Grand Strategy: In Athena's Camp – Section 1', p. 160.
107. Arquilla and Ronfeldt, *A New Epoch*, p. 8.
108. Goodwin, 'Don't Techno for an Answer', p. 220.
109. Arquilla and Ronfeldt, 'Cyberwar is Coming', p. 31.
110. Wylie, *Military Strategy*, p. 19.
111. In this respect, Wylie notes how the strategic aim of control must also include non-military instruments such as diplomacy, economic tools and philosophy. Wylie, *Military Strategy*, p. 89.
112. Clausewitz, *On War*, p. 309.
113. For accounts of the war between England and Spain see Parker, *The Grand Strategy of Philip II*, Martin and Parker, *The Spanish Armada*, Whiting, *The Enterprise of England: The Spanish Armada*, Sugden, *Sir Francis Drake*, Wallace T. MacCaffrey, *Elizabeth I: War and Politics 1588–1603* (Princeton, NJ, Princeton University Press, 1992), Garrett Mattingly, *The Defeat of the Spanish Armada* (London, Book Club Associates, 1972), and Anne Somerset, *Elizabeth I* (London, Phoenix Giant, 1992).
114. Gray, *Modern Strategy*, pp. 37–8.
115. Bennett, *Behind the Battle*, p. xxiii.
116. Ibid., p. 61.
117. Murray and Knox note that those military organisations that have successfully innovated in the past have avoided radical leaps forward. Rather, they have based their innovation on experience, history and an understanding of the nature of war. To support their thesis, they present the example of German adaptation to technological changes during the interwar period. See Murray and Knox, 'Conclusion: The Future Behind Us', and Williamson Murray, 'May 1940: Contingency and Fragility of the German RMA', in Williamson Murray and MacGregor Knox (eds), *The Dynamics of Military Revolution, 1300–2050* (Cambridge, Cambridge University Press, 2001).
118. Clausewitz, *On War*, p. 718.

Bibliography

BOOKS

Adams, James, *The Next World War: The Warriors and Weapons of the New Battlefields in Cyberspace* (London, Hutchinson, 1998).

Aron, Raymond, *Peace and War: A Theory of International Relations*, trans. Richard Howard and Annette Baker Fox (London, Weidenfeld & Nicolson, 1966).

Arquilla, John and David Ronfeldt (eds), *In Athena's Camp: Preparing for Conflict in the Information Age* (Santa Monica, CA, RAND, 1996).

Arquilla, John and David Ronfeldt, *The Advent of Netwar* (Santa Monica, CA, RAND, 1996).

Ashworth, G. J., *War and the City* (London, Routledge, 1991).

Asprey, Robert B., *War in the Shadows* (London, Little, Brown, 1994).

Atkinson, Rick, *Crusade: The Untold Story of the Persian Gulf War* (Boston, MA, Houghton Mifflin, 1993).

Bagnall, Nigel, *The Punic Wars: Rome, Carthage and the Struggle for the Mediterranean* (London, Pimlico, 1999).

Barker, Ralph, *The Thousand Plan: The Story of the First Thousand Bomber Raid on Cologne* (Shrewsbury, Airlife Publishing, 1992).

Beaufre, Andre, *An Introduction to Strategy: With Particular Reference to the Problems of Defence, Politics, Economics, and Diplomacy in the Nuclear Age* (London, Faber & Faber, 1965).

Bellamy, Christopher, *The Evolution of Modern Land Warfare: Theory and Practice* (London, Routledge, 1990).

——, *Knights in White Armour: The New Art of War and Peace* (London, Hutchinson, 1996).

Bennett, Ralph, *Behind the Battle: Intelligence in the War with Germany 1939–1945* (London, Pimlico, 1999).

Black, Jeremy, *War for America: The Fight for Independence 1775–1783* (Stroud, Sutton Publishing, 1991).

Brettingham, Laurie, *Royal Air Force Beam Benders No.80 (Signals) Wing 1940–1945* (Leicester, Midland Publishing, 1997).

Brodie, Bernard, *Strategy in the Missile Age* (Princeton, NJ, Princeton University Press, 1959).

——*War and Politics* (London, Cassell, 1973).

Bull, Hedley, *The Anarchical Society: A Study of Order in World Politics* (London, Macmillan, 1977).

Callwell, C. E., *Small Wars: A Tactical Textbook for Imperial Soldiers* (London, Greenhill Books, 1990).

Campbell, G. A., *The Crusades* (London, Duckworth, 1935).

Chandler, David, *The Campaigns of Napoleon* (London, Weidenfeld & Nicolson, 1966).

Clark, Wesley K., *Waging Modern War: Bosnia, Kosovo, and the Future of Combat* (New York, PublicAffairs, 2001).

Clausewitz, Carl von, *On War*, trans. Michael Howard and Peter Paret (London, David Campbell, 1993).

Clodfelter, Mark, *The Limits of Air Power: The American Bombing of North Vietnam* (New York, Free Press, 1989).

Cohen, Eliot A., *Supreme Command: Soldiers, Statesmen, and Leadership in Wartime* (New York, Free Press, 2002).

Coker, Christopher, *Humane Warfare* (London, Routledge, 2001).

Corbett, Julian S., *Some Principles of Maritime Strategy* (London, Longmans, Green, 1919).

Crane, Conrad C., *Bombs, Cities, and Civilians: American Airpower Strategy in World War II* (Kansas, University Press of Kansas, 1993).

Daalder, Ivo H. and Michael E. O'Hanlon, *Winning Ugly: NATO's War to Save Kosovo* (Washington, DC, Brookings Institution Press, 2000).

Davis, William C., *The American Civil War: A Historical Account of America's War of Secession* (London, Salamander, 1996).

de la Billiere, General Sir Peter, *Storm Command* (London, HarperCollins, 1992).

Denning, Dorothy E., *Information Warfare and Security* (Boston, MA, Addison-Wesley, 1999).

Douhet, Giulio, *The Command of the Air* (London, Faber & Faber, 1943).

Dupuy, T. N., *A Genius for War: The German Army and General Staff, 1807–1945* (London: MacDonald and Jane's, 1977).

Edwards, Sean J. A., *Swarming on the Battlefield* (Santa Monica, CA, RAND, 2000).

Eisenhower, Dwight D., *Crusade in Europe* (London, William Heinemann, 1948).

Ellis, John, *The Fighting Man in World War II: The Sharp End of War* (London, Book Club Associates, 1980).

——*Brute Force: Allied Strategy and Tactics in the Second World War,* (London, Andre Deutsch, 1990).

Fadok, David S., *John Boyd and John Warden: Air Power's Quest for Strategic Paralysis* (Maxwell Air Force Base, AL, Air University Press, 1995).

Ferrill, Arthur, *The Origins of War: From the Stone Age to Alexander the Great* (London, Thames & Hudson, 1985).

Fraser, David, *Knight's Cross: A Life of Field Marshal Erwin Rommel* (London, HarperCollins, 1994).

Fuller, J. F. C., *Armament and History: A Study of the Influence of Armament on History from the Dawn of Classical Warfare to the Second World War* (London, Eyre & Spottiswoode, 1946).

——*The Generalship of Alexander the Great* (Ware, Wordsworth Editions, 1998).

Futrell, R. F., *Ideas, Concepts, Doctrine: Basic Thinking in the United States Air Force 1961–1984,* Vol. 2 (Maxwell, AL, Maxwell Air Force Base Air University, 1984).

Gabriel, Richard A. and Donald W. Boose, Jr, *The Great Battles of Antiquity: A Strategic and Tactical Guide to the Great Battles that Shaped the Development of War* (Westport, CT, Greenwood Press, 1994).

Gat, Azar, *The Development of Military Thought: The Nineteenth Century* (Oxford, Clarendon Press, 1992).

Gordon, Michael R. and General Bernard E. Trainor, *The Generals' War: The Inside Story of the Conflict in the Gulf* (Boston, MA, Little, Brown, 1995).

Grace, Charles S., *Nuclear Weapons: Principles, Effects and Survivability,* Land Warfare: Brassey's New Battlefield Weapons Systems and Technology Series, Vol. 10 (London, Brassey's, 1994).

Gray, Colin S., *Nuclear Strategy and National Style* (Lanham, MD, Hamilton Press, 1986).

——*War, Peace, and Victory: Strategy and Statecraft for the Next Century* (New York, Simon & Schuster, 1990).

——*The Leverage of Sea Power: The Strategic Advantage of Navies in War* (New York, Free Press, 1992).

——*Explorations in Strategy* (Westport, CT, Praeger, 1996).

——*Modern Strategy,* (Oxford, Oxford University Press, 1999).

——*The Second Nuclear Age* (Boulder, CO, Lynne Rienner Publishers, 1999).

Griffith, Paddy, *Battle Tactics of the Western Front: The British Army's Art of Attack 1916–18* (New Haven, CT, Yale University Press, 1994).

Grove, Eric, *The Future of Sea Power* (Annapolis, MD, Naval Institute Press, 1990).

Hallion, Richard P., *Storm over Iraq: Air Power and the Gulf War* (Washington, DC, Smithsonian Institution Press, 1992).

Hammond, Grant T., *The Mind of War: John Boyd and American Security* (Washington, DC, Smithsonian Institution Press, 2001).

Hammond, Nicholas, *The Genius of Alexander the Great* (London, Duckworth, 1998).

Handel, Michael I., *Masters of War: Classical Strategic Thought*, Second, Revised Edition (London, Frank Cass, 1996).

Hartcup, Guy, *The Silent Revolution: Development of Conventional Weapons 1945–85* (London, Brassey's, 1993).

Hastings, Max, *Bomber Command* (London, Michael Joseph, 1979).

Hastings, Max and Simon Jenkins, *The Battle for the Falklands* (London, Pan Books, 1997).

Hawking, Stephen, *A Brief History of Time: From the Big Bang to Black Holes* (London, Bantam Books, 1995).

Hawkins, Joyce M. (ed.), *The Oxford Reference Dictionary* (London, Guild Publishing, 1987).

Hayden, H. T. (ed.), *Warfighting: Manoeuvre Warfare in the US Marine Corps* (London, Greenhill, 1995).

Heisbourg, Francois, *The Future of Warfare* (London, Phoenix, 1997).

Ignatieff, Michael, *Virtual War: Kosovo and Beyond* (New York, Picador USA, 2001).

Jacobsen, Carl G. (ed.), *Strategic Power: USA/USSR* (New York, St Martin's Press, 1990).

Jomini, Baron Antoine Henri de, *The Art of War* (London, Greenhill Books, 1996).

Kahn, Herman, *On Thermonuclear War* (Princeton, NJ, Princeton University Press, 1960).

Katcher, Philip, *The Army of Robert E. Lee* (London, Arms & Armour Press, 1996).

Keegan, John, *The Face of Battle* (London, Barrie & Jenkins, 1988).

——*The Mask of Command* (London, Penguin, 1988).

——*A History of Warfare* (London, Pimlico, 1994).

Keppie, Lawrence, *The Making of the Roman Army: From Republic to Empire* (London, Routledge, 1984).

Kingston-McCloughry, E. J., *War in Three Dimensions: The Impact of Air-Power upon the Classical Principles of War* (London, Jonathan Cape, 1949).

Lambeth, Benjamin S., *NATO's Air War for Kosovo: A Strategic and Operational Assessment* (Santa Monica, CA, RAND, 2001).

Lane Fox, Robin, *Alexander the Great* (Harmondsworth, Penguin, 1986).

Lawrence, T. E., *Seven Pillars of Wisdom* (Ware, Wordsworth Editions, 1997).

Leonhard, Robert R., *The Principles of War for the Information Age* (Novato, CA, Presidio Press, 1998).

Libicki, Martin C., *Defending Cyberspace and Other Metaphors* (Washington, DC, National Defense University, 1997).

Luttwak, Edward N., *The Grand Strategy of the Roman Empire: From the First Century AD to the Third* (Baltimore, MD, Johns Hopkins University Press, 1979).

——*Strategy: The Logic of War and Peace* (Cambridge, MA, Belknap Press, 1987).

MacCaffrey, Wallace T., *Elizabeth I: War and Politics 1588–1603* (Princeton, NJ, Princeton University Press, 1992).

Mackesy, Piers, *The War for America 1775–1783* (Lincoln, NE, Bison Books, 1993).

Mackinder, Halford J., *Democratic Ideals and Reality* (New York, W. W. Norton, 1962).

Mao Tse-Tung, *Selected Military Writings of Mao Tse-Tung* (Beijing, Foreign Languages Press, 1963).

Marshall, S. L. A., *Men Against Fire: The Problem of Battle Command in Future War* (New York, William Murrow, 1947).

Martin, Colin and Geoffrey Parker, *The Spanish Armada,* revised edition (Manchester, Mandolin, 1999).

Mattingly, Garrett, *The Defeat of the Spanish Armada* (London, Book Club Associates, 1972).

McNab, Andy, *Bravo Two Zero* (London, BCA, 1993).

McPherson, James E., *Battle Cry of Freedom: The American Civil War* (London, Penguin, 1990).

Messenger, Charles, *The Art of Blitzkrieg,* 2nd edition (London, Ian Allan, 1991).

Mierzejewski, Alfred C., *The Collapse of the German War Economy 1944–45: Allied Air Power and the German National Railway* (Chapel Hill, NC, University of North Carolina Press, 1988).

Montgomery, Field Marshal, *The Path to Leadership* (London, Collins, 1961).

Moore, Lt-Gen. Harold G. (Ret.) and Joseph L. Galloway, *We Were Soldiers Once ... and Young* (London, Corgi, 2002).

Murray, Williamson, *Air War in the Persian Gulf* (Baltimore, MD, Nautical and Aviation Publishing Company of America, 1995).

——*The Luftwaffe 1933–45: Strategy for Defeat* (Washington, DC, Brassey's, 1996).

Nichiporuk, Brian and Carl H. Builder, *Information Technologies and the Future of Land Warfare* (Santa Monica, CA, RAND, 1995).

O'Hanlon, Michael *Technological Change and the Future of Warfare* (Washington, DC, Brookings Institution Press, 2000).

Ochmanek, David A., Edward R. Harshberger, David E. Thaler and Glenn A. Kent, *To Find and Not to Yield: How Advances in*

Information and Firepower Can Transform Theatre Warfare (Santa Monica, CA, RAND, 1998).

Omissi, David E., *Air Power and Colonial Control: The Royal Air Force 1919–1939* (Manchester, Manchester University Press, 1990).

Overy, Richard, *Why the Allies Won* (London, Pimlico, 1996).

Owens, Admiral William with Ed Offley, *Lifting the Fog of War* (New York, Farrar, Straus & Giroux, 2000).

Pape, Robert A., *Bombing to Win: Air Power and Coercion in War* (Ithaca, NY, Cornell University Press, 1996).

Paret, Peter, *Understanding War: Essays on Clausewitz and the History of Military Power* (Princeton, NJ, Princeton University Press, 1992).

Parker, Geoffrey, *The Grand Strategy of Philip II* (New Haven, CT, Yale University Press, 1998).

Parkinson, Roger, *Clausewitz* (London, Wayland Publishers, 1970).

Payne, Robert, *The Crusades* (Ware, Wordsworth Editions, 1998).

Peddie, John, *The Roman War Machine* (London, Grange Books, 1997).

Peters, Ralph, *Fighting for the Future: Will America Triumph?* (Mechanicsburg, PA, Stackpole Books, 2001).

Puryear, Jr, Edgar F., *Nineteen Stars: A Study in Military Character and Leadership* (Novato, CA, Presidio, 1992).

Rattray, Greg, *Strategic Warfare in Cyberspace* (Cambridge, MA, MIT Press, 2001).

Rosen, Stephen P., *Winning the Next War: Innovation and the Modern Military* (Ithaca, NY, Cornell University Press, 1991).

Schwartau, Winn, *Information Warfare: Cyberterrorism: Protecting Your Personal Security in the Electronic Age*, Second Edition (New York, Thunder's Mouth Press, 1996).

Shy, John, *A People Numerous and Armed: Reflections on the Military Struggle for American Independence* (New York, Oxford University Press, 1976).

Slim, Field Marshal Sir William, *Courage and Other Broadcasts* (London, Cassell, 1957).

——*Defeat into Victory* (London, Reprint Society, 1957).

Somerset, Anne, *Elizabeth I* (London, Phoenix Giant, 1992).

Spector, Ronald H., *Eagle against the Sun: The American War with Japan* (New York, Free Press, 1985).

Strachan, Hew, *European Armies and the Conduct of War* (London, George Allen & Unwin, 1983).

Sugden, John, *Sir Francis Drake* (London, Pimlico, 1996).

Summers, Jr, Harry G., *On Strategy: A Critical Analysis of the Vietnam War* (Novato, CA, Presidio, 1982).

Sun Tzu, *The Art of War*, trans. Samuel B. Griffith (London, Oxford University Press, 1971).

——*The Art of War*, trans. Thomas Cleary, (Boston, MA, Shambhala, 1988).

Terraine, John, *The Right of the Line: The Royal Air Force in the European War 1939–1945* (Sevenoaks, Sceptre, 1988).

Thompson, Leroy, *Ragged War: The Story of Unconventional and Counter-Revolutionary Warfare* (London, Arms & Armour Press, 1996).

Thucydides, *History of the Peloponnesian War*, trans. Rex Warner (London, Penguin, 1972).

Toffler, Alvin and Heidi, *War and Anti-war: Survival at the Dawn of the 21st Century* (London, Little, Brown, 1994).

van Creveld, Martin, *Command in War* (Cambridge, MA, Harvard University Press, 1985).

——*Technology and War*, Revised and Expanded Edition (New York, Free Press, 1991).

——*The Transformation of War* (New York, Free Press, 1991).

——*The Art of War: War and Military Thought* (London, Cassell, 2002).

Vegetius, *Vegetius: Epitome of Military Science*, trans. N. P. Milner (Liverpool, Liverpool University Press, 1993).

Warden III, Colonel John A., *The Air Campaign: Planning for Combat*, Future Warfare Series, Vol. 3 (Washington, DC, Pergamon-Brassey's, 1989).

Wavell, Archibald, *Generals and Generalship* (London, Times Publishing, 1941).

Webster, Sir Charles and Noble Frankland, *The Strategic Air Offensive against Germany 1939–45*, Vol. III, *Victory, Part 5* (HMSO, London, 1961).

Weigley, Russell F., *The Age of Battles: The Quest for Decisive Warfare from Breitenfeld to Waterloo* (London, Pimlico, 1991).

Werrell, Kenneth P., *Blankets of Fire: United States' Bombers over Japan during WWII* (Washington, DC, Smithsonian Institution Press, 1996).

Westmoreland, General William C., *A Soldier Reports* (New York, Doubleday, 1976).

Whiting, Roger, *The Enterprise of England: The Spanish Armada* (Stroud, Alan Sutton Publishing, 1995).

Winters, Harold A., with Gerald E. Galloway, Jr, William J. Reynolds and David W. Rhyne, *Battling the Elements: Weather and Terrain in the Conduct of War* (Baltimore, MD, Johns Hopkins University Press, 1998).

Wohlstetter, Roberta, *Pearl Harbor: Warning and Decision* (Stanford, CA, Stanford University Press, 1962).

Wylie, J. C., *Military Strategy: A General Theory of Power Control*

(Annapolis, MD, Naval Institute Press, 1967).

ARTICLES

Adams, James, 'Anoraks' Apocalypse', *Sunday Times, News Review*, 16 March 1997.
Arkin, William M., 'Baghdad: The Urban Sanctuary in Desert Storm?', www.airpower.maxwell.af.mil/airchronicles/apj/spr97/arkin.html.
Arquilla, John, 'The Strategic Implications of Information Dominance', *Strategic Review*, 22, 3 (1994).
Bacevich, A. J., 'Preserving the Well-Bred Horse', *National Interest*, 37 (1994).
Barnett, Col Jeffery R., 'Defeating Insurgents with Technology', *Airpower Journal*, Summer 1996, www.airpower.maxwell.af.mil/ airchronicles/ apj/barnett.pdf.
Barnett, Thomas P. M., 'The Seven Deadly Sins of Network-Centric Warfare', *Proceedings*, 125, 1 (1999).
Bartlett, Henry C., G. Paul Holman, Jr and Timothy E. Somes, 'Force Planning, Military Revolutions and the Tyranny of Technology', *Strategic Review*, 24, 4 (1996).
Bassford, Christopher, 'John Keegan and the General Tradition of Trashing Clausewitz: A Polemic', *War in History*, 1 (1994).
Bender, Bryan, 'US Cyber-Defence Task Force Is Now Operational', *Jane's Defence Weekly*, 31, 3, 20 January 1999.
——'US Weapons Shortages Risked Success in Kosovo', *Jane's Defence Weekly*, 32, 14, 6 October 1999.
Betts, Richard, 'The Downside of the Cutting Edge', *National Interest*, 45 (1996).
Biddle, Tami Davis, 'British and American Approaches to Strategic Bombing: Their Origins and Implementation in the World War II Combined Bomber Offensive', *Journal of Strategic Studies*, special issue on Airpower: Theory and Practice, John Gooch (ed.), 18, 1 (1995).
Bodnar, Captain John and Second Lieutenant Rebecca Dengler, 'The Emergence of the Command Network', *Naval War College Review*, 49, 4 (1996).
Borger, Julian, 'After the Onslaught, a Leap in the Dark', *Guardian*, 20 March 2003.
Borger, Julian and Richard Norton-Taylor, 'US Generals Embrace New Kind of Warfare', *Guardian*, 22 March 2003.
Bowman, Lt-Col Michael, Gheorghe Tecuci and Mihai Boicu, 'Intelligent Agents in the Command Post', *Military Review*, 81, 2 (2001).

Boyes, Roger, 'Serb Unity is the Deadliest Weapon Confronting NATO Alliance', *Times*, 30 March 1999.

Burkeman, Oliver, 'Shock Tactics', *G2, Guardian*, 25 March 2003.

Burkeman, Oliver, Stuart Millar and Nick Paton Walsh, 'Pentagon Plans for Worst Nightmare', *Guardian*, 3 April 2003.

Byman, Daniel L. and Matthew C. Waxman, 'Kosovo and the Great Air Power Debate', *International Security*, 24, 4 (2000).

Caldwell, W., Jr, 'Promises, Promises', *Proceedings*, 122, 1 (1996).

Campbell, Matthew, 'US at Mercy of Cyber Terrorists', *Sunday Times*, 17 May 1998.

Carlin, John, 'The Netizen: A Farewell to Arms', *Wired*, 5.05 (1997).

Casper, Lawrence E., Irving L. Halter, Earl W. Powers, Paul J. Selva, Thomas W. Steffens and T. LaMar Willis, 'Knowledge-Based Warfare: A Security Strategy for the Next Century', *Joint Force Quarterly*, 13 (1996).

Cebrowski, Vice-Admiral Arthur K., 'Network-Centric Warfare: Its Origin and Future', *Proceedings*, 124, 1 (1998).

Chapman II, Col Robert E., 'Unmanned Combat Aerial Vehicles: Dawn of a New Age?', *Aerospace Power Journal*, 16, 2 (2002), www.airpower. maxwell.af.mil/airchronicles/apj/apj02/sum02/chapman.html.

Cilluffo, Frank J. and Curt H. Gergely, 'Information Warfare and Strategic Terrorism', *Terrorism and Political Violence*, 9, 1 (1997).

Clark, Mark T., 'The Continuing Relevance of Clausewitz', *Strategic Review*, 26, 1 (1998).

Clarke, General Bruce C., 'Leadership, Commandership, Planning, and Success', *Military Review*, 82, 4 (2002).

Coale, John C., 'Fighting Cybercrime', *Military Review*, 78, 2 (1998).

Cohen, Eliot A., 'A Revolution in Warfare', *Foreign Affairs*, 75, 2 (1996).

Coker, Christopher, 'Post-modern War', *RUSI Journal*, 143, 3 (1998).

Conversino, Mark J., 'The Changed Nature of Strategic Air Attack', *Parameters*, 27, 4, carlisle-www.army.mil/usawc/Parameters/97winter/ conversi.htm.

Cook, Nick, 'War of Extremes', *Jane's Defence Weekly*, 7 July 1999.

Craddock, Ashley, 'Netwar and Peace in the Global Village', an interview with John Arquilla, *Wired*, 5.05 (1997).

Davidson, Clive, 'Christine Downton's Brain', www.wired.com/wired/ 4.12/esrobotrader.html.

Davis, Major Norman C., 'An Information-Based Revolution in Military Affairs', *Strategic Review*, 24, 1 (1996).

Dessert, Jr, Colonel Rolland A., 'Mobile Strike Force: An Experiment in Future Battle Command', *Military Review*, 76, 4 (1996).

Devost, Matthew G., Brian K. Houghton and Neal Allen Pollard, 'Response to Cilluffo and Gergely', *Terrorism and Political Violence*,

9, 1 (1997).

DiNardo, R. L. and Daniel J. Hughes, 'Some Cautionary Thoughts on Information Warfare', *Airpower Journal*, 9, 4 (1995).

Dippold, Maj. Mark K., 'Air Occupation: Asking the Right Questions', *Aerospace Power Journal*, Winter 1997, www.airpower.maxwell.af.mil/airchronicles/apj/apj97/win97/dippold.html.

Duffy, Daintry, 'Information is a Weapon. What Will Happen When Every Soldier Is Armed With It?', www.infowar.com/mil_c4i/01/mil_c4i_110501b_j.shtml.

Dunlap, Jr, Charles J., '21st-Century Land Warfare: Four Dangerous Myths', *Parameters*, 27, 3 (1997).

Emmett, Squadron Leader Peter, 'Information Mania – A New Manifestation of Gulf War Syndrome?', *RUSI Journal*, 141, 1 (1996).

Evans, Michael, 'Weather Holds up the Bombs', *Times*, 31 March 1999.

Evans, Michael and James Landale, 'High-Tech Harriers are Blinded by Smoke', *Times*, 26 March 1999.

Ferris, John and Michael I. Handel, 'Clausewitz, Intelligence, Uncertainty and the Art of Command in Military Operations', *Intelligence and National Security*, 10, 1 (1995).

Fitchett, Joseph, 'British Influence US with Tactics in Iraq', *International Herald Tribune*, 24 March, 2003.

——'With New Technology, US Tries Out New Way to Make War', *International Herald Tribune*, 24 March 2003.

Fitzsimonds, James R., 'The Coming Military Revolution: Opportunities and Risks', *Parameters*, 25, 2 (1995).

Forno, Richard, 'September 11th Does Not Mean Cyberwar is Coming', www.infowar.com/mil_c4i/01/mil_c4i_091401b_j.shtml.

Franks, Jr, General Frederick M., 'Battle Command: A Commander's Perspective', *Military Review*, 76, 3 (1996).

Gadsby, Brigadier A. C. I., 'Do We Still Need Tanks?', *RUSI Journal*, 142, 4 (1997).

Garfinkel, Simson, '2001 Double Take', www.wired.com/wired/5.01/features/ffhal.html.

Gertz, Bill, 'Pentagon Fortifying Computer Networks to Block Hackers', www.washtimes.com/nation/national.html.

Gompert, David C., 'The Information Revolution and US National Security', *Naval War College Review*, 51, 4 (1998).

Goodman, Jr, Glenn W., 'The Power of Information: Air Force Clarifies its Misunderstood Virtual Presence Concept', *Armed Forces Journal International*, July 1995.

Goodwin, Brent Stuart, 'Don't Techno for an Answer: The False Promise of Information Warfare', Review Article, *Naval War College Review*, 53, 2 (2000).

Gordon, Michael R., 'Tested on the Battlefield, Rumsfeld's Principles are

Challenged', *International Herald Tribune*, 2 April 2003.

Goulding, Jr, Vincent J., 'From Chancellorsville to Kosovo, Forgetting the Art of War', *Parameters*, 30, 2 (2000).

Gray, Colin S., 'War-Fighting for Deterrence', *Journal of Strategic Studies*, 7, 2 (1984).

——'A Rejoinder by Colin S. Gray', *Orbis*, 40, 2 (1996).

——'Three Visions of Future War', *Queen's Quarterly*, 103, 1 (1996).

Gruber, Michael, 'In Search of the Electronic Brain', *Wired*, 5.05 (1997).

Handel, Michael I., 'Clausewitz in the Age of Technology', in Michael I. Handel (ed.), 'Clausewitz and Modern Strategy', special issue of *Journal of Strategic Studies*, 9, 2/3 (1986).

——'Introduction', in Michael I. Handel (ed.), 'Clausewitz and Modern Strategy', special issue of *Journal of Strategic Studies*, 9, 2/3 (1986).

Harig, Paul T., 'The Digital General: Reflections on Leadership in the Post-Information Age', *Parameters*, 26, 3 (1996).

Harknett, Richard J., 'Information Warfare and Deterrence', *Parameters*, 26, 3 (1996).

Hawkins, Charles F., 'The People's Liberation Army: Looking to the Future', *Joint Force Quarterly*, 25 (2000).

Hawkins, William R., 'Imposing Peace: Total vs. Limited Wars, and the Need to Put Boots on the Ground', *Parameters*, 30, 2 (2000).

Heisbourg, Francois L. J., 'Invitation to the Revolution', Book Review, *Joint Forces Quarterly*, 26 (2000).

Henry, Ryan and C. Edward Peartree, 'Assessing "Byte City": An Insightful or Misleading Vision?', *Washington Quarterly*, 20, 2 (1997).

Herbig, Katherine L., 'Chance and Uncertainty in *On War*', 'Clausewitz and Modern Strategy', special issue of *Journal of Strategic Studies*, in Michael I. Handel (ed.), 9, 2/3 (1986).

Herman, Jr, Paul F., 'The Revolution in "Military" Affairs', *Strategic Review*, 24, 2 (1996).

Hewish, Mark and Rupert Pengelley, 'Warfare in the Global City: The Demands of Modern Military Operations in Urban Terrain', *Jane's International Defense Review*, 31 (1998).

Howard, Michael, 'The Forgotten Dimensions of Strategy', *Foreign Affairs*, 57 (1979).

Jablonsky, David, 'US Military Doctrine and the Revolution in Military Affairs', *Parameters*, 24, 3 (1994).

Jantzen, Major Linda C., 'Taking Charge of Technology', *Military Review*, 81, 2 (2001).

Jensen, Colonel Owen E., 'Information Warfare: Principles of Third-Wave War', *Air Power Journal*, 8, 4 (1994).

Johnston, Alastair I., 'Thinking About Strategic Culture', *International Security*, 19, 4 (1995).

Joint Chiefs of Staff, 'Joint Vision 2010: America's Military – Preparing for Tomorrow', *Joint Force Quarterly*, 12 (1996).

Jones, George and Michael Smith, 'Hacking is Now Bigger Threat than Terrorism', *Telegraph*, 30 March 2001, www.telegraph.co.uk/et.

Kahn, David, 'Clausewitz and Intelligence', in Michael I. Handel (ed.), 'Clausewitz and Modern Strategy', special issue of *Journal of Strategic Studies*, 9, 2/3 (1986).

Keegan, John, 'Please Mr Blair, Never Take Such a Risk Again', *Sunday Telegraph*, 6 June 1999, www.telegraph.co.uk/et.

Kemp, Damian, 'Combat Drones Fly for Casualty-Free War', *Jane's Defence Weekly*, 9 June 1999.

Keohane, Robert O. and Joseph S. Nye, Jr, 'Power and Interdependence in the Information Age', *Foreign Affairs*, 77, 5 (1998).

Kipp, Jacob W. and Lt-Col. Lester W. Grau, 'The Fog and Friction of Technology', *Military Review*, 81, 5 (2001).

Kirin, Lt-Col Stephen J., 'Synchronisation', *Naval War College Review*, 49, 4 (1996).

Klein, Yitzhak, 'A Theory of Strategic Culture', *Comparative Strategy*, 10, 1 (1991).

Krause, Michael D., 'Getting to Know Jomini', Book Review, *Joint Forces Quarterly*, 7 (1995).

Krepinevich, A. F., 'Cavalry to Computer: The Pattern of Military Revolutions', *National Interest*, 37 (1994).

——'Why No Transformation?', *Joint Force Quarterly*, 23 (1999–2000).

Krisinger, Lt-Col Chris J., 'War and Anti-war: *Caveat Emptor*', Review Essay, *Strategic Review*, 24, 2 (1996).

Kuehl, Daniel T., 'Airpower vs. Electricity: Electric Power as a Target For Strategic Air Operations', *Journal of Strategic Studies*, special issue on Airpower: Theory and Practice, John Gooch (ed.), 18, 1 (1995).

Lamont, Robert W., 'A Tale of Two Cities – Hue and Khorramshahr', *Marine Corps Gazette*, 83, 4 (1999).

Laqueur, Walter, 'Postmodern Terrorism', *Foreign Affairs*, 75, 5 (1996).

Lemelin, David J., 'Force XXI: Getting it Right', *Military Review*, 76, 6 (1996).

Libicki, Martin C., 'The Emerging Primacy of Information', *Orbis*, 40, 2 (1996).

Lieven, Anatol, 'The World Turned Upside Down', *Armed Forces Journal International*, August 1998.

Luttwak, Edward N., 'Towards Post-Heroic Warfare', *Foreign Affairs*, 74, 3 (1995).

——'A Post-Heroic Military Policy', *Foreign Affairs*, 75, 4 (1996).

MacAskill, Ewen and Stuart Millar, 'America's Digital Division – the Biggest Advance in Warfare since the Tank', *Guardian*, 7 April 2003.

Mahncke, Frank C., 'Information Warriors', Book Review, *Naval War College Review*, 47, 3 (1994).

Mathews, Jessica T., 'Power Shift', *Foreign Affairs*, 76, 1 (1997).

McInnes, Colin, 'A Different Kind of War? September 11 and the United States' Afghan War', *Review of International Studies*, 29 (2003).

McKenzie, Jr, Kenneth F., 'Beyond Luddites and Magicians: Examining the MTR', *Parameters*, 25, 2 (1995).

McKitrick, Jeffrey, James Blackwell, Fred Littlepage, George Kraws, Richard Blanchfield and Dale Hill, 'The Revolution in Military Affairs', www.airpwr.maxwell.af.mil/airchronicles/battle/chap3.html.

McLamb, Captain Joseph S., 'The Future of Mission Orders', *Military Review*, 77, 5 (1997).

McManners, Hugh, 'Smart Missiles to Spike the Army's Big Guns', *Sunday Times*, 11 October 1998.

——'Plastic Tank is Silent Killer of Battlefield', *Sunday Times*, 7 February 1999.

Meek, James, 'US Advance Grinds to Halt in Teeth of Storm', *Guardian*, 26 March 2003.

Meilinger, Col Phillip S., 'Precision Aerospace Power, Discrimination, and the Future of War', *Aerospace Power Journal*, 15, 3 (2001), www.airpower.maxwell.af.mil/airchronicles/apj/apj01/fal01/meilinger.html.

Metcalf, Marvin G., 'Acoustics on the 21st Century Battlefield', *Joint Force Quarterly*, 10 (Winter 1995–96).

Metz, Steven, 'Non-Lethal Weapons: A Progress Report', *Joint Force Quarterly*, 28 (2001).

Millar, Stuart, 'Hi-Tech Arsenal Decisive – if Targets Can be Found', *Guardian*, 25 March 2003.

Minihan, Kenneth A., 'Defending the Nation against Cyber Attack: Information Assurance in the Global Environment', *CyberThreat: Protecting US Information Networks*, USIA Electronic Journal, 3, 4 (1998), usinfo.state.gov/journals/itps/1198/iipe/toc.htm.

Molander, Roger C., Andrew S. Riddile and Peter A. Wilson, 'Strategic Information Warfare: A New Face of War', *Parameters*, 26, 3 (1996), carlisle-www.army.mil/usawc/Parameters/96autumn/molander.htm.

Moore, Mike, 'Unintended Consequences', *The Bulletin of Atomic Scientists*, 56, 1 (2000),www.bullatomsci.org/issues/2000/jf00/ jf00moore. html.

More, Max, 'Thinking About Thinking', www.wired.com/wired/4.12/features/churchland.html.

Murray, Major Scott F., 'Battle Command, Decisionmaking, and the Battlefield Panopticon', *Military Review*, 82, 4 (2002).

Murray, Williamson, 'Does Military Culture Matter?', *Orbis*, 43, 1 (1999).

——'Thinking about Cities and War', www.mca-marines.org/Gazette/stanton.html.

Mustin, Lt Jeff, 'Future Employment of Unmanned Aerial Vehicles',

Aerospace Power Journal, 16, 2 (2002), www.airpower.maxwell.af.mil/airchronicles/apj/apj02/sum02/vorsum02.html.

Nifong, Lt-Col Michael R., 'The Key to Information Dominance', *Military Review*, 76, 3 (1996).

Odom, Maj. Earl, 'Future Missions for Unmanned Aerial Vehicles: Exploring Outside the Box', *Aerospace Power Journal*, www.airpower.maxwell.af.mil/airchronicles/apj/apj02/sum02/phisum02.html.

Nye, Jr, Joseph S. and William A. Owens, 'America's Information Edge', *Foreign Affairs*, 75, 2 (1996).

Owens, Mackubin Thomas, 'Vietnam as Military History', Review Essay, *Joint Force Quarterly*, 3 (1993–94).

——'Technology, the RMA, and Future War', *Strategic Review*, 26, 2 (1998).

Owens, Admiral William A., 'The Emerging System of Systems', *Military Review*, 75, 3 (1995).

Pape, Robert A., 'The Limits of Precision-Guided Air Power', *Security Studies*, 7, 2 (1997–98).

Peters, Ralph, 'After the Revolution', *Parameters*, 25, 2 (1995).

——'The Future of Armoured Warfare', *Parameters*, 27, 3 (1997).

Posen, Barry R., 'The War for Kosovo: Serbia's Political-Military Strategy', *International Security*, 24, 4 (2000).

Rathmel, Andrew, 'Cyber-Terrorism: The Shape of Future Conflict?', *RUSI Journal*, 142, 5 (1997).

Reed, J., 'Protecting Armoured Vehicles against Helicopter Attack: Stealth, Smoke and Mirrors', *Asian Defence Journal*, July 1996.

Reisweber, Major Deborah, 'Battle Command: Will We Have It When We Need It?', *Military Review*, 77, 5 (1997).

Ritcheson, Phillip L., 'The Future of "Military Affairs": Revolution or Evolution?', *Strategic Review*, 24, 2 (1996).

Robins, W. J. P., 'Information Age Operations', *RUSI Journal*, 142, 3 (1997).

Scales, Jr, Robert H., 'Cycles of War: Speed of Maneuver Will Be the Essential Ingredient of an Information-Age Army', *Armed Forces Journal International*, July 1997.

Schwartz, John, 'Cyberterrorists Sharpening their Tools for Online Warfare', *International Herald Tribune*, 21 March 2003.

Seffers, George I., 'Army War Game Reveals Power of Commercial Data', *Defense News*, 22–28 September 1997.

Segal, Gerald, 'Strategy and Ethnic Chic', *International Affairs*, 60, 1 (1983–84).

Seigle, Greg, 'USMC Receives First MV-22', *Jane's Defence Weekly*, 16 June 1999.

Sherman, Jason, 'Rush to Digitization: Has the Electronic Battlefield

Been Oversold?', *Armed Forces Journal International*, February 1996.

Silverberg, David, 'Tofflermania', *Armed Forces Journal International*, June 1995.

Singh, Ajay, 'Time: The New Dimension in War', *Joint Force Quarterly*, 10 (1995–96).

Smith, George, 'An Electronic Pearl Harbor? Not Likely.', *Issues in Science and Technology Online*, Fall 1998, 205.130.85.236/issues/15.1/smith.htm.

Somerville, Keith, 'US Drones Take Combat Role', news.bbc.co.uk/1/hi/world/2404425.stm.

Soo Hoo, Kevin, Seymour Goodman and Lawrence Greenberg, 'Information Technology and the Terrorist Threat', *Survival*, 39, 3 (1997).

Starr, Barbara, 'Wargames highlight US vulnerability in space', *Jane's Defence Weekly*, 8 October 1997.

Starry, Col. M. D. and Lt-Col. C. W. Arneson Jr, 'FM 100-6: Information Operations', *Military Review*, 76, 6 (1996).

Stone, Janet Andrea, 'Cyberspace: The Next Battlefield', www.infowar.com/mil_c4i/01/mil_c4i_061901a_j.shtml.

Sullivan, General Gordon R., 'A Vision for the Future', *Military Review*, 75, 3 (1995).

Szafranski, Richard and Martin C. Libicki, '... Or Go Down in Flame? Toward an Airpower Manifesto for the Twenty-first Century', *Airpower Journal*, 10, 3 (1996).

Thomas, Timothy L., 'Deterring Information Warfare: A New Strategic Challenge', *Parameters*, 26, 4 (1996–97).

——'The Battle of Grozny: Deadly Classroom for Urban Combat', *Parameters*, 29, 2 (1999), carlisle-www.army.mil/usawc/Parameters/99summer/thomas.htm.

——'Kosovo and the Current Myth of Information Superiority', *Parameters*, 30, 2 (2000), carlisle-www.army.mil/usawc/Parameters/00spring/thomas.htm.

Thomas, Captain Troy S., 'Slumlords: Aerospace Power in Urban Fights', *Aerospace Power Journal*, 16, 1 (2002), www.airpower.maxwell.af.mil/airchronicles/apj/apj02/spr02/thomas.doc.

Thompson, Major Chip, 'F-16 UCAVs: A Bridge to the Future of Air Combat', *Aerospace Power Journal*, Spring 2000, www.airpower.maxwell.af.mil/airchronicles/apj/apj00/spr00/thompson.htm.

Tirpak, John A., 'Send in the UCAVs', *Air Force Magazine*, August 2001, www.infowar.com/mil_c4i/01/mil_c4i_080701a_j.shtml.

Toffler, Alvin, 'Looking at the Future with Alvin Toffler', www.usatoday.com/news/comment/columnists/toffler/toff05.htm.

Toffler, Alvin and Heidi, 'The Discontinuous Future: A Bold but Overoptimistic Forecast', Review Essay, *Foreign Affairs*, 77, 2 (1998).

Tucker, David, 'Fighting Barbarians', *Parameters*, 28, 2 (1998), carlisle-www.army.mil/usawc/Parameters/98summer/tucker.htm.

van Creveld, Martin, 'The Eternal Clausewitz', in Michael I. Handel (ed.), 'Clausewitz and Modern Strategy', special issue of *Journal of Strategic Studies*, 9, 2/3 (1986).

Van Riper, Paul and Robert H. Scales, Jr, 'Preparing for War in the 21st Century', *Parameters*, 27, 3 (1997).

Vincent, 1st Lieutenant Gary A., 'A New Approach to Command and Control: The Cybernetic Design', www.cdsar.af.mil/apj/vincent.html.

Vlahos, Michael, 'The War after Byte City', *Washington Quarterly*, 20, 2 (1997).

Walker, Tom, 'Outgunned Underdogs Await Day of Revenge in a "Man-to-Man" Battle', *Sunday Times*, 28 March 1999.

Waller, Douglas, 'Onward Cyber Soldiers', *Time*, 146, 8 (1995).

Walsh, Mark, 'US Task Force Promotes Cyber Crime-Fighting Team', *Defense News*, 15–21 September 1997.

Warden III, Col. John A., 'The Enemy as a System', www.airpower. maxwell. af.mil/airchronicles/apj/warden.html.

Warner, Col. Volney J., 'Technology Favours Future Land Forces', *Strategic Review*, 26, 3 (1998).

Wass de Czege, Brigadier-General Huba, 'Mobile Strike Force: A 2010 Potential Force', *Military Review*, 76, 4 (1996).

Watts, Barry D., 'Ignoring Reality: Problems of Theory and Evidence in Security Studies', *Security Studies*, 7, 2 (1997–98).

Weinraub, Bernard, 'A Top US Intelligence Officer Admits Army Miscalculations', *International Herald Tribune*, 31 March 2003.

Weinraub, Bernard and Thom Shanker, 'War on the Cheap?', *International Herald Tribune*, 2 April 2003.

Wendt, Diego M., 'Using a Sledgehammer to Kill a Gnat: The Air Force's Failure to Comprehend Insurgent Doctrine during Operation Rolling Thunder', www.airpower.maxwell.af.mil/airchronicles/apj/4sum90.html.

Werrell, Kenneth P., 'Did USAF Technology Fail in Vietnam?: Three Case Studies', www.airpower.maxwell.af.mil/airchronicles/apj/apj98/spr98/werrell.html.

Whitehead, Yulin, 'Information as a Weapon: Reality versus Promises', www.airpower.maxwell.af.mil/airchronicles/apj/apj97/fal97/whitehead.html.

Wohlstetter, Albert, 'Illusions of Distance', *Foreign Affairs*, 46, 2 (1968).

Wolf, Jim, 'US Prepares for Cyberwar – the War Next Time', www. infowar.com/mil_c4i/01/mil_c4i_110801e_j.shtml.

Wright (Ret.), Lt-Col Richard H., 'Information Operations: Doctrine,

Tactics, Techniques and Procedures', *Military Review*, 81, 2 (2001).

Wriston, Walter B., 'Bits, Bytes, and Diplomacy', *Foreign Affairs*, 76, 5 (1997).

'18 Die as US Plane Bombs Kurdish Convoy in Worst Friendly Fire Incident', *Guardian*, 7 April 2003.

'Athene Will Put Canadian Army in Command', *Jane's Defence Weekly*, 29, 2, 4 March 1998.

'Europe Politics Hurt NATO Strikes', news.bbc.co.uk/hi/english/world/europe/newsid_334000/334879.stm.

'New Security Threats Rest in "Cyber Terrorism"', www.infowar.com/CIVIL_DE/civil_c.html-ssi.

'Predator a Lethal Eye in the Sky', www.cnn.com/2002/US/11/04/predator. background/index.html.

'Russia, Not Bombs, Brought End to War in Kosovo, Says Jackson', *Sunday Telegraph*, 1 August 1999, www.telegraph.co.uk/et.

'Sri Lanka Says Navy Will Be Upgraded to Combat Tigers', *Jane's Defence Weekly*, 12 November 1997.

'The Future of Warfare', *Economist*, 8 March 1997.

'US Destroys 6 Iraqi Systems Jamming GPS', *International Herald Tribune*, 26 March 2003.

CHAPTERS IN BOOKS

Applegate, Col Dick, 'Towards the Future Army', in Brian Bond and Mungo Melvin (eds), *The Nature of Future Conflict: Implications for Force Development*, The Occasional, 36 (Camberley, Strategic and Combat Studies Institute, Joint Services Staff College, 1998).

Arquilla, John and David Ronfeldt, 'A New Epoch – and Spectrum – of Conflict', in John Arquilla and David Ronfeldt (eds), *In Athena's Camp: Preparing for Conflict in the Information Age* (Santa Monica, CA, RAND, 1996).

——'Cyberwar is Coming', in John Arquilla and David Ronfeldt (eds), *In Athena's Camp: Preparing for Conflict in the Information Age* (Santa Monica, CA, RAND, 1996).

——'Information, Power, and Grand Strategy: In Athena's Camp – Section 1', in John Arquilla and David Ronfeldt (eds), *In Athena's Camp: Preparing for Conflict in the Information Age* (Santa Monica, CA, RAND, 1996).

——'Information, Power, and Grand Strategy: In Athena's Camp – Section 2', in John Arquilla and David Ronfeldt (eds), *In Athena's Camp: Preparing for Conflict in the Information Age* (Santa Monica, CA, RAND, 1996).

——'Looking Ahead: Preparing for Information-Age Conflict', in John

Arquilla and David Ronfeldt (eds), *In Athena's Camp: Preparing for Conflict in the Information Age* (Santa Monica, CA, RAND, 1996).

——'Afterword (September 2001): The Sharpening Fight for the Future', in John Arquilla and David Ronfeldt (eds), *Networks and Netwars: The Future of Terror, Crime, and Militancy* (Santa Monica, CA, RAND, 2001).

——'The Advent of Netwar (Revisited)', in John Arquilla and David Ronfeldt (eds), *Networks and Netwars: The Future of Terror, Crime, and Militancy* (Santa Monica, CA, RAND, 2001).

Ball, Desmond, 'Modern Technology and Geopolitics', in Ciro E. Zoppo and Charles Zorgbibe (eds), *On Geopolitics: Classical and Nuclear*, NATO ASI Series (Dordrecht, Martinus Nijhoff Publishers, 1985).

Baylis, John and John Garnett, 'Introduction', in John Baylis and John Garnett (eds), *Makers of Nuclear Strategy* (New York, St Martin's Press, 1991).

Baylis, John and James J. Wirtz, 'Introduction', in John Baylis, James Wirtz, Eliot Cohen and Colin S. Gray (eds), *Strategy in the Contemporary World: An Introduction to Strategic Studies* (Oxford, Oxford University Press, 2002).

Biddle, Stephen, 'Land Warfare: Theory and Practice', in John Baylis, James Wirtz, Eliot Cohen and Colin S. Gray (eds), *Strategy in the Contemporary World: An Introduction to Strategic Studies* (Oxford, Oxford University Press, 2002).

Brinton, Crane, Gordon A. Craig and Felix Gilbert, 'Jomini', in Edward Mead Earle (ed.), *Makers of Modern Strategy: Military Thought from Machiavelli to Hitler* (Princeton, NJ, Princeton University Press, 1943).

Brodie, Bernard, 'The Continuing Relevance of *On War*', in Carl von Clausewitz, *On War*, trans. Michael Howard and Peter Paret (London, David Campbell, 1993).

Brown, Michael L., 'The Revolution in Military Affairs: The Information Dimension', in Alan D. Campen, Douglas H. Dearth and R. Thomas Goodden, *Cyberwar: Security, Strategy, and Conflict in the Information Age* (Fairfax, VA, AFCEA International Press, 1996).

Campen, Alan D., 'Introduction', in Alan D. Campen (ed.), *The First Information War* (Fairfax, VA, AFCEA International Press, 1992).

Carter, Ashton B., 'Assessing Command System Vulnerability', in Ashton B. Carter, John D. Steinbruner and Charles A. Zraket (eds), *Managing Nuclear Operations* (Washington, DC, Brookings Institution, 1987).

——'Sources of Error and Uncertainty', in Ashton B. Carter, John D. Steinbruner and Charles A. Zraket (eds), *Managing Nuclear Operations* (Washington, DC, Brookings Institution, 1987).

Carver, M., 'Montgomery', in John Keegan (ed.), *Churchill's Generals* (London, Weidenfeld & Nicolson, 1991).

Cate, James Lea and Wesley Frank Craven, 'Victory', in James Lea Cate and Wesley Frank Craven (eds), *The Army Air Forces in World War II*, Vol. Five, *The Pacific: Matterhorn to Nagasaki June 1944 to August 1945* (Chicago, IL, University of Chicago Press, 1953).

Chaliand, G., 'Warfare and Strategic Culture', in G. Chaliand (ed.), *The Art of War in World History: From Antiquity to the Nuclear Age* (Berkeley, CA, University of California Press, 1994).

Cleary, Thomas, 'Translator's Introduction', in Sun Tzu, *The Art of War*, trans. Thomas Cleary (Boston, MA, Shambhala, 1988).

Cohen, Eliot, 'Technology and Warfare', in John Baylis, James Wirtz, Eliot Cohen and Colin S. Gray (eds), *Strategy in the Contemporary World: An Introduction to Strategic Studies*, (Oxford, Oxford University Press, 2002).

Cooper, Jeffrey, 'Dominant Battlespace Knowledge and Future Warfare', in Stuart E. Johnson and Martin C. Libicki (eds), *Dominant Battlespace Knowledge*, Revised Edition (Washington, DC, National Defense University, 1996).

——'Another View of the Revolution in Military Affairs', in John Arquilla and David Ronfeldt (eds), *In Athena's Camp: Preparing for Conflict in the Information Age* (Santa Monica, CA, RAND, 1996).

Davis, Malcolm R. and Colin S. Gray, 'Weapons of Mass Destruction', in John Baylis, James Wirtz, Eliot Cohen and Colin S. Gray (eds), *Strategy in the Contemporary World: An Introduction to Strategic Studies* (Oxford, Oxford University Press, 2002).

Dolman, Everett C., 'Geostrategy in the Space Age: An Astropolitical Analysis', in Colin S. Gray and Geoffrey Sloan (eds), *Geopolitics: Geography and Strategy* (London, Frank Cass, 1999).

Dunlap, Charles J., 'Sometimes the Dragon Wins: A Perspective on Information Age Warfare', in Winn Schwartau (ed.), *Information Warfare: Cyberterrorism: Protecting Your Personal Security in the Electronic Age*, Second Edition (New York, Thunder's Mouth Press, 1996).

Fagg, John E., 'Mission Accomplished', in Wesley Frank Craven and James Lea Cate (eds), *The Army Air Forces in World War II*, Vol. Three, *Europe: Argument to V-E Day January 1944 to May 1945* (Chicago, IL, University of Chicago Press, 1951).

——'The Climax of Strategic Operations', in Wesley Frank Craven and James Lea Cate (eds), *The Army Air Forces in World War II*, Vol. Three, *Europe: Argument to V-E Day January 1944 to May 1945* (Chicago, IL, University of Chicago Press, 1951).

Freedman, Lawrence, 'Conclusion: The Future of Strategic Studies', in

John Baylis, James Wirtz, Eliot Cohen and Colin S. Gray (eds), *Strategy in the Contemporary World: An Introduction to Strategic Studies* (Oxford, Oxford University Press, 2002).

Fritz, Sandy, 'Introduction', in Sandy Fritz (ed.), *Understanding Artificial Intelligence* (New York, Warner Books, 2002).

Garden, Timothy, 'Air Power: Theory and Practice', in John Baylis, James Wirtz, Eliot Cohen and Colin S. Gray (eds), *Strategy in the Contemporary World: An Introduction to Strategic Studies* (Oxford, Oxford University Press, 2002).

Gray, Colin S., 'Inescapable Geography', in Colin S. Gray and Geoffrey Sloan (eds), *Geopolitics: Geography and Strategy* (London, Frank Cass, 1999).

Griffith, Samuel B., 'Introduction', in Sun Tzu, *The Art of War*, trans. Samuel B. Griffith (London, Oxford University Press, 1971).

Harris, Paul, 'Radicalism in Military Thought', in Brian Bond and Mungo Melvin (eds), *The Nature of Future Conflict: Implications for Force Development*, The Occasional, 36 (Camberley, Strategic and Combat Studies Institute, Joint Services Staff College, 1998).

Hart, B. H. Liddell, 'Foreword', in Sun Tzu, *The Art of War*, trans. Samuel B. Griffith (London, Oxford University Press, 1971).

Hazlett, James, 'Just-in-Time Warfare', in Stuart E. Johnson and Martin C. Libicki (eds), *Dominant Battlespace Knowledge*, Revised Edition (Washington, DC, National Defense University, 1996).

Holden Reid, Brian, 'Enduring Patterns in Modern Warfare', in Brian Bond and Mungo Melvin (eds), *The Nature of Future Conflict: Implications for Force Development*, The Occasional, 36 (Camberley, Strategic and Combat Studies Institute, Joint Services Staff College, 1998).

Howard, Michael, 'The Dimensions of Strategy', in Lawrence Freedman (ed.), *War* (Oxford, Oxford University Press, 1994).

Kiras, James D., 'Terrorism and Irregular Warfare', in John Baylis, James Wirtz, Eliot Cohen and Colin S. Gray (eds), *Strategy in the Contemporary World: An Introduction to Strategic Studies* (Oxford, Oxford University Press, 2002).

Kopp, Carlo, 'The E-Bomb – A Weapon of Electrical Mass Destruction', in Winn Schwartau (ed.), *Information Warfare: Cyberterrorism: Protecting Your Personal Security in the Electronic Age*, Second Edition (New York, Thunder's Mouth Press, 1996).

Kuehl, Daniel T., 'Strategic Information Warfare and Comprehensive Situational Awareness', in Alan D. Campen, Douglas H. Dearth and R. Thomas Goodden, *Cyberwar: Security, Strategy, and Conflict in the Information Age* (Fairfax, VA, AFCEA International Press, 1996).

Kurzweil, Ray, 'The Coming Merging of Mind and Machine', in Sandy Fritz (ed.), *Understanding Artificial Intelligence* (New York, Warner

Books, 2002).

Lamb, Christopher Jon, 'The Impact of Information Age Technologies on Operations Other Than War', in Robert L. Pfaltzgraff, Jr and Richard H. Shultz, Jr (eds), *War in the Information Age: New Challenges for U.S. Security Policy* (Washington, DC, Brassey's, 1997).

Lawrence, T. E., 'Guerrilla Warfare', in Gerard Chaliand (ed.), *The Art of War in World History: From Antiquity to the Nuclear Age* (Berkeley, CA, University of California Press, 1994).

Libicki, Martin C., 'Deterring Information Attacks', in Winn Schwartau (ed.), *Information Warfare: Cyberterrorism: Protecting Your Personal Security in the Electronic Age*, Second Edition (New York, Thunder's Mouth Press, 1996).

——'Dominant Battlespace Knowledge and its Consequences', in Stuart E. Johnson and Martin C. Libicki (eds), *Dominant Battlespace Knowledge*, Revised Edition (Washington, DC, National Defense University, 1996).

——'The Small and the Many', in John Arquilla and David Ronfeldt, *In Athena's Camp: Preparing for Conflict in the Information Age* (Santa Monica, CA, RAND, 1996).

——'Technology and Warfare', in Patrick M. Cronin (ed.), *2015: Power and Progress*, www.ndu.edu/ndu/inss/books/2015/chap4.html.

Libicki, Martin and Jeremy Shapiro, 'Conclusion: The Changing Role of Information in Warfare', in Zalmay Khalizad, John P. White and Andrew W. Marshall (eds), *Strategic Appraisal: The Changing Role of Information in Warfare* (Santa Monica, CA, RAND, 1999)

Moran, Daniel, 'Strategic Theory and the History of War', in John Baylis, James Wirtz, Eliot Cohen and Colin S. Gray (eds), *Strategy in the Contemporary World: An Introduction to Strategic Studies* (Oxford, Oxford University Press, 2002).

Moreman, T. R., 'Small Wars and Imperial Policing: The British Army and the Theory and Practice of Colonial Warfare in the British Empire, 1919–1939', in Brian Holden Reid (ed.), *Military Power: Land Warfare in Theory and Practice* (London, Frank Cass, 1997).

Murray, Williamson, 'Armoured Warfare: The British, French, and German Experiences', in Williamson Murray and Allan R. Millett (eds), *Military Innovation in the Interwar Period* (Cambridge, Cambridge University Press, 1996).

——'Some Thoughts on War and Geography', in Colin S. Gray and Geoffrey Sloan (eds), *Geopolitics: Geography and Strategy* (London, Frank Cass, 1999).

——'May 1940: Contingency and Fragility of the German RMA', in Williamson Murray and MacGregor Knox (eds), *The Dynamics of*

Military Revolution, 1300–2050 (Cambridge, Cambridge University Press, 2001).

Murray, Williamson and Mark Grimsley, 'Introduction: On Strategy', in Williamson Murray, MacGregor Knox and Alvin Bernstein (eds), *The Making of Strategy: Rulers, States, and War* (Cambridge, Cambridge University Press, 1994).

Murray, Williamson and MacGregor Knox, 'Conclusion: The Future Behind Us', in Williamson Murray and MacGregor Knox (eds), *The Dynamics of Military Revolution, 1300–2050* (Cambridge, Cambridge University Press, 2001).

——'Thinking About Revolutions in Warfare', in Williamson Murray and MacGregor Knox (eds), *The Dynamics of Military Revolution, 1300–2050* (Cambridge, Cambridge University Press, 2001).

'Onasander', in G. Chaliand, *The Art of War in World History: From Antiquity to the Nuclear Age* (Berkeley, CA, University of California Press, 1994).

Owens, Admiral William A., 'Introduction', in Stuart E. Johnson and Martin C. Libicki (eds), *Dominant Battlespace Knowledge*, Revised Edition (Washington, DC, National Defense University, 1996).

Parker, Geoffrey, 'The Making of Strategy in Habsburg Spain: Philip II's "bid for mastery," 1556–1598', in Williamson Murray, MacGregor Knox, and Alvin Bernstein (eds), *The Making of Strategy: Rulers, States, and War* (Cambridge, Cambridge University Press, 1994).

Pimlott, John, 'The Theory and Practice of Strategic Bombing', in Colin McInnes and G. D. Sheffield (eds), *Warfare in the Twentieth Century: Theory and Practice* (London, Unwin Hyman, 1988).

Rodger, N. A. M., 'Weather, Geography and Naval Power in the Age of Sail', in Colin S. Gray and Geoffrey Sloan (eds), *Geopolitics: Geography and Strategy* (London, Frank Cass, 1999).

Ronfeldt, David and John Arquilla, 'What Next For Networks and Netwars?', in John Arquilla and David Ronfeldt (eds), *Networks and Netwars: The Future of Terror, Crime, and Militancy* (Santa Monica, CA, RAND, 2001).

Ryan, Danial J. and Julie J. C. H. Ryan, 'Protecting the National Information Infrastructure Against Infowar', in Winn Schwartau (ed.), *Information Warfare: Cyberterrorism: Protecting Your Personal Security in the Electronic Age*, Second Edition (New York, Thunder's Mouth Press, 1996).

Shepperd, Alan, 'Horrocks', in John Keegan (ed.), *Churchill's Generals* (London, Weidenfeld & Nicolson, 1991).

Shy, John, 'Jomini', in Peter Paret (ed.), *Makers of Modern Strategy: From Machiavelli to the Nuclear Age* (Oxford, Clarendon Press, 1986).

Sovereign, Michael, 'DBK with Autonomous Weapons', in Stuart E.

Johnson and Martin C. Libicki (eds), *Dominant Battlespace Knowledge*, Revised Edition (Washington, DC, National Defense University, 1996).

Summers, Harry G., 'A War is a War is a War is a War', in Loren B. Thompson (ed.), *Low-Intensity Conflict: The Pattern of Warfare in the Modern World* (Lexington, MA, Lexington Books, 1989).

Szafranski, Richard, 'Neocortical Warfare? The Acme of Skill', in John Arquilla and David Ronfeldt (eds), *In Athena's Camp: Preparing for Conflict in the Information Age* (Santa Monica, CA, RAND, 1996).

Tangredi, Sam J., 'Sea Power: Theory and Practice', in John Baylis, James Wirtz, Eliot Cohen and Colin S. Gray (eds), *Strategy in the Contemporary World: An Introduction to Strategic Studies* (Oxford, Oxford University Press, 2002).

Thompson, Loren B., 'Low-Intensity Conflict: An Overview', in Loren B. Thompson (ed.), *Low-Intensity Conflict: The Pattern of Warfare in the Modern World* (Lexington, MA, Lexington Books, 1989).

Toffler, Alvin and Heidi, 'Foreword: The New Intangibles', in John Arquilla and David Ronfeldt (eds), *In Athena's Camp: Preparing for Conflict in the Information Age* (Santa Monica, CA, RAND, 1996).

Zanini, Michele and Sean J. A. Edwards, 'The Networking of Terror in the Information Age', in John Arquilla and David Ronfeldt (eds), *Networks and Netwars: The Future of Terror, Crime, and Militancy* (Santa Monica, CA, RAND, 2001).

Zoppo, Ciro E., 'Classical Geopolitics and Beyond', in Ciro E. Zoppo and Charles Zorgbibe (eds), *On Geopolitics: Classical and Nuclear*, NATO ASI Series (Dordrecht, Martinus Nijhoff Publishers, 1985).

PAPERS

Allen, James F., *AI Growing Up: The Changes and Opportunities*, American Association for Artificial Intelligence, www.aaai.org.

Anderson, Robert H., *Securing the US Defense Information Infrastructure: A Proposed Approach*, www.rand.org/publications/mr/mr993.

Baddeley, A. J., 'Insurgency and Counter Insurgency in the Information Age', paper prepared for the BISA Annual Conference, 15–17 December 1997, University of Leeds.

Bailey, Jonathan, *The First World War and the Birth of the Modern Style of Warfare*, The Occasional, 22 (Camberley, Strategic and Combat Studies Institute, Joint Services Staff College, 1997).

Bellamy, Christopher, *Spiral through Time: Beyond 'Conflict Intensity'*, The Occasional, 35 (Camberley, Strategic and Combat Studies Institute, Joint Services Staff College, 1998).

Biddle, Stephen, *Afghanistan and the Future of Warfare: Implications for Army and Defence Policy* (Carlisle, PA, Strategic Studies Institute, US Army War College, 2002).

Blaker, James R., *Understanding the Revolution in Military Affairs: A Guide to America's 21st Century Defense*, Progressive Policy Institute, Defense Working Paper 3 (Washington, DC, January 1997).

Borg, Col Charles M., *Information Operations: Is the Army Doing Enough?* (Carlisle Barracks, PA, US Army War College, 2001).

Cebrowski, Vice-Admiral Arthur K., 'Network-Centric Warfare: An Emerging Military Response to the Information Age', Command and Control Research and Technology Symposium, 29 June 1999.

Freedman, Lawrence, *Information Warfare: Will Battle Ever Be Joined?*, International Centre for Security Analysis (Launch), 14 October 1996.

——*The Revolution in Strategic Affairs*, Adelphi Paper 318 (Oxford, Oxford University Press, 1998).

Gray, Colin S., *The American Revolution in Military Affairs: An Interim Assessment*, The Occasional, 28 (Camberley, Strategic and Combat Studies Institute, 1997).

——'A Contested Vision: The RMA Debate Today', paper presented at The Royal Institute of International Affairs conference 'Revolution in Military Affairs? Challenges to Government and Industry in the Information Age', Chatham House, London, 21–22 May 1997.

Kisseloff, Jeff, 'Kasparov's Back Against the Wall', www.chess.ibm.com/home/may10/story_3.html.

Lamont, Robert W., 'Urban Warrior – A View from North Vietnam', www.geocities.com/Pentagon/6453/uwvietnam.html.

Lawler, Andrew J., 'The Battle for Hue City', www.geocities.com/Pentagon/6453/hue3.html.

Leake, David B., 'Artificial Intelligence', in *Van Norstrand Scientific Encyclopedia* (New York, Wiley, 2002), www.cs.indiana.edu/~leake/papers/p-01-07/p-01-07.html.

Libicki, Martin C., *What is Information Warfare?*, ACIS Paper, 3 (Washington, DC, National Defense University, 1995).

——'Information and Nuclear RMAs Compared', *Strategic Forum*, 82, July 1996, www.ndu.edu/inss/strforum/forum82.html.

——*The Mesh and the Net: Speculation on Armed Conflict In an Age of Free Silicon*, McNair Paper 28 (Washington, DC, National Defense University, Institute for National Strategic Studies, 1996).

——'Information Dominance', *Strategic Forum*, 132, November 1997, http://www.ndu.edu/inss/strforum/SF132/forum132.html.

——*Illuminating Tomorrow's War*, McNair Paper 61, November 1999, www.ndu.edu/inss/mcnair/mcnair61/m61cont.html.

Metz, Steven and James Kievit, *The Revolution in Military Affairs and Conflict Short of War*, 25 July 1994, www.cs.virginia.edu/~alb/

misc/rmawarcollege.html.

O'Hanlon, Michael E., 'Beware the "RMA'nia"!', paper presented at the National Defense University, 9 September 1998.

O'Malley, Chris, *Information Warriors of the 609th: Air Force's 609th Information Warfare Squadron*, www.infowar.com/mil_c4i/mil_c4i_ 100397a.html-ssi.

Owens, Admiral William, 'The Emerging System-of-Systems', *Strategic Forum*, 63, February 1996, www.ndu.edu/inss/strforum/forum63. html.

Parry, Captain Chris, 'Some Recent and Emerging Themes in Maritime Warfare', New Dimensions: Maritime Manoeuvre and the Strategic Defence Review, Conference at the University of Hull, 2 July 1999.

Press, Daryl G., 'Urban Warfare: Options, Problems and the Future', summary of a conference sponsored by the MIT Security Studies Program, 20 May 1998, Hanscom Air Force Base, Massachusetts.

Sloman, Aaron, 'What is Artificial Intelligence?', www.cs.bham.ac.uk/ ~axs/misc/aiforschools.html.

Stork, David G., 'The End of an Era, the Beginning of Another? Hal, Deep Blue and Kasparov', www.chess.ibm.com/learn/html/e.8./c.html.

Thomas, Timothy L., *'Like Adding Wings to a Tiger': Chinese Information War Theory and Practice* (Fort Leavenworth, KS, Foreign Military Studies Office, 2000), www.iwar.org.uk/iwar/ resources/ china/iw/ chinaiw/htm.

Vatis, Michael A., *Cyber Attacks during the War on Terrorism: A Predictive Analysis* (Hanover, NH, Institute for Security Technology Studies, Dartmouth College, 2001).

Villacres, Edward J. and Christopher Bassford, 'Reclaiming the Clausewitzian Trinity', www.clausewitz.com/CWZHOME/Trinity/ TRINITY.htm.

Watts, Barry D., *Clausewitzian Friction and Future War*, McNair Paper 52 (Washington, DC, Institute for National Strategic Studies, National Defense University, October 1996).

Weeks, Stanley B., 'US Maritime Doctrine and Manoeuvre Warfare', New Dimensions: Maritime Manoeuvre and the Strategic Defence Review, Conference at the University of Hull, 2 July 1999.

Wilson, Peter A., 'The Transformation of Military Power, 1997–2027', paper presented at the 1997 Pacific Symposium, Honolulu, Hawaii, 28–29 April 1997.

——*Preparing for Early 21st Century War: Beyond the Bottom-Up Review*, CGSC Monograph, 'Toward 2000' Series, 5 (Centre for Global Security Cooperation).

'Kasparov Down – But Not Out', www.chess.ibm.com/home/may11/ story_2.html.

GOVERNMENTAL PAPERS

Anderson, Robert H., 'Risks to the US Infrastructure from Cyberspace', Verbal testimony to the Permanent Subcommittee on Investigations, 25 June 1996.

British Defence Doctrine: Joint Warfare Publication (JWP) 0-01 (London, HMSO, 1997).

Critical Foundations: Protecting America's Infrastructures, Report of the President's Commission on Critical Infrastructure Protection, October 1997, www.pccip.gov.

Dacey, Robert F., *Critical Infrastructure Protection: Significant Homeland Security Challenges Need to Be Addressed* (Washington, DC, United States General Accounting Office, 2002), www.gao.gov/cgi-bin/getrpt? GAO-02-918T.

Deutch, John M., 'Foreign Information Warfare Programs and Capabilities', Statement for the Record to the US Senate Committee on Governmental Affairs; Permanent Subcommittee on Investigations, 25 June 1996.

Executive Order Establishing the President's Commission on Critical Infrastructure Protection, www.infowar.com/CIVIL_DE/Cyberwar. html-ssi.

FM 100-6 Information Operations (Washington, DC, Headquarters Department of the Army, 1996).

GAO Executive Report, B-266140, http://www.infowar.com/civil_de/gaosum.html-ssi.

Joint Vision 2020 (Washington, DC, US Government Printing Office, 2000).

Keaney, Thomas A. and Eliot A. Cohen, *Gulf War Air Power Survey: Summary Report* (Washington, DC, 1993).

Neumann, P. G., 'Security Risks in the Computer-Communication Infrastructure', Written testimony for the US Senate Permanent Subcommittee on Investigations of the Senate Committee on Governmental Affairs, 25 June 1996.

Nunn, S., 'Opening Statement', US Senate Permanent Subcommittee on Investigations Hearing on Security in Cyberspace, 25 June 1996.

Secretary Rumsfeld Speaks on "21st Century Transformation" of US Armed Forces (transcript of remarks and question and answer period (United States Department of Defense, 31 January 2002), www.defenselink.mil/ speeches/2002/s20020131-secdef.html.

Testimony Delivered on Military Transformation (United States Department of Defense, 9 April 2002), www.defenselink.mil/speeches/2002/ s20020409-depsecdef1.html.

United States Marine Corps, *A Concept for Future Military Operations on Urbanized Terrain,* Marine Corps Concept Paper (Quantico, VA, USMC, 1997).

Index

Printed in the United States
142467LV00001B/2/A